Statistical Methods for Validation of Assessment Scale Data in Counseling and Related Fields

Dimiter M. Dimitrov

AMERICAN COUNSELING ASSOCIATION
5999 Stevenson Avenue
Alexandria, VA 22304
www.counseling.org

Statistical Methods for Validation of Assessment Scale Data in Counseling and Related Fields

10 9 8 7 6 5 4 3 2 1

American Counseling Association
5999 Stevenson Avenue
Alexandria, VA 22304
www.counseling.org

Director of Publications ◆ Carolyn C. Baker

Production Manager ◆ Bonny E. Gaston

Editorial Assistant ◆ Catherine A. Brumley

Copy Editor ◆ Kimberly W. Kinne

Text and cover design by Bonny E. Gaston.

Library of Congress Cataloging-in-Publication Data

Dimitrov, Dimiter M.
Statistical methods for validation of assessment scale data in counseling and related fields/ Dimiter M. Dimitrov.
p. cm.
Includes bibliographical references and index.
ISBN 978-1-55620-295-7 (alk. paper)
1. Counseling—Evaluation. 2. Social sciences—Statistical methods. I. Title.
BF636.6.D56 2012
158′.30727—dc23 2011018595

To the memory of my parents,
Milko and Maria

◆ ◆ ◆

Table of Contents

Preface

The purpose of this book is to present statistical methods and procedures used in contemporary approaches to validation of targeted constructs through the use of assessment scales (tests, inventories, questionnaires, surveys, and so forth). An important clarification in this regard is that *validity* is a property of data and inferences made from data rather than a property of scales (or instruments in general). Although most references and examples are in the context of counseling, the methodology and practical know-how provided in this book directly apply to assessments in psychology, education, and other fields. The text is intended primarily for use by applied researchers, but it can also be useful to faculty and graduate students in their coursework, research, dissertations, and grants that involve development of assessment instruments and/or related validations.

To a large extent, the need for this book stemmed from my six-year work (2005–2011) as editor of *Measurement and Evaluation in Counseling and Development*, the official journal of the Association for Assessment in Counseling and Education, and as a reviewer for numerous professional journals in the areas of counseling, psychology, and education. In general, commonly occurring shortcomings in (mostly unpublished) manuscripts that deal with validation of assessment instruments relate to outdated conceptions of validity, lack of sound methodology, and/or problems with the selection and technical execution of statistical methods used to collect evidence about targeted aspects of validity. The approach to validation of assessment scale data and related statistical procedures presented in this book is based on the unified construct-based conception of validity (Messick, 1989, 1995), which is also reflected in the current *Standards for Educational and Psychological Testing* (American Educational Research Association, American Psychological Association, & National Council on Measurement in Education, 1999). On the technical side, this book presents contemporary statistical methods and related procedures for evaluating psychometric properties of assessment scales. For example, exploratory and confirmatory factor analysis, testing for invariance of constructs across groups, multitrait–multimethod data analysis for validity evidence, and modern scale analysis are elaborated at both methodological and technical levels.

This book is organized in three parts comprising nine chapters. Part I (*Scales, Reliability, and Validity*) consists of four chapters. Chapter 1 presents variables and measurement scales, with focus on the nature of measurement, types of scales, and scaling procedures typical for assessment in the context of counseling, psychology, education, and other fields. Chapter 2 introduces the classical (true-score) model of score reliability, types of reliability, reliability of composite scores, and maximal reliability. Chapter 3 presents the unified construct-based model of validity (Messick, 1989, 1995). Chapter 4 outlines major steps in the development of an assessment instrument within the framework of the adopted validity model.

Part II (*Factor Analysis in Construct Validation*) consists of three chapters. Chapter 5 deals with exploratory factor analysis—a brief introduction of the EFA framework, contemporary approaches to determining the number of factors, and issues of sample size, data adequacy, and categorical data. Chapter 6 deals with confirmatory factor analysis (CFA). As this chapter plays a central role under the conception of validity adopted in the book, topics of critical importance such as CFA model–data fit, evaluation of model adequacy, and testing for factorial invariance of (first- and higher-order) CFA models are addressed with methodological and technical details in the context of construct validation. Chapter 7 presents a variety of CFA-based models of multitrait–multimethod data analysis for collecting convergent and discriminant evidence, as well as evidence of method bias, as related to the external aspect of construct validity.

Part III (*Psychometric Scale Analysis*) consists of two chapters. Chapter 8 deals with classical scale analysis of binary and rating scales, with a focus on procedures that can be useful to researchers in piloting stages of development and validation of an assessment instrument. Chapter 9 presents Rasch-based analysis of binary and rating scales, and particular attention is paid to optimizing the effectiveness of rating scales by addressing issues of disordering in rating scale categories and their thresholds, person–item distribution mapping, and dimensionality of assessment measures.

From a pedagogical perspective, the presentation of topics was guided by the intent to provide applied researchers with understandable treatment of contemporary statistical methods and procedures that they would be able to apply in development and validation of assessment scale data. The hope is that this goal is achieved by minimized use of mathematical symbols and formulas and focus on conceptual understanding of methods and procedures, underlying assumptions, possible pitfalls, and common misconceptions. This strategy is enhanced by the use of numerous illustrative examples, tables, and figures throughout the text. Practical applications of relatively complex procedures are facilitated by the inclusion of operationalized (step-wise) guidance for their implementation and computer code in Mplus (Muthén & Muthén, 2008). Of course, given the description of such procedures, they can be translated into computer source codes for other popular software packages such as LISREL, EQS, or Amos.

Acknowledgments

I would like to thank all colleagues, friends, and family members for their encouragement and support during my work on this book. I truly appreciate the guidance, expertise, and support provided by Carolyn Baker, director of publications for the American Counseling Association (ACA), from the initial idea about the need for such a book to its final publication. I am also grateful to the supportive role of the ACA Publications Committee.

I would like to acknowledge the expertise and contribution of the reviewers, Everett V. Smith, Jr.; Thomas J. Smith; Carolyn Baker; and Catherine Y. Chang, all of whom provided valuable comments and suggestions on improving the book. I am also grateful to my family for their patience and encouragement during the time this book was written.

—*Dimiter M. Dimitrov*
George Mason University

About the Author

Dimiter M. Dimitrov, PhD, is professor of educational measurement and statistics in the Graduate School of Education at George Mason University in Fairfax, Virginia. He earned his bachelor's degree in mathematics and a PhD in mathematics education from the University of Sofia, Bulgaria, in 1984 as well as a PhD in educational psychology from Southern Illinois University at Carbondale in 1995. His teaching experience includes courses on multivariate statistics, quantitative research methods, modern measurement, generalizability theory, and structural equation modeling. Dr. Dimitrov's professional work—which has resulted in numerous journal articles, books, and book chapters—has received national and international recognition. He has served as president of the Mid-Western Educational Research Association (2008–2009), program chair of the SIG Rasch Measurement of the American Educational Research Association, and editor of *Measurement and Evaluation in Counseling and Development*, the official journal of the Association for Assessment in Counseling and Education (2005–2011). Dr. Dimitrov has also lectured on modern measurement and latent variable modeling at universities in Russia and Spain. He has served on the editorial board of prestigious professional journals such as *Educational Researcher*, *Educational and Psychological Measurement*, *Journal of Applied Measurement*, and *Research in the Schools*. Dr. Dimitrov is multilingual and has lectured and published professional work in English, Bulgarian, Russian, and French.

His email address is: ddimitro@gmu.edu.

Part I

Scales, Reliability, and Validity

Chapter 1
Variables and Measurement Scales

The development of instruments for assessment in counseling, psychology, education, and other areas must be addressed within the framework of a more general goal of providing theoretical explanations of behaviors and phenomena in these areas. As Kerlinger (1986) noted, "a theory is a set of interrelated constructs (concepts), definitions, and propositions that present a systematic view of phenomena by specifying relations among variables, with the purpose of explaining and predicting the phenomena" (p. 9). To reach valid interpretations and conclusions through testing hypotheses, researchers must collect accurate measures of the variables involved in the hypothesized relations. Therefore, it is important that researchers understand well the nature of the study variables and the properties of their measurement scales.

In this chapter I describe the nature of variables in social and behavioral research, basic classifications of variables (observable vs. unobservable; discrete vs. continuous), levels of measurement (nominal, ordinal, interval, and ratio), binary scales, rating scales, and scaling. The focus is on binary scales and rating scales that are typically used for assessment in counseling and related fields (e.g., Likert scales, Likert-type scales, and frequency rating scales). Some basic transformation of scales is also discussed.

1.1 VARIABLES IN SOCIAL AND BEHAVIORAL RESEARCH

In general, a *variable* is any characteristic of a person (or an object) that may vary across persons or across different time points. A person's weight, for example, is a variable with different values for different people, although some people may weigh the same. This variable can also take on different values at different points in time, such as when obtaining repeated measurements for one person (say, every month during a one-year period to monitor the effect of a weight-loss treatment). Most often, the capital letters X, Y, and Z (in italics) are used to denote variables. Alternately, if a study involves many variables, a capital letter with subscripts can be used to denote different variables (e.g., X_1, X_2, X_3). Variables can also be described as *observable* versus *unobservable* or *continuous* versus *discrete*. *Constants* (i.e., numbers that remain the same throughout an analysis) are represented by lowercase letters in italics (e.g., a, b, c, d).

1.1.1 Observable Versus Latent Variables

Variables that can be measured directly are referred to as *observable variables*. For example, gender, age, ethnicity, and socioeconomic status are observable variables. Variables such as intelligence, attitude, motivation, anxiety, self-esteem, and verbal ability, on the other hand, are not directly observable and are therefore referred to as *latent* (i.e., unobservable or hidden) *variables* or *constructs*. Typically, a construct is given an operational definition specifying which observed variables are considered to be measurable indicators of the construct. For instance, measurable indicators of anxiety can include the person's responses to items on an anxiety test, the person's heartbeat and skin responses, or his or her reactions to experimental manipulations.

It is important to note that the operational definition for a construct should be based on a specific theory; therefore, the validity of the measurable indicators of the construct will necessarily depend on the level of correctness of this theory. For example, if a theory of creativity assumes, among other things, that people who can provide different approaches to the solution of a given problem are more creative than those who provide fewer approaches, then the number of approaches to solving individual problems (or tasks) can be used as an indicator of creativity. If, however, this theory is proven wrong, then the person's score on this indicator cannot be used for valid assessment of creativity.

1.1.2 Continuous Versus Discrete Variables

It is also important to understand the differences between continuous and discrete variables. *Continuous variables* are those that can take any possible value within a specific numeric interval. For example, the height of the students in a middle school population is a continuous variable because it can take any value (usually rounded to the nearest inch or tenth of an inch) within a numeric interval on the height measuring scale. Other examples of continuous variables are the students' ages, time on task in a classroom observation, and abilities that underlie proficiency outcomes in subject areas such as math, science, or reading. Latent variables that are typically involved in counseling research are continuous in nature—for example, motivation, anxiety, self-efficacy, depression, social skills, multicultural competence, and attitude (e.g., toward school, religion, or minority groups).

Discrete variables, on the other hand, can take only separate values (say, integer numbers). The measurement of a discrete variable usually involves counting or enumeration of how many times something has occurred—for example, the number of spelling errors in a writing sample or the frequency with which a specific behavior (e.g., aggressiveness) has occurred during a period of time. Thus, while the measurement of a continuous variable relates to the question "How much?" the measurement of a discrete variable relates to the question "How many?"

1.2 WHAT IS MEASUREMENT?

Measurement can be thought of as a process that involves three components—an object of measurement, a set of numbers, and a system of rules—that serve to assign numbers to magnitudes of the variable being measured. The object of measurement can be an observable variable (e.g., weight or age) or a latent variable (e.g., self-efficacy, depression, or motivation). Any latent variable can be viewed as a hidden continuum with magnitudes increasing in a given direction, say, from left to right if the continuum is represented with a straight line. A latent variable is usually defined with observable indicators (e.g., test items). The person's total score on these indicators is the number assigned to the hidden magnitude for this person on the latent variable.

Note 1.1

It may be confusing that values of continuous variables are reported as "discrete" values. This confusion arises because the values of a continuous variable are rounded. Take, for example, a weekly weather report on temperature (in Fahrenheit): 45°, 48°, 45°, 58°, 52°, 47°, 51°—values of the continuous variable temperature look discrete because they are rounded to the nearest integer. As another example, GPA scores rounded to the nearest hundredth (e.g., 3.52, 3.37, 4.00, and so forth) also look like discrete values, but they represent a continuous variable (academic achievement).

Let's say, for example, that a researcher measures middle school students' reading comprehension using a test of 20 binary items (1 = correct, 0 = incorrect). These items serve as observable indicators of the latent variable reading comprehension. The total test score of a student is the number assigned to the actual (yet hidden) magnitude of reading comprehension for that student. With 20 binary items, there are 21 discrete numbers (possible test scores: 0, 1, . . ., 20) that can be assigned to magnitudes of the continuous variable reading comprehension. The explanation of this paradox is that each number must be viewed as a midpoint of a *score interval*, so that all score intervals together cover with no gap a continuous interval on the number line. There are 21 such intervals in this case: (–0.5, 0.5) with a midpoint of 0, (0.5, 1.5) with a midpoint of 1, and so on, up to the interval (19.5, 20.5) with a midpoint of 20. It is assumed that all values within a numerical interval represented by an observed score are equally likely to occur. Thus, if eight examinees have a score of 10 on the test, it is assumed that their scores are uniformly distributed between 9.5 and 10.5 (see also Note 1.1).

1.3 LEVELS OF MEASUREMENT

Measurement of variables can take place at four different levels—nominal, ordinal, interval, and ratio—depending on the presence or absence of four characteristics of the relationship between magnitudes of the variable being measured and the scores assigned to these magnitudes: distinctiveness, ordering, equal intervals, and equal ratios. The scales produced at these four levels of measurement are referred to as *nominal scales*, *ordinal scales*, *interval scales*, and *ratio scales*, respectively.

1.3.1 Nominal Scale

A *nominal scale* is used to classify persons (or objects) into mutually exclusive categories, say, by gender, ethnicity, professional occupation, and so forth. The numbers on a nominal scale serve only as names of such categories, hence the name of this scale (in Latin, *nome* means "name"). Thus, the nominal measurement possesses the characteristic of *distinctiveness*. It is important to emphasize, however, that nominal scale numbers do not reflect magnitudes of the classification variable. For example, if one uses the nominal scale "1 = male, 2 = female" to label gender groups, this does not mean that 1 and 2 are numeric values assigned to different gender magnitudes. Therefore, the nominal scale is *not* a true measurement scale because one cannot place individuals in any sort of (increasing or decreasing) order based on their nominal classification. Keeping this in mind, nominal scales are useful for coding categorical data.

Any transformation of numbers that labels different categories in a nominal scale is permissible as long as the resulting new numbers are also different. That is, any transformation that preserves the distinctiveness of the nominal scale is permissible. To illustrate, let's say that we have the nominal scale "1 = White, 2 = Black, and 3 = Asian" for three racial groups. We can, for example, subtract one from each of the original numbers, thus obtaining the nominal scale "0 = White, 1 = Black, and 2 = Asian." However, although transformations are permissible, carrying out arithmetic operations with numbers that label nominal categories is meaningless (e.g., if "1 = male, 2 = female" is a nominal scale for gender groups, it does not make any sense to add, subtract, or average these two numbers).

1.3.2 Ordinal Scale

An *ordinal scale* is one in which the magnitudes of the variable (trait, property) being measured are ordered in the same way as the numbers assigned to these magnitudes. Thus, an ordinal scale possesses the characteristics of distinctiveness and ordering. We can also say that with an ordinal scale, for any two individuals the higher score will be assigned to the person who has more of the variable (trait) being measured. However, the ordinal scale does not show by how much the two individuals differ on this variable. In other words, an ordinal scale provides information about the order of individuals—in terms of their actual magnitudes on the variable being measured—but not about the distances between such magnitudes.

Any transformation of an ordinal scale that preserves the order of the scores originally obtained with this scale is permissible. For example, let's assume that 1, 2, and 3 are ordinal scale numbers that stand for first, second, and third place assigned to three students based on their ranking by popularity among other students. If we square these numbers, the resulting numbers (1, 4, and 9) are in the same order; therefore, they also form an ordinal scale. However, it is not permissible to perform arithmetic operations with these numbers. For example, calculating the arithmetic mean of ordinal numbers (e.g., ranks) for a group of individuals in an attempt to provide an "average rank" for this group would be meaningless. The reason it would be meaningless is because equal differences between ordinal scale numbers do not necessarily represent equal distances between the corresponding magnitudes of the variable being measured.

1.3.3 Interval Scale

An *interval scale* provides information about the order and the distances between actual magnitudes of the variable being measured. Specifically, the interval scale has the characteristics of (a) distinctiveness—that is, different scores represent different magnitudes of the variable; (b) ordering—that is, the variable magnitudes and their respective scores are in the same order; and (c) equal intervals—that is, equal differences between variable magnitudes result in equal differences between the scores assigned to these magnitudes.

It is important to note that the interval scale has an arbitrary zero point. When zero is assigned to a given magnitude of a variable measured on an interval scale, this does not necessarily mean that this magnitude is actually missing (i.e., that there is no magnitude at all). For example, the measurement of temperature is an interval scale, but if at a given moment the temperature is "zero degrees" (in Fahrenheit or Celsius) this does not mean that there is no temperature at all at this moment. The *zero* (origin) of an interval scale is conventional and can be moved up or down using a desired linear transformation. For example, the formula for transformation from Celsius to Fahrenheit is $F = (9/5)C + 32$, where C and F stand for temperature readings in Celsius and Fahrenheit, respectively. Thus, if $C = 0$, then $F = 32$ (i.e., 0° in Celsius corresponds to 32° in Fahrenheit). In the context of counseling research, a score of zero points on an anxiety test does not necessarily indicate a total absence of anxiety.

Note also that because the zero (origin) of an interval scale is arbitrary and does not indicate absence of the trait being measured, the ratio of two numbers on an interval scale does not provide information about the *ratio* of the trait magnitudes that correspond to these two numbers. For example, if the temperature readings on two consecutive days were, say, 60°F on Tuesday and 30°F on Wednesday, we cannot say that "on Tuesday it was twice as hot as on Wednesday." We can only say

> **Note 1.2**
>
> In many scenarios of assessment in counseling, psychology, and education (e.g., teacher-made tests), it is unlikely that the scale is (even close to) interval. Therefore, arithmetic operations with scores in such cases (e.g., calculation of mean and standard deviation) may produce misleading results. Interval (or close to interval) scales can be obtained with appropriate data transformations, which are usually performed with the development of standardized assessment instruments.

that the temperature on Wednesday was 30°F lower than that on Tuesday (or "the temperature dropped by 30°F"). As another example, if Persons A and B have 20 points and 40 points, respectively, on an anxiety test, we cannot say that Person B is twice as anxious as Person A.

If the numbers on an interval scale are changed using a linear transformation, the resulting numbers will also be on an interval scale. The linear transformation of these numbers preserves their distinctiveness, ordering, and equal intervals. Unlike the nominal and ordinal scales, the interval scale allows for arithmetic operations to be carried out on its numerical values; that is, one can add, subtract, multiply, and divide numerical values (scores) obtained with an interval scale. So, given the temperature readings 5°, 10°, 20°, and 25° (say, in Celsius), one can compute the average temperature: $(5° + 10° + 20° + 25°)/4 = 15°$. Thus, interval scales allow for both linear transformation and algebraic operations with their scale values.

1.3.4 Ratio Scale

A ratio scale provides information both about the ratio between magnitudes of the variable being measured and about the distinctiveness of such magnitudes, their order, and distances between them. Thus, the ratio scale possesses the characteristics of distinctiveness, ordering, equal intervals, and equal ratios. The zero (origin) of a ratio scale is naturally fixed; that is, zero indicates absence of the property being measured. For example, zero distance between two points on a straight line indicates that there is no distance between these two points (which is the case when two points perfectly coincide). Also, the origin of all ratio scales for distance measurement is the same (e.g., zero inches and zero centimeters indicate the same thing—absence of distance). As a reminder, this is *not* the case with interval scales; for example, 0°C and 0°F stand for different magnitudes of temperature and do not indicate absence of temperature. Furthermore, let's assume that the property being measured on a ratio scale is length of objects. If two objects are 50 feet and 25 feet long, respectively, we can say that "the first object is *twice as long* as the second object." Unfortunately, it is not possible to measure latent variables that we deal with in counseling (or other) assessments. Therefore, we cannot say, for example, that "Mary is twice as motivated as John" if Mary has 100 points and John has 50 points on a motivation scale. The best we can try to achieve is that latent variables are measured on interval scales.

If we multiply (or divide) each of the numbers on a ratio scale by a (non-zero) constant, the resulting new numbers will also be on a ratio scale. The multiplication (or division) of ratio scale numbers by a non-zero constant maintains the ratio scale as it preserves the properties of distinctiveness, ordering, equal intervals, and equal ratios (indeed, when both the numerator and denominator of a ratio are multiplied by the same constant, the ratio does not change). In addition, arithmetic operations with ratio scale numbers are permissible. As noted earlier, typical ratio scales are those that measure distance, weight, age, time, and counting (e.g., number of spelling errors in a writing test).

1.4 TYPICAL SCALES FOR ASSESSMENT IN COUNSELING

Different approaches to measuring variables (constructs, in particular) are used in each type of assessment in counseling, for example, assessments of clinical, personality, and behavioral constructs; assessments of intelligence, aptitudes, and achievement; assessments in career counseling; and assessment in counseling of couples and families. A detailed description of such assessments can be found in Erford (2007). Typically, measurement scales in a variety of assessments are based on scores that represent the sum (or mean) of numbers assigned to responses of examinees, clients, or patients on individual items of the assessment instrument. For example, referring to a *binary scale* means that the scale scores represent the sum (or mean) of binary item scores (e.g., 1 = true, 0 = false). Likewise, referring to a *rating scale* means that the scale scores represent the sum (or mean) of numbers assigned to the response categories of individual items (e.g., from 1 = *strongly disagree* to 5 = *strongly agree* in five-level Likert items). Briefly described here are scales typically used for assessment in counseling, such as binary scales, Likert scales, Likert-type scales, and other rating scales.

1.4.1 Binary Scales

A *binary scale* is obtained by adding (or averaging) binary scores (1/0) assigned to people's responses on individual items (e.g., 1 = true, 0 = false) in an assessment instrument. In a test of 20 binary items, for example, the binary scale consists of 21 possible scores, from 0 to 20, if the scale scores are obtained by summing the binary scores on the individual items. The raw scale scores can be submitted to appropriate transformations to facilitate the score interpretation or to meet underlying assumptions, such as that of interval scales or normal distribution of scores.

Examples of binary scales for assessment in counseling include the following: (a) the Minnesota Multiphasic Personality Inventory—Second Edition (Butcher et al., 1989), a 56-item, true–false self-report inventory designed to assess major patterns of personality in adults aged 18–90 years; (b) the Substance Abuse Subtle Screening Inventory—3 (Miller & Lazowski, 1999), in which the scales consist of 67 true–false items regarding substance dependence; (c) the Jackson Personality Inventory—Revised (D. N. Jackson, 1997), an inventory of 300 true–false statements designed to measure 15 personality traits grouped into five higher order categories: Analytical, Emotional, Extroverted, Opportunistic, and Dependable; (d) Otis–Lennon School Ability Test (Otis & Lennon, 2004), a school ability test for students in Grades K–12 that includes seven levels (A–G), with binary scored items (1 = correct, 0 = incorrect) measuring five cognitive skills: verbal comprehension, verbal reasoning, pictorial reasoning, figural reasoning, and quantitative reasoning; and (e) TerraNova—Second Edition (CTB/McGraw-Hill, 2001), a multiple-skills test battery for students in Grades K–12 that uses binary scored multiple-choice items (1 = correct, 0 = incorrect) grouped into four scales to assess Reading/Language Arts, Mathematics, Science, and Social Studies (school systems can choose both multiple-choice items and constructed-response items).

1.4.2 Rating Scales

A rating scale is represented by a set of ordered-category statements that express attitude, satisfaction, or perception about something (e.g., how often a specific behavior occurs). For each statement (scale item), the respondents are asked to select a category label from a list indicating the level of their attitude, satisfaction, or perception related to the statement. The numeric value associated with the category selected by a person represents the person's item score. The scale score for a person is obtained by summing (or averaging) the scores of that person on all individual items. Some clarifications on the legitimacy of summing (or averaging) scores are provided later in this chapter (Section 1.5.6). The most common examples of rating scales, Likert scale and Likert-type scale, are presented next.

Likert Scale. The widely used Likert scales were developed by the American sociologist Rensis Likert (1903–1981). (Likert pronounced his name with a short *i* sound.) A distinction must be made first between a *Likert scale* and a *Likert item*. The Likert scale is the sum of responses on several Likert items, whereas a Likert item is a statement that the respondent is asked to evaluate according to (subjective or objective) criteria—usually, five levels of agreement or disagreement with the statement, where 1= *strongly disagree*, 2 = *disagree*, 3 = *neither agree nor disagree*, 4 = *agree*, 5 = *strongly agree*.

With, say, 20 Likert items, the Likert scale scores produced by the summation of the item scores will vary from 20 to 100: A score of 20 will have people who answered "strongly disagree" to all 20 items, and a score of 100, people who answered "strongly agree" to all 20 items. Instead of the sum, one can use the average of the 20 item scores as Likert scale value in this case. In general, a Likert scale that is obtained by summing (or averaging) five-level Likert items is usually referred to in the literature as a *5-point Likert scale.* This term is also used here, primarily for consistency with references to published studies and assessment instruments, but it should be kept in mind that a 5-point Likert scale refers to a scale composed of five-level Likert items. Likewise, a 7-point Likert scale is composed of seven-level Likert items: 1= *strongly disagree*, 2 = *disagree*, 3 = *slightly disagree*, 4 = *neutral*, 5 = *slightly agree*, 6 = *agree*, and 7 = *strongly agree*. Table 1.1 provides three Likert items from the Career-Related Parent Support Scale (Turner, Alliman-Brissett, Lapan, Udipi, & Ergun, 2003).

Uebersax (2006) summarized the characteristics of a "genuine" Likert scale as follows:

1. The scale contains several items.
2. Response levels are arranged horizontally.
3. Response levels are anchored with consecutive integers.
4. Response levels are also anchored with verbal labels that connote more or less evenly spaced gradations.
5. Verbal labels are bivalent and symmetrical about a neutral middle.
6. In Likert's usage, the scale always measures *attitude* in terms of level of agreement or disagreement to a target statement.

Of course, there is no need to strictly apply all of the above six criteria when using the Likert scale concept. For example, Criterion 6 can be relaxed to allow for applications of Likert's methodology to domains other than attitude measurement. Also, Criterion 5 implies that the Likert scale is based on an odd number of item response levels, but sometimes it might be more reasonable to use four-level Likert items by omitting the middle (neutral) category. This method is referred to as *forced-choice* because the middle option of *neither agree nor disagree* is omitted, for example, to avoid the so-called central tendency bias that

TABLE 1.1

Three Five-Level Likert Items From the Career-Related Parent Support Scale (CRPSS)

CRPSS Item	**Response Scale**				
Please indicate how much you agree or disagree with each of the following statements:					
	Strongly Disagree	*Disagree*	*Neither Agree nor Disagree*	*Agree*	*Strongly Agree*
My parents help me do my homework.	1	2	3	4	5
My parents encourage me to make good grades.	1	2	3	4	5
My parents praise me when I learn job-related skills.	1	2	3	4	5

Note. Adapted from "The Career-Related Parent Support Scale," by S. L. Turner, A. Alliman-Brissett, R. T. Lapan, S. Udipi, and D. Ergun, 2003, *Measurement and Evaluation in Counseling and Development, 36,* p. 89. Copyright 2003 by the American Counseling Association. No further reproduction is authorized without written permission of the American Counseling Association.

occurs when the respondents tend to avoid the extreme categories. Response options other than "agree/disagree" can be used in Likert items as long as Criteria 2 to 4 in the Likert scale definition are in place (see the first scale type and item in Table 1.2).

Likert-Type Scale. When Criteria 2–4 in the definition of a genuine Likert scale, described in the previous section, are in place for a given item but Criterion 5 is somewhat relaxed, the item can be referred to as a *Likert-type item* (Uebersax, 2006). For example, the second (middle) item in Table 1.2 is a Likert-type item. Indeed, Criteria 2–4 are in place, but Criterion 5 regarding bivalent and symmetrical verbal levels is not fully satisfied because the lowest level (*never*) is not exactly the opposite of the highest level (*very often*). However, the item levels can still be interpretable as evenly spaced, especially when associated with consecutive integers in an evenly spaced printed format, as shown in Table 1.2 (middle item). A Likert-type scale, then, is a scale that consists of Likert-type items.

Likert scales and Likert-type scales are widely used in instruments for assessment in counseling. Examples include (a) the Revised NEO Personality Inventory (Costa & McCrae, 1992), an inventory designed to measure the five major dimensions of personality using a 5-point Likert scale ranging from 1 (*strongly agree*) to 5 (*strongly disagree*); (b) the Tennessee Self-Concept Scale—Second Edition (Fitts & Warren, 1996), an inventory of self-report measures of self-concept on a 5-point Likert scale ranging from 1 (*always false*) to 5 (*always true*); (c) the Career Beliefs Inventory (Krumboltz, 1997), an inventory designed to identify career beliefs and assumptions that may block clients from taking constructive action and that uses a 5-point Likert scale ranging from 1 (*strongly disagree*) to 5 (*strongly agree*); (d) the Reynolds Adolescent Depression Scale—Second Edition (Reynolds, 2002), a 4-point Likert-type scale (*almost never*, *hardly ever*, *sometimes*, *most of the time*) on scale items such as "I feel lonely" and "I feel like running away"; and (e) the Symptom Checklist–90—Revised (Derogatis, 1992), a 4-point Likert-type scale on which the clients are asked to rate their level of discomfort with a given problem, ranging from 0 (*not at all*) to 4 (*extremely*).

Likert scales may be subject to distortion attributable to (a) *central tendency bias*—respondents avoid using extreme response categories, (b) *acquiescence bias*—respondents agree with the statements as presented, and/or (c) *social desirability bias*—respondents try to portray themselves or their organization in a more favorable light. Designing a scale with an equal

TABLE 1.2

Examples of a Five-Level Likert Item for Approval on Same-Sex Marriage, a Five-Level Likert-Type Item on Frequency of Alcohol Consumption, and a Four-Level Ordered Category Item on Frequency of Library Visits

Scale Type and Item	Response Scale				
	Strongly Disapprove	*Disapprove*	*Neutral*	*Approve*	*Strongly Approve*
Likert scale How do you feel about same-sex marriage?	1	2	3	4	5
	Never	*Sometimes*	*Average*	*Often*	*Very Often*
Likert-type scale How often do you consume alcohol?	1	2	3	4	5
	Never	*Once*	*2–3 Times*	*More Than 3 Times*	
Frequency response scale How often do you visit a library monthly?	1	2	3	4	

Note. In Likert-type items, the criterion of "bivalent and symmetrical verbal levels" is not fully satisfied.

number of positively and negatively worded statements can avert the problem of acquiescence bias, but central tendency and social desirability are somewhat more problematic. As noted earlier, researchers often try to avoid the central tendency bias by using a forced-choice method, that is, by omitting the middle option (e.g., *neither agree nor disagree*) in Likert or Likert-type items.

Frequency Rating Scale. Rating scales represented by a set of statements about frequency levels of an event (e.g., how often a particular behavior has been observed) are referred to here as *frequency rating scales*. Some frequency rating scales consist of ordered-category items that are not Likert items or Likert-type items. This is the case, for example, with the third (bottom) item in Table 1.2: The verbal labels of the ordered categories in this item are not symmetrical about a neutral middle and do not connote evenly spaced gradations.

As shown in Table 1.2 (middle item), however, some frequency rating scales are developed with the intent to satisfy the criteria for a Likert-type scale (e.g., 1 = *never*, 2 = *sometimes*, 3 = *average*, 4 = *often*, and 5 = *very often*). Examples of frequency rating scales in instruments for assessment in counseling are (a) the Disruptive Behavior Rating Scale (Erford, 1993), which measures disruptive behaviors of children aged 5–10 years, with the answer on each item indicating the frequency of a displayed behavior: 0 = *rarely/hardly*, 1 = *occasionally*, 2 = *frequently*, and 3 = *most of the time*; and (b) the Attention Deficit Disorders Evaluation Scale—Third Edition (McCarney & Arthaud, 2004a, 2004b), a scale designed to assess symptoms of attention deficit hyperactivity disorder in children and youths based on input provided by primary observers (parents or educators), with a child's demonstration of behavior rated on a frequency rating scale (which, clearly, is not a Likert-type scale): 0 = *not developmentally appropriate*, 1 = *not observed*, 2 = *one to several times per month*, 3 = *one to several times per week*, 4 = *one to several times per day*.

Descriptive Rating Scale. Rating scales represented by a set of statements that describe levels of a particular trait, state, or feelings (e.g., sadness, mood, or guilt) are usually referred to as *descriptive rating scales*. Consider, for example, the descriptive rating scales used on the item about "feelings of guilt" from the Hamilton Rating Scale for Depression Scale (Hamilton, 1960):

0 = *Absent*
1 = *Self reproach, feels he has let people down*
2 = *Ideas of guilt or rumination over past errors or sinful deeds*
3 = *Present illness is a punishment. Delusions of guilt*
4 = *Hears accusatory or denunciatory voices and/or experiences threatening visual hallucinations*

Clearly, the ordered categories of "feelings of guilt" described with this item do not represent a Likert scale or Likert-type scale (they are not symmetrical about a neutral middle and do not connote evenly spaced gradations).

Visual Analog Scale. A visual analog scale (VAS) is represented by a straight line with two end anchors that are labeled as the extreme boundaries of the intensity of a phenomenon being measured, for example, pain, anxiety, satisfaction, and so forth. For instance, a VAS to measure intensity of pain could be labeled "*No pain*" on one end and "*Pain as bad as it could possibly be*" on the other, whereas a VAS to measure intensity of anxiety could be labeled "*Not anxious*" on one end and "*As anxious as I could be*" on the other end (see Figure 1.1 a). The patients mark on the line the point that they feel represents their perception of their current state. It is recommended that the VAS line be horizontal (instead of vertical), with a distance of 100 millimeters (mm) between the two ends (e.g., Wewers & Lowe, 1990).

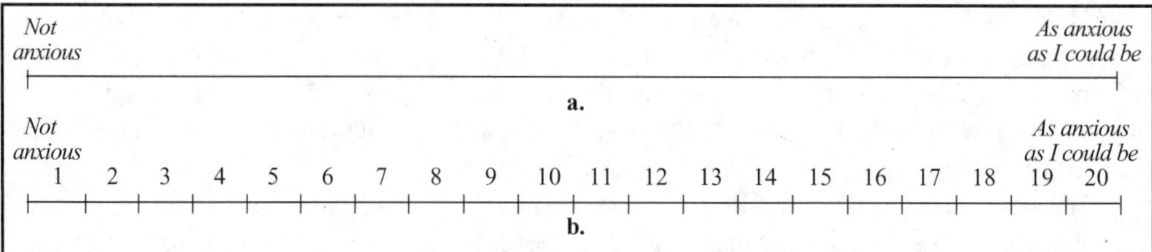

FIGURE 1.1

An Example of a Visual Analog Scale (VAS) Measuring Intensity of Anxiety

The VAS is scored by measuring the distance (in millimeters) from one end of the scale to the subject's mark on the line. Alternatively, a VAS may be scored by superimposing a key grid or stencil divided into predetermined intervals, such as 20 half-centimeter (5-millimeter) intervals, resulting in a possible range of scores of 0 to 20—see Figure 1.1 b (Guiffre, 1983). As a point of comparison, previous research shows that, compared with 5-point Likert-type scales, VAS are less sensitive to mode differences between computer-assisted and self-administered interviews (Gerich, 2007). This finding, however, cannot be generalized as an overall advantage of VAS over Likert-type scales in terms of psychometric characteristics. In a study on optimizing scale categories for self-efficacy (and other) research, E. V. Smith, Wakely, de Kruif, and Swartz (2003) pointed out some potential problems using the 0 to 100 scale with 10-point increments and argued that "specific methods should be used to optimize the number of rating points for each application of a self-efficacy scale in a given research context and be replicated to support the modifications made" (p. 373).

There are numerous studies using VAS, particularly in the area of hospital counseling. For example, Khazaal et al. (2008) used VAS (horizontal lines, 100 mm in length, anchored by word descriptions at each end) to assess attitudes toward stopping smoking, with ratings from 0 (*not at all*) to 100 (*absolutely*). D. R. Thompson, Webster, and Meddis (1990) also used typical VAS (horizontal lines, 100 mm in length, anchored by word descriptions at each end) to assess first-time myocardial infarction patients and spouses' satisfaction with in-hospital counseling, with ratings from 0 (*not at all satisfied*) to 100 (*extremely satisfied*).

Discussing strengths and limitations of VAS, Wewers and Lowe (1990) pointed out that (a) careful instruction and repeated use of a VAS is necessary to eliminate problems with conceptual understanding of the method, especially with an elderly population; (b) inaccurate reproduction of the instrument (e.g., in photocopying) may distort the length of the line; (c) the placement of the mark on the line can be altered because of factors such as the angle at which a subject views the VAS, the effects of medication on hand–eye coordination, and other perceptual/motor limitations caused by the subject's clinical status; (d) scales that contain bipolar anchors (i.e., depression–elation) are not recommended because they introduce two phenomena, thus increasing conceptual difficulties; and (e) although an extreme boundary such as *no pain* is easily understood by subjects, the other extreme boundary, *pain as bad as it can be*, is subjectively interpreted, thus affecting the placement of the mark along the line between these two extremes.

Semantic Differential. The semantic differential scale measures people's reactions to stimulus words and concepts in terms of 7-point ratings on bipolar scales defined with contrasting adjectives at each end (Osgood, Tannenbaum, & Suci, 1957; Snider & Osgood, 1969). Using an exploratory factor analysis of large collections of semantic differential scales, Osgood (1962) identified three attitude dimensions that people use to evaluate words and phrases: Evaluation, Potency, and Activity. Specifically, Evaluation is defined by the adjective pair *good–bad*, Potency by the adjective pair *strong–weak*, and Activity by the adjective pair *active–passive*. These three dimensions of affective meaning were found to be cross-cultural universals in a study of dozens of cultures (Osgood, May, & Miron, 1975).

An example of a semantic differential item is shown in Figure 1.2. Usually the position marked 0 is labeled *neutral*, the 1 positions are labeled *slightly*, the 2 positions *quite*, and the 3 positions *extremely* (e.g., Heise, 1970).

The semantic differential scale measures both the directionality (e.g., tense vs. relaxed) and intensity (e.g., slight through extreme) of the person's reaction to the respective stimulus. A readable discussion of methodology and scaling related to semantic differential was provided by Heise (1970). As he noted (p. 235), ratings on bipolar adjective scales tend to be correlated, and three basic dimensions of response account for most of the covariation in ratings: Evaluation, Potency, and Activity (EPA). Thus, unlike the unidimensional Likert scales, the semantic differential scale has a three-dimensional (EPA) structure. Prior to combining the item scores into separate factor scores, numerical values (–3, –2, –1, 0, 1, 2, 3) are assigned to the scale positions (see Figure 1.2), going from one end of the scale to the other. Then the EPA factor scores (e, p, and a, respectively) can be used separately or to produce a general polarization index, $P = \sqrt{e^2 + p^2 + a^2}$, which indicates the distance from the origin (zero) of the scale and the particular concept under consideration. When the interest is in comparing two concepts (or two groups on the same concept), collectively on all three EPA dimensions, one can use the so-called D score: $D = \sqrt{(e_1 - e_2)^2 + (p_1 - p_2)^2 + (a_1 - a_2)^2}$, where e_1, p_1, and a_1 are the factor scores on Evaluation, Potency, and Activity, respectively, for the first concept (or group), and e_2, p_2, and a_2 are their counterparts for the second concept (or group; see Heise, p. 342).

1.5 SCALING

1.5.1 What Is Scaling?

Scaling is a type of measurement in which one first focuses on rationales and statistical techniques in order to generate an initial pool of items (questions). Then one selects the items (or questions) that represent valid indicators of the construct (ability, trait, property) being measured, and one determines what numbers should be used to represent different magnitudes of the construct. That is, the purpose of scaling is to develop scales with desirable measurement characteristics. The number assigned to a person based on his or her responses to the scale items is called a *scale value*. The scale value for a person is referred to as the *observed score* (or *raw score*) when it is obtained as the sum of the person's scores on the scale items. For example, using a 5-point Likert scale with 20 items, each scored from 1 (*strongly disagree*) to 5 (*strongly agree*), the raw scores can vary from 20 to 100.

1.5.2 Dimensionality

A scale is *unidimensional* when it measures a single trait (property, ability)—that is, there is a single latent factor that underlies the person's responses on the set of scale items. For example, scales that measure height or weight are unidimensional. Typically, rating scales

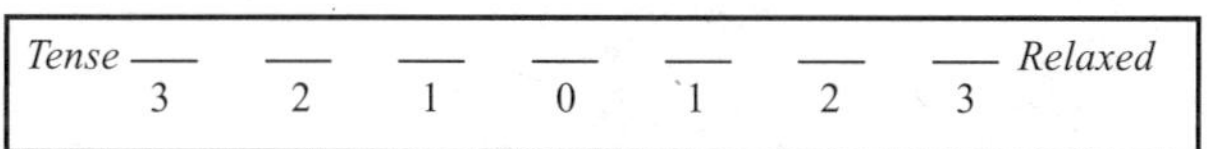

FIGURE 1.2

An Example of a Semantic Differential Item

(e.g., Likert or Likert-type scales) are developed to measure unidimensional constructs, such as job satisfaction, attitude toward smoking, and so forth.

In contrast, a scale is *multidimensional* when it measures two or more traits (properties, abilities). For example, scales that measure intelligence are multidimensional because the theoretical models of intelligence postulate dimensions such as verbal ability, quantitative ability, visual–spatial reasoning, and so forth (e.g., see Erford, Klein, & McNinch, 2007). A semantic differential scale that measures the meaning of a term is also multidimensional, as the general theory of meaning postulates three dimensions: evaluation, potency, and activity (see the description of semantic differential scales in Section 1.4.2). Typically, the scales for assessment in counseling are multidimensional, referring to each dimension as a subscale (factor, facet). For example, the Attention Deficit Disorders Evaluation Scale—Third Edition (McCarney & Arthaud, 2004b) consists of two subscales: Inattentive and Hyperactive–Impulsive. As another example, the Disruptive Behavior Rating Scale (Erford, 1993) consists of four subscales: Distractible, Oppositional, Impulsive–Hyperactivity, and Antisocial Conduct. Testing for dimensionality, which is a major step in scale development, is discussed later in this book from both exploratory and confirmatory perspectives.

1.5.3 Likert Scaling

The development of a Likert (or Likert-type) scale is a process of unidimensional scaling. Trochim (2006) described this as a five-step process. The first step is to define the trait that is being measured, assuming that this is a unidimensional trait (e.g., self-esteem, ability, motivation, and so forth). The next step is to generate a pool of potential Likert items, preferably 80–100 items rated on a 15 or 17 *disagree–agree* response scale. The third step is to have a group of judges rate the items on how favorable they are to the concept (trait), say using a 1–5 scale: 1 = *strongly unfavorable*, 2 = *somewhat unfavorable*, 3 = *undecided*, 4 = *somewhat favorable*, 5 = *strongly favorable*.

The fourth step is to make judgments about which items to retain for the final scale. This step involves a variety of analyses, such as (a) computing the intercorrelations between all pairs of items based on the judges' ratings; (b) throwing out items that have a low correlation with the total score across all items; (c) performing a t test for each item of the differences between the mean values for the item using the top quarter and the bottom quarter of ranking numbers for the item provided by the judges—items with higher t values are better discriminators; and (d) taking into account the merits and practical considerations of retaining various items (though items with high item–total correlations and high discrimination are preferred).

Finally, the fifth step is to administer the scale, with each respondent rating each item on its response scale, and to use the sum of the respondent's ratings for all items as his or her raw score on the scale. If some items are reversed in meaning from the overall direction of the scale, their response values must be reversed prior to using them in the summation for the total raw score. Because the overall assessment with an instrument is based on the respondent's scores on all items, the measurement quality of the total score is of particular interest.

The Likert scaling process described above can be viewed as a classical approach to initial scale development, which can be further refined using more sophisticated procedures in the framework of item response theory and latent trait modeling. More information in this regard is provided in Chapters 8 and 9.

1.5.4 Guttman Scaling

The Guttman scale (Guttman, 1944, 1950) presents a list of hierarchically arranged statements to which the person is requested to agree or not agree. Questions in a Guttman scale gradually increase in specificity. The intent of the scale is that the person will agree with all statements up to a point and then will stop agreeing. The scale may be used to determine how extreme a view is, with successive statements showing increasingly extremist positions. The Guttman scale is also known as a *scalogram analysis*, *deterministic scaling*, or *cumulative scaling*. The rating is scaled by summing all responses until the first negative response in the list (hence the name *cumulative scale* as one of the references to a Guttman scale). R. L. Thorndike (2005, p. 393) provided the following example of a Guttman scale:

1. Abortion should be available to any woman who wishes one.
2. Abortion should be legal if a doctor recommends it.
3. Abortion should be legal whenever the pregnancy is the result of rape or incest.
4. Abortion should be legal whenever the health or well-being of the mother is endangered.
5. Abortion should be legal only when the life of the mother is endangered.

With this Guttman scale, it is presumed that a respondent selecting Choice 3 also agrees with the conditions listed in Choices 1 and 2 but not with those listed in Choices 4 and 5. The scale score for that respondent would be 3 (i.e., the sum 1 + 1 + 1 for "positive" responses on the first three items). Another example of a Guttman scale is the Bogardus Social Distance Scale (Bogardus, 1925). The scale measures people's willingness to participate in social contacts of varying degrees of closeness with members of diverse social groups, such as other racial and ethnic groups, or with sex offenders. Following is an example of a Bogardus Social Distance Scale:

Place a check-mark against any item with which you agree that illegal immigrants

☐ should be deported immediately
☐ can live in this country
☐ can live in your town
☐ can live in your neighborhood
☐ can be your next door neighbors
☐ can be your close friends

The Bogardus Social Distance Scale is a Guttman scale because agreement with any item implies agreement with all preceding items. In the above example, the respondent is assigned (a) a score of 1 if only the first item is checked, (b) a score of 2 if the first two items are checked, (c) a score of 3 if the first three items are checked, (d) a score of 4 if the first four items are checked, (e) a score of 5 if the first five items are checked, and (f) a score of 6 if all six items are checked. Under such scoring, the maximum score (here, a score of 6) would indicate *no* social distance. Harris (1980) used Guttman scale analysis in a study on coercive child behavior. Specifically, Guttman scaling was used to determine if there were regular, unidimensional progressions across eight coercive response categories, that is, that children who performed high probability coercive behaviors would also tend to perform all of the lower probability coercive behaviors. Hofmann (1979) discussed the Guttman scale from the viewpoint of errors in response patterns and a significance test for such errors. Hays and Ellickson (1990–1991) described an extension of the traditional Guttman scaling to a longitudinal scalogram analysis and illustrated its application in a study on drug use involvement.

1.5.5 Thurstone Scaling

Louis Thurstone (1887–1955) proposed three methods for developing a unidimensional scale: the method of equal-appearing intervals, the method of successive intervals, and the method of paired comparisons. Briefly described here is the method of equal-appearing intervals. Just like with Likert scaling, the first step is to define the concept (trait) of interest and to generate a pool of (say, 80–100) potential items that reflect this concept. Then a group of judges (the larger, the better) rate the items on how favorable they are to the concept—typically using a scale ranging from 1 (*least favorable to the concept*) to 11 (*most favorable to the concept*). It is important to make sure that all of the statements are worded similarly, that is, that they don't differ in grammar or structure. For example, there should not be a mixture of questions and statements that the respondents are asked to agree or disagree with.

The next step is to compute the median and interquartile range of the ratings for each item and to sort the items in ascending order by the median; items with equal medians are sorted in descending order by the interquartile range (IRQ; the difference between the third and first quartiles). Furthermore, the items that are at equal intervals across the range of medians are selected to form the scale; among items with the same median, the choice is based on the criteria of smaller IRQ and better substantive meaning. The median associated with each selected item represents its scale value. For example, if the items are statements of attitude toward school, items with higher scale values should indicate more favorable reflection of attitude toward school. Finally, the respondents are asked to either agree or disagree with each of the selected scale items. A respondent's total score is computed as the average of the scale values of the items that he or she agreed with (e.g., see Trochim, 2006).

The other Thurstone scaling methods (successive intervals and paired comparisons) are somewhat similar to the method of equally appearing intervals, but the judges' data are collected differently. Under the method of paired comparisons, for example, each judge is asked to make a judgment about each pair of items regarding which item is more favorable to the concept (trait) of interest. As demonstrated by Thurstone (1927a, 1927b, 1928), this method can yield an interval-scale ordering of items along a dimension such as preference or importance. However, as the initial pool of items for an assessment instrument is usually large, the paired comparisons are time consuming and difficult to process. For details on the method of paired comparisons, the reader may refer to David (1988). The Thurstone scaling method of successive intervals was first reported by Safir (1937) along with a computational procedure. Under this method, a set of stimuli (e.g., items) are sorted by judges into categories ordered according to some stated property. Two parameters—a scale value and a discrimination variance—are estimated for each stimulus, and two parameters—a scale value and a variance—are estimated for each boundary between categories. Numerous computational procedures that have been proposed for estimations with the method of successive intervals include graphical approaches, algebraic solutions, least squares fitting, and likelihood solutions (e.g., Adams & Messick, 1958; Blischke, Bush, & Kaplan, 1975; Schonemann & Tucker, 1967; Torgerson, 1958, pp. 214–240).

1.5.6 Transformations of Scale Scores

Transformations of scale scores are often necessary for interpreting, score equating (presenting scores on a common scale), and performing various statistical and psychometric analyses. The transformations can be linear or nonlinear. The general form of a linear transformation is $Y = bX + a$, where X is the raw score, b and a are constants (referred to as the *slope* and *intercept*, respectively), and Y is the transformed score. For example, if the raw scores X (say, 2, 10, and 24) are submitted to the linear transformation $Y = 0.5X - 1$, the resulting transformed scores are Y: 0, 4, and 11, respectively.

Important properties of linear transformations are that they (a) maintain the interval scale, that is, if the X scores are on an interval scale, so are the Y scores; (b) do not alter the shape of the score distribution, for example, if the distribution of X scores is normal, the distribution of Y scores is also normal (or, if the distribution of X scores is positively [negatively] skewed, the distribution of Y scores is also positively [negatively] skewed), and (c) do not alter the size of correlations, that is, if the raw scores on two variables, X_1 and X_2, are linearly transformed, say $Y_1 = bX_1 + a$ and $Y_2 = cX_2 + d$, the correlation between X_1 and X_2 is of the same size as that between Y_1 and Y_2; specifically, $r_{Y_1 Y_2} = r_{X_1 X_2}$ when the coefficients b and c are of the same sign (both positive or both negative), and $r_{Y_1 Y_2} = -r_{X_1 X_2}$ when b and c have opposite signs. The raw score transformations discussed here are all *monotonic* transformations; that is, they preserve the rank order of raw scores. All linear transformations $Y = bX + a$, with a positive coefficient for X ($b > 0$), are monotonic transformations. Presented next are transformations of raw scores that are useful in scale development and analysis. The group of people whose raw scores are used in this process is referred to here as a *norm group*—typically a random sample of people (e.g., test examinees or clients) selected from a population of interest.

Percentiles. To understand the relative standing of people in a norm group with respect to their score values on a continuous latent trait (e.g., verbal ability or anxiety), the raw scores are transformed into percentile ranks. Specifically, the *percentile rank* of a given raw score, X, is defined as the percentage of people in a norm group who have scores less than or equal to X. For example, if 82% of the examinees in a norm group have a score less than or equal to 25, then the percentile rank of 25 is 82 (denoted as $PR_{25} = 82$). Conversely, the score of 25 in this example represents the 82nd percentile (denoted $P_{82} = 25$). Thus, *percentile* and *percentile rank* are closely related, but they are not identical; any percentile is a score at or below which a certain percentage of all other scores fall, whereas the percentile rank of a particular score is the percentage of scores that are less than or equal to that score. The median of a score distribution is the 50th percentile ($Mdn = P_{50}$), the first quartile is the 25th percentile ($Q_1 = P_{25}$), the second quartile is the 50th percentile ($Q_2 = P_{50} = Mdn$), and the third quartile is the 75th percentile ($Q_3 = P_{75}$). For any score distribution, the middle 50% of the scores fall between the first and third quartiles. The distance between these two quartiles is called the *interquartile range*: $IQR = Q_3 - Q_1$. The computation of percentiles is provided with standard statistical packages such as SPSS or SAS.

Stanines. When the distribution of raw scores, X, is normal, stanine (*Sta*ndard *nine*) is a method of scaling test scores on a 9-point standard scale with a mean of 5 and a standard deviation of 2. Specifically, (a) a stanine of 1 is assigned to the lowest 4% of the scores—scores below the 4th percentile, P_4; (b) a stanine of 2, to the next 7% of the scores—between P_4 and P_{11}; (c) a stanine of 3, to the next 12% of the scores—between P_{11} and P_{23}; (d) a stanine of 4, to the next 17% of the scores—between P_{23} and P_{40}; (e) a stanine of 5, to the next 20%—between P_{40} and P_{60}; (f) a stanine of 6, to the next 17% of the scores—between P_{60} and P_{77}; (g) a stanine of 7, to the next 12% of the scores—between P_{77} and P_{89}; (h) a stanine of 8, to the next 7% of the scores—between P_{89} and P_{96}; and (i) a stanine of 9, to the next 4% of the scores—above P_{96}. Thus, using stanines, the raw scores are converted into single-digit numbers (1, . . . , 9). A disadvantage of stanines is that it is possible that two raw scores in a single stanine can be further apart than two raw scores that fall in adjacent stanines.

Standard Scores. To obtain the *standard score* (or z score) that corresponds to any raw score, X, the mean of the raw scores in a norm group, $\bar{X}$, is subtracted from the raw score X, and the resulting number is divided by the standard deviation of the raw scores, s; that is, $z = (X - \bar{X})/s$ The standard score of X indicates how many standard deviations X is below or above the mean. For example, $z = 2$ indicates that X is two standard deviations above the mean, whereas $z = -1.5$ indicates that X is one and one-half standard deviations below the mean. Standard scores always have a mean of zero and a standard deviation of 1.

As the z score formula represents a linear transformation of the raw scores, X, the shape of the z score distribution will be the same as the shape of the raw-score distribution, and correlations will not be affected. When the raw-score distribution is positively (or negatively) skewed, the z score distribution is also positively (or negatively) skewed. Thus, contrary to popular belief, the z score distribution is *not* always normal. Only when the raw-score distribution is normal is the z score distribution normal—in which case it is referred to as a *standard normal distribution*, denoted $N(0, 1)$. This distribution is depicted in Figure 1.3, with graphical illustration of the basic properties of the normal distribution, such as (a) symmetry around the mean; (b) "one-sigma rule": about 68% of the scores fall within the interval $\mu \pm \sigma$; (c) "two-sigma rule": about 95% of the scores fall within the interval $\mu \pm 2\sigma$; and (d) "three-sigma rule": 99.7% of the scores fall within the interval $\mu \pm 3\sigma$. Note that for the z score distribution the mean is zero ($\mu = 0$) and the standard deviation is one ($\sigma = 1$).

Standardized Scores. To avoid problems with negative values of standard scores in reports and interpretations, the standard scores can be transformed into a scale with a desired mean and standard deviation using a linear transformation. The resulting scores are referred to as *standardized scores*. Specifically, let μ and σ denote the mean and standard deviation of the population distribution of raw scores, X. To transform the X-score distribution into a distribution of Y scores with desired mean and standard deviation (denoted μ^* and σ^*, respectively), it is necessary to (a) transform the X scores into z scores, $z = (X - \mu)/\sigma$, and (b) transform the z scores into Y scores using the linear transformation $Y = z\sigma^* + \mu^*$. For example, when $\mu^* = 50$ and $\sigma^* = 10$, the scale of standardized scores is referred to as the T scale: $Y = 10z + 50$.

It is important to note that the distributions of the original raw scores, the standard (z) scores, and the standardized scores all have the same shape. This similar shape occurs because the original scores, X, are transformed into z scores using a linear transforma-

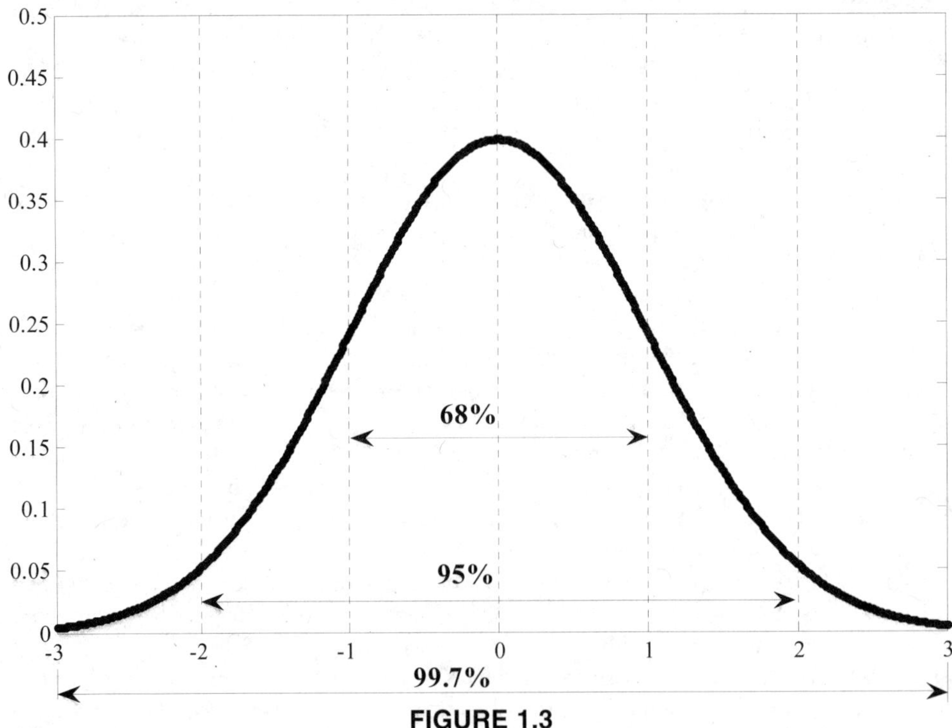

FIGURE 1.3

The Standard Normal Distribution, *N* (0, 1)

tion and then the z scores are transformed into standardized scores, Y, also using a linear transformation. Thus, it is not correct to compare scores on two standardized scales unless their frequency distributions have the same shape.

Normalized Scores. Most statistical and psychometric procedures assume that the score distribution is normal. Tests for normality are provided with standard statistical packages, for example, the normal quantile–quantile plot (Q–Q plot) in SPSS (e.g., see Dimitrov, 2008, p. 89). When the original raw scores are not normally distributed, they can be normalized by smoothing out departures from normality in their distribution. The resulting scores from such a transformation are called *normalized scores*. Normalizing scores is appropriate only if there is a reasonable expectation that the underlying trait (ability, property) being measured is distributed normally for the population of interest. Under this assumption, the normalization of raw scores is performed by following these steps: (a) transform the raw scores to percentiles, (b) find the z scores in the standard normal distribution that correspond to the percentiles, and (c) transform the z scores to standardized scores with a desired mean and standard deviation, for example, T scores ($\mu = 50$, $\sigma = 10$) or stanines ($\mu = 5$, $\sigma = 2$). Keep in mind, however, that if the raw-score distribution in a norm group is highly skewed, small raw-score differences between extreme scores may be artificially extended or compressed with the normalization. Even if it is expected that the distribution of scores on the underlying trait is normal, such an expectation would be reasonable only if the scores are reliable and valid. Therefore, one should not normalize scores obtained with a poor assessment tool. Example of normalized scales are the T scale ($\mu = 50$, $\sigma = 10$), normal curve equivalent scale (NCE; $\mu = 50$, $\sigma = 21$), IQ scale ($\mu = 100$, $\sigma = 15$), and school ability index ($\mu = 50$, $\sigma = 16$).

Interval Scales. Along with the assumption that the score distribution is normal, the assumption that the scale is interval (see Section 1.3.3) is critical for statistical and psychometric procedures used in the development and validation of assessment tools. Typically, the initial raw scores on rating scales do not form an interval scale; that is, equal differences between scale scores do not necessarily reflect equal differences between trait magnitudes (e.g., see Merbitz, Morris, & Grip, 1989; Wright & Linacre, 1989). For example, the raw scores on Likert items are considered as ordinal data because one cannot assume that respondents perceive all pairs of adjacent levels as equidistant. On the other hand, the symmetry of response levels about a middle category implies that, at the very least, such items fall between ordinal- and interval-level measurement. This argument becomes even stronger when the items are accompanied by a visual analog scale, where equal spacing of response levels is clearly indicated (of course, this does not mean that the observed scores form an interval scale). Reips and Funke (2008) described an online-based approach to creating visual analog scales that approximate an interval-scale level of measurement. They developed a tool called the VAS Generator (www.vasgenerator.net), which represents "a free Web service for creating a wide range of visual analog scales that can be used as measurement devices in Web surveys and Web experimentations, as well as for local computerized assessments" (Reips & Funke, 2008, p. 699).

Wright and Linacre (1989) emphasized that "meaningful measurement is based on the arithmetical properties of interval scales" (p. 857); therefore, it is important to transform the initial observations (e.g., rating-scale counts) into linear measures (i.e., scores on an interval scale). They also argued that a psychometrically rigorous solution to this task is provided by use of Rasch data analysis (e.g., Andrich, 1988; Rasch, 1960; Wright & Masters, 1982). More details on such analysis are provided in Chapter 9.

When the preliminary conditions for Rasch analysis (e.g., sufficiently large sample and data fit) are not in place, one can use conventional methods, such as Thurstone's absolute scaling method, to construct interval scales. This method works under the assumptions that (a) the trait being measured is continuous and normally distributed in the study population; and (b) the raw scores are monotonically related to the trait magnitudes that they represent, that is, the raw scores increase with the increase of the trait magnitudes. If these two assumptions are met, an interval scale is obtained by normalizing the raw scores (as described in the previous section). To test whether the two required assumptions are met, the raw scores on the trait of interest are normalized separately for two independent samples. Thus, each raw score is associated with a normalized score in one sample and with another normalized score in the other sample. If the two sets of normalized scores are linearly related, then the normalized scores for either sample form an interval scale.

Most inventories for assessment in counseling provide conversion of the raw scores into percentiles, stanines, and normalized scores. Some examples include the Piers–Harris Children's Self-Concept Scale—Second Edition (Piers & Herzberg, 2002), which uses percentile ranks, stanines, and T scores; the Conners' Rating Scales—Revised (Conners, 1997), which uses percentile ranks and T scores; the Otis–Lennon School Ability Test (Otis & Lennon, 2004), which uses percentile ranks, stanines, NCE scores, and school ability indexes; the Wechsler Abbreviated Scale of Intelligence (Wechsler, 1999), which uses percentile ranks, standard scores, T scores, and IQ scores; and the Marital Satisfaction Inventory—Revised (Snyder, 1997), which uses T scores.

The binary and rating scales described in this chapter are called *subject-centered scales* because they reflect differences among the respondents in terms of their standing along the trait (ability, property) being measured. There are also stimulus-centered scales, which reflect differences among items (e.g., Thurstone's paired comparison scale; see Trochim, 2006). As noted earlier, such scales are not addressed here as they are not that typical for assessment in counseling. Later in this book, I describe scales referred to as *response scales* in which differences among respondents and differences among items are measured on the same scale (e.g., Rasch calibrated scales; Andrich, 1978a, 1978b, 1988, 1996; Rasch, 1960, 1966; Wright & Masters, 1982).

SUMMARY

1. Variables that can be measured directly are referred to as *observable* variables (e.g., gender, age, ethnicity, time), whereas variables that cannot be measured directly are referred to as *unobservable* (or *latent*) variables (e.g., verbal ability, self-efficacy, anxiety, depression, and attitude [say, toward school]).
2. A *construct* is a latent (hidden) variable that is given an operational definition to specify which observed variables represent measurable indicators of the construct.
3. Continuous variable*s* are those that can take any possible value within a specific numeric interval (e.g., time on task, temperature, anxiety, and motivation). Discrete variables, on the other hand, can take only separate values (say, integer numbers).
4. Measurement is a process that involves three components—an object of measurement, a set of numbers, and a system of rules—that serve to assign numbers to magnitudes of the variable being measured.
5. A nominal scale is used to classify persons (or objects) into mutually exclusive categories. An ordinal scale is one in which the magnitudes of the variable being measured are ordered in the same way as the numbers assigned to these magnitudes. An interval scale provides information about the order and the distances between actual magnitudes of the variable being measured. A ratio scale provides information

about the ratio between magnitudes of the variable being measured; in addition, it provides information about the distinctiveness of such magnitudes, their order, and distances between them.

6. A binary scale is obtained by adding (or averaging) binary scores (1/0) assigned to the person's responses on individual items in an assessment instrument.
7. A rating scale is represented by a set of ordered-category statements that express attitude, satisfaction, or perception about something. Typical rating scales are the Likert scale, Likert-type scale, frequency rating scale, descriptive rating scale, visual analog scale, and semantic differential.
8. In a Likert item (a) the response levels are arranged horizontally and anchored with consecutive integers as well as with verbal labels that connote more or less evenly spaced gradations, and (b) the verbal labels are bivalent and symmetrical about a neutral middle category (which, when appropriate, can be omitted). If the second condition, (b), is not fully satisfied, this results in a Likert-type item.
9. The purpose of scaling is to develop scales with desirable measurement characteristics. The number assigned to a person based on his or her responses to the scale items is called a *scale value*.
10. A scale is unidimensional when it measures a single trait (property, ability)—that is, there is a single latent factor that underlies the person's responses on the set of scale items.
11. The development of a Likert (or Likert-type) scale is a process of unidimensional scaling.
12. The Guttman scale presents a list of hierarchically arranged statements to which the person is requested to agree or not agree. The questions gradually increase in specificity, and the person will agree with all statements up to a point and then will stop agreeing.
13. The Thurstone scale is a unidimensional scale that can be developed by the method of (a) equal-appearing intervals, (b) successive intervals, or (c) paired comparisons.
14. Transformations of raw scores are often necessary for purposes of interpreting, score equating (presenting scores on a common scale), and performing various statistical and psychometric analyses. The frequently used linear transformation ($Y = bX + a$) maintains the interval scale. Also, the distribution of the resulting Y scores has the same shape as that of the original scores, X; thus, the distribution of raw scores, X, does not change in shape under linear transformation to standard, z, scores.

Chapter 2
Reliability

Reliability is a key concept in measurement and plays an important role in evaluating the validity of assessment data. Generally speaking, the reliability of measurements indicates the degree to which they are free of random error. I want to clarify from the beginning here that reliability refers to the measurement data (scores) obtained with an instrument, *not* to the instrument itself. Tests cannot be accurate, stable, or unstable, but observations (scores) can. Therefore, any reference to reliability of a test should be interpreted to mean the reliability of the measurement data derived from a test.

In this chapter I present the concept of reliability in the framework of classical (true-score) theory of measurement. Assumptions that underlie the computation of reliability estimates such as Cronbach's coefficient alpha are clarified under the congeneric model of an assessment scale. Types of reliability are also discussed, with some elaboration on internal consistency reliability, criterion-referenced reliability, and interrater reliability. In addition, the concept of stratified alpha is introduced for estimation of reliability when scores from two or more scales are combined into a multidimensional composite score to measure and interpret a more general construct related to those scales. Finally, the concept of maximal reliability for congeneric measures is discussed.

2.1 WHAT IS RELIABILITY?

Measurements in social and behavioral sciences, and even physical measurements, are not completely accurate and consistent. For example, although the height of a person remains constant throughout repeated measurements using the same scale within a short period of time (say, 20 minutes), the observed values would be scattered around this constant because of imperfection in the visual acuity of the individual(s) performing the repeated measurements. It is even less likely that the scores of students on a given test are error free. When a person takes a test, there is always some error involved because of the test taker's emotional, physical, and/or psychological state (e.g., mood or fatigue) and/or because of external conditions (e.g., noise) that may randomly occur during the measurement process. The instrument of measurement (tests, inventories, or raters) may also affect the accuracy of the scores. For example, it is unlikely that an examinee's scores on two different forms of a reading comprehension test would be equal. Also, different scores are likely to be assigned to a student when different teachers evaluate, say, specific behavioral characteristics of that student. In another scenario, if a group of people take the same test twice within a short period of time, one can expect the rank order of their scores on the two test administrations to be somewhat similar but not exactly the same. In other words, one can expect a relatively high, yet not perfect, positive correlation of test–retest scores for the group of examinees. Inconsistency may occur also in criterion-referenced classification of people, say, on mastery/nonmastery of a particular content knowledge, based on subjective judgments of raters (e.g., teachers or school counselors).

In measurement parlance, the higher the accuracy and consistency of measurement scores, the higher their reliability. The reliability of measurements indicates the degree to which they are accurate, consistent, and replicable when (a) different people conduct the measurement, (b) different instruments are used that purport to measure the same trait (e.g., proficiency, ability, attitude, anxiety), and (c) there is incidental variation in measurement conditions (e.g., lighting, seating, temperature). That is, the reliability of scores shows the degree to which they are free of random error. Most important, the reliability of scores is a necessary condition for their valid interpretations and data-driven decisions in counseling, education, and other fields.

2.2 CLASSICAL CONCEPT OF RELIABILITY

2.2.1 True-Score Model

A fundamental assumption in the classical treatment of reliability is that the observed score, X, that a person receives on an assessment instrument is affected by random error, referred to as *error of measurement* (E). If we subtract the random error from the observed score, $X - E$, we will obtain the person's "true" score, T, on this particular test. In other words, the observed score, X, that a person may receive on a single test administration consists of two components: the true score, T, and the error of measurement, E. That is,

$$X = T + E. \tag{2.1}$$

> **Note 2.1**
>
> A person's true score is not a crystal ball value for the actual location of this person on a continuum of the trait (or ability) being measured, because the true score depends on the difficulty of the test and, therefore, will vary across tests with different levels of difficulty. Thus, a person with a given ability in, say, math will have different true scores on math tests with different levels of difficulty. As discussed later in this book (cf. Chapter 9), estimates of the person's actual ability (or trait) level, regardless of test difficulty, can be obtained in the framework of item response theory (IRT) or Rasch measurement.

To further explain the meaning of a *true score*, imagine that a person takes a standardized test each day for, say, 100 days in a row. The person would likely obtain a number of different observed scores over these 100 test administrations. The mean of all observed scores would represent an approximation of the person's true score, T, on this test. In general, a person's true score is the mean of the theoretical distribution of scores that would be observed for this person in repeated independent measurements using the same test. The true score is a hypothetical concept because it is not practically possible to test a person an infinite number of times in independent repeated administrations of the same test, given that each testing could influence the subsequent testing (e.g., because of carry over effects of practice or memory).

2.2.2 Congeneric Measures

To better understand the nature of observed scores and their reliability, it is necessary to introduce the concepts of parallel measures, tau-equivalent measures, and essentially tau-equivalent measures as obtained through restrictions on the more general concept of congeneric measures of a particular unidimensional trait. For specificity, consider three items (X_1, X_2, and X_3) with the assumption that they are linearly related to a single underlying latent trait, say η. Graphically, this model is depicted in Figure 2.1.

As the items are linearly related with the underlying latent trait, η, each of them can be predicted from η through a simple linear regression. That is,

$$\begin{aligned} X_1 &= (\lambda_1\eta + a_1) + E_1, \\ X_2 &= (\lambda_2\eta + a_2) + E_2, \\ X_3 &= (\lambda_3\eta + a_3) + E_3, \end{aligned} \tag{2.2}$$

where λ_1 is the slope, a_i is the intercept, and E_i is the residual (error term) in the linear regression (i = 1, 2, 3).

In Equations 2.2., the predicted score (in parentheses) for each item represents, in fact, the person's true score on the item:

$$\begin{aligned} T_1 &= \lambda_1\eta + a_1, \\ T_2 &= \lambda_2\eta + a_2, \\ T_3 &= \lambda_3\eta + a_3. \end{aligned} \tag{2.3}$$

In this example, the total score on the set of three items ($X = X_1 + X_2 + X_3$) has two components: the true score ($T = T_1 + T_2 + T_3$) and random error ($E = E_1 + E_2 + E_3$; cf. Equation 2.1).

Congeneric Measures. The observed scores in Equations 2.2 (X_1, X_2, and X_3) are called *congeneric measures* when they are allowed to have (a) different units of measurement—the slopes (λ_i) can be different; (b) dissimilar scale origins—the intercepts (a_i) can be different; and (c) unequal error variances—the variances of error terms, VAR(E_i) can be different (i = 1, 2, 3). Note also from Equations 2.3 that as the slopes (λ_i) can be different, the true scores can have different variances. Thus, the congeneric model of an assessment scale states that the scale items measure a single trait and they may have different true score variances and different error variances.

Parallel Measures. The most restricted case of congeneric measures, referred to as *parallel measures*, occurs when the following three conditions are in place: (a) all slopes are equal,

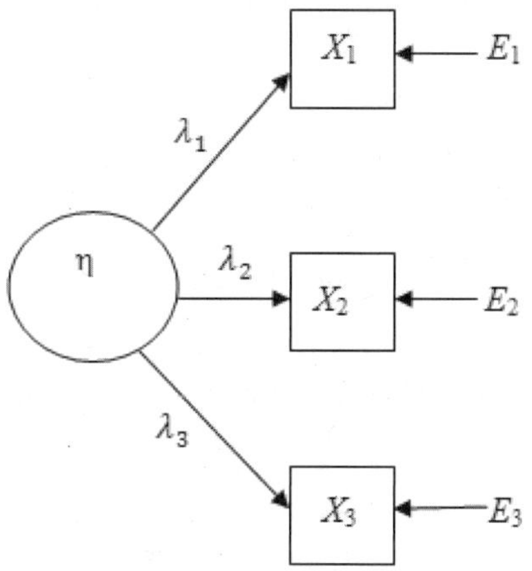

FIGURE 2.1

Latent Variable η Measured by Three Observed Variables: X_1, X_2, and X_3

$\lambda_1 = \lambda_2 = \lambda_3$; (b) all intercepts are equal, $a_1 = a_2 = a_3$; and (c) all error variances are equal, $\text{VAR}(E_1) = \text{VAR}(E_2) = \text{VAR}(E_3)$. Thus, parallel measures have the same units of measurement, scale origins, and error variances. Given Equations 2.3, the first two conditions imply that parallel measures have equal true scores ($T_1 = T_2 = T_3$). One can say then that parallel measures have equal true scores and equal error variances.

Tau-Equivalent Measures. A less restricted case of congeneric measures, referred to as *tau-equivalent measures*, occurs when only the first two conditions are in place: $\lambda_1 = \lambda_2 = \lambda_3$ and $a_1 = a_2 = a_3$. As already noted, these two conditions imply that the true scores are equal (i.e., $T_1 = T_2 = T_3$). That is, tau-equivalent measures have the same units of measurement and scale origins, but their error variances may differ. Or, equivalently, one can say that the tau-equivalent measures have equal true scores but unequal error variances.

Essentially Tau-Equivalent Measures. An even less restricted case of congeneric measures, referred to as *essentially tau-equivalent measures*, occurs when only the first condition is in place: $\lambda_1 = \lambda_2 = \lambda_3$. That is, essentially tau-equivalent measures have the same units of measurement but dissimilar origins and unequal error variances. Also, given Equations 2.3, the condition $\lambda_1 = \lambda_2 = \lambda_3$ implies that the true scores of any two essentially tau-equivalent measures differ by a constant. As variables that differ by a constant have equal variances, one can say that essentially tau-equivalent measures have equal true score variances but unequal error variances.

Without loss of generality, when the slopes are equal, one can set them equal to 1 (i.e., $\lambda_1 = \lambda_2 = \lambda_3 = 1$). Under this condition, which holds for parallel, tau-equivalent, and essentially tau-equivalent measures, the units of measurement of the observed scores, X_1, X_2, and X_3, will be identical to the unit of measurement for the underlying trait, η. This is because the regression coefficient (λ_i) in Equations 2.2 is the ratio of the scale unit of X_i to the scale unit of η; thus, these two scale units are equal when $\lambda_i = 1$. For theoretical presentation of congeneric models, the reader may refer to Werts, Grabdy, and Schabacker (1980) and to Millsap and Everson (1991).

2.2.3 Calibration of Measures

The process of transforming two or more measures so that they have the same units and origins is called *calibration of measures*. That is, to calibrate congeneric measures is equivalent to transforming them to tau-equivalent measures. For example, for the case of three indicators of a single trait, the calibration is performed by using Equations 2.2 with (a) subtracting the intercepts, a_i, from their respective observed scores, X_i; and then (b) dividing each X_i by the slope, λ_i ($i = 1, 2, 3$). With this, the transformed observed scores become the following:

$$X_i^* = \eta + E_i^*, \tag{2.4}$$

where $X_i^* = (X_i - a_i)/\lambda_i$, and $E_i^* = E_i/\lambda_i$.

In Equation 2.4, the slope equals one ($\lambda_i = 1$), and the intercept equals zero ($a_i = 0$). This indicates that X_1^*, X_2^*, and X_3^* (obtained from Equation 2.4 for $i = 1$, 2, and 3) are tau-equivalent measures; that is, they have the same units and origins (only their error variances may differ). Note that if the above transformation is limited to only dividing both sides in Equations 2.2 by λ_i (i.e., without subtracting the intercept, a_i), the transformed X_i scores (say, denoted X_i^{**}) represent essentially tau-equivalent measures; that is, they have the same units but may have nonzero intercepts and their error variances may differ:

$$X_i^{**} = \eta + a_i^{**} + E_i^{**}, \tag{2.5}$$

where $X_i^{**} = X_i/\lambda_i$, $a_i^{**} = a_i/\lambda_i$, and $E_i^{**} = E_i/\lambda_i$ (estimates of λ_i are discussed in Chapter 6).

> **Note 2.2**
>
> The calibration approach described in this section is appropriate only when there is a linear relationship (correlation) between the observed variables and the underlying trait. As the errors (E_i) are randomly distributed, the observed scores (X_i) will have about the same distribution. If this is not the case but the observed-score distributions are roughly unimodal, it would be reasonable to normalize the observed variables (see Chapter 1, Section 1.5.6). This method will result in same-shape distributions and improved linearity.

2.2.4 Definition of Reliability

Equation 2.1 represents the classical assumption that any observed score consists of a true score and error of measurement ($X = T + E$). Because errors are random, they do not correlate with the true scores (i.e., $r_{TE} = 0$). Indeed, there is no reason to expect that persons with higher true scores would have systematically larger (or smaller) measurement errors than persons with lower true scores. Given that $r_{TE} = 0$, the following is true for the *variances* of observed scores, true scores, and errors for a population of test takers:

$$\sigma_X^2 = \sigma_T^2 + \sigma_E^2. \tag{2.6}$$

Thus, the observed score variance, σ_X^2, is the sum of true score variance, σ_T^2, and error variance, σ_E^2. Given this, the reliability of scores (denoted ρ_{XX}) indicates what proportion of the observed score variance is true score variance. The analytic form of this definition is as follows:

$$\rho_{XX} = \sigma_T^2/\sigma_X^2 = \sigma_T^2/(\sigma_T^2 + \sigma_E^2). \tag{2.7}$$

> **Note 2.3**
>
> The notation for reliability, ρ_{XX}, stems from the definition that reliability is the correlation between the observed scores on two parallel tests (i.e., tests with equal true scores and equal error variances for every population of people).

The definition of reliability implies that ρ_{XX} takes values from 0.00 to 1.00. The closer ρ_{XX} is to 1.00, the higher the reliability; conversely, the closer ρ_{XX} is to zero, the lower the reliability. Perfect reliability ($\rho_{XX} = 1.00$) can theoretically occur when the total observed score variance equals the true score variance ($\sigma_X^2 = \sigma_T^2$) or, equivalently, when the error variance equals zero ($\sigma_E^2 = 0$). In general, a ρ_{XX} of .90 (or higher) is desirable for achievement tests and a ρ_{XX} of .75 (or higher) is good for inventories that measure more stable traits, such as self-esteem.

2.2.5 Standard Error of Measurement (*SEM*)

The classical treatment of reliability also assumes that (a) the distribution of observed scores that a person may obtain under repeated independent administrations of the same test is normal, and (b) the standard deviation of this normal distribution, referred to as the *standard error of measurement* (*SEM*), is the same for all persons taking the test. Figure 2.2 represents a hypothetical normal distribution of observed scores for a person with a true

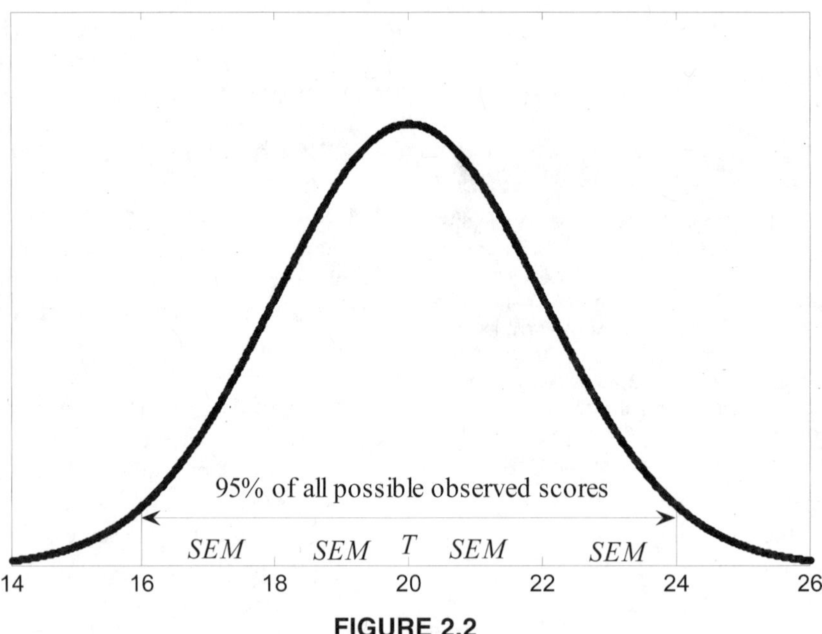

FIGURE 2.2

Theoretical Distribution of Observed Scores for One Person Over Repeated Independent Administrations of the Test

Note. $T = 20$ = true score; *SEM* = standard error of measurement.

score of 20 on a specific test. The mean of the distribution is the person's true score ($T = 20$), and the standard deviation is the standard error of measurement ($SEM = 2$).

Based on the statistical properties of normal distributions, about 95% of the scores fall in the interval between two standard deviations below the mean, $T - 2(SEM)$, and two standard deviations above the mean, $T + 2(SEM)$ (in Figure 2.2, this is the interval from 16 to 24). This property can be used to construct (approximately) a 95% confidence interval of a person's true score, T, given this person's observed score, X. Specifically, in 95% of the cases, the true score of a person with an observed score X will fall in the interval from $X - 2(SEM)$ to $X + 2(SEM)$. For example, with $SEM = 2$, the (approximate) 95% confidence interval for the true score of a person with an observed score of 17 is from 13 to 21. Smaller *SEMs* will produce smaller confidence intervals for the person's true score, thus improving the accuracy of measurement. Because the *SEM* is inversely related to the accuracy of measurement, a low *SEM* indicates high reliability. If the reliability, $\rho_{XX'}$, and the standard deviation of the observed scores, σ_X are given, the *SEM* can be computed as follows:

$$SEM = \sigma_X \sqrt{1 - \rho_{XX}} \,. \qquad (2.8)$$

For example, if the reliability is .80 and the standard deviation of the person's observed scores is 10, the standard error of measurement is as follows: $SEM = (10)\sqrt{1 - .80} = 4.47$.

2.3 TYPES OF RELIABILITY

The reliability of test scores for a population of examinees shows what proportion of the variance in the observed scores is true score variance (see Equation 2.7). In empirical research, however,

Note 2.4

Although the reliability coefficient is a unitless number between 0 and 1, conveniently used to report reliability in empirical studies, the *SEM* relates directly to the meaning of the test's scale of measurement (e.g., number-right score, deviation IQ score, T score, or *z* score) and is, therefore, more useful for score interpretations.

true scores cannot be directly determined. Therefore, the reliability is typically estimated by coefficients of internal consistency, test–retest, alternate forms, and other types of reliability estimates discussed in the measurement literature. It is important to emphasize that different types of reliability relate to different sources of measurement error and, contrary to common misconceptions, are generally not interchangeable.

2.3.1 Internal Consistency Reliability

Internal consistency estimates of reliability are based on the average correlation among items within a test in a single administration of this test. A widely known method for determining internal consistency of test scores yields a split-half reliability estimate. With this method, the test is split into two halves—for example, by assigning the odd-numbered test items to one half and the even-numbered test items to the other half (this is particularly appropriate when the items are presented in order of increasing difficulty). If ρ_{12} is the Pearson correlation between the scores on the two test halves, the reliability for the whole test is estimated using the Spearman–Brown Prophecy formula:

$$\rho_{XX} = \frac{2\rho_{12}}{1 + \rho_{12}}. \tag{2.9}$$

For example, if the correlation between the two test halves is 0.7, the split-half reliability estimate is calculated as follows: $\rho_{YY} = (2)(0.7)/(1 + 0.7) = 0.82$. A general premise is that with all other things being equal, the more items on a test, the more reliable the test scores will be.

The Spearman–Brown formula assumes that the two halves of the test are parallel (see Section 2.2.2). Whereas Equation 2.9 "predicts" the reliability of a test from the reliability of two parallel components (two halves) of the test, the general form of the Spearman–Brown formula predicts the reliability of a test, ρ_{XX}, from the reliability of *n* parallel components of the test:

$$\rho_{XX} = \frac{n\rho_{YY}}{1 + (n-1)\rho_{YY}}, \tag{2.10}$$

where ρ_{YY} is the reliability of any of the *n* parallel components (e.g., *n* parallel test items). For example, if $\rho_{YY} = .70$ is the reliability of a 20-item test, one can use Equation 2.10 to predict the reliability after increasing the test length, say, three times—that is, adding 40 items that are parallel to the original 20 items:

$$\rho_{XX} = \frac{(3)(.70)}{1 + (3-1)(.70)} = .875.$$

When there are indications that the test halves are not parallel, the internal consistency of the scores for the whole test can be estimated with Cronbach's coefficient alpha using the following formula (Cronbach, 1951):

$$\alpha = \frac{n}{n-1}\left[1 - \frac{\Sigma \text{VAR}(X_i)}{VAR\ (X)}\right], \tag{2.11}$$

where: n is the number of test items, X_i is the observed score on the ith test item, $\text{VAR}(X_i)$ is the variance of X_i (the summation, Σ, is for $i = 1, 2, \ldots, n$), X is the observed score for the whole test (i.e., $X = X_1 + X_2 + \ldots + X_n$), and VAR($X$) is the variance of X.

The estimation of reliability for the general case of congeneric measures, when the assumptions of Cronbach's alpha may not hold, is addressed in the framework of covariance structure analysis (e.g., Feldt & Brenan, 1989; Gilmer & Feldt, 1983; Raykov, 2001b) and, even more efficiently, via latent trait modeling (e.g., Jöreskog, 1971b; Raykov, 2009; Raykov, Dimitrov, & Asparouhov, 2010). More details on the estimation of reliability in the framework of latent trait modeling are provided later in this book (cf. Chapter 8, Section 8.3).

Note 2.5

The Spearman–Brown formula assumes that the items in the composite test, whose score is the simple total of all items, measure the same trait and have an exchangeable covariance structure; that is, the items summed to create the test score have the same variance, and all pairs of items have the same correlation. When these assumptions are badly violated, or when the items are differently weighted to form the test score, the Spearman–Brown equation and its implications are no longer valid (e.g., Charter, 2001; H. Li, Rosenthal, & Rubin, 1996).

2.3.2 Test–Retest Reliability

When the goal is to assess the extent to which people respond consistently to the same test or questionnaire administered on different occasions, this is a matter of test–retest reliability (or stability) of test scores. Test–retest reliability is estimated by calculating the correlation between the observed scores of the same participants taking the same test on two separate occasions. The resulting correlation coefficient is also referred to as the *coefficient of stability* because the primary source of measurement error is a lack of stability over time.

The major problem with test–retest reliability estimates is the potential for carry-over effects between the two test administrations. Readministrations of a test within a short period of time (e.g., a few days or even a couple of weeks) may produce carry-over effects attributable to memory and/or practice. For example, students who take a math or vocabulary test may look up some answers they were unsure of after the first administration of the test, thus changing their true knowledge of the content measured by the test. Or, if an individual learns a lot about math between the first and second administration of a math achievement test, the scores of this individual may vary substantially. Indeed, if the construct being measured varies over time (e.g., cognitive skills, depression), a long period of time between the two administrations of the instrument may produce score changes attributable to biologi-

Note 2.6

Cronbach's alpha is an accurate estimate of the internal consistency reliability of test scores if the test components (e.g., test items) satisfy two assumptions: (a) there is no correlation among errors associated with item scores, and (b) the items are essentially tau-equivalent (see Section 2.2.2). When the latter is not true, Cronbach's alpha underestimates the reliability. If, however, there are items with correlated errors, Cronbach's alpha overestimates the reliability. Correlated errors may occur, for example, when different items relate to a common piece of test information (e.g., the same graph or reading passage) or when tests are presented in a speeded fashion.

Note 2.7

Test-retest reliability and internal consistency reliability are independent concepts. They are affected by different sources of error; therefore, it may happen that measures with low internal consistency have high temporal stability and vice versa.

cal maturation, cognitive development, experience, and/or mood shifts. Thus, test–retest reliability estimates are most appropriate for measurements of traits that are stable over the period of time between the two administrations of the assessment instrument (e.g., visual acuity, personality, and work values).

2.3.3 Alternate Forms Reliability

If two versions of an instrument (test or questionnaire) have very similar observed score means, variances, and correlations with other measures, they are referred to as *alternate forms* of the instrument. Any decent attempt to construct parallel tests is expected to result in alternate test forms, as it is practically impossible to obtain perfectly parallel tests. Alternate forms are usually easier to develop for instruments that measure ability/aptitude or proficiency in specific academic subjects than for instruments that measure constructs such as personality, motivation, and anxiety.

Alternate forms reliability is a measure of the consistency of scores obtained from the administration of alternate test forms to the same group of individuals. The correlation between observed scores on two alternate test forms provides an estimate of the reliability of either one of the alternate forms. Just like the test–retest reliability coefficients, the estimates of alternate form reliability are subject to carry-over (practice) effects but to a lesser degree because the participants are not tested twice on the same items. A recommended rule of thumb is to have a two-week time period between administrations of alternate test forms.

Whenever possible, it is better to obtain both internal consistency coefficients and alternate forms correlations for a test. If the correlation between alternate forms is much lower than the internal consistency coefficient (e.g., a difference of 0.20 or more), it may indicate (a) differences in content, (b) subjectivity of scoring, and/or (c) changes in the trait being measured over the time period between the administrations of alternate forms. When scores on alternate forms of an instrument are assigned by raters (e.g., teachers or counselors), scoring errors attributable to subjectivity can be reduced by training the raters how to use the instrument and providing clear guidelines for scoring the traits being measured.

2.3.4 Criterion-Referenced Reliability

Criterion-referenced measurements show how the examinees' performance compares with a specific criterion. In education, the criterion is usually some specific performance objective, such as "knowing how to solve simple algebra equations." Most teacher-made tests are criterion-referenced because the teacher is more interested in how well students master the coursework (criterion-referenced) than how students compare with other students (norm-referenced). Likewise, counselors frequently want to know whether or not a client has "enough" of a mental disorder (e.g., depression) to warrant a diagnosis.

When the results of criterion-referenced measurements are used for classifications (e.g., related to mastery or nonmastery of the criterion), the reliability of such classifications is often referred to as *classification consistency*. It shows the consistency with which classifications are made, either by the same test administered on two occasions or by alternate test forms.

Two widely known indices of classification consistency are P_0, the observed proportion of consistent classifications, and Cohen's kappa (κ), the proportion of nonrandom consistent classifications. Let's examine Figure 2.3, where the entries are proportions of people classified as masters or nonmasters by two alternate forms of a criterion-referenced test (Form A and Form B). The marginal proportions are as follows: $P_{A1} = p_{11} + p_{10}$, $P_{A0} = p_{01} + p_{00}$, $P_{B1} = p_{11} + p_{01}$, and $P_{B0} = p_{10} + p_{00}$. The observed proportion of consistent classifications (masters or nonmasters) is as follows:

$$P_o = p_{11} + p_{00}\,. \qquad (2.12)$$

Typically, the observed proportion of correct classifications, P_o, is inflated because part of P_o may occur by chance. Cohen's kappa takes into account the proportion of consistent classifications that is theoretically expected to occur by chance, P_e, and provides a ratio of nonrandom consistent classifications (J. Cohen, 1960):

$$\kappa = \frac{P_o - P_e}{1 - P_e}, \qquad (2.13)$$

where P_e is obtained by summing the cross-products of marginal proportions in Figure 2.3, that is, $P_e = P_{A1}P_{B1} + P_{A0}P_{B0}$. The numerator $(P_o - P_e)$ is the proportion of nonrandom consistent classifications being detected, whereas the denominator $(1 - P_e)$ is the maximum proportion of nonrandom consistent classifications that may occur. Thus, Cohen's kappa shows what proportion of the maximum possible nonrandom consistent classifications is found with the data.

Example 2.1. Assume that the task is to evaluate how well a teacher-made math test (Form A) compares with the pass–fail classification produced by a state proficiency math test (Form B) for ninth-grade students in a given school. Let's say that the student records on the two tests (Form A and Form B) yield the following specific values for the proportions in Figure 2.3: $p_{11} = 0.4$, $p_{10} = 0.2$, $p_{01} = 0.1$, and $p_{00} = 0.3$. The marginal proportions in this case are as follows: $P_{A1} = 0.4 + 0.2 = 0.6$, $P_{A0} = 0.1 + 0.3 = 0.4$, $P_{B1} = 0.4 + 0.1 = 0.5$, and $P_{B0} = 0.2 + 0.3 = 0.5$. These results are presented in Figure 2.4.

		Form B		
		Master	*Nonmaster*	
Form A	*Master*	p_{11}	p_{10}	P_{A1}
	Nonmaster	p_{01}	p_{00}	P_{A0}
		P_{B1}	P_{B0}	

FIGURE 2.3

Mastery–Nonmastery Classification Table

Note. Form A and Form B are two alternate forms of a criterion-referenced test; *p* = cell proportion; *P* = marginal proportion.

		Form B: State Proficiency Test		
		Pass	Fail	
Form A: Teacher-Made Test	Pass	0.4	0.2	$P_{A1} = 0.6$
	Fail	0.1	0.3	$P_{A0} = 0.4$
		$P_{B1} = 0.5$	$P_{B0} = 0.5$	

FIGURE 2.4

Classification Table for Pass–Fail on a Math Proficiency Test

Note. P = marginal proportion.

The observed proportion of consistent classifications is as follows: $P_o = 0.4 + 0.3 = 0.7$. The proportion of consistent classifications that may occur by chance is as follows: $P_e = (0.6)(0.5) + (0.4)(0.5) = 0.50$. Using Equation 2.13, Cohen's kappa (κ) is $(0.7 - 0.50)/(1 - 0.50) = .20/.50 = .40$. Thus, the initially obtained 70% of observed consistent classifications ($P_o = 0.7$) is reduced to 40% consistent classifications after controlling for those that may occur by chance. As kappa is a conservative estimate of consistency, it would be reasonable to report in this case that the classification consistency is between .40 and .70 (i.e., between κ and P_o).

It should be noted, however, that some authors prefer P_o to κ as an index of classification consistency in the context of criterion-referenced tests. For example, on the basis of assumptions and statistical properties of P_o and κ, Berk (1980) suggested that "P_o should be the index of agreement for criterion-referenced tests where an absolute cutting score is chosen and for other tests that may contain short subtests and/or yield low score variance. While κ may be a legitimate index of agreement for tests where relative cutting scores are set according to the consequences of passing or failing a particular proportion of the students, the problems with κ render it less useful than P_o" (p. 333; see also, Berk, 2000). For an estimation of classification consistency under a single test administration, the reader may refer to Subkoviak (1976).

2.3.5 Interrater Reliability

Cohen's Kappa. The chances of measurement error increase when the scores are based on raters' subjective judgments. Such subjectivity may occur, for example, with portfolio assessments or pass–fail decisions where raters (e.g., teachers) are the instrument of assessment. In situations of rater-based scoring, it is important to estimate the degree to which the scores are unduly affected by the raters' subjective judgments. Such estimation is provided by coefficients of interrater reliability, referred to also as *coefficients of interrater agreement.*

Frequently used measures of interrater reliability are the observed proportion of consistent classifications, P_o, and Cohen's kappa coefficient, κ. When more than two categories are used by two raters to classify persons (or their products), one can still use Equations 2.12 and 2.13, but P_o and P_e should be calculated with a contingency table for the respective number of categories. For example, let two raters (A and B) classify student portfolios in three performance categories (e.g., 1 = low, 2 = medium, and 3 = high). Let also p_{11}, p_{22}, and p_{33} denote the proportion of consistent classifications in Categories 1 (low), 2 (medium), and 3 (high), respectively. The marginal proportions for Rater A are denoted P_{A1}, P_{A2}, and P_{A3}, whereas those for Rater B are P_{B1}, P_{B2}, and P_{B3}, across Categories 1, 2, and 3, respectively. We can now calculate Cohen's kappa using Equation 2.13, with $P_o = p_{11} + p_{22} + p_{33}$ and $P_e = P_{A1}P_{B1} + P_{A2}P_{B2} + P_{A3}P_{B3}$.

Intraclass Correlations. In general, when *n* "targets" (e.g., persons, products, and so forth) are rated by *k* judges, an intraclass correlation coefficient (ICC) is often used as a measure of interrater reliability. The targets, which represent the object of measurement, are treated as randomly selected, thus representing a random source of variation (random factor). The logic of ICC stems from the definition of reliability as a ratio of true variance to total variance (see Equation 2.7). In the context of analysis of variance (ANOVA), the ICC is defined by the following ratio:

$$\text{ICC} = \sigma_B^2/(\sigma_B^2 + \sigma_W^2), \tag{2.14}$$

where σ_B^2 is the variance between targets and σ_W^2 is the variance within targets (error variance).

Shrout and Fleiss (1979) discussed the estimation of ICC for interrater reliability in three cases: Case 1—each target is rated by a different set of judges, randomly selected from a larger population of judges; Case 2—a random sample of judges is selected from a larger population, and each judge rates each target; that is, each judge rates *n* targets altogether; and Case 3—each target is rated by each of the same judges, who are the only judges of interest. The variance components in Equation 2.14 are estimated through the respective mean squares values in an ANOVA design that is (a) in Case 1, one-way ANOVA, where the targets represent a random factor; (b) in Case 2, two-way ANOVA, where both the targets and judges are random factors; and (c) in Case 3, two-way ANOVA, where the targets are treated as a random factor and the judges as a fixed factor (i.e., a two-way mixed ANOVA design). In each case, ICC is estimated as a single measure reliability (where the unit of analysis is an individual rating) and average measure reliability (where the unit of analysis is the average of the ratings provided by all judges for the respective target).

In the case of a two-way ANOVA design (Case 2 or Case 3), Targets × Judges (T × J), there is an option for computing ICC of consistency versus ICC of absolute agreement. Under the ICC of consistency, the column variance in the (T × J) ANOVA is deemed irrelevant and thus ignored in the denominator of the ratio in Equation 2.14. In contrast, the ICC of absolute agreement keeps the column variance in the denominator of this ratio (e.g., McGraw & Wong, 1996; Shavelson & Webb, 1991, pp. 84–87). The ICCs of consistency, referred to also as Type C ICCs, indicate the degree of agreement on the relative standing (rank order) of the targets' ratings. The ICCs of absolute agreement, referred to as Type A ICCs, indicate the degree of agreement on the absolute values of the ratings. McGraw and Wong (1996) illustrated this point with ratings of 2, 4, and 6 for three targets by one judge and ratings of 4, 6, and 8 for the same targets by another judge, reporting a perfect consistency (Type C ICC = 1.0) but lower level of agreement on their absolute ratings (Type A ICC = .67). Thus, Type C ICCs are appropriate for norm-referenced interpretations, and Type A ICCs for criterion-referenced interpretations.

Some additional clarifications on the use of ICCs also need to be made. First, ICCs are defined under the assumption of equal column variances in the (T × J) ANOVA data structure; that is, the error variance is uniform across judges. When this assumption is not met, it is meaningless to use ICCs. Second, under the one-way ANOVA design, only ICC for absolute agreement is measurable. Third, in case of two judges, both the Pearson correlation coefficient, r, and the Type C ICC measure consistency (as a single measure reliability), but the latter is attenuated because of its sensitivity to disagreement indicated by differences between the column variances in the (T × J) sample data (e.g., see McGraw & Wong, 1996). Consider, for example, the ratings given by Judge 1 (X_1: 1, 3, 5) and those given by Judge 2 (X_2: 3, 7, 11) on three targets. As these ratings are linearly related (note that $X_2 = 2X_1 + 1$), the Person correlation coefficient indicates perfect consistency ($r = 1.0$), but the Type C ICC does not (for these data, ICC = .80) because the ratings do not differ by a constant, and, thus, their variances are not equal (see also McGraw & Wong, 1996). If the ratings given by two judges differ by a constant (e.g., 1, 3, 5 and 3, 5, 7), both the Pearson r and Type C ICC would indicate perfect consistency (r = ICC = 1.0).

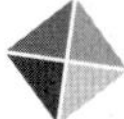

Example 2.2. The purpose of the example is to illustrate the computation of ICCs using SPSS. Specifically, SPSS version 18.0 (now PASW 18.0) or higher versions report ICCs for consistency and absolute agreement under all ANOVA cases, with choices for single measure reliability or average measure reliability. The data for this example consist of ratings for 10 students (as "targets") provided by three randomly selected teachers (as "judges") on disruptive behavior. Both students and teachers are randomly selected (see Table 2.1).

TABLE 2.1

Ratings for 10 Students by Three Teachers (Judges) on Disruptive Behavior

Student	Teacher 1	Teacher 2	Teacher 3
1	8	5	8
2	8	6	7
3	7	7	5
4	10	8	10
5	5	3	8
6	4	4	5
7	2	3	2
8	1	1	3
9	7	6	4
10	9	8	6

In SPSS, the computation of ICCs is available in the dialog box "Reliability Analysis: Statistics" (which is reached via the path Analyze → Scale → Reliability Analysis → Statistics). Checking the option "Intraclass correlation coefficient" activates the menu for "Model and Type of ICCs." Because in this example student and teachers are random, we select the "Two-way random" model. First we run an analysis under type "Consistency" and then a separate analysis under type "Absolute agreement." The results are provided in Table 2.2. The upper panel provides ICCs of consistency for single measures (ICC = .724) and average measures (ICC = .887). The lower panel provides ICCs of absolute agreement for single measures (ICC = .717) and average measures (ICC = .884). By default, 95% confidence intervals for the ICCs are also provided as well as F tests for statistical significance at the .05 level (see also Yaffee, 1998).

2.4 STRATIFIED ALPHA

In many situations, scores from two or more scales are combined into a *multidimensional composite score* (MCS) to measure and interpret a more general construct related to these scales. MCSs are often used with test batteries for aptitude, achievement, intelligence, or depression as well as with local school measurements, such as performance and portfolio assessments. One frequently reported MCS, for example, is the sum of verbal and quan-

TABLE 2.2

SPSS Output for Type C and Type A Intraclass Correlation Coefficients (ICCs) Under the Two-Way Random ANOVA Model (Data in Table 2.1)

		95% Confidence Interval		F Test With True Value 0			
Measure	Intraclass Correlation[a]	Lower Bound	Upper Bound	Value	*df* 1	*df* 2	*p*
			Type C				
Single	.724[b]	.404	.914	8.885	9	18	.000
Average	.887	.670	.970	8.885	9	18	.000
			Type A				
Single	.717[b]	.406	.910	8.885	9	18	.000
Average	.884	.672	.968	8.885	9	18	.000

Note. Two way random effects model where both people effects and measures effects are random. ANOVA = analysis of variance.
[a]Type C ICCs use a consistency definition—the between-measure variance is excluded from the denominator variance. Type A ICCs use absolute agreement definition. [b]The estimator is the same, whether interaction effect is present or not.

titative scores on the Graduate Record Examination. MCSs are typically computed for most assessment instruments used in counseling. For example, the Tennessee Self-Concept Scale–Second Edition (Fitts & Warren, 1996) reports MCS as summary scores on different self-concept scales (e.g., Physical, Moral, Personal, Family, Social, and Academic/Work).

Research has shown that when the items in an assessment instrument do not assess the same underlying dimension, Cronbach's alpha is not suitable to estimate the reliability of multidimensional scores (e.g., Komaroff, 1997; H. G. Osborn, 2000; Raykov, 1998, 2001a). Instead, a coefficient referred to as *stratified alpha* is a better estimate of the true reliability (e.g., Kamata, Turhan, & Darandari, 2003; H. G. Osborn, 2000). Stratified alpha was proposed by Cronbach, Shönenmann, and McKie (1965) to estimate the reliability of items that are grouped into strata (subtests, scales) on the basis of content (see also Kane & Case, 2004). Feldt and Brennan (1989) gave the following formula for stratified alpha (α_S):

$$\alpha_S = 1 - \frac{\Sigma(1 - \alpha_k)\text{VAR}(X_k)}{\text{VAR(X)}}, \tag{2.15}$$

Note 2.8

The principle behind improving reliability is to maximize the variance of relevant individual differences and minimize the error variance. Researchers can do this by (a) writing items clearly, (b) providing complete and understandable test instructions, (c) administering the instrument under prescribed conditions, (d) reducing subjectivity in scoring, (e) training raters and providing them with clear scoring instructions, (f) using heterogeneous respondent samples to increase the variance of observed scores, and (g) increasing the length of the test by adding items that are (ideally) parallel to those that are already in the test.

where α_k = is the Cronbach's *alpha* for the *k*th stratum, VAR(X_k) is the score variance for the *k*th stratum, and VAR(X) is the score variance for the entire assessment instrument ($k = 1, 2, \ldots, K$).

A careful examination of Equation 2.15 shows that α_S will be a better estimate of the true reliability if (a) the correlation among the items within the same stratum is high, thus producing large α_k and small VAR(X_k); and (b) the correlations among different strata are low, which leads to a large VAR(X)—the denominator in the right-hand term in Formula 2.15. Also,

Rae (2008) showed that α_S equals the true reliability if the item scores within each stratum are essentially tau-equivalent and their error terms are not correlated.

2.4.1 Stratified Alpha for Two Scales

If X is a composite score obtained by adding together the scores of two scales, X_1 and X_2 ($X = X_1 + X_2$), Equation 2.15 for the stratified alpha becomes the following:

$$\alpha_S = 1 - \frac{(1-\alpha_1)\text{VAR}(X_1) + (1-\alpha_2)\text{VAR}(X_2)}{\text{VAR}(X)}, \tag{2.16}$$

where VAR(X_1), VAR(X_2), and VAR (X) stand for the variances of X_1, X_2, and X, respectively, whereas α_1 and α_2 are Cronbach's alphas for X_1 and X_2, respectively.

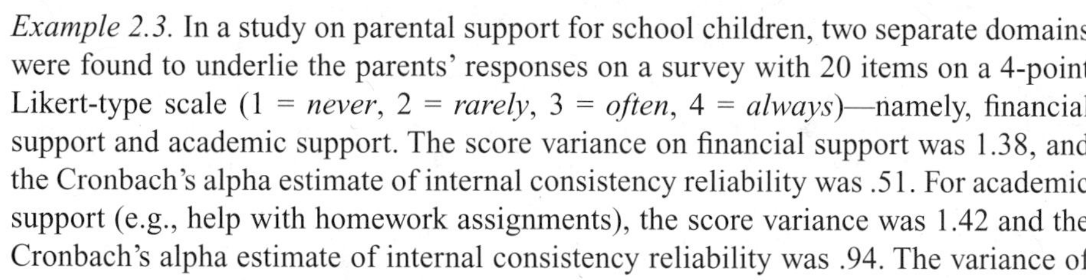

Example 2.3. In a study on parental support for school children, two separate domains were found to underlie the parents' responses on a survey with 20 items on a 4-point Likert-type scale (1 = *never*, 2 = *rarely*, 3 = *often*, 4 = *always*)—namely, financial support and academic support. The score variance on financial support was 1.38, and the Cronbach's alpha estimate of internal consistency reliability was .51. For academic support (e.g., help with homework assignments), the score variance was 1.42 and the Cronbach's alpha estimate of internal consistency reliability was .94. The variance of the sum of the respondents' scores on these two domains was 2.66. These results are based on a sample of 60 observations.

Note 2.9

Although not explicitly shown in Equation 2.16, a correlation between X_1 and X_2 affects the reliability of the composite score, α_S. When X_1 and X_2 do not correlate ($r_{12} = 0$), the reliability of their sum ($X = X_1 + X_2$) is simply the average of their reliabilities: $\alpha_S = (\alpha_1 + \alpha_2)/2$.

With the notations in Equation 2.16, we have X_1 = financial support, X_2 = academic support, $X = X_1 + X_2$ (composite score), α_1 = .51, VAR(X_1) = 1.38, α_2 = .94, VAR(X_2) = 1.42, and VAR(X) = 2.66. Thus, replacing these values in Equation 2.16, the stratified alpha in this case is as follows:

$$\alpha_S = 1 - \frac{(1-.51)(1.38) + (1-.94)(1.42)}{2.66} = 0.714.$$

As can be noticed, the reliability of the composite score (α_S = .714) is very close to the mean of the reliabilities of the two domains: (.51 + .94)/2 = .72. As stated in Note 2.9, this similarity is due to the lack of correlation between X_1 and X_2. Specifically, for the data in this example, it was found that r_{12} = –.05 (not statistically significant for the sample of 60 observations).

When the scores that are combined into a composite score come from scales with different units of measurement (e.g., 4-point and 5-point Likert scales), it is appropriate to present them on a common scale—for example, by converting them into standard scores (z scores)—before summing them. Then Equation 2.16 translates into a simpler form:

$$\alpha_S = 1 - \frac{2 - (\alpha_1 + \alpha_2)}{\text{VAR}(Z_{12})}, \tag{2.17}$$

where VAR(Z_{12}) is the variance of the sum of the z scores of X_1 and X_2 ($Z_{12} = z_1 + z_2$).

2.4.2 Stratified Alpha for Three Scales

For a composite score on three scales (strata), $X = X_1 + X_2 + X_3$, Equation 2.15 takes the following specific form:

$$\alpha_S = 1 - \frac{(1 - \alpha_1)\text{VAR}(X_1) + (1 - \alpha_2)\text{VAR}(X_2) + (1 - \alpha_3)\text{VAR}(X_3)}{\text{VAR(X)}},$$

where VAR(X_1), VAR(X_2), VAR(X_3), and VAR (X) stand for the variances of X_1, X_2, X_3, and X, respectively, whereas α_1, α_2, and α_3 are Cronbach's alphas for X_1, X_2, and X_3, respectively.

When X_1, X_2, and X_3 are converted to standard scores (z scores) before being summed, and are thus presented on a common scale, the stratified alpha is obtained as follows:

$$\alpha_S = 1 - \frac{3 - (\alpha_1 + \alpha_2 + \alpha_3)}{\text{VAR}(Z_{123})}, \tag{2.18}$$

where VAR(Z_{123}) is the variance of the sum of the standard (z) scores for X_1, X_2, and X_3.

Following the specifications of Formula 2.15 for the cases of two scales and three scales, one can compute stratified alphas for composite scores on four scales, five scales, and so forth.

2.5 MAXIMAL RELIABILITY OF CONGENERIC MEASURES

As discussed in Section 2.2.2, congeneric items ($X_1, X_2, \ldots, X_n$) measure a single underlying construct (η; e.g., depression, self-esteem, and so forth) with different units, different scale origins, and different precision (see Equations 2.2). Under the congeneric model, the total scores represent the sum of item scores: $X = X_1 + X_2 + \ldots + X_n$. If the items are assigned weights, the total scores are $X = w_1X_1 + w_2X_2 + \ldots + w_nX_n$. Weights that will produce the highest possible internal consistency reliability (maximal reliability) of X are referred to as *optimal weights*.

Recent approaches to estimation of optimal weights are based on covariance analysis (e.g., Conger, 1980; H. Li, 1997; H. Li et al., 1996; Raykov, 2004; T. Wang, 1998) or latent trait modeling (e.g., Bentler, 2004; Raykov, 2007b; Raykov & Hancock, 2005). For example, H. Li et al. (1996) proposed an approach to estimating maximal reliability for the case when the items in a test can be grouped into subtests with parallel items; all items together produce congeneric measures, that is, items from different subtests may have different true score variances and different error variances. For the general case of congeneric measures, without assuming their breakdown into subsets of parallel measures, T. Wang (1998) proposed an approach to maximal reliability based on computations that involve the elements of the variance–covariance matrix of the congeneric measures.

Most efficiently, the task of determining optimal weights and maximal reliability for congeneric measures is addressed in the framework of latent trait modeling. Specifically, using the presentation of congeneric measures as shown in Equations 2.2, $X_i = (\lambda_i\eta + a_i) + E_i$, the optimal weights can be computed as follows:

$$w_i = \lambda_i / \text{VAR}(E_i)\,, \tag{2.19}$$

where λ_i is the slope and VAR(E_i) is the variance of the error. With this, the maximal reliability for the weighted composite score of congeneric measures, $X = w_1X_1 + w_2X_2 + \ldots + w_nX_n$, denoted here r^*_{XX}, is given by the squared correlation between X and the underlying latent trait, η, that is,

$$r^*_{XX} = [\text{Corr}(X, \eta)]^2. \tag{2.20}$$

Efficient estimation of the components necessary for the computation of optimal weights and maximal reliability via Equations 2.19 and 2.20, respectively, is provided in the framework of latent variable modeling (LVM; Bartholomew, 1996; Jöreskog, 1971b; Raykov, 2004, 2007b). LVM-based approaches to estimating internal consistency reliability for congeneric measures are also preferable to classical approaches based on, say, Cronbach's alpha coefficient (e.g., Bollen, 1989; Raykov, 2009; Raykov & Shrout, 2002). Related procedures are discussed and illustrated in Chapter 8, Section 8.3.

SUMMARY

1. The reliability of measurements indicates the degree to which they are accurate, consistent, and replicable when (a) different people conduct the measurement; (b) different instruments that purport to measure the same trait are used; and (c) there is incidental variation in measurement conditions. *Reliability* refers to the measurement data obtained with an instrument, *not* to the instrument itself.
2. The *true score* of a person is the mean of the theoretical distribution of scores that would be observed for this person in repeated independent measurements using the same test. It is assumed that this theoretical distribution is normal, and its standard deviation is referred to as *standard error of measurement.*
3. Congeneric measures are unidimensional measures that allow for different units of measurement, dissimilar scale origins, and unequal error variances. Restricted cases of congeneric measures are (a) parallel measures, which must have the same units of measurement, the same scale origin, and equal error variances; (b) tau-equivalent measures, which must have the same units of measurement and scale origins, but their error variances may differ; and (c) essentially tau-equivalent measures, which must have the same units of measurement but allow for dissimilar origins and unequal error variances.
4. Under the classical (true-score) model, the reliability of scores is defined by the ratio of true score variance to observed score variance.
5. Internal consistency reliability of test scores is based on the average correlation among items within a test in a single administration of this test.
6. Cronbach's coefficient alpha is an accurate estimate of the internal consistency reliability of test scores only under the assumptions that (a) there is *no* correlation among errors associated with item scores, and (b) the items are essentially tau-equivalent.
7. Test-retest reliability (temporal stability) is estimated by the correlation between the observed scores of the same participants taking the same test on two separate occasions. The major problem with test–retest reliability estimates is the potential for carry-over effects between the two test administrations.
8. Test-retest reliability and internal consistency reliability are independent concepts. They are affected by different sources of error; therefore, it may happen that measures with low internal consistency have high temporal stability and vice versa.
9. Alternate forms reliability is a measure of the consistency of scores obtained from the administration of alternate test forms to the same group of individuals. The correlation between observed scores on two alternate test forms provides an estimate of the reliability of either one of the alternate forms.

10. When the results of criterion-referenced measurements are used for classifications, the consistency with which classifications are made, either by the same test administered on two occasions or by alternate test forms, is referred to as *criterion-referenced reliability* (or *classification consistency*). Two widely known indices of classification consistency are the observed proportion of consistent classifications and Cohen's kappa, κ.
11. In situations of rater-based scoring, interrater reliability (or interrater agreement) shows the degree to which the scores are unduly affected by the raters' subjective judgments. Frequently used measures of interrater reliability are Cohen's kappa and an appropriate intraclass correlation—in general, the ratio of between-targets (persons or objects) variance to total variance.
12. Stratified alpha is used to estimate the reliability of multidimensional composite scores, which are obtained by combining the scores from two or more scales to measure and interpret a more general construct related to these scales.
13. When the test items are assigned weights under the congeneric model, the weights that will produce the highest possible internal consistency reliability (maximal reliability) of the scale scores are referred to as *optimal weights*. The process of determining optimal weights and maximal reliability for congeneric measures is most efficiently achieved in the framework of latent trait modeling.

Chapter 3
Validity

The model of validity discussed in this chapter played a key role in the selection of content, procedures, and methodological guidelines for the validation of assessment scale data presented in this book. In general terms, validity has to do with whether an instrument (e.g., test or questionnaire) measures what it purports to measure. It is important to emphasize that an instrument per se cannot be labeled as valid (or invalid) as validity relates to an interpretation of data obtained through the use of an instrument, *not* to the instrument itself. When the term *scale validation* is used occasionally in this book, it should be interpreted to mean "validation of scale data (scale scores)" obtained through the use of the scale at issue.

In this chapter I present the current conception of validity that is referred to as *unified construct-based model of validity*, which is based on Messick's (1989) definition of validity and is reflected in the *Standards for Educational and Psychological Testing* (American Educational Research Association [AERA], American Psychological Association [APA], & National Council on Measurement in Education [NCME], 1999). The focus is on the following six aspects of validity: content aspect, substantive aspect, structural aspect, generalizability aspect, external aspect, and consequential aspect of validity. However, I also discuss an alternative view on the consequential aspect of validity and provide additional notes on validity regarding responsiveness, interpretability, and sources of invalidity.

3.1 WHAT IS VALIDITY?

Whereas reliability of scores deals with their accuracy and consistency, validity has to do with whether an instrument (e.g., test or questionnaire) measures what it purports to measure. As shown later in this chapter, reliability is a necessary, albeit not sufficient, condition for validity. That is, high reliability of test scores does not guarantee validity but represents an important condition for valid interpretation of test scores. As Cronbach (1971) noted, "one validates not a test, but an *interpretation of data arising from a specified procedure*" (p. 447). Take, for example, student scores on a test consisting of arithmetic computations items. An example of an invalid interpretation of these scores would be to make inferences about the students' "mathematics ability" based on the results, because the test measures computational skills, not mathematics ability. On the other hand, a valid interpretation of these test scores would be to say that the score differences reflect meaningful differences in the students' computational skills. Likewise, a valid anxiety test must generate scores that reflect meaningful differences in anxiety among persons taking the test.

Historically, three major validity models have developed over the years: (a) the criterion-based model (Cronbach & Gleser, 1965; Cureton, 1950; E. L. Thorndike, 1918), in which validity of measures is viewed as the degree to which these measures are consistent with (or predict) the measures on a specific criterion; (b) the construct-based model (Cronbach

& Meehl, 1955), which considers three different types of validity—content validity, criterion validity, and construct validity; and (c) the unified construct-based model of validity (Messick, 1989, 1995). A comprehensive review of the history of validity can be found in Kane (2001).

Under the criterion-based model, the validity of test scores is depicted as the degree to which these scores are accurate representations of the values of a specified criterion. A major drawback of the criterion-based conception of validity is that (a) it is too limited and does not capture some basic (e.g., content-related) aspects of validity, and (b) it is not possible to identify criterion measures in some domains. Although the construct-based model (Cronbach & Meehl, 1955) does a better job in this regard, the major problem of this model is that content validity, criterion validity, and construct validity are depicted as different types of validity. Even if the instrument is initially validated using content or criterion validity, construct validation is just added to provide deeper understanding of the constructs or processes accounting for observed responses. However, as Kane (2001, p. 321) noted, "if the observations are not consistent with the theory, some part of the network would be rejected, but it would generally not be clear whether the fault is in the axioms [of the adopted theory], the correspondence rules, or in the details of the measurement procedures." The discrete treatment of content validity, criterion validity, and construct validity under the construct-based model of Cronbach and Meehl (1955) can mislead test developers and users to believe that these three "types of validity" are comparable or, even worse, that they are equivalent and, thus, collecting evidence for any of them is sufficient to label an assessment instrument as valid. Such problems are avoided under the current conception of validity in the framework of the unified construct-based model (Messick, 1989, 1995), which is discussed next.

3.2 UNIFIED CONSTRUCT-BASED MODEL OF VALIDITY

The current conception of validity, referred to as the *unified construct-based model of validity*, stems from Messick's (1989) definition of *validity*: "Validity is an integrated evaluative judgment of the degree to which empirical evidence and theoretical rationales support the *adequacy* and *appropriateness of inferences* and *actions* based on test scores or other modes of assessment" (p. 13). This definition is also reflected in the recent *Standards for Educational and Psychological Testing* (AERA, APA, & NCME, 1999), where it is stated that "validity refers to the degree to which evidence and theory support the interpretation of test scores entailed by proposed uses of tests" (p. 9). The unified construct-based model of validity integrates content-related and criterion-related evidence into a unified framework of construct validity and empirical evaluation of the meaning and consequences of measurement. Messick (1995) specified six aspects of the unified conception of construct validity: content, substantive, structural, generalizability, external, and consequential aspects of validity. In the following sections, I provide a brief description of these validity aspects and how one collects evidence of their manifestation, as described by Messick (1995). Technical details on procedures for collecting validity evidence are discussed later in this book.

3.2.1 Content Aspect of Validity

The *content aspect of validity* includes evidence of content relevance, representativeness, and technical quality (Lennon, 1956; Messick, 1989). Typically, this definition is interpreted with some variations in different assessment contexts. In employment assessment, for example, evidence of content validity is provided when the assessment includes a representative sample of tasks, behaviors, knowledge, skills, abilities, or other characteristics necessary to perform the job. In general, the content aspect of validity is investigated through the collection of face validity evidence and logical validity evidence. Specifically, face validity evidence is established through subjective judgments of experts and/or examinees regarding whether the test content is relevant to the purpose of the test. Logical validity evidence involves developing a logical design of test items in order to cover all the important aspects of the target content domain organized in a two-way (Content Area × Test Objective) table. Experts' judgments regarding readability, suitability, and fairness of the items in the assessment instrument should also be documented in collecting evidence about the content aspect of validity.

Note 3.1

The terms *face validity* and *logical validity* should be avoided as they are used to indicate content validity as a separate type of validity under the outdated conception of validity (Cronbach & Meehl, 1955). Instead, under the unified construct-based model of validity (Messick, 1989, 1995), it would be more appropriate to refer, for example, to *face validity evidence* and *logical validity evidence* as manifestations of the content aspect of validity.

The technical quality of the items also relates to the content aspect of validity. The evaluation of individual items in this regard usually takes place during the piloting stage in the development of an assessment instrument (e.g., see Chapter 4, Section 4.3.3). An important index of the technical quality of an item that serves as an indicator for a given construct (subscale) in the instrument is the Pearson correlation between the scores on this item and the average score across the remaining items that serve as indicators for the same construct (subscale). This index, referred to as *item-total correlation* for raw scores, must be positive in order to provide support to the content aspect of validity. When the item-total correlation is close to zero, it indicates that (a) the item is either very easy or very difficult to answer, or (b) the item may not measure the target construct in the same manner as the remaining items that serve as indicators of this construct. Negative item-total correlation may occur when the item is negatively worded but its scoring is not reversed for consistency with the remaining (positively worded) items. A more sophisticated analog to the item-total correlation, referred to as *item-measure correlation*, is typically estimated in the context of Rasch measures (e.g., Wolfe & Smith, 2007b). More information on the item-measure correlation and some other indices of items' technical quality is provided later in this book (see Chapter 9).

3.2.2 Substantive Aspect of Validity

The *substantive aspect of validity* refers to theoretical rationales for the observed consistencies in test responses, including process models of task performance along with empirical evidence that the theoretical processes are actually engaged by respondents in the assessment tasks (Messick, 1995). The substantive aspect adds to the content aspect of construct validity the need for empirical evidence of response consistencies or performance regularities reflective of domain processes (Loevinger, 1957). Evidence about the substantive aspect of validity can be collected through cognitive modeling of the examinees' response processes, observations of behaviors exhibited by the examinees when answering the items, analysis of scale functioning, consistency between expected and empirical item difficulties, and person-fit analysis (e.g., when the test items are developed in the framework of Rasch measurement; see Chapter 9).

Cognitive Modeling. One way to collect evidence about the substantive aspect of validity is by identifying and modeling the cognitive processes that underlie people's responses on test items. This task can be accomplished by using (a) existing theory and empirical research on cognitive processes related to the construct of interest, (b) "think aloud" protocols or retrospective reflections through which examinees explain the reasoning they used in responding to each item, (c) experts' judgments, and/or (d) other sources of relevant information. When such techniques identify cognitive processes that also exist in the processing model of the construct, it provides strong support to the substantive aspect of validity.

A comprehensive illustration of cognitive modeling for construct validation is provided in a study by Carpenter, Just, and Shell (1990) on cognitive processes in the Raven's Progressive Matrices Test (J. C. Raven, 1936; J. Raven, J. C. Raven, & Court, 2003). In this multiple-choice test of abstract reasoning, examinees are asked to identify missing segments required to complete given patterns. The test is designed to measure two main components of general intelligence: deductive ability (the ability to think clearly and make sense of complexity) and reproductive ability (the ability to store and reproduce information). Specifically, Carpenter et al. (1990) analyzed a form of the Raven test called the Raven Advanced Progressive Matrices (APM) in terms of which processes distinguish between higher scoring and lower scoring subjects and which processes are common to all subjects and all items on the test. The analysis is based on performance characteristics such as verbal protocols, eye-fixation patterns, and errors. They found that even the simplest types of figural analogies in APM were decomposed and incrementally processed through a sequence of pairwise comparisons, and that this segmentation is an inherent part of problem solving and a facet of thinking that is common across domains in various tasks requiring analytic intelligence. A critically important feature of Carpenter et al.'s approach is the search for observable support to the theoretical models used as a framework of the cognitive modeling.

Perhaps the validation of cognitive processes that govern people's responses on observable indicators of the construct is best performed in the framework of cognitive diagnosis modeling (CDM)—a modern discipline that integrates cognitive psychology and psychometrics. Key steps in CDM are (a) identification of a hypothetical set of cognitive processes required for correct responses (or endorsement) of the items in an instrument; (b) development of a matrix (rows = items; columns = cognitive processes), called the Q-matrix, in which the entry in cell (i, k) equals 1 if item i requires cognitive process k and equals 0 if it does not; and (c) validation of the Q-matrix by means of a psychometric model adopted by the researcher (e.g., De La Torre & Douglas, 2004; Dimitrov, 2007; Embretson, 1995; Tatsuoka & Tatsuoka, 1983).

Behavioral Correlates. Documentation of correlations between examinees' behaviors while answering items and their responses on these items can also support the substantive aspect of validity. Examples of observable behaviors are eye movements, time of accomplishing specific subtasks, note taking, graphics, computations, and so forth. For example, Carpenter et al. (1990) found that eye-fixation data provided clear evidence supporting the following theoretically based prediction: As the number of cognitive rules increases, so should the number of pairwise similarities and differences to be encoded and, consequently, the number of pairwise comparisons (the subjects' eye fixations were monitored remotely with an Applied Science Laboratories corneal and pupil-centered eye tracker). They also concluded that "many of the performance commonalities occur at the microstructure of the processing, which is revealed in the eye-fixation patterns. Such processes are too fast for conscious awareness or for inclusion in a verbal report. The eye-fixation analysis reveals iterations through small units of processing; the task is decomposed into manageable units of processing, each governed by a subgoal" (Carpenter et al., 1990, p. 429).

Scale Functioning. Yet another piece of evidence related to the substantive aspect of validity is provided when examinees' observed responses on (multiple-choice or rating scale) items are consistent with the intended response characteristics of these items as targeted by the item developer(s). With multiple-choice items, for example, typical expectations are (a) that response options that are incorrect (i.e., distractors) for an item will be equally attractive to examinees who don't know the correct answer of that item, and (b) each distractor should attract more examinees at the lower level of ability than examinees at the higher level of the ability that is measured by the test. When the observed responses for an item deviate from these expectations, this item should be examined for validity problems. Technical procedures for such analyses are illustrated later in Chapter 8. Other methodological and technical characteristics of multiple-choice items, discussed in Chapter 4, Section 4.3, should also be taken into account.

When rating scale items are used, the substantive aspect of validity is supported if the observed item responses are consistent with the intended response characteristics of the items as targeted by the item developer(s). Useful in this regard are the methodological comments provided in Chapter 4, Section 4.3, on item formats in rating scales (using a middle response category, using negatively phrased items, labeling response categories, and so forth). Wolfe and Smith (2007b) described some guidelines for rating scale functioning that stem from research on rating scales in the context of Rasch measurement (e.g., Linacre, 2002; Wright & Linacre, 1992; Zhu, 2002). Four primary guidelines that they consider essential conditions for measurement stability, measurement accuracy, accurate description of the sample, and/or inferences to the target population are as follows:

> - Each rating category should contain a minimum of 10 observations to ensure the precision of the relevant indices [of rating scale functioning].
> - The shape of each rating scale distribution should be smooth and unimodal to support the argument that rating scale categories are not being used in idiosyncratic ways.
> - The average respondent measure [ability score] associated with each category should increase with the values of the rating scale categories to support the argument that the rating scale is used fairly consistently across items.
> - The unweighted mean-squared fit statistics [for discrepancies between the observed and expected values associated with a particular item] should be less than 2.00 to support the notion that the responses in each rating category are in accord with the Rasch model expectations. (Wolfe & Smith, 2007b, p. 210)

Although these guidelines are useful for rating scales in general, some technical guidelines that are specific to Rasch-based assessment are discussed in Chapter 9.

3.2.3 Structural Aspect of Validity

As described by Messick (1995), the *structural aspect of validity* appraises the fidelity of the scoring structure to the structure of the construct domain at issue. Messick (1995) emphasized that "the theory of the construct domain should guide not only the selection or construction of relevant assessment tasks but also the rational development of construct-based scoring criteria and rubrics" (p. 746). He defined *structural fidelity* as a property of the construct-based scoring model under which "the internal structure of the assessment (i.e., interrelations among the scored aspects of task and subtask performance) should be consistent with what is known about the internal structure of the construct domain" (p. 746).

Typically, evidence of the structural aspect of validity is sought by correlational and measurement consistency between the target constructs and their indicators (items). This task is done primarily by using (exploratory and/or confirmatory) factor analysis. An exploratory factor analysis (EFA) is used when the instrument developers do not have enough theoretical or empirical information to hypothesize how many constructs (factors) underlie the initial set of items and which items form which factor. Therefore, EFA is typically used earlier in the process of scale development and construct validation.

A confirmatory factor analysis (CFA) is used in later phases of scale validation after the underlying structure has been established on prior empirical and/or theoretical grounds. Thus, CFA is used when the goal is to test the validity of a hypothesized model of constructs (factors) and their relationships with a set of observable variables (items, indicators). Factor analyses (EFA, CFA, or both) are widely used and play a key role in the process of development and structural validation of instruments used in counseling, education, psychology, and other fields. Validity studies that use factor analysis are widely represented in professional journals such as *Measurement and Evaluation in Counseling and Development* (*MECD*), *Educational and Psychological Measurement*, *Developmental Psychology*, *Journal of Personality Assessment*, *Journal of Clinical Psychology*, *Psychological Assessment*, and others. Methodological and technical aspects of EFA and CFA in collecting evidence about the structural aspect of validity of assessment instruments are discussed in Chapters 5 and 6.

3.2.4 Generalizability Aspect of Validity

As described by Messick (1995), the *generalizability aspect of validity* examines the extent to which score properties and interpretations generalize to and across population groups, settings, and tasks, including validity generalization of test criterion relationships. Collecting evidence related to the generalizability aspect of validity involves identifying the boundaries of the meaning of the scores across tasks and contexts. Typical procedures for collecting such evidence deal with testing for factorial invariance of target constructs across groups and/or time points, item bias, differential prediction, contextual stability, and reliability.

Factorial Invariance. Testing for factorial invariance across population groups is used to provide evidence that the properties and interpretations of scores are generalizable across these groups. There are three stages in testing for factorial invariance: (a) testing for configural invariance to ensure that the baseline factor structure of the scores resulting from the instrument is the same for each group; (b) testing for measurement invariance to ensure that that the meaning and interpretation of the test score is the same for all groups; and (c) testing for structural invariance to ensure that the variability of construct scores (and the correlations among them in case of two or more constructs) is the same across the groups.

In measurement parlance, the lack of measurement invariance indicates the presence of differential item functioning. By definition, an item is functioning differentially when respondents at the same level of the construct being measured differ in their responses on the item because they belong to different groups for example, majority versus minority groups. For narrative texts, for example, cultural differences are the most likely source of irrelevant difficulty for students with limited English proficiency, because although the narrative genre is universal, narration varies across cultures in terms of types used, their function, their content, thematic emphasis, structural organization, and style (Westby, 1994). Typically, CFA methods in the framework of structural equation modeling are used to determine the extent to which two groups exhibit structurally invariant patterns of associations among the constructs. Item response theory methods that deal with differential item functioning are also used for establishing measurement invariance across groups. In Chapter 6, I give a detailed discussion of testing for factorial invariance and include illustrative examples using CFA-based methods.

Differential Prediction. The consistency of the relationship between the target construct and an external criterion across population groups also provides support to the generalizability aspect of validity. As previously noted, the relationship between the scores on a test under development and an external criterion is referred to as *criterion validity* under the obsolete conception of validity (Cronbach & Meehl, 1955). The respective correlation coefficient is called the *predictive validity coefficient* when the criterion is a future "behavior" of the examinees—for example, using SAT scores to predict the future performance (college grade point average) of college applicants. Under the unified construct-based model of validity (Messick, 1995), changes to the predictive validity coefficient across groups is referred to as *differential prediction* or *differential validity*. Studies of differential prediction typically examine group differences in linear regression slopes or intercepts for predicting criterion scores from one or more test scores. The lack of differential prediction provides support to the generalizability aspect of validity. Testing for differential prediction can be done by testing for interaction between the grouping variable and the predictor (i.e., the scale under validation) through classical regression analysis (e.g., Allen & Yen, 1979; Humphreys, 1986; Nunnally & Bernstein, 1994) or, even better, in the framework of structural equation modeling (e.g., Millsap, 1998; L. K. Muthén & B. O. Muthén, 2008). See also Chapman and Hayslip (2005) for an application of the so-called incremental validity approach to evaluating differential prediction.

Contextual Stability. Evidence in support of the generalizability aspect of validity is also provided in the presence of contextual stability—that is, when the measures under validation are (a) stable across contexts of administration of the assessment instrument and (b) relate to external criteria in a consistent manner across contexts of decision making. The former type of stability is referred to as *situational specificity*, whereas the latter is referred to as *cross-sectional consistency* (e.g., James, Demaree, & Mulaik, 1986; Wolfe & Smith, 2007b). These two types of contextual stability should be evaluated, for example, when the assessment instrument is administered in paper-based and computer-based formats (situational specificity) or when it is used to predict attitude toward school and academic achievement (cross-sectional consistency).

In a study on correlations between a job performance criterion and personality measures reflecting achievement motivation and an interpersonal orientation, Helmreich, Sawin, and Carsrud (1986) found that although correlations between the personality predictors and performance were small and nonsignificant for the three-month period after beginning the job, by the end of six and eight months a number of significant relationships had emerged. The lack of contextual stability across time in this example clearly indicates problems with the validity of personality measures in selection and performance prediction (Helmreich et al., 1986). There are different approaches to evaluating validity generalization (e.g., Burke, 1986; Raju & Burke, 1983; Schmidt & Hunter, 1977; Schmidt, Hunter, & Caplan, 1981). Comparing six procedures for validity generalization, Burke (1986) showed that the Taylor Series Approximations (Raju & Burke, 1983) yielded the highest true validity estimates.

Reliability. As described in Chapter 2, the reliability of measurements indicates the degree to which they are accurate, consistent, and replicable when (a) different people conduct the measurement, (b) different instruments that purport to measure the same trait are used, and (c) there is incidental variation in measurement. The reliability of scores is a necessary condition for their valid interpretation and generalization across samples of items, time points, raters, and testing conditions. One can compute coefficients of different types of reliability—for example, internal consistency reliability, test–retest reliability, alternate forms reliability, criterion-referenced reliability, and interrater reliability (cf. Chapter 2). Coefficients of reliability in the framework of generalizability theory are particularly useful in evaluating the generalizability aspect of validity as such coefficients take into account different sources of error attributable, for example, to different test forms, raters, testing conditions, and so forth (e.g., Brennan, 2004; Shavelson & Webb, 1991). Changes in reliability across groups and/or modification of an instrument during the process of its development should also be taken into account in evaluating the generalizability aspect of validity (e.g., Raykov, 2002; Raykov & Grayson, 2003).

3.2.5 External Aspect of Validity

As described by Messick (1995), the *external aspect of validity* includes convergent and discriminant evidence from multitrait–multimethod (MTMM) comparisons as well as evidence of criterion relevance and applied utility. The convergent evidence indicates a correspondence between measures of the same trait, whereas the discriminant evidence indicates a distinctness from measures of other traits. The MTMM approach to collecting convergent and discriminant evidence, in both classical and confirmatory factor modeling, is described in Chapter 7. An exploratory factor modeling approach to collecting convergent and discriminant evidence is described in Chapter 5, Section 5.11.

Along with convergent and discriminant evidence, the external aspect of validity is supported by evidence of criterion relevance (referred to also as criterion validity). Examples from previous research that provide such evidence using correlational analysis are provided in Chapter 4, Section 4.2.2 (e.g., Bodenhorn & Skaggs, 2005; S. M. Lee et al., 2007). Between-group differences and within-person (e.g., pretest–posttest) changes that are expected with the construct model can also be tested to support the external aspect of validity. For example, in support of external validity of the Beck Depression Inventory—Second Edition (BDI–II), Beck, Steer, and Brown (1996) reported that outpatients with mood disorders scored significantly higher on the BDI–II than outpatients with anxiety or adjustment disorders. A contemporary approach to evaluating criterion relevance, with a computer code in Mplus (L. K. Muthén & B. O. Muthén, 2008), is presented by Raykov (2007a).

Evidence of applied utility can also provide support to the external aspect of validity. For example, Pistole and Roberts (2011) used a logistic regression analysis to examine the applied utility for the scores of a long-distance romantic relationship (LDR) measure under the expectation that the LDR index would correctly classify people into self-selected categories of LDR relationships or geographically close relationships.

3.2.6 Consequential Aspect of Validity

As described by Messick (1995), the consequential aspect of validity appraises the value implications of score interpretations as a basis for action as well as the actual and potential consequences of test use, especially in regard to sources of invalidity related to issues of bias, fairness, and distributive justice. Both short-term and long-term consequences (positive and/or negative) should be evaluated in searching for evidence to support this aspect of validity. It is particularly important to make sure that negative consequences have not resulted from drawbacks of the assessment, such as (a) construct underrepresentation—the assessment is too narrow and fails to measure important dimensions or facets of the construct; and/or (b) construct-irrelevant variance—the assessment allows for variance generated by sources unrelated to the target construct (e.g., item bias).

Also, as Wolfe and Smith (2007b, p. 224) noted, "the processes of standard setting, and the resulting applications of the cut score(s), have a direct relationship with the consequential aspect of validity." Therefore, instrument developers must properly document all players and steps in such processes, for example, the number and qualifications of experts (as well as the reliability of their judgments), model of standard setting, dependability of the cutoff scores, consistency of classifications, and so forth. In this book, the issues of criterion-related reliability, interrater reliability, and dependability of cutoff scores were addressed in Chapter 2, whereas the expert review process in standard setting is addressed later in Chapter 4. A readable treatment of decision theory in counseling, with an example of setting a cutoff score to identify adults at risk for depression, is provided by Basham and Erford (2007).

An Alternative View on the Consequential Aspect of Validity. There is an ongoing debate in the literature regarding the appropriateness of including the consequential aspect of validity under the unified construct-based model of validity. For example, two recent studies (Cizek, Bowen, & Church, 2010; Cizek, Rosenberg, & Koons, 2008) reported that the consequential aspect of validity has been routinely ignored in the presentations of validity evidence published in *Mental Measurements Yearbook* and all articles published in the past 10 years in several applied journals devoted to educational assessment and educational policy (presentations at recent annual meetings of the AERA, APA, and NCME were also examined). Cizek et al. (2010) concluded that "researchers and practitioners do not gather or report evidence on validity based on consequences because it is not possible to include consequences as a logical part of validation . . . and that consequential validity is simply a flaw in modern validity theory" (p. 739). At the same time, however, they argued that "the error of including consequences in modern validity theory should not simplistically be redressed by simply excising consequences from the theory. The consequences of testing are real, diverse, important, and warrant consideration and evaluation" (p. 740). Further clarifying this point, Cizek et al. (2010) suggested that validity theory must be refined to differentiate between validation of score inferences and justification of test use. Without doubt, researchers and developers of assessment instruments can only benefit from understanding the logic behind different conceptions of the nature and role of the consequential aspect of validity, as well as the differentiation between *validity* as a property and *validation* as an activity (e.g., see Borsboom, Mellenbergh, & van Heerden, 2004).

3.2.7 Additional Notes on Validity

Responsiveness and Interpretability. In a study related to instrument development tools and validation activities, Wolfe and Smith (2007a) adopted Messick's framework of validity with two additional criteria proposed by the Medical Outcomes Trust Scientific Advisory Committee (1995): responsiveness and interpretability. *Responsiveness*, referred to also as sensitivity, is the capacity of the assessment instrument to detect change (e.g., after an intervention) in a specific population. *Interpretability* is the degree to which qualitative meaning can be assigned to quantitative measures (see http://www.outcomes-trust.org). Whereas responsiveness is considered for support to the external aspect of validity, interpretability is considered as an aspect of validity that reveals the degree to which qualitative meaning can be assigned to quantitative measures. Thus, the interpretability aspect of validity indicates how well the meaning of assessment scores is communicated to people who may interpret the scores but are not necessarily familiar with the psychometric terminology and concepts in assessment. For example, the proper communication of norm-referenced versus criterion-referenced assessment scores is critical for their valid interpretation by a relatively large audience (e.g., practitioners, clients, parents, social workers, policymakers, and so forth) Wolfe and Smith (2007b) discussed the interpretability aspect of validity in the context of Rasch measurement, but the underlying logic holds for other (e.g., CFA-based) frameworks of construct measurement.

Sources of Invalidity. Messick (1995) specified two major sources of invalidity: (a) construct underrepresentation—the assessment is too narrow and fails to measure important dimensions or facets of the construct; and (b) construct-irrelevant variance—the assessment is too broad and allows for variance generated by sources unrelated to the construct(s) of interest (e.g., item difficulty or bias unrelated to the target construct or, conversely, extraneous clues in the presentation of some items that unduly facilitate responses on these items).

SUMMARY

1. In general terms, validity has to do with whether an instrument measures what it purports to measure. Validity is *not* a property of an instrument but, instead, relates to an interpretation of data obtained through the use of the instrument.
2. Historically, there are three major stages in the development of validity models: (a) criterion-based model (Cronbach & Gleser, 1965; Cureton, 1950; E. L. Thorndike, 1918), in which validity of measures is viewed as the degree to which these measures are consistent with (or "predict") the measures on a specific criterion; (b) construct-based model (Cronbach & Meehl, 1955), which considers three different types of validity—content validity, criterion validity, and construct validity; and (c) unified construct-based model of validity (Messick, 1989, 1995).
3. Major drawbacks of the criterion-based conception of validity are that it is too limited, it does not capture some basic (e.g., content-related) aspects of validity, and it is not always possible to identify appropriate criterion measures.
4. Under the construct-based model, the discrete treatment of content validity, criterion validity, and construct validity can mislead test developers and users to believe that these three "types of validity" are comparable or, even worse, that they are equivalent and, thus, collecting evidence for any of them is sufficient to label an assessment instrument as valid.
5. Under the unified construct-based model of validity (Messick, 1989, 1995), validity is as an integrated evaluative judgment of the degree to which empirical evidence and theoretical rationales support the adequacy and appropriateness of inferences and actions based on test scores or other modes of assessment. This model of validity integrates content-related and criterion-related evidence into a unified framework of construct validity and empirical evaluation of the meaning and consequences of measurement.
6. Messick (1995) specified six aspects of the unified conception of construct validity: content, substantive, structural, generalizability, external, and consequential aspects of validity.
7. The content aspect of validity includes evidence of content relevance, representativeness, and technical quality. Face validity evidence, logical validity evidence, and technical quality of the items relate to the content aspect of validity.
8. The substantive aspect of validity refers to theoretical rationales for the observed consistencies in test responses, including process models of task performance along with empirical evidence that the theoretical processes are actually engaged by respondents in the assessment tasks.
9. The structural aspect of validity appraises the degree of consistency between the scoring structure and the structure of the target construct domain. Key evidence of the structural aspect of validity is sought by correlational and measurement consistency between the target constructs and their indicators (items)—primarily through the use of factor analysis.

10. An exploratory factor analysis (EFA) is used when there is not enough theoretical or empirical information to hypothesize how many latent factors underlie the initial set of items and which items form which factor. EFA is typically used earlier in the process of scale development and construct validation.
11. A confirmatory factor analysis (CFA) is used in later phases of scale validation after the underlying structure has been established on prior empirical and/or theoretical grounds.
12. The generalizability aspect of validity examines the extent to which score properties and interpretations generalize to and across population groups, settings, and tasks, including validity generalization of test criterion relationships. Collecting generalizability evidence typically involves testing for factorial invariance of the target constructs across groups and/or time points, item bias, differential prediction, contextual stability, and reliability.
13. The external aspect of validity includes convergent and discriminant evidence from multitrait–multimethod comparisons as well as evidence of criterion relevance and applied utility.
14. The consequential aspect of validity appraises the value implications of score interpretations as a basis for action as well as the actual and potential consequences of test use, especially in regard to sources of invalidity related to issues of bias, fairness, and distributive justice.
15. The Medical Outcomes Trust Scientific Advisory Committee (1995) proposed two additional criteria under Messick's framework of validity: (a) responsiveness—the capacity of the assessment instrument to detect change in a specific population; and (b) interpretability—the degree to which qualitative meaning can be assigned to quantitative measures.
16. Major sources of invalidity are (a) construct underrepresentation—the assessment is too narrow and fails to measure important dimensions or facets of the construct; and (b) construct-irrelevant variance—the assessment is too broad, thus allowing for variance generated by sources unrelated to the construct(s) of interest.
17. An alternative view on the consequential aspect of validity suggests that validity theory must be refined to differentiate between validation of score inferences and justification of test use (e.g., Cizek et al., 2010). Also, some authors argue about the need to differentiate between validity as a property and validation as an activity (Borsboom et al., 2004).

Chapter 4
Steps in Instrument Development

The unified conception of construct validity provides the blueprints for the theoretical framework (construct map) of the assessment instrument. Wolfe and Smith (2007a) noted that "nearly all of the evidence that is collected to support the validity of inferences that are drawn and decisions that are made based on measures from an instrument relies on a detailed theoretical specification of the construct being measured" (p. 100). They outlined five groups of activities that test developers can use to specify the construct of interest and to collect validation evidence: definition of purpose (of the assessment), test specifications, item development, expert review, and pilot studies. Using the description provided by Wolfe and Smith (2007a), I discuss in this chapter those five activities in light of their relation to the validity of the construct that is being measured by the assessment instrument under development.

4.1 DEFINITION OF PURPOSE

It is critical that the instrument developers define the purpose of the assessment as clearly and completely as possible to facilitate the alignment of that purpose with subsequent steps in the development of the instrument. The purpose of an assessment instrument is defined within a specific domain—for example, clinical, personality, or behavioral assessments; assessments of intelligence, aptitudes, or achievement; assessments in career counseling; or assessments of couples and families. After specifying the domain of assessment, the instrument developers must identify the intended decision for the instrument, constraints related to its development and data collection, and frame of reference (norm-referenced or criterion-referenced assessment).

4.1.1 Intended Decision

The purpose of most assessment instruments in counseling is to determine the status of individuals (e.g., diagnostic assessments related to depression, anxiety, academic strengths and weaknesses, interests, self-esteem, disruptive behavior, and so forth). For example, the purpose of the BDI–II is to assess the severity of depression of individuals ages 13 years or older, the Strong Interest Inventory (Harmon, Hansen, Borgen, & Hammer, 1994) aims to help determine clients' likes and dislikes as they relate to occupations, and the Gray Oral Reading Test—Fourth Edition is designed to measure growth in oral reading as well as to aid in the diagnosis of oral reading difficulties.

4.1.2 Constraints

Instrument developers should consider both objective and subjective constraints related to instrument development and data collection. Objective constraints may relate, for example, to money, policies, and external factors of time frame (e.g., a semester, school year, and so forth). Subjective constraints stem from instrument developers' considerations about length of time and mode of data collection (e.g., paper-based vs. electronic form, individual vs. group administration of the instrument, and so forth).

4.1.3 Frame of Reference

The instrument's purpose, including what decisions will be based on data collected by the instrument, should guide the frame of reference, which can be norm-based, criterion-based, or both. With a norm-referenced assessment, the interpretation of a score reveals its relative position with regard to the other scores in the target population. The sample used to represent the target population is referred to as the standardization sample (or normative sample). The comparison scores in norm-referenced interpretations are placed into two groups: developmental scores and scores of relative standing (Salvia & Ysseldyke, 2004). Two common types of developmental scores, referred to as developmental equivalents, are age-equivalent and grade-equivalent scores. Major types of scores of relative standing include standard (z) scores, standardized scores (e.g., T scores, IQ scores, and NCE scores), stanines, and percentiles (see Chapter 1, Section 1.5.6).

With a criterion-referenced assessment, the interpretation of a score is relative to a prespecified cutting score that represents an absolute standard (criterion) of performance. The purpose can be, for example, to make instructional decisions regarding mastery or nonmastery of specified curriculum goals and objectives or diagnostic decisions based on a level of severity in, say, assessment of depression or anxiety. A recent variation of criterion-referenced assessment is referred to as standards-based assessment. For example, many states have adopted content standards that describe what students should know and be able to do in different subjects at various grade levels. They also have performance standards that define how much of the content standards students should know to reach the basic, proficient, or advanced level in the subject area. In some cases, the assessment instrument is designed to allow for both norm-referenced and criterion-referenced interpretations. For more information on norm-referenced and criterion-referenced interpretations in the context of assessment for counselors, the reader may refer to Doggett, Sheperis, Eaves, Mong, and Erford (2007).

4.2 INSTRUMENT SPECIFICATIONS

After defining the purpose of an assessment instrument (test, inventory, and so forth), the next step in developing the instrument and its validation framework is to create a set of instrument specifications that, according to Wolfe and Smith (2007a), "define the construct by outlining the domain to be measured; and create various construct models for the purpose of illustrating the internal structure of the construct, the place of that construct in a theoretical framework, the hierarchical association of elements of the construct, and the processes through which the construct produces observable behaviors" (p. 102). Key elements in the process of instrument specifications are the theoretical definition of the construct and models of the construct stemming from its definition.

4.2.1 Construct Definition

A comprehensive definition of the construct under consideration is of critical importance for adequate specifications of the assessment instrument. As noted by Wolfe and Smith

(2007a), "through the process of construct definition, instrument developers begin to formally identify the behavioral boundaries of the construct, differentiate the construct from other constructs, and imply relationships between the construct and other constructs" (p. 102). For example, the construct measured by the reading comprehension section on the verbal part of a large-scale standardized test is defined as "one's ability to reason with words in solving problems," and it is expected that "reasoning effectively in a verbal medium depends primarily on ability to discern, comprehend, and analyze relationships among words or groups of words and within larger units of discourse such as sentences and written passages" (Educational Testing Service, 2002, p. 2).

Typically, the definition of a construct is embedded into a more general theory and then operationalized in the context of the theory and practice in which inferences and decisions are to be made based on assessment scores. For instance, various definitions of the construct "self-efficacy" in the context of health behavior are based on definitions of this construct in general theories and models such the Social Cognitive Theory (Bandura, 1997), the Theory of Planned Behavior (Ajzen, 1991), the Transtheoretical Model (Prochaska, Norcross, Fowler, Follick, & Abrams, 1992), and the Health Action Process Approach (Schwarzer, 2001). For example, Schwarzer and Luszczynska (2008, p. 1) translated Bandura's (1997) definition of self-efficacy in the context of health behavior theories as follows:

> Self-efficacy pertains to a sense of **control over one's environment and behavior**. Self-efficacy beliefs are cognitions that determine whether health behavior change will be initiated, how much effort will be expended, and how long it will be sustained in the face of obstacles and failures. Self-efficacy influences the effort one puts forth to change risky behavior and the persistence to continue striving despite barriers and setbacks that may undermine motivation. Self-efficacy is directly related to health behavior, but it also affects health behaviors indirectly through its impact on goals. Self-efficacy influences the challenges that people take on as well as how high they set their goals (e.g., "I intend to reduce my smoking," or "I intend to quit smoking altogether"). Individuals with strong self-efficacy select more challenging goals (DeVellis & DeVellis, 2000. Self-efficacy and health. In: A. Baum, T. A. Revenson, & J. E. Singer [Eds.], Handbook of Health Psychology [pp. 235–247]. Mahwah, NJ: Erlbaum.) They focus on opportunities, not on obstacles (e.g., "At my university there is a smoking ban, anyway," instead of "There are still a lot of ashtrays at my university.").

As another example, Wood, Linley, Maltby, Baliousis, and Joseph (2008) based the development of the Authenticity Scale on a model presented in Figure 4.1. This model, in turn, stems from Rogers's (1959, 1961) theory of therapy, personality, and interpersonal relationships (see also Barrett-Lennard, 1998).

4.2.2 Construct Models

Based on the adopted construct definition, instrument developers should build a detailed construct model that specifies (a) the internal structure of the construct (i.e., its componential structure), (b) the external relationships of the construct to other constructs, (c) potential types of indicators (e.g., item formats) for measuring behaviors that are relevant to assessing individuals on the construct, and (d) construct-related processes (e.g., causal impacts that the construct is expected to have on the specific behavior). As described by Wolfe and Smith (2007a), the development of a construct model is based on information that may come from a variety of sources related to the construct or similar constructs, such as (a) reviews of previous theoretical and/or empirical research, (b) reviews of existing assessment instruments, (c) content and task analysis within the domain of the construct,

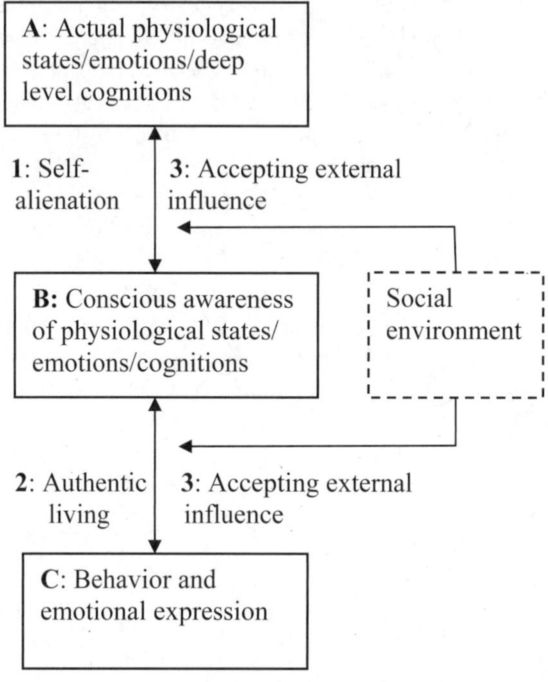

FIGURE 4.1

The Person-Centered Conception of Authenticity

Note. From "The Authentic Personality: A Theoretical and Empirical Conceptualization and the Development of the Authenticity Scale," by A. M. Wood, P. A. Linley, J. Maltby, M. Baliousis, and S. Joseph, 2008, *Journal of Counseling Psychology, 55,* p. 386. Copyright 2008 by the American Psychological Association. Reprinted with permission.

(d) expert-based conceptions, and (e) empirical experiences and observations. The whole structure of a construct model can be presented as an integration of four model components: internal, external, developmental, and processing.

Internal Model. An internal model of a construct specifies the components of the construct and the relationships among them. That is, an internal model depicts the expected internal structure of the measures (scores) that will be produced by the instrument, thus providing an explicit framework for structural validity arguments. Illustrations of internal models and their use in evaluating the structural aspect of validity are provided in Chapter 6.

External Model. An external model of a construct specifies the relationships between the construct and other constructs and/or relevant criterion variable(s). Testing hypotheses generated from the external model provides evidence related to the external aspect of construct validity. This testing can be correlation analysis, MTMM analysis, or factorial approaches to convergent and discriminant evidence of construct validity.

For example, the external model in the development of the School Counselor Efficacy Scale (SCE; Bodenhorn & Skaggs, 2005) is based, among other things, on Bandura's (1997) theory that states that self-efficacy reduces anxiety and avoidant behavior. To check the expected negative correlation between the anxiety level of school counselors and their self-efficacy level, Bodenhorn and Skaggs (2005) correlated the observed scores on the instrument under development (SCE) with those obtained on the State–Trait Anxiety Inventory (Spielberger, Gorsuch, Lushene, Vagg, & Jacobs, 1983). In a study on the development of the Counselor Burnout Inventory (CBI; S. M. Lee et al., 2007), evidence about the external aspect of the target construct (counselor burnout) was based on previous findings that counselors experiencing burnout were dissatisfied with their job and had poor self-esteem (e.g., Kirk-Brown & Wallace, 2004; C. J. Osborn, 2004). Therefore, as the authors stated, CBI subscales were correlated with the job satisfaction and self-esteem scales to check for criterion-related validity of the CBI (S. M. Lee et al., 2007). The use of MTMM analysis and other approaches to collecting evidence about the external aspect of construct validity is described in Chapter 7.

Developmental Model. A developmental model of a construct specifies changes in the construct and/or its relations with other variables that are expected to occur over time based on a specific theory and/or empirical research related to the construct. Developmental models provide a framework for validation arguments related to (a) the substantive aspect of validity—by allowing for comparisons between theoretical expectations versus empirical evidence collected over an appropriate time period; and (b) the external aspect of validity—for example, by allowing the testing of expected differences between groups defined by characteristics of interest, such as gender, ethnicity, severity of depression, and so forth.

Developmental models provide valuable information to instrument developers during the process of item writing. For example, Wolfe and Smith (2007a) discussed this issue in reference to developing an instrument to measure levels of acculturation to the U.S. culture among Chinese immigrants (Hsu, 2005). This model specifies three levels of increasing adaptation to the U.S. culture: (a) superficial changes—learning historical facts and traditions and eating food commonly available in the United States; (b) intermediate changes—changing language use, increasing interactions with the dominant culture, and participating in cultural and leisure activities; and (c) significant changes—adopting beliefs, values, and norms of the dominant society in the United States. Comparing the observed and expected matching of measures for persons at different levels of acculturation and the psychometric characteristic of items capturing those levels can provide evidence related to the substantive aspect of validity, whereas comparing the measures of persons at different levels of acculturation can provide evidence related to the external aspect of validity.

Some developmental models specify stability of the construct over a period of time and/or changes in relationships of the construct with other variables (e.g., other constructs or grouping variables, such as gender, ethnicity, depression status, and so forth). It is critical that such models be based on previous theoretical and/or empirical findings and take into account possible differential effects in the manifestation of the construct and its relationships with other variables. For example, investigating the stability of the perfectionism construct and its relationships with prior and concurrent depression, Rice and Aldea (2006) discriminated between (a) absolute stability, which refers to whether average group scores on perfectionism changed over time, and (b) relative stability, which refers to the extent to which relative differences among individuals on measures of personality remain stable. Among other things, they found greater absolute stability in perfectionism for individuals with remission of depressive symptoms. As an implication of this finding for the counseling practice, Rice and Aldea (2006, p. 210) pointed out that "interventions aimed at improving the depressed mood of maladaptively perfectionistic clients may be beneficial in the short run, but without additional attention to, and lowering of, perfectionistic self-critical characteristics, the client may remain at risk for relapse." In the context of validity, this implication relates to the consequential aspect in the validation of instruments for assessment of perfectionism.

As another example, considering that the existing self-concept literature has been phrased largely as a change versus stability question, Young and Mroczek (2003) used growth curve modeling to investigate changes over time in self-concept of adolescents aged 11–20. They assessed self-concept with the Self-Perception Profile for Adolescents (Harter, 1988), a widely used 45-item questionnaire that measures global self-worth and eight specific domains of self-concept. Six of the self-concept domains were found to be stable over time, but a significant increase in perceived competency was found in three domains: job competence, romantic appeal, and physical appearance. The authors attributed some of these changes to social changes that occur during puberty (Young & Mroczek, 2003). They also found that age at baseline was a significant predictor of level of self-concept for several of the domains. Older adolescents had higher job competence and romantic appeal ratings than younger adolescents. According to the authors, this finding likely reflects normal developmental processes whereby adolescents become increasingly more involved in jobs and romantic relationships as they get older. Gender was also a significant predictor of level of self-concept for several of the domains. Specifically, females had lower global self-worth, scholastic competence, athletic competence, and physical appearance ratings than males (Young & Mroczek, 2003). Clearly, such findings provide useful information for creating a developmental model of self-concept and collecting evidence related to the substantive and external aspects of validity for measures of self-concept.

Processing Model. A processing model of a construct specifies a set of internal attributes (states or cognitive operations and processes) that govern the person's responses on observable indicators of the construct (e.g., test items). The specification and validation of internal attributes is best performed in the framework of cognitive diagnosis modeling a modern discipline that integrates cognitive psychology and psychometrics (e.g., De La Torre & Douglas, 2004; DiBello, Stout, & Roussos, 1995; Dimitrov, 2007; Dimitrov & Raykov, 2003; Embretson, 1983, 1994, 1995; Embretson & Wetzel, 1987; Gitomer & Rock, 1993; Henson & Douglas, 2005; Irvine & Kyllonen, 2002; Mislevy, 1993, 1994, 1995; Snow & Lohman, 1989; Tatsuoka, Corter, & Tatsuoka, 2004; Tatsuoka & Tatsuoka, 1983; Templin & Henson, 2006; von Davier, 2005).

Knowledge about internal attributes can help test developers to construct test items with desirable cognitive characteristics and/or to test hypotheses related to the substantive aspect of validity. For example, Henson and Douglas (2005) used pathological gambling as an example to demonstrate that an instrument developed for psychological assessment of factors underlying a clinical disorder can provide diagnostic information via cognitive diagnosis modeling. They used criteria of pathological gambling as defined in the *Diagnostic and Statistical Manual of Mental Disorders* (4th ed., text rev.; *DSM–IV–TR*; American Psychiatric Association, 2000). Specifically, persistent and recurrent maladaptive gambling behavior is indicated by the presence of at least five (out of 10) criteria, such as (a) is preoccupied with gambling, (b) needs to gamble with increasing amounts of money in order to achieve the desired excitement, (c) has repeated unsuccessful efforts to control, cut back, or stop gambling, and so forth.

In the area of educational assessment, cognitive models of the operations and processes required for correct responses on individual test items can provide valuable information for the process of construct definition, item writing, and construct validation (e.g., Embretson, 1994; Mislevy, 1994). Leighton (2004) described three types of cognitive models: domain mastery, test specifications, and task performance. For purposes of construct definition, the cognitive model of domain mastery seems most relevant, as it describes relationships between various skills and knowledge that comprise expertise in a given content area. Such relationships can be operationalized, for example, using a construct map (M. Wilson, 2005). As the construct map specifies the development of skills and associated knowledge within a content domain, it can be useful in developing explicit criteria to evaluate individual items during the process of their development and substantive validation. For a comprehensive review of cognitively based test development and validation, the reader may refer to Gorin (2006).

4.2.3 Content Specification

The content specification of an instrument that measures a construct of interest requires that the instrument developers (a) operationalize the construct by developing a fairly exhaustive list of potential observable indicators of the construct, (b) select from this list a representative sample of indicators, and (c) develop item formats for the selected sample of indicators—for example, multiple-choice item format, Likert (or Likert-type) item format, open-ended item format, and so forth. This process is facilitated by developing a blueprint that maps specific models of the construct onto its content domain—most often in a two-way table (grid format) where the elements of the content domain are described in the rows of the table and the elements of the construct model in columns. The entries in the cells of this two-way table indicate the number of items allocated to the respective content and model elements.

4.2.4 Scoring and Scaling Models

As described by Wolfe and Smith (2007a), the scoring model for an assessment instrument translates the observed responses on construct indicators (items) into numerical codes. These numerical codes can be (a) dichotomous (or binary), in which the responses are assigned to one of two categories (e.g., 1 = true, 0 = false); or (b) polytomous, in which responses are assigned to more than two categories (e.g., Likert items). When the observed responses do not follow a fixed-response format (e.g., in open-ended items, essays, or think aloud protocols), it is necessary to develop a scoring rubric in order to standardize the assignment of numeric codes to observed responses.

The scoring model maps the observed responses onto scoring categories for individual items, thus producing item scores. The next step is to develop a scaling model that combines the individual item scores into overall measures (raw scores) of the target construct. In a test of 20 binary items, for example, the summation of individual item scores (0 or 1) will produce a scale with 21 possible raw scores: 0, 1, 2, . . ., 20. Likewise, the summation of 10 item scores obtained with a 5-point Likert scale ranging from 1 (*strongly disagree*) to 5 (*strongly agree*) will produce a scale with 41 possible raw scores: 10, 11, 12, . . ., 50. If necessary, the initially obtained raw scores can be transformed to obtain a scale with desired measurement features and quality (e.g., see Chapter 1, Section 1.5.6).

It is important to emphasize also that the process of developing scoring and scaling models relates to the structural aspect of validity. As Messick (1995, p. 746) noted, "the theory of the construct domain should guide not only the selection or construction of relevant assessment tasks but also the rational development of construct-based scoring criteria and rubrics. Ideally, the manner in which behavioral instances are combined to produce a score should rest on knowledge of how the processes underlying those behaviors combine dynamically to produce effects."

4.3 ITEM DEVELOPMENT

Item development must be guided by the purpose of the assessment, frame of reference (norm-referenced, criterion-referenced, or both), definition of the target construct, structure of the construct model (internal, external, developmental, or processing), and instrument specifications (blueprint, scoring, and scaling). The process of item development and the analysis of item responses provide primary (item-level) evidence of construct validity. A careful documentation of this process includes both qualitative and quantitative forms of evidence. Downing and Haladyna (1997) described a qualitative framework of item-validity evidence and activities related to (a) content definition, (b) test specifications, (c) item writer training, (d) adherence to item-writing principles, (e) cognitive behavior, (f) item content verification, (g) item editing, (h) bias-sensitivity review, (i) item tryout and pretesting, (j) validation and verification of the keyed answer, and (k) test security plan (see also, Downing & Haladyna, 2006; Haladyna, 1996).

The qualitative aspects of item validity are complemented by quantitative item analysis to further evaluate the psychometric quality of individual items in measuring the target construct (e.g., Ackerman, 1992; Allen & Yen, 1979; Anastasi & Urbina, 1997; Clauser, 2000; R. J. Cohen & Swerdlik, 1999; Crocker & Algina, 1986; Haladyna, 1999; Janda, 1998; M. Wilson, 2005; Wright & Masters, 1982). As technical aspects of item analysis are addressed in Chapters 8 and 9, here I provide only some validity-related notes on item format and basic concepts of item difficulty, item discrimination, and item bias.

4.3.1 Selection of Item Format

Instrument developers select the format of the items based on their own preferences, the type of information needed, relevant characteristics of the examinees, and the setting in which the instrument is used (e.g., Janda, 1998). True–false format is used primarily for achievement, personality, or attitude tests (e.g., Whiston, 2005). A major disadvantage of using a true–false format for items in educational achievement tests is that the examinees have a 50% chance of guessing the correct answer.

Multiple-choice (MC) format is used mostly in achievement tests. Haladyna, Downing, and Rodriguez (2002) provided a taxonomy of 31 guidelines for writing MC items based on two sources of evidence. These guidelines are grouped in clusters by content concerns, formatting concerns, style concerns, composition of the item stem, and composition of the response choices. One of the rules for writing the response choices, for example, is to use typical errors of students to write the distractors. One way the test developer can achieve this is first to conduct a pilot test in which the items are provided in open-ended format and then to use the most frequently occurring wrong answers to generate MC distractors. Another way is to use think-aloud protocols to determine how students think when searching for a solution to the problem, and then use students' common errors and misconceptions to generate MC distractors.

Regarding writing the item stem, Haladyna et al. (2002) recommended that test developers "word the stem positively, avoid negatives such as NOT and EXCEPT. If negative words are used, use the word cautiously and always ensure that the word appears capitalized and boldface" (p. 312). With respect to the role of stem wording, Barnette (2000) noted that "negated items are not considered the exact opposite of directly worded items, and this is one of the major factors in the reduction of the reliability and validity of scores on surveys using mixed items" (p. 369). In general, following the guidelines for MC item writing reduces the chances of construct-irrelevant variance, which, in turn, provides support to the substantive aspect of construct validity.

Rating scale format is frequently used in assessment instruments. In the area of counseling, for example, the Likert format is often used in personality, attitude, career, and aptitude tests (e.g., Whiston, 2005). Previous research has identified several characteristics of the rating scale format that may affect the substantive and structural aspects of validity:

(a) the number of response categories (e.g., Aiken, 1983; Lam & Stevens, 1994), (b) using a middle response category (e.g., Bishop, 1987; Kalton, Roberts, & Holt, 1980; Narayan & Krosnick, 1996), (c) using negatively phrased items (e.g., Ahlawat, 1985; Barnette, 2000; L. Chang, 1995; Marsh, 1996; Motl & DiStefano, 2002), and (d) labeling response categories (e.g., Klockars & Yamagishi, 1988; Lam & Stevens, 1994). Following are some highlights in this regard:

- The number of response categories relates to score variability, thus affecting the internal consistency reliability and, therefore, the structural aspect of validity. Specifically, increasing the number of response categories increases the score reliability, but this is true only up to a certain point. For example, Masters (1974) reported that in situations where opinion varied widely in regard to the content being measured, reliability appeared to be independent of the number of response categories. Also, Wolfe and Smith (2007b) argued that when the number of available categories exceeds the number of levels of a construct that participants can discriminate, one begins introducing error variance rather than information into the ratings. This finding is supported by C. Cook, Heath, Thompson, and Thompson (2001), who studied the dependence of reliability on the type of scale in Web- or Internet-based surveys. Specifically, they indicated that "although greater score variance is possible when more score intervals are employed, if participants do not cognitively process so many score intervals when dealing with unnumbered graphic scales [a continuous line drawn between two antonyms], then the use of excessive intervals may not improve score reliability and might even lessen reliability" (p. 705). Typically, up to seven response categories are recommended for adults, and fewer (say, three) categories should be used for assessments of younger participants or of persons from special needs populations.
- The effects of using a middle response category have also been investigated in previous research. For example, Kalton et al. (1980) reported that offering a middle option increases the proportion of respondents stating a neutral view by between 15% and 49%. Bishop (1987) also concluded that people are more likely to select the middle response category when it is explicitly offered to them as part of the question than when it is omitted from the question yet provided as an optional rating choice. He also noted that "people who select a middle response alternative when it is offered would not necessarily answer the question in the same way as other respondents if forced to choose sides on the issue" (Bishop, 1987, p. 220). In yet another study, Presser and Schuman (1980) found that the decline in the polar response categories associated with an explicit offering of a middle category is proportional; therefore, the univariate distribution of opinion is not affected when middle responses are excluded from analysis. However, they supported a point made by Payne (1951) that "if the direction in which people are *leaning* on the issue is the type of information wanted, it is better not to suggest the middle ground . . . If it is desired to sort out those with more definite convictions on the issue, then it is better to suggest the middle ground" (p. 64; emphasis in original). Further discussion on dealing with problems related to a middle response category (e.g., undecided or neutral in Likert items)—for example, to treat the responses in this category as missing—is provided in Chapter 9.
- Using negatively phrased items is another issue to take into consideration in selecting item formats and evaluating construct validity. The primary intent of wording items positively and negatively has been to avoid acquiescence, affirmation, or

agreement bias (R. F. DeVellis, 1991; Nunnally, 1978). In other words, the purpose of using positively and negatively worded items within the same instrument is to prevent possible response bias—that is, the "tendency to respond in a particular way or style to items on a test that yields systematic, construct-irrelevant error in test scores" (Motl & DiStefano, 2000, p. 562). It has been found, however, that positively and negatively worded items tend to produce correlated, but distinct, traits when the instrument measures are submitted to factor analysis (e.g., Carmines & Zeller, 1979; L. Chang, 1995; Conroy, 2002; Corwyn, 2000; DiStefano & Motl, 2002; Marsh, 1996; Motl, Conroy, & Horan, 2000; Tomás & Oliver, 1999). Thus, positively and negatively worded items produce method effects that threaten the structural aspect of validity.

Whereas some researchers have considered method effects associated with positive/negative wording of items to be substantively irrelevant (e.g., Ahlawat, 1985; Marsh, 1996), others have suggested that such effects may represent something that is substantively meaningful (e.g., Motl et al., 2000; Motl & DiStefano, 2002; Tomás & Oliver, 1999). For example, some studies found that method effects associated with negatively worded items demonstrate longitudinal invariance, which is attributed to behavioral consistency across time (Billiet & McClendon, 2000; Motl & DiStefano, 2002). Discussing this finding in the context of self-esteem assessment, Motl and DiStefano (2002) noted that if method effects associated with negatively worded items are substantively meaningful, one possible interpretation might be the presence of a response style. Bentler, Jackson, and Messick (1971, p. 188) described response style as a potentially measurable personality trait that can be "identified by the existence of a latent variable" and described as "a behavioral consistency operating across measures of several conceptually distinct content traits." Motl and DiStefano (2002) attributed the presence of a response style associated with negatively worded items to potential causes such as social desirability (Crowne & Marlowe, 1964), avoidance behavioral tendencies (Davidson, 1998), and sentence syntax or semantics and neural processing (Vigliocco, 2000).

An important implication for the practice of using assessment instruments with positively and negatively worded items is that the researchers must provide evidence that the reversed scoring of negatively worded items results in comparable meaning with the scores of positively worded items. For example, L. Chang (1995) stated that construct unidimensionality cannot be maintained by simply reversing the scale points associated with negatively worded items. Another point made by L. Chang (1995) also deserves attention—namely, the connotation of an item as positive or negative depends on the context in which the item is presented. For example, as values are culturally defined, positive/negative connotations for the items of an instrument can be inconsistent and confusing in cross-cultural assessments using this instrument.

- The labeling of response categories in a rating scale also affects the validity of measures produced by the scale. Usually, instrument developers attach verbal labels to the response options that are intended to be as equally spaced as possible across the entire response continuum. Sometimes, however, the labels are packed with positive descriptions with the intent to overcome people's tendencies to be lenient in their description of others—for example, by using the labels *poor, fair, good, very good,* and *excellent* for a 5-point evaluative rating scale (Symonds, 1931). However, research on labeling response categories in rating scales shows that (a) whether the options are letters or numbers has no significant effect on responses,

(b) the use of labeled versus unlabeled intermediate alternatives has a small but systematic effect on the responses, (c) packing a rating scale with verbal labels from either the upper or the lower end of the underlying continuum can affect how subjects respond to the scale, (d) the use of rating scales containing verbal anchors predominantly from one end of the continuum provides increased discrimination in that portion of the scale, and (e) the labeled position of a response is interpreted as a combination of the meaning of the label and the position in which the label is used (Lam & Klockars, 1982; Klockars & Yamagishi, 1988). Wolfe and Smith (2007a) described two basic principles that instrument developers should keep in mind when labeling rating scale categories: (a) label all categories, because each respondent will most likely assign a slightly different meaning to unlabeled categories, which, in turn, may introduce construct irrelevant variance into the ratings; and (2) verify that the rating category labels are conceptually consistent and that they indicate distinguishable magnitudes across categories.

4.3.2 Expert Review

The process of item development also involves the collection of feedback from experts. The pool of experts may include persons with expertise in the construct of interest, persons who are familiar with the target population for the assessment, and persons who may use the instrument, analyze the data, and/or make assessment-based decisions. As Wolfe and Smith (2007a) suggested, the information collected during the expert review process should be documented and used in arguments related to the content aspect of construct validity. Such information includes expert judgments about the content representativeness of individual items and their sensitivity.

The bulleted list presented next follows the description provided by Wolfe and Smith (2007a) on how expert reviews of content, sensitivity, and standard setting contribute to collecting validity evidence.

- Content reviews can be conducted at different stages of item development. Content experts may provide input about the initial pool of items in terms of their relevance, accuracy, and completeness in representing the content domain. During item development, experts may provide suggestions on selection of items and adjustments in item formats, scoring models, and so forth. After item development, reviewers may provide evaluative judgments regarding the content representativeness (relevance, accuracy, and completeness) of the selected items and the relevance of the measures they generate to the intended purpose of the assessment instrument.
- Sensitivity reviews address issues of potential item bias. In the assessment literature, the concept of item bias is defined from different perspectives, but all the definitions convey the idea that item bias occurs when respondents at the same level of the construct being measured differ in their responses because they belong to different groups, such as majority versus minority groups. For example, an item would be biased against a minority group if the difficulties that the members of this group experience with the item are attributable to its cultural irrelevance, offensive language, and/or other contextual characteristics that affect the responses of the minority group on that item. It is also said that in this case the item is functioning differentially in regard to the two groups.

The presence of item bias poses a serious threat to construct validity. As stated by Whiston (2005), the term *bias* "refers to the degree that construct-irrelevant factors systematically affect a group's performance" (p. 211). For example, Abedi (2006) noted that, when administering items to nonnative English speakers, the linguistic complexity of the items may contribute construct-irrelevant variance to the measurement process. It is important to distinguish between item bias and item impact. If two groups differ on an item, it does not necessarily mean that this item is biased. As Ackerman (1992) noted, "if all the items are measuring only the valid skills or constructs, any group differences reflect impact, not bias." For a detailed review on issues related to fairness in assessment, the reader may refer to Hood and Johnson (2007; pp. 211–225) and Zieky (2006). Statistical aspects of differential item functioning in the validation of assessment instruments are discussed in Chapters 6 and 9.

- Standard setting is a process in which experts identify cutoff scores for criterion-referenced decisions on levels of performance or diagnostic classifications. For example, on a depression screening test, experts may come to an agreement that a client with a score of 20 or higher requires further diagnostic evaluation. Typically, expert-based standard settings for assessment in counseling are developed in the framework of a decision theory (Anastasi & Urbina, 1997), which involves determining a screening test score and a criterion cutoff score, either at the same point (concurrent decision) or at some point in the future (predictive decision). A readable treatment of decision theory in counseling, with an example of setting a cutoff score to identify adults at risk for depression, is provided by Basham and Erford (2007).

4.3.3 Pilot Studies

As described by Wolfe and Smith (2007a, p. 118), "the process of instrument development typically involves two or three phases of data collection and item revision in conjunction with expert reviews." Phase one, referred to also as *item tryout* or *pilot test*, is used to evaluate individual items based on their measurement characteristics and expert judgments about their quality and relevance as indicators of the target construct. Phase two, referred to also as a *field test*, is used to administer an initial form of the instrument to an appropriate sample of respondents. The goal is to refine the initial form and to create a final form (or alternate forms) of the instrument. Phase three, called a *validation study*, is used to collect data for establishing and documenting the structures and measurement characteristics of the final form(s) of the instrument and (if relevant) for establishing standards for criterion-based decisions. On the basis of the results, some items can be revised or dropped (e.g., if an item is found to display item bias). The sample of respondents at this phase must be representative of the population for which the instrument is designed, and the administration conditions should be similar to those in future practical uses of the instrument. For additional reading on construction of instruments for assessment in counseling, the reader may refer to Sheperis (2001) and Sheperis, Davis, and Doggett (2007).

SUMMARY

1. Instrument developers must first define the purpose of the assessment instrument within a specific domain and then identify the intended decision for the instrument, constraints related to its development and data collection, and frame of reference (norm-referenced or criterion-referenced assessment).
2. The purpose of most assessment instruments used in counseling is to determine status of individuals—for example, diagnostic assessments related to depression,

anxiety, academic strengths and weaknesses, interests, self-esteem, disruptive behavior, and so forth.

3. Instrument developers should consider both objective constraints (e.g., money and/or policies) and subjective constraints (e.g., paper-based vs. electronic form) related to instrument development and data collection.
4. With a norm-referenced assessment, the interpretation of a score reveals its relative position with regard to the other scores in the target population. The sample used to represent the target population is called *standardization sample* (or *normative sample*).
5. With a criterion-referenced assessment, the interpretation of a score is relative to a prespecified cutting score that represents an absolute standard (criterion) of performance.
6. Key elements in the process of instrument specifications are the theoretical definition of the construct and models of the construct stemming from its definition. Typically, the definition of a construct is embedded into a more general theory and then operationalized in the context of the theory and practice in which inferences and decisions are to be made based on assessment scores.
7. The construct model specifies (a) the internal structure of the construct, (b) the external relationships of the construct to other constructs, (c) potential types of relevant indicators, and (d) construct-related processes.
8. An internal model of a construct specifies the components of the construct and the relationships among them.
9. An external model of a construct specifies the relationships between the construct and other constructs and/or relevant criterion variable(s).
10. A developmental model of a construct specifies changes in the construct and/or its relations with other variables that are expected to occur over time based on a specific theory and/or empirical research related to the construct.
11. A processing model of a construct specifies internal attributes (states or cognitive operations and processes) that govern people's responses on observable indicators of the construct. The specification and validation of internal attributes is best performed in the framework of cognitive diagnosis modeling.
12. The content specification of an instrument that measures a construct of interest requires that the instrument developers (a) operationalize the construct by developing a fairly exhaustive list of potential observable indicators of the construct, (b) select from this list a representative sample of indicators, and (c) develop item formats for the selected sample of indicators.
13. The scoring model for an assessment instrument translates the observed responses on construct indicators into (binary or polytomous) numerical codes.
14. The item development must be guided by the purpose of the assessment, its frame of reference (norm-referenced, criterion-referenced, or both), definition of the target construct, structure of the construct model, and instrument specifications (blueprint, scoring, and scaling).
15. True–false format is used primarily for achievement, personality, or attitude assessment. A major disadvantage is that respondents have a 50% chance of guessing the correct answer.
16. Multiple-choice (MC) format is used mostly in achievement tests. One of the rules for writing the response choices is to use typical errors of students to write the distractors.
17. Rating scale format is frequently used in assessment instruments used in counseling and related fields (e.g., Likert format is often used in personality, attitude, career,

and aptitude tests). Characteristics of the rating scale format that may affect substantive and structural aspects of validity are (a) number of response categories, (b) use of a middle response category, and (c) use of negatively phrased items.

18. Expert reviews, involved in the process of item development, include (a) content reviews, which provide input about the initial pool of items in terms of their relevance, accuracy, and completeness in representing the content domain; (b) sensitivity reviews, which address issues of potential item bias; and (c) standard setting, a process in which experts identify cutoff scores for criterion-referenced decisions on levels of performance or diagnostic classifications.
19. Along with expert reviews, the process of item development involves pilot test (item tryout), field test, and validation study.

Part II

Factor Analysis in Construct Validation

Chapter 5
Exploratory Factor Analysis

Researchers in counseling and other social and behavioral sciences often try to simplify and explain the complexity of variables and relationships among them by determining a smaller number of factors that underlie such relationships. Factor analysis plays a key role in validation of assessment scale data. In general, factor analysis is used to determine (a) how many factors underlie a set of variables, (b) which variables form which factor, (c) the correlations between individual variables and factors, (d) the correlations (if any) among factors, and (e) what proportion of the variance in the variables is accounted for by the factors.

An exploratory factor analysis (EFA) is typically used when researchers do not have enough theoretical or empirical information to hypothesize how many factors underlie the set of observable variables and which variables form which factor. In this chapter I discuss basic concepts in EFA and methodological principles of using EFA to validate assessment scale data. After introducing basic EFA models and principles of extracting factors, I cover topics related to determining the proper number of factors, including parallel analysis and Velicer's MAP Test, higher order factors, sample size and data adequacy, EFA with categorical data, and use of EFA in validating assessment scale data. Illustrations of discussed procedures and related software are also provided.

5.1 CORRELATED VARIABLES AND UNDERLYING FACTORS

Let's examine the correlation matrix in Table 5.1, where the Pearson product–moment correlation coefficients are based on the scores of 30 children on spelling (X_1), reading (X_2), coloring (X_3), and cutting (X_4) on a 5-point scale. There is a statistically significant correlation between X_1 and X_2, $r_{12} = .644$, $p < .001$, as well as between X_3 and X_4, $r_{34} = .660$, $p < .001$, but none of the variables in the (X_1, X_2) pair correlates with a variable in the (X_3, X_4) pair.

The correlation between the variables X_3 and X_4 (.660) indicates that they have something

TABLE 5.1

Pearson Correlations Between Four Variables

Variable	X_1	*p* (two-tailed)	X_2	*p* (two-tailed)	X_3	*p* (two-tailed)	X_4	*p* (two-tailed)
X_1	1.000		.644**	.000	–.241	.200	–.173	.362
X_2	.644**	.000	1.000		–.039	.839	–.178	.348
X_3	–.241	.200	–.039	.839	1.000		.660**	.000
X_4	–.173	.362	–.178	.348	.660**	.000	1.000	

Note. $N = 30$. Correlations are based on children's scores on spelling (X_1), reading (X_2), coloring (X_3), and cutting (X_4).
**Correlation is significant at $p < .01$ (two-tailed).

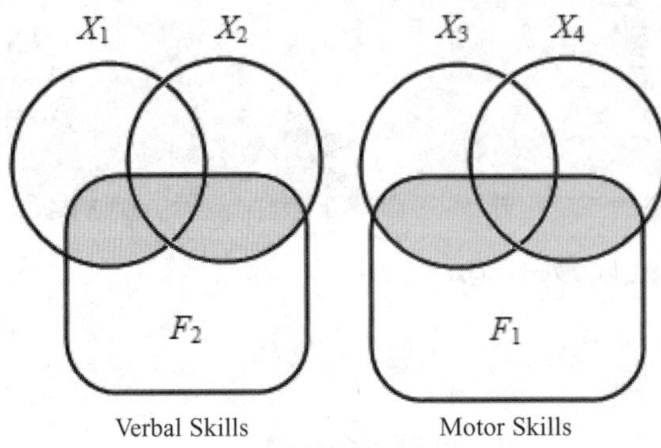

FIGURE 5.1

Four Variables and Two Orthogonal Factors

Note. The variables are spelling (X_1), reading (X_2), coloring (X_3), and cutting (X_4). F = factor.

in common—a factor, denoted here F_1, that accounts for some part of their variance. Likewise, the correlation between X_1 and X_2 (.644) suggests that they relate to a second factor, F_2, accounting for some part of their variance. As X_3 and X_4 do not correlate with X_1 and X_2, we can expect that the two factors, F_1 and F_2, are uncorrelated (orthogonal)—see Figure 5.1. The labeling of a factor depends on the meaning of the variables that correlate with this factor. In this case, the variables are spelling (X_1), reading (X_2), coloring (X_3), and cutting (X_4). Given that factor F_1 correlates with X_3 and X_4, this factor can be labeled *Motor Skills*, whereas factor F_2 can be labeled *Verbal Skills* because it correlates with X_1 and X_2.

With a small number of variables, the examination of the correlation matrix may provide some general information about factors that underlie these correlations. However, situations in which there are just a few variables and a "clean" underlying structure of orthogonal factors are exceptions in educational research. Therefore, although the correlation matrix in Table 5.1, with four variables yielding two factors, is conveniently used for illustrations throughout this chapter, more accurate and valid information about the factorial structure of a set of variables is obtained via factor analysis with a larger ratio for number of variables to number of factors.

5.2 BASIC EFA MODELS

An EFA defines factors through a mathematical procedure that usually maximizes the total variance in the observed variables accounted for by the factors. There are several types of EFA procedures, each with different assumptions and yielding somewhat different results. Under the commonly used principal factor methods in the EFA, the first factor to be extracted from the correlation matrix of observed variables is a weighted linear combination of all observed variables that produces the highest squared correlation between the variables and the factor. The second factor maximizes the variance extracted from the residual correlation matrix obtained after removing the effect of the first factor. Therefore, the second factor is orthogonal to (uncorrelated with) the first factor. Then, the third factor maximizes the variance extracted from the residual correlation matrix after removing the effect of the first two factors. Thus, the third factor is orthogonal to the first two factors. This process continues until all factors that meet a prespecified statistical criterion are extracted. Any two factors are orthogonal to one another because the extraction of any factor is based on the residualized correlation matrix, after removing the effects of all preceding factors.

5.2.1 Full Component Model

Suppose there are two factors (F_1 and F_2) that underlie a set of four variables, X_1, X_2, X_3, and X_4. Under the full component model, the score of an individual, i, on any variable, X_m, is perfectly reproduced (with *no* error) with the equation

$$X_{im} = w_{m1}F_{1i} + w_{m2}F_{2i}, \tag{5.1}$$

where w_{m1} and w_{m2} are the "weights" for variable X_m on the factors F_1 and F_2, respectively, whereas F_{1i} and F_{2i} are the scores of individual i on F_1 and F_2, respectively ($m = 1, 2, 3, 4$). The weights for the case of four variables and two factors are tabulated in Table 5.2. In the general case of k factors (components), the full component model equation is

$$X_{im} = w_{m1}F_{1i} + w_{m2}F_{2i} + \ldots + w_{mk}F_{ki}. \tag{5.2}$$

5.2.2 Common Factor Model

Note 5.1

Under the full component model, the number of factors is usually the same as the number of variables being analyzed except for cases in which the smaller components are dismissed as being attributable to inaccuracy in the model's data fit for a particular sample. Truncated components are the usual form of a component analysis (Gorsuch, 1983, p. 21).

TABLE 5.2

Full Component Model With Four Variables and Two Factors

Variable	Factor	
	F_1	F_2
X_1	w_{11}	w_{12}
X_2	w_{21}	w_{22}
X_3	w_{31}	w_{32}
X_4	w_{41}	w_{42}

Under the common factor model, an additional term, $w_{mu}U_{im}$, is added to Equation 5.2 to reflect the assumption that there is a "unique" factor (U_m) for each variable, X_m. The extended form of Equation 5.2 under the common factor model is

$$X_{im} = w_{m1}F_{1i} + w_{m2}F_{2i} + \ldots + w_{mk}F_{ki} + w_{mu}U_{im}. \tag{5.3}$$

Table 5.3 shows the common factor model with four variables and two common factors. In the general case, the weights for an observed variable ($w_{m1}, w_{m2}, \ldots, w_{mk}$) are called *pattern coefficients*, whereas the correlations between a factor and the observed variables are referred to as *structure coefficients* for that factor. The pattern coefficients are also referred to as *factor coefficients* or *factor loadings*, although both terms are occasionally used to refer to the structure coefficients as well. The structure coefficients are used to determine which variables form which factors, thus allowing the researchers to interpret and label the factors. In case of orthogonal factors, the pattern coefficients equal the structure coefficients.

Communalities. The proportion of the variance in a given variable that is accounted for by the common factors is called *communality* of this variable. The communality of a variable X_m is denoted h^2_m (h^2_1 is the communality of X_1, h^2_2 is the communality of X_2, and so on). Suppose that the two common factors in Table 5.3 are correlated, and r_{12} is their Pearson

TABLE 5.3

Common Factor Model With Four Variables and Two Common Factors

Variable	Common Factor		Unique Factor			
	F_1	F_2	U_1	U_2	U_3	U_4
X_1	w_{11}	w_{12}	w_{1U_1}	0	0	0
X_2	w_{21}	w_{22}	0	w_{2U_2}	0	0
X_3	w_{31}	w_{32}	0	0	w_{3U_3}	0
X_4	w_{41}	w_{42}	0	0	0	w_{4U_4}

correlation coefficient. The communality h^2_m in this case is

$$h^2_m = \frac{w^2_{m1} + w^2_{m2} + 2w_{m1}w_{m2}r_{12}}{\sigma^2_m}, \tag{5.4}$$

where σ^2_m is the variance of the variable, X_m ($m = 1, 2, 3, 4$). When the scores are presented in standard form (z scores), which is typically the case in factor analysis, then $\sigma^2_m = 1$. In this case, Equation 5.4 becomes

$$h^2_m = w^2_{m1} + w^2_{m2} + 2w_{m1}w_{m2}r_{12}. \tag{5.5}$$

Further simplification is obtained when the two factors are orthogonal ($r_{12} = 0$) and the observed scores on the variables are standardized ($\sigma^2_m = 1$):

$$h^2_m = w^2_{m1} + w^2_{m2}. \tag{5.6}$$

Theoretically, the lowest value that the communality of a given variable can take is 0.0, if the variable does not correlate with any other variable in the correlation matrix, whereas its highest possible value is 1.0, if the variance of this variable is entirely accounted for by the set of factors that underlie the correlation matrix.

The initial estimate of communality for a variable, X_j, is usually provided by the squared multiple correlation, R^2_j, which is obtained when X_j is taken as a dependent variable predicted by all other variables in the set of variables being analyzed (recall that in the context of multiple regression analysis, the difference $1 - R^2_j$, referred to as *tolerance* for X_j, is used to estimate the contribution of the predictor variable X_j to multicollinearity among the predictors). Then, within the process of factor extraction, communality estimates are adjusted by iterative procedures to fit the correlation matrix produced by the factor extraction to the observed correlation matrix with the smallest number of factors. Iteration stops when successive communality estimates are very similar. The final communality estimate for a variable represents the proportion of the variance in the variable that is accounted for by the common factors (e.g., see Gorsuch, 1983, p. 102; Tabachnick & Fidell, 2007, p. 643).

Example 5.1 This example illustrates the computation of communalities for the four variables spelling (X_1), reading (X_2), coloring (X_3), and cutting (X_4), described in Section 5.1. The correlation matrix for these variables is provided in Table 5.1, and their empirical grouping into two orthogonal factors is depicted in Figure 5.1. An analysis of the correlation matrix in Table 5.1 under the common factor model, referred to as *principal-axis factoring*, was conducted using the computer program SPSS. The pattern/structure coefficients for the resulting orthogonal factors F_1 and F_2 are provided in Table 5.4 (with another example, the SPSS output for this analysis is provided in Table 5.5). As the two factors are orthogonal, the communality of each variable was computed through the use of Equation 5.6. For example, using the notations in Table 5.3, the communality of variable X_1 (spelling) is obtained as follows: $h^2_1 = w^2_{11} + w^2_{12} = (-.177)^2 + (.727)^2 = .560$. This indicates that the two common factors, F_1 (Motor Skills) and F_2 (Verbal Skills) account for 56.0% of the variance in variable X_1 (spelling). Similarly, one can check that $h^2_2 = .770$, $h^2_3 = .892$, and $h^2_4 = .491$ (cf. the estimates from SPSS output in Table 5.5 in the column labeled "Extraction" under the column spanner "Communalities").

TABLE 5.4

Pattern/Structure Coefficients and Communalities Under the Extraction of Two Orthogonal Factors

Variable	Factor F_1	Factor F_2	Communality h^2
X_1: Spelling	−.18	**.73**	.56
X_2: Reading	−.02	**.88**	.77
X_3: Coloring	**.94**	−.05	.89
X_4: Cutting	**.69**	−.14	.49

Note. The pattern/structure coefficients in bold show that the first factor (F_1), Motor Skills, is defined by the variables X_3 and X_4, whereas the second factor (F_2), Verbal Skills, is defined by variables X_1 and X_2.

5.3 THE PRINCIPAL FACTOR METHOD OF EXTRACTING FACTORS

5.3.1 Principal Factor Extraction

Let **R** denote the correlation matrix of v variables ($X_1, X_2, \ldots, X_v$), and let **P** denote the matrix of pattern coefficients for the v variables and k underlying factors ($F_1, F_2, \ldots, F_k$). For the case of four variables and two factors in Table 5.3, for example, **P** will be the (4 × 2) matrix of pattern coefficients (the unique factor loadings are not included in **P**). Furthermore, let **P′** denote the *transposed* matrix of **P**—that is, **P′** is obtained by changing the roles of rows and columns in matrix **P**. For example, for a (4 × 2) factor pattern matrix, the transposed matrix will be a (2 × 4) matrix. When the factors ($F_1, F_2, \ldots, F_k$) are orthogonal, the correlation matrix **R** is decomposed into the product of the factor pattern matrix and its transposed matrix:

$$\mathbf{R} = \mathbf{P}\mathbf{P}'. \qquad (5.7)$$

Equation 5.7 is referred to as the *fundamental equation of factor analysis*. When the factors are not orthogonal, Equation 5.7 is extended to take into account the correlations among them and the unique factor loadings (e.g., Table 5.3, right panel). The resulting matrix algebra equation and related technical transformations are beyond the scope of this book (e.g., Gorsuch, 1983).

Solutions of the matrix algebra Equation 5.7 are obtained by using methods referred to as the *principal factor method***.** Under this method, the solution for the first factor for a set of p variables ($X_1, X_2, \ldots, X_p$) represents a vector of p factor loadings ($w_{11}, w_{21}, \ldots w_{p1}$) so that the linear combination $w_{11}X_1 + w_{21}X_2 + \ldots + w_{p1}X_p$ maximally correlates with the factor. That is, the first factor accounts for the maximum possible amount of the variance extracted from the correlation matrix **R**. The sum of squared factor loadings (SSLs) for the first factor is called the *eigenvalue* for this factor. After the first factor is extracted, its effect is removed from the correlation matrix **R**, so a residualized correlation matrix is produced. The solution of factor loadings for the second factor ($w_{12}, w_{22}, \ldots w_{p2}$) is obtained so that this factor maximizes the amount of variance extracted from the residualized correlation matrix. Therefore, the second factor is uncorrelated with the first factor. The SSLs for the second factor is called the *eigenvalue* for this factor. Then a third factor is extracted so that it is uncorrelated with the first two factors, and so on.

The number of principal factors obtained under this procedure equals the number of the variables in the correlation matrix **R** in Equation 5.7. Thus, the number of resulting eigenvalues in this process equals the number of observed variables being analyzed, p. The correlation matrix obtained from the extracted factors is called the *reproduced correlation matrix*. A noteworthy property of the principal factor method is that it minimizes the sums of squared differences between the original and reproduced correlations. However, as described in the following, not all principal factors are retained; instead, the goal is to retain enough (not all) factors to ensure an adequate fit between the original and reproduced correlation matrix. In general, factors that do not contribute to fit improvement according to a certain criterion are not retained in the solution.

TABLE 5.5

SPSS Output for Principal-Axis Factoring With Varimax Rotation for Four Variables

	Total Variance Explained														
	Initial Eigenvalues			Extraction Sums of Squared Loadings			Rotation Sums of Squared Loadings			Communalities		Factor Matrix		Rotated Factor Matrix	
	Total	% Var.	Cum. %	Total	% Var.	Cum. %	Total	% Var.	Cum. %	Initial	Extraction	Factor 1	Factor 2	Factor 1	Factor 2
Factor															
1	1.970	49.247	49.247	1.652	41.310	41.310	1.393	34.825	34.825						
2	1.343	33.568	82.815	1.060	26.500	67.809	1.319	32.985	67.809						
3	0.446	11.155	93.970												
4	0.241	6.030	100.000												
Variable															
X_1										.474	.560	−.614	.428	.687	−.139
X_2										.465	.770	−.598	.642	−.177	.727
X_3										.495	.892	.742	.585	.943	−.053
X_4										.471	.491	.607	.350	−.023	.877

Note. Extraction method: principal-axis factoring. Rotation method: varimax with Kaiser normalization. % Var. = percentage variance; Cum. % = cummulative percentage.

5.3.2 Principal Component Analysis

The principal factor method under the full component model is referred to as *principal component analysis* (PCA). All diagonal elements in the analyzed correlation matrix, **R**, are kept at their conventional value of 1 (recall that the variance of each standardized variable is also 1). The full component model produces as many factors (components) as variables. However, as noted earlier, the smaller components are usually dismissed, and the inaccuracies in reproducing the correlations and variable scores are attributed to errors in the model's data fit for the sample being used. Thus, the PCA produces truncated component solution results obtained by using the principal factor method under the component model.

5.3.3 Principal Factor Analysis

The principal factor method under the common factor model is called *principal factor analysis* (PFA). Recall that the common factor model takes into account unique components (U_m)—see Equation 5.3 and Table 5.3 (right panel). The diagonal elements in the analyzed correlation matrix, **R**, are set equal to estimates of the communalities for the respective observed variables in **R**. The PFA is then conducted by first subtracting the correlation matrix of unique components, **U**, from the original correlation matrix, **R** (this causes changes only in the diagonal elements of **R** because **U** is a diagonal matrix). The principal factor method is then applied directly to the resulting correlation matrix (**R** – **U**), thus providing principal common factors. When the principal factor method is applied to a correlation matrix with communality estimates in the diagonal, the resulting factor solutions are called *principal axis*. This procedure is called *principal axis factoring* (PAF). With PAF, caution is needed with the so-called Haywood cases that occur when the estimation of communalities results in diagonal elements that are greater than 1.0. As noted earlier, the communalities can take on values from 0.0 to 1.0. However, it is recommended that in PAF the lower bound for the communality of a variable is its squared multiple correlation with all the other variables in the matrix, whereas the upper bound is its reliability coefficient (e.g., Gorsuch, 1983, p. 102).

5.3.4 Component Analysis Versus Factor Analysis

The PCA is usually discussed in the literature under the topic of EFA. However, although factor analytic procedures based on the common factor model represent EFA, the PCA is conceptually and mathematically different from EFA. Under PCA, the diagonal values equal 1.0, so the total variance being analyzed equals the number of the variables in the correlation matrix. Thus, the distinction between common and unique variance is *not* recognized in PCA. In contrast, under the common factor (EFA) model, the diagonal elements are the communality estimates for the variables, so the variance being analyzed is the part of the total variance in the set of variables accounted for by the common factors. By analyzing the sum of communalities, EFA provides separate estimates of common and unique sources of variance, thus taking into account the presence of error (e.g., Gorsuch, 1990; Fabrigar, Wegener, MacCallum, & Strahan, 1999; Fava & Velicer, 1992a, 1992b; Mulaik, 1990; Reise, Waller, & Comrey, 2000; Steiger, 1990a; Widaman, 1993).

In general, the motivation behind using PCA is based on the PCA's relative simplicity and the fact that some studies showed no practical differences in estimates of factor patterns using PCA and EFA (e.g., Gorsuch, 1990; Velicer & Jackson, 1990). This, however, is the case only when the data are relatively consistent with the assumptions of PCA (e.g., when the unique variance in the observed variables is small). For example, Gorsuch (1983) reported that "when the number of variables is moderately large, for example, greater than 30, and the analysis contains virtually no variables expected to have low communalities (e.g., .4), practically any of the exploratory procedures other than diagonal or multiple-group analysis will lead to the same interpretations" (p. 123). At the same time, research has also shown that under certain conditions—when the communalities are low (e.g., .40), the factors (or components) have few salient loadings, and the number of observed variables per factor is small (e.g., three)—the PCA overestimates the factor loadings and yields component correlations that are negatively biased (e.g., Borgatta, Kercher, & Stull, 1986; Widaman, 1993).

In the context of construct validation, which is of primary interest here, the implication from sound technical and methodological studies on EFA versus PCA is that EFA should be preferred to PCA (e.g., Fabrigar et al., 1999; Mulaik, 1990; Preacher & MacCallum, 2003; Reise et al., 2000; Widaman, 1993; Wood, Tataryn, & Gorsuch, 1996). One commonly used approach of conducting PCA, retaining components with eigenvalues greater than 1.0 and then performing a varimax rotation of these components, has been shown to have potentially negative consequences (e.g., Widaman, 1993; Wood et al., 1996). For example, Wood et al. (1996) noted that "when overextraction occurs, false factors are more likely to look 'real' with principal-components analysis than with principal axis analysis" (p. 361). Most important, EFA factors are considered to be the hypothetical causes that account for the item intercorrelations, whereas PCA is used to create summaries of observed variables; that is, the principal components can be viewed as effects rather than causes of the variable correlations (e.g., Fabrigar et al., 1999; Mulaik, 1990; Preacher & MacCallum, 2003).

Overall, it is recommended that researchers base their PCA/EFA choice on the specific context (goals, data fit, and so forth) of the study. As Tabachnick and Fidell (2007) noted, "if you are interested in a theoretical solution uncontaminated by unique and error variability and have designed your study on the basis of underlying constructs that are expected to produce scores on your observed variables, FA [factor analysis] is your choice. If, on the other hand, you simply want an empirical summary of the data set, PCA is the better choice" (p. 635). Bentler and Kano (1990) also suggested that, particularly with small number of variables, "the factor model is typically more appropriate to understanding the structure of the covariance or correlation matrix, especially the pattern of intercorrelations among variables," but "when one is concerned solely with data summarization, especially, dimension reduction, principal component analysis may be fruitfully employed" (p. 73). As discussed later in this book, PCA is widely used in testing for dimensionality within the framework of Rasch analysis (see Chapter 9, Section 9.2.6).

5.4 ROTATION OF FACTORS

Factors extracted with the initial orthogonal solutions under the principal factor method are usually difficult to interpret. To address this problem, the initial factors are rotated to more desirable positions. A rotated factor represents a linear combination of the initial factors and is much easier to interpret. In fact, the rotated factors explain the same amount of the total variance of the observed variables, but they divide it up in a way that facilitates their interpretation. When orthogonal (uncorrelated) factors are expected, an orthogonal rotation of the initial factors is appropriate. However, when a minor to medium correlation among the factors is expected, then an oblique rotation of the initial factors should be used. Note that an oblique rotation is not recommended in case of highly correlated factors. Instead, as Gorsuch (1983) noted, "if two factors ever did become highly correlated, most investigators would redo the analysis with one less factor" (p. 188).

5.4.1 Simple Structure

Typically, the rotation of factors is guided by the goal of obtaining a simple structure for meaningful interpretation of the extracted factors. For example, the two-factor solution in Table 5.4 provides a descriptive indication of a simple structure in the sense that each variable has a large factor loading estimate on one actor and negligible factor loading estimate (perhaps zero in the population) on the other factor (estimates of factor loadings that fall between –.10 and .10 are usually assumed to be random variations from zero; e.g., Gorsuch, 1983, p. 180). Under criteria suggested by Thurstone (1947, p. 335), there is a simple structure when (a) each variable has at least one zero loading; (b) each factor has a set of linearly independent variables whose factor loadings are zero; (c) for every pair of factors, there are variables whose loadings are zero for one factor but not for the other; (d) for every pair of factors, a large proportion of the variables have zero loadings on both factors whenever more than about four factors are extracted; and (e) for every pair of factors, there is only a small number of variables with nonzero loadings on both (see also Gorsuch, 1983, pp. 177–182).

For testing purposes, some researchers use a less comprehensive definition of simple structure. For example, Sass (2010) adopted the conception that "the test for simple structure assumes that items possess large estimated factor loadings on one factor and small cross-loadings (i.e., small estimated factor loadings on other factors), with the assumption that these cross-loadings are essentially zero in the population" (p. 558). However, as Sass emphasized, to test whether the cross-loadings are essentially zero in the population, researchers should use (and report) the standard errors associated with the estimated factor loadings. A good candidate for simple structure testing would be, for example, the two-factor structure presented in Table 5.4 (this table comes from the SPSS output table under the column spanner titled "Rotated Factor Matrix" in Table 5.5). It should be noted also that the accuracy of estimates for standard errors of factor loadings depends on many elements, such as magnitude of the factor loadings, sample size, type of factor rotation, and magnitude of interfactor correlations (e.g., see Browne, 2001; Cliff & Hamburger, 1967; Cudeck & O'Dell, 1994; Sass, 2010).

5.4.2 Orthogonal Rotation

As already noted, an orthogonal rotation is appropriate when there is a justified expectation that the underlying factors are uncorrelated. An orthogonal rotation of the initial factors, which are always orthogonal, yields rotated factors that are also orthogonal. Under a frequently used orthogonal rotation called *varimax*, the variance of the squared factor loadings across all factors is maximized. The rotation position that maximizes the variance across all factors is referred to as the *varimax solution*. Keep in mind, however, that the varimax rotation is inappropriate when there is a tendency that a single general factor underlies the set of observable variables (e.g., Gorsuch, 1983, p. 185).

Example 5.2 Table 5.5 provides the SPSS output for EFA for the correlation matrix in Table 5.1 using principal-axis factoring under the varimax rotation. As described earlier, the four variables are spelling (X_1), reading (X_2), coloring (X_3), and cutting (X_4). The empirical grouping of these variables into two orthogonal factors is depicted in Figure 5.1. In Table 5.5, the section labeled "Factor Matrix" provides the initial (unrotated) solution. As can be seen, this solution is difficult to interpret as it does not provide a clear picture of which variables relate to which factor. For example, the initial coordinates of the variable X_3 are .742 on the first factor and .585 on the second factor, thus

making it difficult to decide whether X_3 relates to the first or to the second factor. The varimax rotated solution is provided under the table spanner labeled "Rotated Factor Matrix." In this section, the coordinates of X_3 are .943 on the first factor and –.053 on the second factor, thus clearly indicating that variable X_3 correlates with the first factor after the rotation. This finding, along with the examination of the loadings of the other three variables on the rotated solution, indicates that (a) the first factor is defined by the variables X_3 (coloring) and X_4 (cutting), so this factor can be labeled "motor skills," and (b) the second factor is defined by the variables X_2 (reading) and X_1 (spelling), so this factor can be labeled "reading skills." As the two factors are orthogonal, the factor loadings in each (initial and orthogonal solution) table are both pattern coefficients *and* structure coefficients (i.e., pattern/structure coefficients).

In Table 5.5, also note that under the column spanner titled "Communalities" in the SPSS output, the column labeled "Initial" provides the initial (starting) estimates of communalities, whereas the column labeled "Extraction" provides the final estimates of communalities, obtained with the factor extraction. As noted earlier, the initial communality estimate for a variable indicates the proportion in the variance of this variable that is accounted for by the other variables. The final communality estimate represents the proportion in the variance of the variable accounted for by the set of extracted factors. Keep in mind also that communality estimates do not change with orthogonal rotation. As shown in Equation 5.6 for orthogonal factors, the final communalities are obtained by summing the squared factor loadings—horizontally by rows for each variable in either the "Factor Matrix" or the "Rotated Factor Matrix" section of the table (the orthogonal rotation of factors does not change the amount of variance that they account for in the variance of each variable).

5.4.3 Oblique Rotations

When correlated factors are expected, an oblique rotation should be used instead. With an oblique rotation, the angles between the factors are no longer orthogonal when represented geometrically. As noted earlier, an oblique rotation is appropriate when the correlations between factors are minor to moderate in magnitude. The main approaches to an oblique rotation (e.g., available in SPSS) are the following:

- Quartimax rotation minimizes the sum of the cross-products of the squared variable loadings. This rotation is not very helpful to exploratory research goals as it often yields to a general factor with which most variables correlate to a high or moderate degree.
- Equimax rotation compromises between varimax and quartimax criteria.
- Direct oblimin rotation produces higher eigenvalues but diminishes the interpretability of the factors.
- Promax rotation uses the initial orthogonal solution (e.g., obtained via varimax) as a basis for producing an ideal oblique solution. An improved solution using promax versus an orthogonal solution is indicated when (a) the moderate and low loadings with promax are lower than in the orthogonal solution, and (b) the high loadings in the orthogonal solution remain relatively high with promax. Decreasing factor loadings is obtained in promax by raising them to a higher power. In SPSS, for example, the power index with promax, denoted $\boldsymbol{k}$, is set to four ($\boldsymbol{k} = 4$), but one can vary the power in a search for the simplest structure with the least correlation between factors.

It is useful to start with an oblique rotation (e.g., promax) and examine the results. If the correlations between the oblique factors are negligible, then use the varimax rotation and interpret the resulting orthogonal solution (e.g., Gorsuch, 1983; Henson & Roberts, 2006).

5.4.4 Interpreting Factors

The interpretation of factors is based primarily on the factor structure matrix, **S**, and factor pattern matrix, **P**. As noted earlier (Section 5.2.2), in case of orthogonal factors the two matrices are identical (**S** = **P**); that is, the pattern coefficients equal the structure coefficients. Therefore, an orthogonal (e.g., varimax) rotation yields a single matrix of pattern/structure coefficients. Under correlated factors, the pattern coefficients are generally different from the structure coefficients (**S** ≠ **P**). For proper interpretation of a set of factors, both the structure and pattern coefficients should be examined. Some clarifications in this regard, however, are necessary. As Gorsuch (1983) noted, "the basic matrix for interpreting the factors is the factor structure" (p. 207). This statement is correct primarily because the structure coefficient of a variable on a specific factor shows the full relationship (correlation) between the variable and the factor. In contrast, the respective pattern coefficient reflects only the unique contribution of the factor to the variable (i.e., excluding the overlap between the factor and other factors). That is why, as Gorsuch (1983) suggested, "to use **P** for interpretation, the meaning of the factors should already be known" (p. 207). To summarize, test developers are highly urged to examine (and report) both **S** and **P** for proper interpretation of the factors.

Another concept involved in the interpretation of factors is that of a salient loading—a structure (or pattern) coefficient that is sufficiently high to warrant the existence of a relationship between a variable and a factor. Although there is no universal and exact way to determine salient loadings, a widely used general recommendation is that a salient loading of a variable should be at least .30 (in absolute value) and the relationship between the variable and the factor should be substantively meaningful (e.g., Gorsuch, 1983, pp. 208–210). As to labeling factors, Thompson and Daniel (1996) suggested that "factors should be given names that do not invoke the labels of observed variables because the latent constructs are not observed variables themselves" (p. 202). This opinion was reiterated in EFA-related recommendations provided by Henson and Roberts (2006), who also went on to emphasize that at least two variables are needed to define a factor because "sufficient component saturation is needed to warrant factor interpretation and to assume some level of replicability" (p. 410). Researchers should also keep in mind that interpretations of factors and resulting factor names should not be viewed as final until hypothesis testing has been conducted (e.g., in a confirmatory cross-validation testing; see Gorsuch, 1983, p. 212).

5.5 SOME BASIC PROPERTIES

5.5.1 Eigenvalues and Related Properties

As described in Section 5.3.1, the number of factors (or components) initially extracted under the principal factor method is equal to the number of variables in the original correlation matrix, **R**. The eigenvalue of a factor is given by the SSLs for this factor. Thus, with p variables in **R**, there will be p initial factors (or components) and, hence, p eigenvalues (denoted, say, $\lambda_1, \lambda_2, \ldots \lambda_p$). The following properties relate to eigenvalues produced with the solution for initial factors (or components) under the principal factor method:

- The number of eigenvalues equals the number of variables in the correlation matrix, **R**.
- The SSLs for a principal factor is equal to the eigenvalue for this factor (SSLs = λ). However, this statement is true only for the initial principal factor solution under EFA (or PCA). After factor rotation (under EFA or PCA), this property is no longer valid—the SSLs for rotated factors are important, but they are *not* eigenvalues.
- The sum of the eigenvalues, also called the **trace**, equals the sum of the communality estimates used in the diagonal of the correlation matrix, **R**; that is, **trace** = $\Sigma\lambda_j = \Sigma h_j^2$. If **R** has unities in the diagonal, the **trace** is equal to the number of variables in **R**.
- The ratio λ_j/p—the eigenvalue for a factor divided by the number of variables in **R**—indicates the proportion of the total variance in the set of variables being analyzed accounted for by this factor.

5.5.2 Sum of Squared Loadings

As noted in the previous section, eigenvalues are defined only for initial solutions under the principal factor method for EFA (or PCA). The SSLs for a principal factor equals its eigenvalue. After extraction, the SSLs for a retained factor (before or after its rotation) is *not* an eigenvalue. Some basic properties of the SSLs under orthogonal rotation are as follows:

- The sum of SSLs for all factors equals the sum of communalities (upon extraction); that is, $\Sigma\text{SSLs} = \Sigma h_j^2$.
- The SSLs for a factor (or component) divided by the number of variables (SSLs/p) indicates what proportion of the total variance is accounted for by this factor (or component).
- The SSLs for a factor divided by the sum of final communalities (SSLs/ Σh_j^2) shows what proportion of the common variance being analyzed is accounted for by this factor. Recall that the common variance being analyzed under EFA is the part of the total variance accounted for by all common factors.

Example 5.3 This example illustrates properties of eigenvalues and SSLs for the case of EFA on four variables presented with the SPSS output in Table 5.5. First, the eigenvalues for the initial four principal factors are as follows: $\lambda_1 = 1.970$, $\lambda_2 = 1.343$, $\lambda_3 = 0.446$, and $\lambda_4 = 0.241$. Note that the sum of eigenvalues equals the number of variables being analyzed: $\lambda_1 + \lambda_2 + \lambda_3 + \lambda_4 = 1.970 + 1.343 + 0.446 + 0.241 = 4$. The reason this calculation holds true is because although the extraction procedure here is principal axis factoring, the initial principal factor extraction in SPSS starts with unities in the diagonal of the correlation matrix **R** (thus, the initial eigenvalues reported in SPSS are the same under EFA and PCA). The subsequent EFA extraction of factors is then based on a correlation matrix with communality estimates in the diagonal. The communalities reported in the column titled "Extraction" sum to 2.71: $\Sigma h_j^2 = .560 + .770 + .892 + .491 = 2.71$ (rounded to the nearest hundredth). Also, the SSLs for the extracted and rotated factors is the same and is equal to the sum of communalities. Specifically, (a) for extracted factors, $\Sigma\text{SSLs} = 1.652 + 1.060 = 2.71$, and (b) for rotated factors, $\Sigma\text{SSLs} = 1.393 + 1.319 = 2.71$. Thus, $\Sigma\text{SSLs} = \Sigma h_j^2 = 2.71$.

Furthermore, the SSLs for the first rotated factor (SSLs = 1.393) divided by the number of variables ($p = 4$) is 1.393/4 = 0.3483, thus indicating that 34.83% of the total variance in the set of four variables is accounted for by the first factor (cf. Table 5.5). On the other side, the ratio of the SSLs for this factor to the sum of communalities (1.393/2.71 = 0.5140) indicates that 51.40% of the common variance being analyzed is accounted for by the first factor (this is not reported in the SPSS output in Table 5.5). The corresponding results for the second rotated factor, SSLs/p = 1.319/4 = 0.3297 and SSLs/ Σh^2_j = 1.319/2.71 = 0.4867, are interpreted in a similar manner.

5.6 DETERMINING THE NUMBER OF FACTORS

In typical applications of EFA (or PCA), researchers do not have enough theoretical or empirical information to hypothesize how many factors underlie the set of observable variables. Hence, there is a question as to the proper number of factors to be extracted from the correlation matrix. The statistical translation of this question is whether there is a statistically significant variance left in the residual correlation matrix after a certain number of factors have been extracted. Recall that the residual correlation matrix is obtained as a difference between the original correlation matrix and the correlation matrix reproduced by the extracted factors. If the residual correlation matrix is statistically significant, then the search for additional factors continues. If not, the proper number of factors has been found and the extraction of factors terminates.

5.6.1 "Eigenvalues of One or Higher" Criterion

A quick first step in determining the number of factors is to examine the eigenvalues obtained with a principal components extraction. A factor with an eigenvalue smaller than 1 is not considered important because the variance that each standardized variable contributes to a principal component extraction equals 1. This argument is the basis for the "eigenvalues of one or higher" criterion for determining the proper number of factors. This approach is known as the *root ≥ 1 criterion* (the eigenvalues are referred to also as *characteristic roots*—mathematical solutions in extracting factors). The root ≥ 1 criterion works relatively well when the number of variables, v, is 40 or smaller ($v \leq 40$) and the sample size is large. In this case, a rule of thumb is that the number of factors is expected to be between the number of variables divided by 5 and the number of variables divided by 3 (i.e., from $v/5$ to $v/3$). For example, a principal component extraction with 30 variables is expected to produce between 6 and 10 factors: $v/5$ = 30/5 = 6 and $v/3$ = 30/3 = 10. In other situations, the root ≥ 1 (eigenvalues of one or higher) criterion tends to overestimate the number of factors (cf. Gorsuch, 1983, pp. 162–164). Again, this criterion is applicable only under PCA where the roots are extracted from a correlation matrix with unities in the diagonal (e.g., Gorsuch, 1983, p. 161).

5.6.2 Scree Test

A reasonably accurate approach to determining the number of factors is the so-called scree test (Cattell, 1966). This test involves plotting the eigenvalues in descending order of their magnitude against their factor numbers and determining where they level off (i.e., form a *scree*—a term taken from the geological description of the rubble at the bottom of a mountain). The proper number of factors is determined by the number of eigenvalues plotted above the so-called elbow—the break between the steep slope and the leveling-off (scree). This visual approach is referred to also as a *pencil test* because a pencil can be laid on the scree, so the proper number of factors is determined by the number of eigenvalues plotted above the pencil. The scree plot in Figure 5.2, from the SPSS output for a PCA of 11 variables, indicates that there are two factors that underlie the set of 11 variables. Keep in mind, however, that the scree plot approach to selecting the number of factors involves a certain amount of subjective judgment.

5.6.3 Parallel Analysis

A major limitation of the root ≥ 1 criterion for retaining factors is that it tends to overestimate the number of factors because of sampling error. In an attempt to overcome this limitation, Horn (1965) proposed an approach to retaining factors referred to as *parallel analysis* (PA). The logic behind PA is that the eigenvalues of meaningful factors that underlie a set of variables should be larger than the eigenvalues of parallel factors derived from random data sets with the same sample size and number of variables as the original data set. Presented next are two versions of PA that use random data sets and permutations of raw data, respectively.

PA Using Random Data Sets. The PA using random data sets is a stepwise procedure under which (a) a data set of normally distributed variables with the same sample size and number of variables as the real data set is randomly generated, (b) the eigenvalues of all factors extracted from the random data under the PCA are computed and stored, (c) these two steps are repeated a sufficiently large number of times (e.g., > 1,000), and (d) the eigenvalues obtained from all random data sets are averaged and compared with the

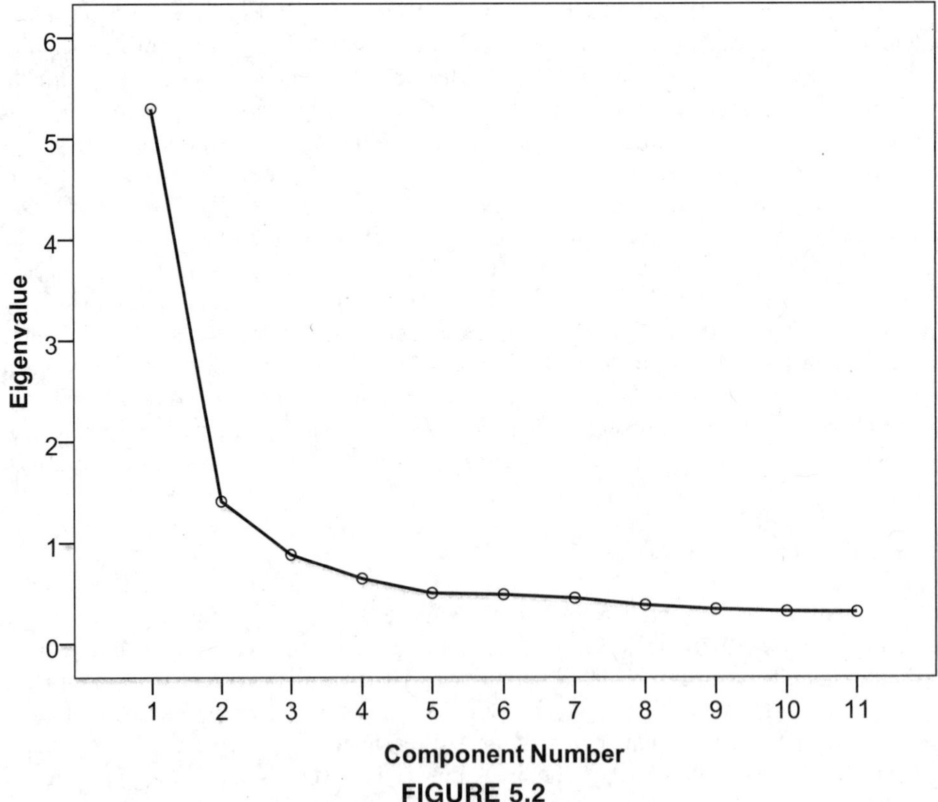

FIGURE 5.2

Scree Plot for the Principal Component Analysis of 11 Variables

eigenvalues obtained from the real data set. The first real eigenvalue is compared with the first average random eigenvalue, the second real eigenvalue is compared with the second average random eigenvalue, and so on. Factors corresponding to the real eigenvalues that are greater than the parallel average random eigenvalues are retained. Actual eigenvalues less than or equal to the parallel average random eigenvalues are considered to be a result of sampling error. Glorfeld (1995) suggested that instead of using average random eigenvalues, it is better to use an upper percentile (usually the 95th percentile) in simulated distributions of eigenvalues to determine whether the real eigenvalues are larger than what could be expected by chance.

PA Using Permutations of Raw Data. Under this PA method, each column of the original data matrix is permuted, so that the response vector in a matrix at a given step consists of responses from previous steps in the permutation processing of raw data (Buja & Eyuboglu, 1992). With the permutation approach, the assumption of normality for the variables in PA with random data sets is not required (thus, the permutation PA can be viewed as a nonparametric version of the PA with random data sets). The permutation PA can be based on either PCA or PFA. However, as Buja and Eyuboglu (1992) demonstrated, the PFA tends to indicate a slightly higher number of factors compared with the PCA in permutation-based PA. They also found that the benefit of using the permutation-based PA over the PA based on random data sets is of secondary importance because the latter approach proved sufficiently robust to violations of the normality assumption. An advantage of using permutation-based PA is that it allows for comparison of results obtained under the PCA and PFA, which can be of importance to the goals in some studies.

5.6.4 Velicer's MAP Test

Velicer (1976) developed a procedure for determining the number of proper factors referred to as the *minimum average partial* (MAP) test. Velicer's MAP test uses a PCA followed by the examination of a series of matrices of partial correlations. The first (largest) principal component is partialed out of the correlations between the variables being analyzed (say, p variables), and then the average squared coefficient in the off-diagonals of the resulting partial correlation matrix is computed. Next, the first two principal components are partialed out of the original correlation matrix, and the average squared partial correlation is computed. This process is repeated in $p - 1$ steps, and the number of components is determined by the sequential number of the step that has produced the lowest average squared partial correlation. However, if the average squared coefficient in the original correlation matrix is smaller than the lowest average squared partial correlation (i.e., the systematic variance is proportionally smaller than the unsystematic variance), then no components are extracted at all from the correlation matrix.

5.6.5 Computer Programs for PA and Velicer's MAP Test

Popular statistical packages such as SPSS and SAS do not provide procedures for PA or Velicer's MAP test. Fortunately, the computer syntax for such procedures is available in SPSS, SAS, and other environments of computer programming. For example, Table 5.6 provides a list of computer programs in SPSS, SAS, and MATLAB that O'Connor (2000) developed and that is available online at http://people.ok.ubc.ca/brioconn/nfactors/nfactors.html.

As shown in Table 5.6, the "map" computer program (SPSS, SAS, or MATLAB version) is for Velicer's MAP test. For example, with the SPSS syntax of the program (map.sps), the user can (a) enter a correlation matrix directly into the program, without having SPSS save

TABLE 5.6

Computer Programs in SPSS, SAS, and MATLAB for the Velicer's Minimum Average Partial (MAP) Test and Parallel Analysis (O'Connor, 2000)

Computer Program			
SPSS	**SAS**	**MATLAB**	**Purpose**
map.sps	map.sas	map.m	Velicer's MAP test
parallel.sps	parallel.sas	parallel.m	Parallel analysis
rawpar.sps	rawpar.sas	rawpar.m	Parallel analysis using raw data

Note. Adapted from http://people.ok.ubc.ca/brioconn/nfactors/nfactors.html

and then read a matrix out file; or (b) have the program read a correlation matrix that was saved by an SPSS procedure (detailed descriptions are provided by syntax comments in the program). The latter option in map.sps was used with a real-data SPSS file containing the responses of 1,028 people on 11 survey items scored on a 5-point Likert scale. (Please note that this SPSS file is available under the name "EXAMPLE23_1.sav" at the website for another book, Dimitrov, 2008: http://cehd.gmu.edu/book/dimitrov.) The output of the map.sps program is shown in Table 5.7.

The results in Table 5.7 show that the Velicer's MAP test retains two factors that underlie the survey data in this example. As described in the previous section, this is because the smallest average squared partial correlation (.0664) occurs for the case of two factors.

Back to Table 5.6, the "parallel" computer program (SPSS, SAS, or MATLAB version) is for PA using random data sets. As an example, the SPSS version of this program (parallel.sps), used again with the SPSS file for the responses of 1,028 people on 11 Likert items, provided the results shown in Table 5.8 (left panel). Under the column spanner labeled "PA/PCA-Random," the eigenvalues in the column labeled "Real" are obtained from the actual data using the PCA option in SPSS. The next two columns, "Mean" and "P_{95}," contain eigenvalues obtained also via PCA but for random data sets of normally distributed variables generated by the SPSS syntax parallel.sps. The results suggest the retention of two factors (F_1 and F_2), because the eigenvalues of these two factors for the real-data PCA (5.295 and 1.410) exceed their counterparts for the random data sets (at both the mean and the 95th percentile, P_{95}). Thus, the two-factor solution found under the section titled "PA/PCA-Random" is consistent with that suggested by the Velicer's MAP test for the same data.

TABLE 5.7

Velicer's Minimum Average Partial (MAP) Test as map.sps Output

Velicer's MAP Test		Average Partial Correlation	
Eigenvalue	**Factor**	**Value Squared**	**Value to 4th Power**
4.6729	0.0000	0.3125	0.1551
1.7710	1.0000	0.2451	0.0736
0.4810	2.0000	0.0664	0.0119
0.4214	3.0000	0.1276	0.0519
0.2332	4.0000	0.2042	0.1160
0.1867	5.0000	0.2718	0.1526
0.1373	6.0000	0.4346	0.3312
0.0965	7.0000	1.0000	1.0000

Note. The smallest average squared partial correlation = .0664. The smallest average fourth power partial correlation = .0119. The number of components according to the original (Velicer, 1976) MAP Test = 2. The number of components according to the revised (O'Conner, 2000) MAP Test = 2.

TABLE 5.8

Eigenvalues From Parallel Analysis (PA) of 11 Variables Through the Use of the SPSS Syntax Programs parallel.sps (for PA With Random Data Sets) and rawpar.sps (for PA With Permutations of Raw Data)

	PA/PCA-Random			PA/PCA-Raw			PA/PFA-Raw		
Factor	Real[a]	Mean	P_{95}	Real[b]	Mean	P_{95}	Real[c]	Mean	P_{95}
F_1	5.295	1.151	1.185	5.295	1.166	1.209	4.803	0.179	0.222
F_2	1.410	1.108	1.131	1.410	1.122	1.163	0.921	0.133	0.176
F_3	0.883	1.078	1.101	0.883	1.083	1.109	0.123	0.093	0.121
F_4	0.643	1.049	1.067	0.643	1.055	1.076	0.081	0.064	0.086
F_5	0.498	1.023	1.041	0.498	1.026	1.050	0.000	0.035	0.058
F_6	0.483	0.998	1.017	0.483	0.997	1.023	–0.016	0.005	0.032
F_7	0.448	0.973	0.994	0.448	0.971	0.995	–0.091	–0.020	0.002
F_8	0.379	0.948	0.966	0.379	0.943	0.962	–0.104	–0.048	–0.030
F_9	0.337	0.920	0.939	0.337	0.913	0.938	–0.130	–0.078	–0,056
F_{10}	0.316	0.892	0.913	0.316	0.880	0.916	–0.158	–0.109	–0.076
F_{11}	0.309	0.859	0.884	0.309	0.842	0.880	–0.167	–0.146	–0.111

Note. Shading indicates factors for which the eigenvalues for the real data exceed the mean and the 95th percentile (P_{95}) of the eigenvalues for the simulated data under PA. PCA = principal component analysis; PFA = principal factor analysis; SPSS syntax programs are by O'Connor (2000).
[a]Eigenvalues for the real data were obtained via the PCA option in SPSS. [b]Eigenvalues for the real data obtained under the PCA option with permutations of raw data. [c]Eigenvalues for the real data obtained under the PFA option with permutations of raw data.

The "rawpar" computer program (SPSS, SAS, or MATLAB version) conducts PA using raw data permutations after first reading a raw data matrix, wherein the rows of the data matrix are cases/individuals and the columns are variables. The user must specify one of the following four options available with this program: (a) PCA with normally distributed random data sets, (b) PFA with normally distributed random data sets, (c) PCA with permutations of the original raw data, or (d) PFA with permutations of the original raw data. Under the last two options, the distributions of raw data for the original variables are exactly preserved, which makes the permutations accurate and particularly relevant when the raw data distributions are not normal.

In Table 5.8, the eigenvalues in the middle and right panels are produced by the SPSS version of the program (rawpar.sps) using again the same SPSS data file. Specifically, the section labeled "PA/PCA-Raw" indicates the use of PCA with permutations of the original raw data, whereas the section labeled "PA/PFA-Raw" indicates the use of PFA with permutations of the original raw data. As the results show, the PA/PCA-Raw option yields two factors, which is consistent with the two-factor solutions produced by the Velicer's MAP test and the PA with random sets using parallel.sps—that is, the PA/PCA-Random data in the left panel in Table 5.8. On the other hand, the PA/PFA-Raw option suggests the retention of three factors (F_1, F_2, and F_3), because the eigenvalues for the real data in this case (4.803, 0.921, and 0.123, respectively) exceed their counterparts under the permutations (at both the mean and the 95th percentile, P_{95}). This finding is not a surprise because, as noted earlier, the PFA tends to indicate a slightly higher number of factors compared with the PCA in permutation-based PA.

5.6.6 Modified PA of Ordered Categorical Data

Although O'Connor's (2000) procedure for PA has many advantages, it has some drawbacks in dealing with missing data and ordinal variables. Specifically, O'Connor's procedure does not allow for missing values in the original data matrix—it is assumed that the user will deal with missing values (e.g., via imputations) prior to using any of the computer programs listed in Table 5.6. Also, the O'Connor procedure using permutations of raw data produces data dependency as the values for a given case are determined by the values of the other cases. To address these two problems, Liu and Rijmen (2008) modified O'Connor's procedure to allow for missing values in the original data matrix and to avoid data dependency. Specifically, instead of permuting the rows of the original data matrix, they estimate the relative frequencies for each variable in the original data matrix and then use these relative frequencies to simulate the data for that variable in subsequent new data sets. This process is done by using independent draws from a multinomial distribution, the probabilities for which are given by the relative frequencies. Also, the frequencies of each variable are computed for all available cases, and the simulated data do not contain missing values. Liu and Rijmen (2008) also provided a computer program in SAS that offers an efficient solution to problems with missing cases in categorical data based on their approach to PA. Such problems occur, for example, with the use of assessment instruments in counseling, education, and other behavioral fields.

5.7 HIGHER-ORDER FACTORS

The factors that are extracted from the correlations among a set of observed variables are referred to as *first-order* (or *primary*) factors. If the first-order factors are correlated, one can use the correlations among them to extract second-order factors. If the second-order factors are correlated, one can extract third-order factors, and so forth. This process can continue until only a single higher order factor or uncorrelated higher-order factors are reached. Gorsuch (1983) noted that "the essential difference between the primary factors and the higher-order factors is that the primary factors are concerned with narrow areas of generalization where the accuracy is great. The higher-order factors reduce accuracy for an increase in the breadth of generalization" (p. 240). In regard to how higher-order factors can help researchers to better understand the factorial structure of the data, B. Thompson (1990) provided the following description: "The first-order analysis is a close-up view that focuses on the details of the valleys and peaks in mountains. The first-order analysis is looking at the mountains. The second-order analysis is like looking at the mountains at a greater distance, and yields a potentially different perspective on the mountains as constituents of a range. Both perspectives may be useful in facilitating understanding of data" (p. 579).

Typically, second-order factors are interpreted directly as factors that underlie first-order factors. However, Gorsuch (1983) argued that this type of interpretation is not desirable and that the interpretation of second-order factors is enhanced by relating them to the observed variables. He noted that "to avoid basing interpretations upon interpretations, the relationships of the original variables to each level of the higher-order factors are determined" (p. 245). Gorsuch (1983, p. 247) also suggested that one way to avoid this "interpretations of interpretations" was to postmultiply the first-order factor pattern matrix times the orthogonally rotated second-order factor pattern matrix. In addition, B. Thompson (1990) suggested that, if rotation is used to facilitate interpretations of other structures, it also seems logical to rotate the product matrix itself to the varimax criterion. Using this approach, W. L. Johnson and A. M. Johnson (1995) developed a SAS-based computer program for second-order factor analysis. An SPSS version of this computer program is also available (W. L. Johnson & A. M. Johnson, 2000). SPSS syntax for second-order EFA, with examples and interpretations, is provided by B. Thompson (2004, pp. 72–81). For examples of studies that use higher-order EFA in the validation of assessment scale data, the reader may refer to Baldwin et al. (2005); W. L. Johnson, Johnson, and Heimberg (1999); and Nelson, Canivez, Lindstrom, and Hatt (2007).

5.8 SAMPLE SIZE FOR EFA

There is a strong evidence in the literature on EFA that the quality of factor solutions depends, among other things, on the sample size (e.g., Guadagnoli & Velicer, 1988; Hogarty, Hines, Kromrey, Ferron, & Mumford, 2005; MacCallum, Widaman, Zhang, & Hong, 1999). Simple rules of thumb for sample size in EFA such as "a minimum of 100 to 250" (e.g., Cattell, 1978; Gorsuch, 1983), "500 or more whenever possible" (Comrey & Lee, 1992), "a ratio of at least 10:1 for sample size to number of variables" (Everitt, 1975), and so forth, do not take into account important issues such as estimation method, factor rotation, magnitude of structure coefficients, and so forth. Also problematic are rules of thumb related to magnitudes of cutting factor loadings that are used to determine which variables are substantially related to a given factor—for example, the rule of "factor loadings of .30 or higher" (e.g., Nunnally, 1978) or "factor loadings of .32 or higher" (Comrey & Lee, 1992). For details in this regard, the reader may refer to Cudeck and O'Dell (1994).

Guadagnoli and Velicer (1988) conducted a Monte Carlo study to investigate the stability of sample factor pattern relative to the population pattern under four conditions: sample size (*N*s = 50, 100, 150, 200, 300, 500, and 1,000), number of variables (*p*s) in the range from 36 to 144, magnitude of structure coefficients (*a*s = .40, .60, and .80), and number of factors (*m*s = 3, 6, and 9). Conditions in which the sample size is smaller than the number of variables (*N*s < *p*s) were not considered because of strong arguments in the literature against such conditions for EFA (e.g., Nunnally & Bernstein, 1994). The results from this study suggested that a good match to the population pattern was attained (a) for $a = .80$ across all conditions, (b) for $a = .60$ when $N \geq 150$, and (c) for $a = .40$ (and low p/m ratio), when $300 \leq N \leq 400$ (Guadagnoli & Velicer, 1988, p. 274). In any case, the larger the sample size, the higher the quality of factor solutions.

5.9 DATA ADEQUACY FOR EFA

5.9.1 Bartlett's Test of Sphericity

Before conducting EFA, the researcher should test for significance the correlation matrix for the variables being analyzed in order to decide whether factoring the variables is appropriate. When all correlations between the variables are zero, the correlation matrix is an *identity matrix*—a matrix with unities on the main diagonal and all off-diagonal elements equal to zero. A widely used test of the null hypothesis that "a correlation matrix is an identity matrix" is known as the *Bartlett's sphericity test* (Bartlett, 1950). This test is based on a chi-square approximation with degrees of freedom $p(p - 1)/2$, where *p* is the number of variables being analyzed (e.g., Gorsuch, 1983, p. 149). Under this test, a chi-square value associated with a probability less than .05 yields a rejection of the null hypotheses that the correlation matrix is an identity matrix (i.e., one can consider that the correlation matrix is significant). Keep in mind, however, that the Bartlett's sphericity test is very sensitive to sample size; that is, the test is likely to be significant with large samples even if correlations are very low. In this regard, Tabachnick and Fidell (2007) stated that "use of the [Bartlett's sphericity] test is recommended only if there are fewer than, say, five cases per variable" (p. 614).

5.9.2 Measures of Sampling Adequacy

Kaiser–Meyer–Olkin (KMO) Measure of Sampling Adequacy. The KMO measure of sampling adequacy provides information about the degree of common variance among variables, which helps researchers decide whether a factor analysis is appropriate. This measure is based on the logic that if two variables share a common variance with other variables, the partial correlation between these two variables, controlling for the other variables, should be small. Specifically, KMO = $SSC/(SSC + SSPC)$, where SSC is the sum of squared correlations and $SSPC$ is the sum of squared partial correlations over *all* variable pairs in the correlation matrix. Thus, KMO is a ratio between 0 and 1. If the partial correlations are close to zero ($SSPC \approx 0$), KMO is close to 1.0, thus indicating that the variables share a common factor. KMO values of .60 or higher (KMO ≥ .60) are required to warrant factor analysis (Kaiser, 1974).

Individual Measures of Sampling Adequacy. Along with the omnibus KMO index, a measure of sampling adequacy (MSA) for each individual variable is also useful for decisions on factorability of a correlation matrix. The MSA for a given variable X_i (MSA_i) is computed like the overall KMO, but the summation is only over those variable pairs in the correlation matrix that contain X_i (not over all pairs of variables as in KMO). That is, $MSA_i = SSC_i/SSPC_i$, where SSC_i is the sum of the squared correlations between X_i and the other variables, and $SSPC_i$ is the sum of the partial correlations between X_i and the other variables. MSA values of .60 or higher (MSA ≥ .60) can be considered acceptable for factorability of the correlation matrix.

Typically (e.g., in SPSS outputs for EFA), MSA values are reported in the main diagonal of the so-called *anti-image correlation matrix* (AIC). The off-diagonal elements of the AIC are the negatives of partial correlations between pairs of variables controlling for the other variables. Although the MSA values on the main diagonal should be large (MSA ≥ .60), the off-diagonal values in the AIC should be mostly negligible to warrant factorability of the correlation matrix.

Example 5.3 This example illustrates interpretations of the Bartlett's sphericity test, the KMO, and individual MSAs reported in an SPSS output for EFA. Specifically, two factors were extracted under PCA of six variables using the varimax rotation. Provided in Table 5.9 are only results related to the purpose of this example.

TABLE 5.9

SPSS Output for the Bartlett's Test of Sphericity, Kaiser–Meyer–Olkin (KMO) Measure of Sampling Adequacy, and Individual Measures of Sampling Adequacy Under Principal Component Analysis With Varimax Rotation

	Anti-Image Matrices					
Variable	X_1	X_2	X_3	X_4	X_5	X_6
Anti-image covariance						
X_1	.646	–.293	.002	.073	.018	.008
X_2	–.293	.599	.070	.074	–.014	.050
X_3	.002	.070	.449	–.135	–.184	–.060
X_4	.073	.074	–.135	.499	–.127	–.052
X_5	.018	–.014	–.184	–.127	.436	–.156
X_6	.008	.050	–.060	–.052	–.156	.665
Anti-image correlation						
X_1	.759[a]	–.470	.003	.129	.003	.011
X_2	–.470	.774[a]	.136	.135	–.027	.079
X_3	.003	.136	.827[a]	–.286	–.417	–.110
X_4	.129	.135	–.286	.869[a]	–.272	–.090
X_5	.003	–.027	–.417	–.272	.803[a]	–.289
X_6	.011	.079	–.110	–.090	.289	.890[a]

Note. KMO Measure of Sampling Adequacy = .822. Bartlett's Test of Sphericity, approximate χ^2 = 1,068.002, df = 15, and p = .000.
[a]Measures of sampling adequacy.

According to the Bartlett's sphericity test, the correlation matrix is *not* an identity matrix, $\chi^2(15, N = 461) = 1{,}068.00$, $p < .001$. That is, the correlation matrix is significant, which opens the door for conducting factor analysis. Also, the overall KMO measure of sampling adequacy (KMO = .822) is higher than the cutting value of .60, thus supporting factorability of the correlation matrix. An additional support in this regard is provided by the AIC, which is reported in the lower panel of Table 5.9 (the anti-image covariance matrix, in the upper panel in this table, has an intermediate role in the development of the AIC, so it is not of interest here). As can be seen, the individual MSA values, provided in the main diagonal of the AIC, range from .759 to .890, thus exceeding the cutting value of .60 for acceptable factorability of the correlation matrix. At the same time, the off-diagonal elements of the AIC (negatives of partial correlations) are relatively small, which is in support of sampling adequacy for individual variables. An exception are the relatively high values of two off-diagonal elements—namely, the negatives of partial correlations between X_1 and X_2 (–.470), and between X_3 and X_5 (–.417). Whether or not this should be a concern would depend on the psychometric quality of the respective variables (e.g., their structure loadings, standard errors, possible cross-loading, and so forth), but this is beyond the scope of this example. For additional reading on assessing correlation matrices and their factorability in the context of instrument development, the reader may refer to Pett, Lackey, and Sullivan (2003).

5.10 EFA WITH CATEGORICAL DATA

Several researchers have cautioned about the use of factor analysis with (binary or polytomous) categorical data (e.g., Cattell, 1978; Gorsuch, 1983; J. Kim & Mueller, 1985; Mislevy, 1986; Nunnally & Bernstein, 1994). Using binary data (e.g., 1 = true, 0 = false) usually causes attenuated correlations and artificial factors. Attenuated correlations, which occur when multiple respondents choose the same response for the same item, affect the factor grouping of variables (e.g., Cattell, 1978). Discussing this issue, J. Kim and Mueller (1985) suggested that if the research goal is to look for clustering patterns, factor analysis with binary data may be justified. Another problem that usually occurs with the use of binary data in factor analysis is the creation of artificial factors referred to as *difficulty factors*. Specifically, a difficulty factor is created by items with similar difficulty (mean item score) or when one of the binary values (1 or 0) is proportionally overrepresented (e.g., Gorsuch, 1983; Rummel, 1970). Thus, extra factors tend to occur in EFA with binary items because of similar response distributions rather than similar item content. When a higher order factor analysis is used, it provides some correction to the problem as the extra factors are regrouped into more general factors (e.g., J. Kim & Mueller, 1985). The problems faced when using factor analysis with binary data also apply with polytomous data, such as scores on Likert items (e.g., Mislevy, 1986; B. O. Muthén, 1984). Theoretically, binary or polytomous scores on a variable that is continuous in nature (e.g., verbal ability, anxiety, or depression) are associated with respective cutting values (thresholds) on the latent continuum of this variable.

From technical perspectives, EFA (or PCA) with Pearson correlations is appropriate for continuous variables but *not* for binary or polytomous variables, because EFA for binary data should be based on tetrachoric correlations and EFA for polytomous data should be based on polychoric correlations. Thus, it is *not* appropriate to use computer programs that run EFA based on Pearson correlations (e.g., SPSS) when the data are binary or polytomous. Instead, computer programs that run EFA based on tetrachoric/polychoric correlations should be used; MicroFACT (Waller, 2001), TESTFACT (D. Wilson, Wood, & Gibbons, 1991), FACTOR (Lorenzo-Seva & Ferrando, 2006), and Mplus (L. K. Muthén & B. O. Muthén, 2008) are appropriate. For example, Donnellan (2008) used FACTOR and Mplus for EFA with Likert items in psychometric analysis of achievement goal inventories (the results produced by FACTOR and Mplus were essentially the same). A useful feature of FACTOR is that it provides the option to conduct a PA with 500 random matrices (FACTOR is available at: http://psico.fcep.urv.es/utilitats/factor). In Mplus, EFA can be performed with continuous items, categorical items (binary or ordered polytomous), or a combination of continuous and categorical items (for underlying theory, see B. O. Muthén, 1984).

5.11 EFA IN COLLECTING EVIDENCE OF CONSTRUCT VALIDITY

As noted at the introduction of this chapter, EFA is typically used when researchers do not have enough theoretical or empirical information to hypothesize how many factors underlie the set of observable variables and which variables form which factor. In the context of construct validation, EFA is used primarily (a) for collecting evidence about the structural aspect of validity in replication studies on existing scales or (b) for collecting evidence in the initial (pilot) stages of developing new scales for assessment. In either case, researchers are strongly recommended to cross-validate the EFA results in the framework of CFA using an independent sample of respondents (CFA-based methods of construct validation are discussed in Chapters 6 and 7). As described next, EFA can also be used in collecting convergent and discriminant evidence of the external aspect of validity. Unfortunately, there are very few (almost no) reports on using this option in studies that have used EFA in validation of assessment scale data in counseling and other fields. Some new trends in using EFA for validation purposes are also noted in this section.

5.11.1 EFA for Convergent and Discriminant Evidence of Validity

The EFA-based approach to collecting convergent and discriminant evidence of the external aspect of validity consists of conducting EFA on data collected with the assessment scale that is being evaluated and data collected with other scales called *marker scales*. Some of the marker scales should be known to measure the construct under validation, and other marker scales should measure something else. For example, if the scale under validation (target scale) is hypothesized to measure anxiety, this scale would be administered to a representative sample from the population of interest along with a battery of marker scales that measure anxiety and something else (say, motivation). The data on all scales together would then be submitted to EFA. Ideally, two factors would emerge: an anxiety factor and a motivation factor. Convergent evidence would be demonstrated if all (target and marker) anxiety scales converged on the anxiety factor. Discriminant evidence would be demonstrated if the anxiety scale items did not load highly on the motivation factor. Any deviations from this scenario (e.g., some items of the target anxiety scale load on a third factor) should cause the test developer to question the external validity aspect of the target anxiety scale. For additional discussion and examples of the EFA-based approach to collecting convergent and discriminant evidence of validity, the reader may refer to Allen and Yen (1979, pp. 111–113).

5.11.2 Some New Trends in Using EFA for Validation Purposes

Relying solely of EFA is, one can say, unfinished business in the validation of assessment scale data. As already noted, it is advisable to cross-validate the EFA results via CFA with an independent sample (e.g., Derby & Smith, 2008; Floyd & Widaman, 1995; Koth, Bradshaw, & Leaf, 2009; Tovar & Simon, 2010; Tovar, Simon, & Lee, 2009). This EFA-then-CFA approach is recommended even when EFA is conducted to investigate unsatisfactory or discrepant results from CFA reported in previous studies—a situation frequently addressed in validation research in counseling and related fields (e.g., Donnellan, 2008; Immekus & Imbrie, 2010). In another scenario, as Jöreskog (1969) suggested, one can use EFA in a CFA framework to obtain preliminary statistical information (e.g., on standard errors of factor loadings) that can be useful in a subsequent CFA (e.g., to select appropriate anchor items). In this case EFA is used to provide a technical jump-start for CFA, *not* to generate hypotheses about the factor structure of interest.

A new approach to integrating EFA and CFA is based on a method referred to as *exploratory structural equation modeling* (ESEM; Asparouhov & Muthén, 2009). The ESEM, currently implemented in the Mplus computer program (L. K. Muthén & B. O. Muthén, 2008), is designed to integrate advantages of EFA and CFA in the framework of structural equation modeling (SEM). The ESEM is motivated by the argument that in many situations the requirement of zero cross-loadings in CFA is too restrictive and does not reflect the actual structure of the data. This situation leads to extensive CFA modifications that, according to Browne (2001), are exploratory in nature, and in such cases "the discovery of misspecified loadings is more direct through rotation of the factor matrix than through the examination of model modification indices" (p. 113). Related to this argument, Asparouhov and Muthén (2009) also noted that "a measurement instrument often has many small cross-loadings that are well motivated by either substantive theory or by the formulation of the measurements. The CFA approach of fixing many or all cross-loadings at zero may therefore force a researcher to specify a more parsimonious model than is suitable for the data" (p. 398). They clarified, however, that there are many situations where CFA is the method of choice, and that the ESEM is intended to "add further modeling flexibility by providing an option that in some cases is more closely aligned with reality, reflecting more limited measurement knowledge of the researcher or a more complex measurement structure" (Asparouhov & Muthén, 2009, p. 399). For additional methodological discussion and practical illustration of the ESEM, the reader may refer to Marsh et al. (2009).

SUMMARY

1. An *exploratory factor analysis* (EFA) is typically used when researchers do not have enough theoretical or empirical information to hypothesize how many factors underlie the set of observable variables and which variables form which factor.
2. An EFA defines factors through a mathematical procedure that usually maximizes the total variance in the observed variables accounted for by the factors.
3. Under the full component model, the score of a person on any variable is perfectly reproduced (with *no* error) as a linear combination of the person's scores on a set of factors (see Equation 5.2).
4. Under the common factor model, an additional term is added to the equation of the full component model to reflect the assumption that, along with the common factors, there is a unique factor for each variable (see Equation 5.3).
5. The proportion of the variance in a given variable that is accounted for by the common factors is called *communality* of this variable.
6. The principal factor method under the full component model is referred to as *principal component analysis* (PCA).
7. The principal factor method under the common factor model is called *principal factor analysis* (PFA). When PFA is applied to a correlation matrix with communality estimates in the diagonal, this is referred to as *principal-axis factoring* (PAF).

8. The PCA is conceptually and mathematically different from EFA—PAF or other factoring procedures with estimated communalities. The distinction between common and unique variance is *not* recognized in PCA, whereas EFA provides separate estimates of common and unique sources of variance, thus taking into account the presence of error.
9. EFA is more appropriate, compared with PCA, for understanding the underlying structure of intercorrelations between observed variables, especially under the conditions of a relatively small number of variables (e.g., 30 or less) and low communalities (e.g., 0.4). PCA can be more useful for empirical summary of the data, especially for dimension reduction.
10. In the context of construct validation, EFA should be preferred to PCA in collecting evidence about the structural aspect of validity. The PCA has more limited applications—for example, in determining the proper number of factors (a) the "root ≥ 1" (eigenvalues of one or higher) criterion works only under PCA, (b) PCA performs somewhat better than the PFA under the permutation-based approach to parallel analysis, and (c) the Velicer's MAP test uses PCA.
11. In both EFA and PCA, the interpretation of factors is based on rotated factor solutions. Typically, the rotation of factors is guided by the goal of obtaining a simple structure for meaningful interpretation of the extracted factors.
12. Under a practically useful conception of simple structure, the items should have large estimated factor loadings on one factor and small cross-loadings, with the assumption that these cross-loadings are essentially zero in the population.
13. Varimax is an orthogonal rotation under which the variance of the squared factor loadings across all factors is maximized. The varimax rotation is inappropriate when there is a tendency that a single general factor underlies the set of observable variables.
14. An oblique rotation is appropriate when the correlations between factors are minor to moderate in magnitude. Commonly used oblique rotations are quartimax, equimax, direct oblimin, and promax.
15. It is useful to start with an oblique rotation (e.g., promax) and examine the results. If the correlations between the oblique factors are negligible, then use the varimax rotation and interpret the resulting orthogonal solution.
16. For proper interpretation of a set of factors, both the structure and pattern coefficients should be examined. The structure coefficients show the full relationship (correlation) between the variables and the factors, whereas the pattern coefficients reflect the unique contribution of the factor to the variable (under orthogonal rotation, the structure and pattern coefficients are the same).
17. The eigenvalue of a principal factor is the sum of squared loadings (SSLs) for this factor obtained under the initial (unrotated) extraction of factors. After factor rotation this property is no longer valid—the SSLs for rotated factors are important, but they are *not* eigenvalues.
18. The "root ≥ 1" (eigenvalues greater than 1.00) criterion for determining the number of factors is applicable only under PCA. This criterion works relatively well when the number of variables is 40 (or smaller) and the sample size is large.
19. The scree test for determining the number of factors involves plotting the eigenvalues in descending order of their magnitude against their factor numbers and determining where they level off. The number of factors is determined by the number of dots (eigenvalues) on the plot above the elbow—the break between the steep slope and the leveling off.

20. The logic behind the parallel analysis (PA) approach to determining the proper number of factors is that the eigenvalues of meaningful factors that underlie a set of variables should be larger than the eigenvalues of parallel factors derived from random data sets with the same sample size and number of variables as the original data set.
21. The Velicer's minimum average partial (MAP) test uses PCA followed by the examination of a series of matrices of partial correlations. The proper number of components is determined by the sequential number of the step that has produced the lowest average squared partial correlation.
22. The essential difference between the primary (first-order) factors and the higher-order factors is that the primary factors are concerned with narrow areas of generalization where the accuracy is great, whereas the higher-order factors reduce accuracy for an increase in the breadth of generalization.
23. Simple rules of thumb for sample size in EFA (e.g., "a minimum of 100 to 250") do not take into account important issues such as estimation method, factor rotation, magnitude of structure coefficients, and so forth.
24. Under the Bartlett's test of sphericity, a chi-square value associated with a probability less than .05 ($p < .05$) indicates that the correlation matrix is significant.
25. The Kaiser–Meyer–Olkin (KMO) measure of sampling adequacy provides information about the degree of common variance among variables, which can help the researcher decide whether a factor analysis is appropriate. KMO values of .60 or higher (KMO $\geq$ .60) are required to warrant factor analysis.
26. EFA with Pearson correlations is appropriate for continuous variables, whereas EFA for binary data should be based on tetrachoric correlations and EFA for polytomous data should be based on polychoric correlations.
27. In the context of construct validation, EFA is used primarily for collecting evidence about the structural aspect of validity in replication studies on existing scales or in the initial (pilot) stages of developing new scales for assessment. Researchers are strongly recommended to cross-validate the EFA results in the framework of confirmatory factor analysis (CFA) using an independent sample of respondents.
28. The EFA-based approach to collecting convergent and discriminant evidence of the external aspect of validity consists of conducting EFA on data collected with the assessment scale under validation and data collected with other scales called *marker scales*.
29. A new approach to integrating EFA and CFA is based on a method referred to as *exploratory structural equation modeling* (ESEM). The rationale behind ESEM is that in some situations the requirement of zero cross-loadings in CFA is too restrictive and does not reflect the actual structure of the data.

Chapter 6
Confirmatory Factor Analysis

As discussed in Chapter 5, an exploratory factor analysis (EFA) is typically used when a researcher does not have enough theoretical and/or empirical information to hypothesize how many factors underlie the set of observable variables and which variables form which factor. In contrast, a confirmatory factor analysis (CFA) is used when the goal is to test the validity of a hypothesized model of factors and those factors' relationships to a set of observed variables. Factor analysis (EFA and/or CFA) is widely used and plays a key role in the process of developing and validating assessment scale data in counseling, education, psychology, and other behavioral fields. Validity studies that use factor analysis are widely represented in professional journals such as *Measurement and Evaluation in Counseling and Development*, *Educational and Psychological Measurement*, *Developmental Psychology*, *Journal of Personality Assessment*, *Journal of Clinical Psychology*, *Psychological Assessment*, *Psychological Methods*, and others. Theoretical and technical aspects of factor analysis are addressed in professional journals such as *Structural Equation Modeling*, *Multivariate Behavioral Research*, and *Journal of Educational and Behavioral Statistics*.

In this chapter I outline similarities and differences of EFA and CFA and describe CFA concepts and methodological principles of CFA applications related to construct validation. The focus is on issues of CFA model specification, model adequacy, and testing for factorial invariance across groups. Higher order CFA models are also discussed, with focus on their identification, acceptability, interpretation (through the use of Schmidt–Leiman transformation), and testing for invariance across groups.

6.1 SIMILARITIES AND DIFFERENCES OF EFA AND CFA

The purpose of both EFA and CFA is to identify (one or more) latent factors that account for variation and covariation among a set of observable variables. In EFA and CFA the factors represent unobservable variables, called *latent variables*, *factors*, or *constructs*, whereas the observed variables are referred to as *indicators* of such latent variables. The set of factors and indicators associated with them define the factorial structure underlying the set of indicators. As both EFA and CFA are based on the common factor model, many EFA concepts, such as factor loadings, residuals, and unique variances, apply to CFA as well.

The basic features of CFA are better understood in comparison with their counterparts in EFA. The main conceptual difference is that EFA is a data-driven approach to "discovering" unknown factorial structures, whereas CFA is a theory-driven approach to "confirming" hypothesized factorial structures. Listed below are some differences between EFA and CFA, the first two of which are depicted in Figure 6.1 for the case of two common factors underlying a set of five observable variables (X_1, X_2, X_3, X_4 and X_5). It is assumed that the first factor, F_1, is identified through its correlations with X_1, X_2, and X_3, whereas the second

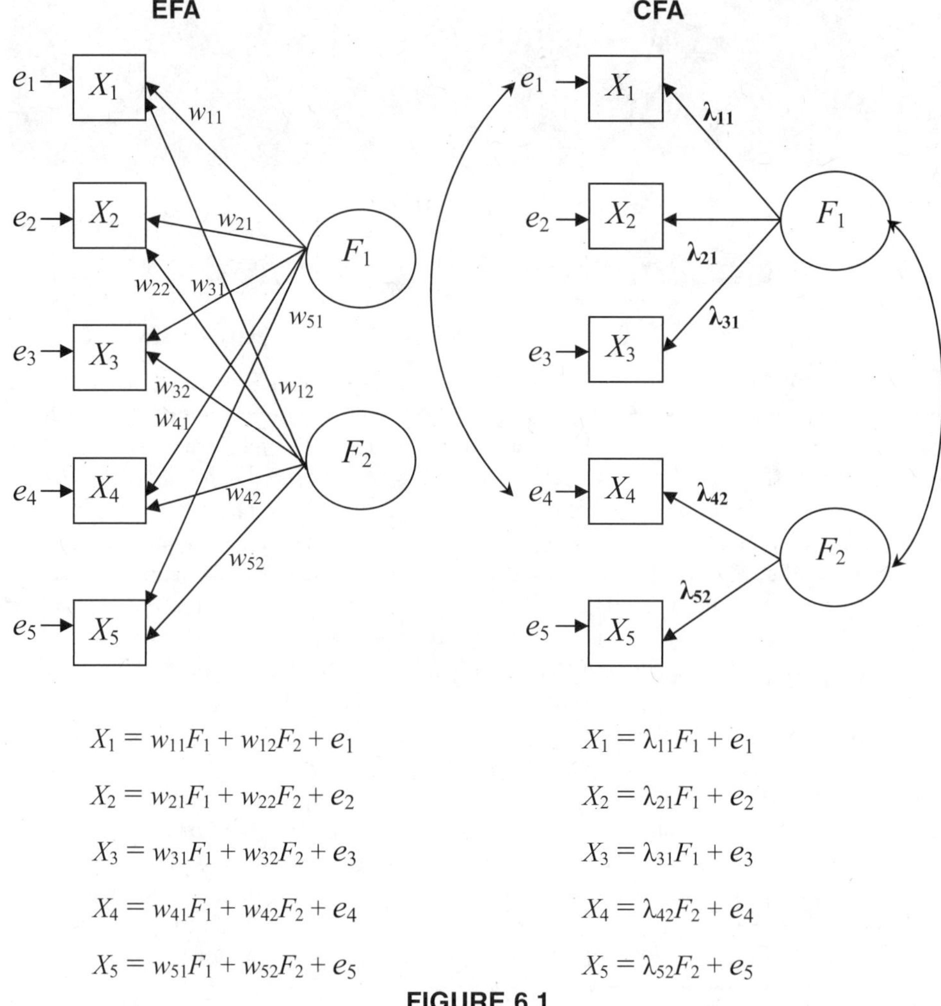

FIGURE 6.1

Exploratory Factor Ananlysis (EFA) and Confirmatory Factor Analysis (CFA) Models for Two Common Factors and Five Variables

factor, F_2, correlates primarily with X_4 and X_5. Although both the EFA (left panel) and CFA (right panel) are common factor models, they have the following differences:

1. Under the EFA model, all observed variables are assumed to correlate with all factors, whereas the under CFA model the correlations between factors and observable variables are restricted to previously hypothesized relationships among them. For example, under the EFA model, X_1 is predicted from both F_1 and F_2, so $X_1 = w_{11}F_1 + w_{12}F_2 + e_1$, where the standardized regression coefficients w_{11} and w_{12} are the pattern coefficients for X_1, and e_1 is the error term in the prediction of X_1. Under the CFA model, it is hypothesized that X_1 is predicted *only* from F_1, so $X_1 = \lambda_{11}F_1 + e_1$. Thus, the regression coefficient of F_2 for the prediction of X_1 is fixed to zero ($\lambda_{12} = 0$). The equations for the prediction of all five indicators from the two common factors, F_1 and F_2, under the EFA and CFA models are provided with Figure 6.1 (lower panel).

2. The EFA model assumes that all common factors are either correlated or uncorrelated. In contrast, CFA allows researchers to specify in advance only those correlations between factors that are considered substantively meaningful. In Figure 6.1, the two-way arrow connecting F_1 and F_2 indicates that the correlation between them is hypothesized a priori and will be tested for significance in the CFA model.
3. EFA uses a correlation matrix as input data and renders completely standardized solutions for latent factors and indicators—that is, the factor variances equal 1.0 and the factor loadings are interpreted as correlations or standardized regression coefficients. In contrast, CFA typically uses a variance–covariance matrix to produce (a) unstandardized solutions (factor loadings and other parameters are estimated in the original metrics of the indicators), (b) standardized solutions (parameter estimates are based on unstandardized indicators and standardized latent factors), and (c) completely standardized solutions (parameter estimates are based on standardized indicators and standardized latent factors).
4. Whereas the EFA model assumes no correlations between errors associated with indicators, the CFA model allows for testing hypotheses about the presence of such correlations. In Figure 6.1, the two-way arrow connecting the errors associated with X_1 and X_4 means that it is expected these two error terms will correlate. Typically, correlations between errors are expected when, for the most part, these errors have common sources—for example, the indicators are test items that relate to the same reading passage or same figure.
5. Unlike EFA, CFA allows for testing hypotheses about (a) equal factor loadings, (b) equal factor variances, (c) equal error variances, (d) validity of the factorial structure with data across different populations or across time points, and (e) comparison of alternative ("rival") factorial structures for a set of indicators—a procedure of critical importance to the process of construct validation.
6. There are situations in factorial validations of assessment scale data when it is not clear whether some factors have substantive meaning or are simply attributable to statistical artifacts stemming from (a) positively and negatively worded items, with positively worded items loading on one factor and negatively worded items on another; (b) different methods of measurement—for example, multiple-choice items and open-ended items; or (c) differential item difficulty—for example, with easy test items loading on one factor and difficult test items on another. Problems of this kind cannot be solved in EFA, whereas they can be efficiently addressed in the framework of CFA.

6.2 CFA MODEL SPECIFICATION

The first step in CFA is to specify a hypothesized CFA model based on theoretical and/or empirical knowledge about latent factors and relationships among them. This process includes specifying how many factors are expected, which factors relate to which observed variables, which factors (if any) are expected to correlate, which errors (if any) are expected to correlate, which factor loadings (if any) should be held equal, and so forth. As illustrated in Figure 6.1 (right panel), a CFA model is depicted as a path diagram, where (a) circles (or ellipses) depict latent factors; (b) a one-way arrow from a factor to an indicator means that the indicator is influenced by the factor (statistically, the indicator is predicted from the factor); (c) a curved two-way arrow connecting two factors (or two error terms) represents a correlation between them; and (d) an error term (e), referred to also as a *residual*, with a short one-way arrow ending at an indicator, represents the error (residual) in the prediction of the indicator from a factor.

A table that describes the items related to the hypothesized factors is also very useful. For example, Table 6.1 provides the description of seven items from a survey for people with multiple sclerosis, with four items being indicators for a hypothesized factor labeled *Psychosocial Distress* and three items being indicators for another hypothesized factor labeled *Successful Coping*. The path diagram of this CFA model is presented in Figure 6.2. The numbers associated with one-way arrows from the two factors to their indicators represent the unstandardized factor loadings for this model obtained with a CFA analysis described later in this chapter (see Example 6.1).

When it is hypothesized that a given factor does not relate to some indicators, the factor loadings (regression coefficients) in the prediction of these indicators from the factor are fixed to zero. In Figure 6.2, for example, the lack of one-way arrows from Psychosocial Distress to Items 5, 6, and 7 indicates that the respective three factor loadings are fixed to zero. Likewise, the lack of one-way arrows from Successful Coping to Items 1, 2, 3, and 4 means that the respective four factor loadings are fixed to zero. Furthermore, for any given factor, the measurement scale of one specific indicator is selected to represent the metric of this factor. This indicator, called the *reference indicator* for the factor, is specified by fixing its loading to 1. For the CFA model in Figure 6.2, Item 1 is selected as a reference indicator for Psychosocial Distress; therefore, the factor loading for Item 1 is fixed to 1. In this way, Psychosocial Distress is measured on the scale of Item 1. Likewise, Item 5 is the reference indicator for Successful Coping; that is, Successful Coping is measured on the scale of Item 5. The remaining five factor loadings will be estimated "freely." The selection of a reference indicator is based on its statistical and substantive representativeness for the respective hypothesized factor. For example, one can select reference indicators based on information obtained from a preliminary EFA. Yet another way to define a metric of a latent factor is to set its variance to a constant, usually 1.0 (e.g., Bentler, 2004; L. K. Muthén & B. O. Muthén, 2008).

6.3 DEPENDENT AND INDEPENDENT VARIABLES IN CFA

In the general case of a structural equation model (SEM), dependent variables are those that receive at least one path (one-way arrow) from another variable in the model, whereas independent variables are those that emanate paths (one-way arrows) but never receive a path. For the CFA model in Figure 6.1 (right panel), for example, there are five dependent

TABLE 6.1

Confirmatory Factor Analysis Model for Two Hypothesized Constructs (Psychosocial Distress and Successful Coping) Underlying Seven Survey Items for People With Multiple Sclerosis

Construct/Indicator	Survey Item In the last month, how often have you . . .
Psychosocial Distress	
Item 1	felt that you were unable to control the important things in life?
Item 2	felt nervous and distressed?
Item 3	been angered because of things that happened outside of your control?
Item 4	found that you cannot cope with all the things you had to do?
Successful Coping	
Item 5	felt confident about your ability to handle your personal problems?
Item 6	been able to control irritations in your life?
Item 7	felt that you were effectively coping with important changes that were occurring in your life?

Note. Adapted from "Testing for Factorial Invariance in the Context of Construct Validation," by D. M. Dimitrov, 2010, *Measurement and Evaluation in Counseling and Development, 43,* p. 128. Copyright 2010 by Sage Publications. Reprinted with permission.

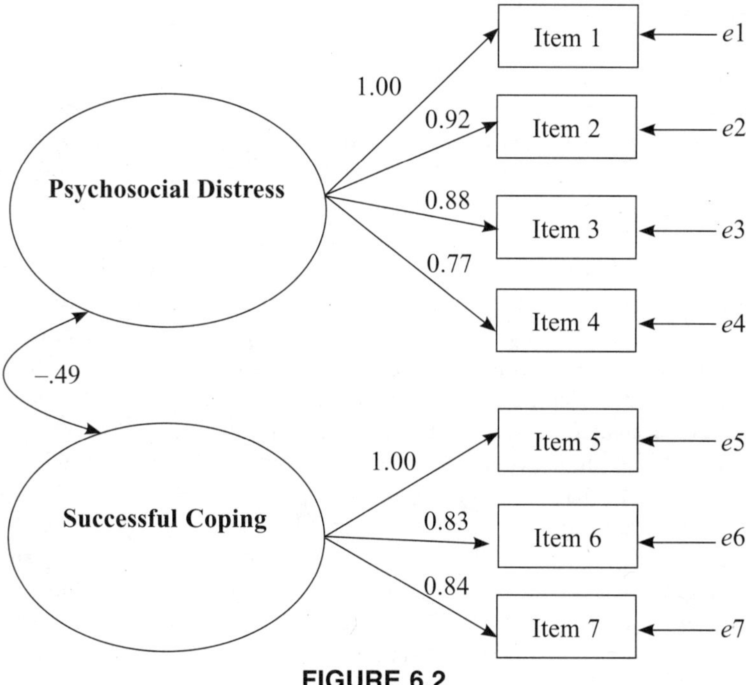

FIGURE 6.2

Two-Factor Confirmatory Factor Analysis Model for Psychosocial Distress and Successful Coping for People With Multiple Sclerosis

Note. From "Testing for Factorial Invariance in the Context of Construct Validation," by D. M. Dimitrov, 2010, *Measurement and Evaluation in Counseling and Development, 43,* p. 128. Copyright 2010 by Sage Publications. Reprinted with permission.

variables (X_1, X_2, X_3, X_4, and X_5) and seven independent variables—two latent variables (F_1 and F_2) and five error terms: e_1, e_2, e_3, e_4, and e_5. The definition equations for this model are also provided in Figure 6.1. Note also that the CFA model in Figure 6.1 hypothesizes that the error terms e_1 and e_4 are correlated. Correlated errors may occur, although they are not typical for CFA models in structural validations of counseling assessment instruments.

6.4 CFA MODEL PARAMETERS

The parameters in a CFA model are determined by rules that apply in general to SEM (e.g., Bentler, 2004; Raykov & Marcoulides, 2006a). Specifically, model parameters are (a) all variances of independent variables, (b) all covariances between independent variables (unless the model states that some of them are equal to 0 or to a given constant), (c) all factor loadings connecting the latent variables with their indicators (unless the model states that some of them are equal to zero or to a given constant), and (d) all regression coefficients between observed or latent variables (unless the model states that some of them are equal to 0 or to a given constant). When applying these "rules" for model parameters, keep in mind that the variances of dependent variables, the covariances between dependent variables, and the covariances between dependent and independent variables are *not* model parameters as they are explained in terms of model parameters. Also, as described in the previous section, the metric of each factor in CFA is established by setting either its variance or a factor loading of a reference indicator to a constant, usually 1.

6.5 CFA MODEL IDENTIFICATION

A CFA model is identified if, given the input variance–covariance matrix, it is possible to obtain a unique set of estimates for all unknown parameters in the model (e.g., factor loadings, residual variances, factor variances and covariances, and so forth). Mathematically, this can happen only if the number of known elements is greater than or equal to the number of unknown parameters. Unknown parameters in a CFA model are all freely estimated parameters, whereas known elements are the variances and covariances in the input data matrix. For a CFA model with p indicators, the number of known elements (in the input variance–covariance matrix) equals $p(p + 1)/2$. Thus, in the case of six indicators, there are 21 known elements: $6(6 + 1)/2 = 21$. The difference in the number of known elements and freely estimated parameters in a model constitutes its degrees of freedom (*df*).

A CFA model is underidentified when the number of known elements is smaller than the number of freely estimated parameters (this yields negative *df*, i.e., $df < 0$). An underidentified model cannot produce unique estimates of the unknown parameters because, as known in linear algebra, a set of equations produces an infinite number of solutions when the number of known elements is smaller than the number of unknown elements. Thus, there are an infinite number of parameter estimates that produce a perfect fit in an underidentified CFA model. Consider the CFA model in Figure 6.3A, where only two items (Item 1 and Item 2) serve as indicators of a latent factor, *F*. Assuming that the latent factor is scaled by fixing its variance to unity, $Var(F_1) = 1.0$, there are four freely estimated parameters: two factor loadings (λ_1 and λ_2) and two error variances [$Var(e_1)$ and $Var(e_2)$]. The number of unknown parameters would remain the same if the latent factor is scaled by using a reference indicator, say Item 1 (i.e., by fixing the factor loading of Item 1 to unity: $\lambda_1 = 1.0$). At the same time, there are three known elements in the matrix of indicator variances and covariances: two variances of two indicators and one covariance between them. Thus, the model in Figure 6.3A is underidentified because the number of known elements is smaller than the number of freely estimated parameters (there are negative degrees of freedom: $df = 3 - 4 = -1$).

When a CFA is identified, it is either just-identified or overidentified. Specifically, the model is just-identified if the number of known elements in the input variance–covariance matrix equals the number of freely estimated model parameters (thus, there are no degrees of freedom, $df = 0$). Although it yields a unique solution for all unknown parameters, the just-identified model is not of scientific interest because it always produces a perfect fit ($df = 0$) and, therefore, can never be rejected. The model in Figure 6.3B is just identified because the number of known elements (three variances of the indicators and three covariances among them) equals the number of freely estimated parameters: three factor loadings and three error variances. Indeed, assuming that the latent factor is scaled by fixing its variance to unity, $Var(F_1) = 1.0$, there are six freely estimated parameters: three factor loadings (λ_1, λ_2, λ_3) and three error variances: $Var(e_1)$, $Var(e_2)$, and $Var(e_3)$. The number of unknown parameters would remain the same if the latent factor is scaled by using a reference indicator, say Item 1 (i.e., the factor loading of Item 1 is fixed to 1: $\lambda_1 = 1$).

A CFA model is overidentified if the number of known elements in the input variance–covariance matrix exceeds the number of freely estimated parameters in the model (this yields positive degrees of freedom, $df > 0$). For example, the model in Figure 6.3C is overidentified. That is, with four indicators in this model, the number of known elements is $4(4 + 1)/2 = 10$. On the other hand, assuming that the two correlated latent factors are scaled by fixing their variances to 1.0, there are nine freely estimated model parameters: four factor loadings, four error variances, and one factor covariance ($df = 10 - 9 = 1$).

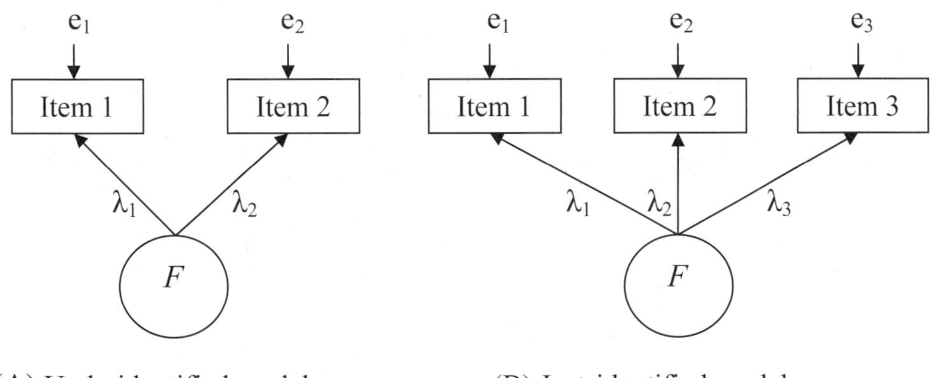

(A) Underidentified model

(B) Just-identified model

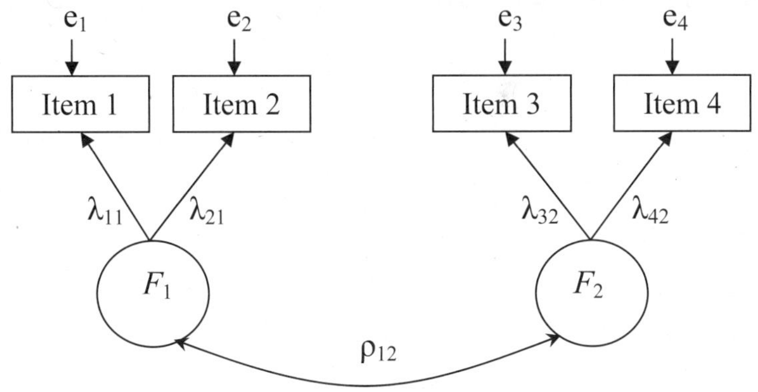

(C) Overidentified model

FIGURE 6.3

Examples of Underidentified, Just-Identified, and Overidentified Confirmatory Factor Analysis Models

Likewise, the model in Figure 6.2 is also overidentified. Indeed, with seven indicators in this model ($p = 7$), there are 28 known elements in the input variance–covariance matrix: $7(7 + 1)/2 = 28$. At the same time, there are 15 freely estimated parameters: five factor loadings (for Items 2, 3, 4, 6, and 7), seven error variances, two factor variances, and one factor covariance (the factor loadings of two reference indicators, Items 1 and 5, are fixed to 1). Thus, there are 13 degrees of freedom in this model ($df = 28 - 15 = 13$). Overidentified models are of scientific interest as they allow researchers to test model fit and to compare alternative models in CFA-based construct validation. One can obtain an overidentified model by imposing restrictions on particular model parameters. Such restrictions, however, must be based on meaningful substantive considerations.

It should also be noted that the specification of an overidentified model is a necessary, albeit not sufficient, condition to resolve the identification problem. Kenny (1979) introduced the term *empirical underidentification* for situations in which a model is statistically identified (i.e., just-identified or overidentified) but does not yield a unique set of parameter estimates because of a sample-based anomaly in the input variance–covariance matrix or in the estimates of some model parameters. Typically, an empirical underidentification occurs when a certain relationship (e.g., a correlation between two factors) is specified in the model but is practically dismissed from the model because the empirical estimate of this relationship equals zero as a consequence of sampling fluctuation. For example, as already shown, the CFA model in Figure 6.3C is overidentified. However, if for a given sample of data the input variance–covariance matrix contains values that yield an estimate of zero for the correlation between the two latent factors (i.e., $\hat{\rho}_{12} = 0$), the model would no longer be identified because its estimation would be reduced to a simultaneous estimation of two underidentified models, each of which has the structure of the model depicted in Figure 6.3A. As Kenny (1979) noted, the threat of empirical underidentification means that researchers must always be alert for signs of identification problems, even when a model is nominally identified based on its structure. To avoid such problems, researchers should use at least three indicators per latent factor in a CFA model. See also Brown (2006, pp. 62–72) for additional details and examples on CFA model identification. The reader may also refer to Hair, Anderson, Tatham, and Black (1998) for an approach to testing for identification problems based on multiple estimation of the CFA model with varying starting values (solution convergence at the same point across the estimation is indicative of model identification).

Brown (2006, p. 71) summarized four basic guidelines for model identification:

- Each latent factor must be scaled either by fixing its variance to a constant (usually 1.0) or by specifying a reference indicator by fixing its loading to 1.0.
- The number of known elements in the input variance–covariance matrix must be greater than or equal to the number of freely estimated parameters in the model (i.e., model $df \geq 0$).
- In a model with one latent factor, at least three indicators are required (if there are no correlated errors, three indicators yield a just-identified model, but more than three indicators yield an overidentified model).
- In a model with two or more latent factors, with two indicators per factor, the solution will be overidentified only if each latent factor is correlated with at least one other latent factor and their indicator errors are uncorrelated. It would be safer to use at least three indicators per latent factor to guard against empirical underidentification that may occur with such models.

6.6 EVALUATION OF CFA MODEL ADEQUACY

Typically, CFA models are tested for data fit using maximum likelihood tests within the framework of SEM. When a CFA model is tested for data fit, the factor loadings are estimated to minimize the discrepancy between the sample covariance matrix for the observed variables, **S**, and the population covariance matrix implied by the model, Σ (i.e., **S** – Σ = minimum). The function describing such discrepancy is denoted F(**S**, Σ). The smallest (minimal) value of this function, denoted F_{min}, is used as a measure of the difference (residual) between **S** and Σ.

6.6.1 The Assumption of Multivariate Normality

Testing for CFA data fit is valid under the SEM assumption of multivariate normality; that is, (a) the distribution of each observed variable is normal, (b) the joint distributions for all combinations of observed variables are normal, and (c) all bivariate scatter plots are linear and homoscedastic (all conditional distributions have equal variances). Violations of this assumption can cause distortion of the goodness-of-fit statistics (Curran, West, & Finch, 1996; Hu, Bentler, & Kano, 1992) and inflation of the Type I error rate in testing factor loadings, correlations, and other model parameters for statistical significance (Kline, 1998). Slight deviations of the data from multivariate normality are handled relatively well by major SEM programs such as LISREL (Jöreskog & Sörbom, 1996), Mplus (L. K. Muthén & B. O. Muthén, 2008), EQS (Bentler, 2004), and Amos (Arbuckle & Wothke, 1999).

Testing for Multivariate Normality. A first step in testing for multivariate normality is to test each observable variable for univariate normality. This step is taken first because the normality of individual variables is a necessary (albeit not sufficient) condition for their multivariate normality. Testing for univariate normality can be accomplished through the examination of skewness, kurtosis, and statistical tests available in most statistical packages (e.g., SPSS and SAS). Skewness reflects deviation from symmetry in a univariate distribution. Kurtosis indicates the degree to which the distribution is peaked or flat relative to the shape of a normal distribution. The skewness and kurtosis of a normal distribution are equal to zero (e.g., Glass & Hopkins, 1996, pp. 89–94). In the context of CFA, previous research found that significant problems occur with univariate skewness of 2.0 or higher and kurtosis of 7.0 or higher (e.g., Curran et al., 1996; B. O. Muthén & Kaplan, 1992). An examination for outliers in the sample of observations is also recommended at this stage. After univariate normality for individual variables is established, and outliers (if any) are dealt with, the next step is to test for multivariate skewness and kurtosis.

A widely used test of multivariate normality is based on Mardia's coefficients for multivariate skewness and kurtosis (Mardia, 1970, 1974, 1980; Mardia, Kent, & Bibby, 1979). In SAS (using macro MULTNORM), two Mardia's (1970) coefficients are available: k_1 (kappa 1), based on skewness, and k_2 (kappa 2), based on kurtosis. Under multivariate normality, (a) k_1 follows the chi-square distribution with $df = p(p + 1)(p + 2)/6$, where p is the number of variables; and (b) k_2 follows the standard normal distribution, $N(0, 1)$. Statistical significance of k_1 and k_2 indicates departure from multivariate normality. For details on these two coefficients and related SAS-based examples, the reader may refer to Ravindra and Naik (1999). SPSS does not support Mardia's coefficients. However, a detailed treatment of the meaning and use of kurtosis is provided by DeCarlo (1997), and an SPSS macro for univariate and multivariate tests of skew and kurtosis is available at his website: http://www.columbia.edu/%7Eld208.

Yet another Mardia's coefficient, known as *Mardia's normalized estimate* (e.g., Mardia et al., 1979, p. 21), is also available. Mardia's normalized estimate should be less than 3 to indicate that the assumption of multivariate normality is met (e.g., Bentler & Wu, 2002). This coefficient can be obtained with popular software such as PRELIS (a companion software for LISREL), Mplus, Amos, and EQS (e.g., the reader may refer to Tabachnick and Fidell [2007, p. 753] for EQS output on Mardia's normalized estimate). In Mplus, skewness and kurtosis values are available under the TECH12 option in the OUTPUT command. One can also obtain the Mardia's normalized estimate in Mplus under the TECH 13 option in the OUTPUT command but in the framework of mixture modeling (TYPE = MIXTURE) with CLASSES = c(1) (i.e., using a single latent class when the CFA does not involve mixture modeling; L. K. Muthén & B. O. Muthén, 2008).

Dealing With Multivariate Nonnormality. In the framework of CFA-based validation of constructs, which is of primary interest here, the usual maximum-likelihood (ML) method of estimation is based on the assumption of multivariate normality for the observed variables (indicators). If this assumption is not met, estimates of standard errors, chi-square, and related fit indices can be misleading. For example, under violation of multivariate normality, the usual ML chi-square (MLχ^2) is too large, thus inflating the Type I error in testing hypotheses based on chi-square tests. This problem can be avoided by using the ML (*mean-adjusted*; MLM) estimator (or ML robust [MLR] estimator), which was developed by Satorra and Bentler (1994). The *Satorra–Bentler scaled (mean-adjusted) chi-square*, MLMχ^2 (denoted also SBχ^2), is the usual MLχ^2 divided by a scaling correction to better approximate chi-square under nonnormality. The ML and MLM estimators are both available in Mplus, LISREL, Amos, and EQS. It should be noted, however, that although the difference of two usual MLχ^2 values for two nested CFA models follows a chi-square distribution, the difference of two SBχ^2 values for such models is *not* distributed as chi-square (e.g., Satorra, 2000). This issue is addressed in more detail in the discussion of testing for factorial invariance in Section 6.8.

Other approaches to correcting for nonnormality are based on bootstrap resampling (e.g., Bollen & Stine, 1992; Boomsma, 1986; Yung & Bentler, 1996). In the context of factor analysis, Bollen and Stine (1992) proposed a bootstrap approach to estimating chi-square under conditions of multivariate nonnormality. For a comprehensive evaluation of the bootstrap method under different scenarios of nonnormality, sample size, model specification, and number of bootstrap samples, the reader may refer to Nevitt and Hancock (2001). Bootstrap resampling is available in Mplus, EQS, Amos, and LISREL.

Note 6.1

The robust ML estimator (MLM), which is designed for continuous variables, yields efficient parameter estimates with minimal bias in CFA with ordinal (e.g., Likert) indicators with five or more categories, but in the case of ordinal indicators with less than five categories, SEM estimation methods for categorical variables should be used to avoid estimation bias (e.g., Brosseau-Liard, Rhemtulla, & Savalei, 2010; D. R. Johnson & Creech, 1983). This task can be done by using the robust weighted least squares (WLS) approach, which is implemented with some variations in Mplus, LISREL, and EQS. The WLS-based estimations work well if the sample size is 200 or higher (e.g., see Flora & Curran, 2004; B. O. Muthén, 1984; Wirth & Edwards, 2007). Amos supports a Bayesian approach to estimation of categorical variables (S.-Y. Lee & Tang, 2006). The reader may also refer to DiStefano (2002), Finney and DiStefano (2006), and Hutchinson and Olmos (1998) for treatments of nonnormal and categorical data in CFA.

6.6.2 Goodness-of-Fit Indices

Numerous inferential and descriptive fit indices have been developed to assist the evaluation of goodness-of-fit of a CFA model as a whole. Typically, the evaluation of model fit is based on an inferential goodness-of-fit index, called the *chi-square value*, in combination with several descriptive indices. The chi-square value is, in fact, the test statistic $T = (N - 1)F_{min}$, where N is the sample size and F_{min} is the computed minimal difference (*residual*) between the covariance matrices **S** and Σ obtained with the actual sample data and implied for the population by the model, respectively. When the CFA model fits the data, the T statistic approaches a central chi-square distribution, hence the name *chi-square value*. The degrees of freedom for the chi-square distribution of T are computed as $df = v(v + 1)/2 - p$, where v is the number of observed variables and p is the number of model parameters (factor loadings, variances, and covariances) to be estimated. Thus, evidence of data fit is provided when the chi-square value is *not* statistically significant (say, $p > .05$). However, when the sample size, n, increases, the T statistic also increases, thus yielding smaller p values and, therefore, an artificial tendency to reject the model fit. On the other hand, an artificial tendency to support the model fit occurs with small samples, as T tends to remain small and thus its p value remains large. Hence, the chi-square value alone does *not* provide sufficiently valid evidence for the presence (or lack) of model fit (e.g., see Bentler & Bonnett, 1980; Raykov & Marcoulides, 2006a). Other goodness-of-fit indices must also be examined when evaluating CFA model fit. The following descriptive indices of model fit are commonly reported in empirical studies:

- *Goodness-of-fit index* (GFI). This index (similar to R^2 in multiple regression) tends to represent the proportion of the variance and covariance accounted for by the CFA model. A GFI value higher than .95 (GFI > .95) is considered an indication of a reasonable model fit (Hu & Bentler, 1999). The same holds for its adjusted-for-population value (AGFI). In general, the GFI must be above .90 (GFI > .90) to be interpreted as "somewhat acceptable" for model fit.
- *Chi-square to degrees of freedom ratio* (χ^2/df). When the ratio obtained by dividing the chi-square value by its degrees of freedom is smaller than 2.00 (i.e., $\chi^2/df < 2$), this indicates an acceptable model fit (Bollen, 1989).
- *Comparative fit index* (CFI; Bentler, 1990). Generally speaking, the CFI indicates the ratio of improvement from a null model to the hypothesized CFA model (the null model is defined as model with zero variances and covariances). A CFI greater than .95 (CFI > .95) is considered as evidence of a good model fit (Hu & Bentler, 1999). The following criteria are also used for determining fit: (a) unacceptable fit: CFI < .85; (b) mediocre fit: CFI between .85 and .89; (c) acceptable fit: CFI between .90 and .95; (d) close fit: CFI between .95 and .99; and (e) exact fit: CFI = 1.00.
- *Tucker–Lewis Index* (TLI; Tucker & Lewis, 1973). Similar to the CFI, the Tucker-Lewis index (TLI), referred to also as the *non-normed fit index* (NNFI), is a comparative fit index, but it compensates for the effect of model complexity. Specifically, the TLI provides a penalty for adding freely estimated parameters that do not substantially improve the model fit. The cutoff criteria for the TLI are the same as those for the CFI (Hu & Bentler, 1999).
- *Standardized root mean square residual* (SRMR). This index represents the standardized difference between the observed covariance and the covariance implied by the model. A value of zero indicates perfect fit, whereas a value less than .08 (SRMR < .08) is considered to indicate a good model fit. Keep in mind, however, that this index tends to get smaller as the sample size increases and as the number of parameters in the model increases.
- *Root mean square error of approximation* (RMSEA; Steiger, 1990b). This fit index is a function of the chi-square (χ^2) value, degrees of freedom for the model (*df*), and the sample size, *N*. An RMSEA of .05 or less (RMSEA ≤ .05) indicates a good model fit (Browne & Cudeck, 1993). Conversely, models with RMSEA of .10 or higher have a poor fit. A 90% confidence interval (CI) for the RMSEA is also used in fit evaluations. An excellent model fit is indicated when the lower value of the interval is close to (or includes) zero and its upper value is smaller than .08. Keep in mind, however, that the RMSEA can be misleading when the degrees of freedom for the model are small and the sample size is not large. In a study on the use of fixed cutoff points in RMSEA, Chen, Curran, Bollen, Kirby, and Paxton (2008) found that for properly specified models, a 0.05 cutoff value of the RMSEA rejects too many models in small sample sizes ($n \leq 100$) but performs better with large sample sizes (although it tends to overaccept model fit when $n \geq 800$). An advantage of the RMSEA over other goodness-of-fit indices is that its value is not affected by variations in the number of indicators per factor and number of factors in the model. However, models with fewer indicators and factors are typically associated with larger standard error of the RMSEA (Cheung & Rensvold, 2002).
- *Akaike information criterion* (AIC; Akaike, 1987). This index is very useful in cross-validations and comparing alternative CFA models estimated from the same data set. The AIC takes into account both the measure of fit and model

complexity (it places a penalty of two for every estimated parameter). The AIC measures the degree to which a hypothesized CFA model is expected to replicate in another sample taken from the same population. A version of the AIC, known as the *consistent AIC* (CAIC; Bozdogan, 1987), is also available. The CAIC makes the AIC asymptotically consistent and penalizes overparameterization more stringently to pick only the simplest of the "true" models. For two models estimated from the same data set, the model with the smaller AIC (or CAIC) value is to be preferred.

- *Bayesian Information Criterion* (BIC; Schwarz, 1978). Like the AIC, the BIC is used to compare the fit of two or more models estimated from the same data set. The BIC also takes into account the measure of fit and model complexity, but it increases the penalty with the increase of the sample size. As the BIC penalty per estimated parameter seems to be too high, the adjusted BIC, which lowers the penalty, can be used (e.g., the adjusted BIC is given in Mplus). For two models estimated from the same data set, the model with the smaller BIC (of adjusted BIC) is to be preferred.

Hu and Bentler (1999) recommended that the assessments of model fit should be based on a joint evaluation of several fit indices. In a Monte Carlo analysis, they demonstrated that the combined use of the SRMR and the CFI led to the lowest sum of Type I and Type II errors, and they suggested that a reasonably good fit is supported when the following fit criteria are met: SRMR ≤ .08, RMSEA ≤ .06, CFI ≥ .95, and TLI ≥ .95 (Hu & Bentler, 1999). However, less stringent criteria of a reasonable data fit (RMSEA ≤ .08, CFI ≥ .90, and TLI ≥ .90) can also be useful in some practical applications (e.g., Marsh, Hau, & Wen, 2004). The recommendation for a joint evaluation of goodness-of-fit indices in making decisions regarding model fit is in line with findings and discussions on this issue in numerous empirical studies (e.g., Bentler, 1990; Browne & Cudeck, 1993; Jöreskog & Sörbom, 1996; MacCallum, Wegener, Uchino, & Fabrigar, 1993; Marsh, Balla, & McDonald, 1988; Yuan, 2005). Keep in mind, however, that goodness-of-fit indices are typically overestimated for small samples (n < 200), although RMSEA and CFI are less sensitive to sample size than other indices (e.g., Fan, Thompson, & Wang, 1999). Also, it is important that researchers base their decision about the validity of a CFA model on a joint examination of overall fit indices, model complexity, adequacy and interpretability of model parameters, and other issues relevant to the goals of their study (e.g., Hu & Bentler, 1998, 1999; Marsh et al., 2004).

Note 6.2

When using robust estimators to correct for multivariate nonnormality (see Note 6.1), researchers should check whether the corrected chi-square (SB χ^2) was also used to re-estimate the goodness-of-fit indices reported by the respective software (e.g., this is done in Mplus and EQS). For example, Hutchinson and Olmos (1998) argued that under robust estimation based on weighted least squares (WLS; e.g., WLSMV in Mplus), the RMSEA performs well with nonnormal Likert-type data. Also, Yu and Muthén (2002) recommended the weighted root mean square residual (WRMR) index in testing for fit to categorical data (WRMR < 1.0 indicates a good fit).

6.6.3 Analysis of Residuals

Along with the indices discussed in the previous section, which provide information about the overall fit of the model, the covariance residuals should also be examined for possible misfit in some parts of the model (covariance residuals are elements of the matrix representing the difference between the sample covariance matrix and the reproduced covariance matrix). If the measurement scale is not the same across the observed variables, it is better to examine the standardized covariance residuals. As Raykov and Marcoulides (2006a, p. 48) noted, a model underexplains or overexplains the relationship between two variables if their standardized residual is above 2.0 or smaller than –2.0, respectively. They also recommended the Q plot of the standardized residuals (against their expectations under a well-fitting model) as a useful tool for checking the plausibility of a proposed model. As they stated, "marked departures [of the Q plot dots] from a straight line indicate serious model misspecifications or possibly violations of the normality assumption (e.g., nonlinear trends in the relationships between some observable variables" (Raykov & Marcoulides, 2006a, p. 49).

6.6.4 Modification Indices

If the initially hypothesized model does not fit, an immediate task is to determine which parameters in the model are misspecified. A parameter is considered specified when it is statistically significant (the estimate of the parameter divided by its standard error must exceed the z-critical value of 1.96, at the .05 level of significance). In Figure 6.2, for example, the absence of a path from the Successful Coping factor to Item 4 represents a constraint that the loading of Item 4 on this factor is fixed to 0. Another example of a constraint is to fix all (or some) factor loadings to be equal. If a parameter under constraint is freed from that constraint, the chi-square value for the model will decrease by a certain amount measured by the so-called *modification index* (MI). Thus, the MI value for a parameter gives the expected drop in the model chi-square value if this parameter is freely estimated (e.g., Byrne, 2001; Jöreskog & Sörbom, 1979).

A single change (e.g., freeing one factor loading) can affect the estimates of parameters in the model (e.g., Jöreskog & Sörbom, 1979). Therefore, if there are several parameters with statistically significant MIs, they should be freed one at a time, starting with the parameter that has the largest MI. It should be emphasized, however, that changes suggested by MIs must be made only if they allow for substantive interpretations in the framework of the theory behind the initial model and its possible modifications. Therefore, if there is no substantive reason for freeing the parameter with the largest MI, the parameter associated with the second largest MI should be considered, and so on. Models that result from such changes must be cross-validated (i.e., tested with an independent sample) before final decisions related to model fit are made. MI values are reported with Mplus, LISREL, EQS, and Amos (in EQS, the MIs are referred to as *Lagrange multiplier statistics*).

6.6.5 Interpretability of Model Parameters

In addition to evaluating goodness-of-fit indices, the researcher must further verify the model fit by determining whether the parameter estimates make both statistical and substantive sense. For example, statistical problems are signaled by out-of-range values of parameter estimates, referred to as *improper solutions* (or *Heywood cases*)—for instance, factor correlations that exceed 1.0 in absolute value, negative factor variances, or negative variances of errors terms. Heywood cases can be attributable to model identification problems, outliers, sampling fluctuations, or misspecifications in the model (e.g., see Bollen, 1987; Dillon, Kumar, & Mulani, 1987; Gerbing & Anderson, 1987; Wothke, 1993).

Discussing Heywood cases related to negative estimates of error variances, Dillon et al. (1987) emphasized that corrective action to avoid such cases can be taken only after determining the cause(s) of the offending (improper) variance estimates. For example, they stated that "if the model provides a reasonable fit, the respective confidence interval for the offensive estimate covers zero, and the magnitude of the corresponding estimated standard error is roughly the same as the other estimates' standard errors, the Heywood case is likely due to sampling fluctuations, and the model can be reestimated with the offending estimate set to zero" (p. 134). Still, in case of a good model fit, statistically significant negative error variances may be attributable to overfitting (i.e., there are unnecessary parameters in the model), so a more parsimonious model should be specified.

Researchers must be cautious in dealing with Heywood cases because, as Dillon et al. (1987) noted, (a) attempts to restrict all of the error variances to be strictly positive will generally result in identification problems, and (b) post hoc remedial measures can rarely if ever correct for theoretical deficiency in the model (signaled, e.g., by cases suffering from lack of fit or large negative estimates of error variances). Other CFA methodologists have also urged caution with model respecifications even when there are reasonable arguments for doing so (e.g., Brown, 2006; MacCallum, 1986; MacCallum, Roznowski, & Necowitz, 1992).

Another point of caution also deserves attention. Namely, researchers often use a chi-square difference test to detect an improvement in model fit with a more parsimonious model that is nested within an initial CFA model—for example, by restricting some model parameters to be equal or fixing a factor correlation parameter to zero. Although this action is permissible with nested models, it is not appropriate when some indicators have been deleted from the initial model, because the resulting model is *not* nested within the initial model (i.e., the two models do *not* have the same data structure). Hence, it is not correct to compare two such models using a chi-square difference test for nested models (neither is it appropriate to compare them using the AIC).

From substantive perspective, the interpretability of model parameters is supported when the direction (positive or negative) of the parameter estimates, their statistical significance, and magnitude are consistent with the context-specific theoretical and/or empirical expectations. For example, in a CFA model of the NEO Five-Factor Inventory (Costa & McCrae, 1991, 2003), it is reasonable to expect a negative estimate of the correlation between the Neuroticism factor and the Extraversion factor because the two are inversely related (neuroticism involves a general tendency to experience negative affect and poor emotional stability; extraversion involves social orientation combined with the tendency to experience positive affect).

Example 6.1 The purpose of this example is to illustrate the use of the CFA model depicted in Figure 6.2 (see also Table 6.1) in collecting evidence on the validity of the constructs Psychosocial Distress and Successful Coping for a population of people with multiple sclerosis. The data are from an existing data pool produced through the Employment Preparation Survey Project funded by the National Multiple Sclerosis Society (Dimitrov, 2006; Roessler, Rumrill, & Hennessey, 2001). The CFA was performed using the computer program Mplus (L. K. Muthén & B. O. Muthén, 2008).

As shown in Figure 6.2, Psychosocial Distress relates to four items and Successful Coping relates to three items of the Employment Preparation Survey. Item 1 is the reference indicator for Psychosocial Distress (factor loading fixed to 1.00), thus indicating that the scale of Item 1 is selected as a scale of Psychosocial Distress. On the other side, the scale of Item 5 is selected as a scale of Successful Coping. The choice of Items 1 and 5 as reference indicators was based on their high factor loadings obtained with a preliminary EFA (with Promax rotation for correlated factors) and their substantive relation to the hypothesized constructs. It is also hypothesized that Psychosocial Distress and Successful Coping are negatively correlated. The Mplus code for this CFA model is provided in Table 6.2.

The goodness-of-fit statistics indicated an acceptable model fit according to the criteria discussed earlier in this section. The chi-square value was statistically significant, $\chi^2(28) =$

28.50, $p < .05$. However, given the sensitivity of the chi-square value to sample size, its statistical significance for the data in this case ($N = 1{,}028$) should not be taken as definite inferential evidence of poor data fit. A reasonably good fit of the model was suggested by the joint evaluation of the following fit indices: CFI = .99, TLI = .99, SRMR = .014, and RMSEA = .034, with 90% CI [.017, .051]. Model fit was also supported by the lack of large MIs. Specifically, the MIs reported in the Mplus output (but not shown here) were smaller than 3.84—the critical chi-square value for one degree of freedom at the .05 level—thus indicating a lack of potential cross-loading for some items on the two hypothesized factors.

TABLE 6.2

Mplus Code for the Confirmatory Factor Analysis Model in Figure 6.2

DATA:	FILE IS "C:\EXAMPLE_6_1.dat";
VARIABLE:	NAMES ARE group X1-X7
	USEVARIABLES ARE X1-X7;
ANALYSIS:	TYPE IS GENERAL;
MODEL:	DISTRESS BY X1-X4;
	COPING BY X5-X7;
OUTPUT:	MODINDICES (3.84) STANDARDIZED;

Note. DISTRESS = Psychosocial Distress; COPING = Successful Coping.

As noted earlier, after the researcher evaluates the model fit, it is important to determine whether the parameter estimates are proper solutions (i.e., there are no Heywood cases) and make substantive sense. In Figure 6.2, the numbers associated with the one-way arrows from the two constructs to their indicators are the unstandardized factor loadings (the indicators are on a 5-point scale). As the parameter estimates in Figure 6.2 are unstandardized solutions, the number associated with the two-way arrow connecting Psychosocial Distress and Successful Coping (.49) is an estimate of their covariance. The estimate of the correlation between the two constructs, reported with the completely standardized solutions in the Mplus output, was –.681 (see Table 6.3). The lack of improper solutions, such as out-of-range correlations or negative estimates of residual variances, indicates that the parameter estimates are statistically viable.

Substantive support to the model fit was provided by expected directions of the parameter estimates and their statistical significance. For example, the negative estimate of the correlation between Psychosocial Distress and Successful Coping (–.681) is not a surprise because these two constructs are inversely related. Furthermore, as can be seen in Table 6.3, the estimates of all factor loadings are statistically significant, positive, and of substantial magnitude, which is consistent with the expected substantive relationship between the two constructs and their indicators (see Table 6.1). As annotated in Table 6.3 (see the column titled "Comment"), the squared values of a (completely) standardized factor loading for an indicator shows what proportion of its variance is explained by the latent factor measured by that indicator. For example, the squared value of the factor loading on the indicator denoted X1 is $(0.798)^2 = 0.6368$, thus indicating that a substantial proportion of the variance of X1 is explained by its underlying factor. Given that X1 denotes Item 1 in Table 6.1, one can say that Psychosocial Distress explains 63.68 % of the variability in the statement of people with multiple sclerosis that they are "unable to control important things in life." The factor loadings on the remaining six indicators are interpreted in a similar fashion. One can conclude that the CFA results in this example support a good overall model fit and provide both statistical and substantive evidence of fit at the level of individual model parameters.

6.6.6 Cross-Validation

Researchers are strongly advised to conduct a CFA cross-validation of the hypothesized model with an independent sample, especially when model modifications have been made.

TABLE 6.3

Selected Mplus Output With Standardized Solutions for the Confirmatory Factor Analysis Model of Psychosocial Distress and Successful Coping for People With Multiple Sclerosis (Comments Added)

Mplus Item	Est.	*SE*	Est./*SE*	*p* value	Comment
DISTRESS by					
X1	0.798	0.016	49.721	.000	Standardized factor loadings for Psychosocial
X2	0.752	0.018	42.814	.000	Distress. The squared value of the loading
X3	0.713	0.019	37.217	.000	for an indicator equals its R^2, that is, the
X4	0.638	0.022	29.101	.000	proportion of the variance in the indicator
COPING by					that is explained by Psychosocial Distress.
X5	0.850	0.014	59.867	.000	Standardized factor loadings for Successful
X6	0.760	0.017	44.546	.000	Coping. The squared value of the loading
X7	0.766	0.017	45.858	.000	for an indicator equals its R^2, that is, the
					proportion of the variance in the indicator
COPING WITH					that is explained by Successful Coping.
DISTRESS	−0.681	0.023	−28.983	.000	Negative correlation between Psychosocial
					Distress and Successful Coping (−.681).
Residual Variances					
X1	0.363	0.026	14.195	.000	Error term variance, Var(*e*), indicating the
X2	0.434	0.026	16.401	.000	proportion of the variance of an indicator that
X3	0.492	0.027	18.036	.000	is unexplained by the the factor measured
X4	0.593	0.028	21.208	.000	by that indicator. The proportion of indicator
X5	0.277	0.024	11.450	.000	variance explained by the factor is, therefore,
X6	0.422	0.026	16.241	.000	$R^2 = 1 - \text{Var}(e)$.
X7	0.414	0.026	16.184	.000	

Note. Est. = Estimate of the factor loading; *SE* = standard error; Est./*SE* = critical ratio; *p* value = *p* value associated with the critical ratio (under the standard normal distribution). DISTRESS = Psychosocial Distress; COPING = Successful Coping. All parameter estimates are statistically significant ($p < .001$).

If the initially available sample is large enough, it can be randomly split into two subsamples to be used in a cross-validation. In another scenario, cross-validation would be useful if there is no sufficient theoretical and/or empirical information to start directly with a hypothesized CFA model. If this is the case, an EFA can be used first to help in specifying the model, followed by a CFA with an independent sample to test the hypothesized model.

6.7 FACTORIAL INVARIANCE ACROSS GROUPS

6.7.1 What Is Factorial Invariance?

Testing for model fit relates to collecting evidence of the structural aspect of validity, but it does not tap on the generalizability aspect of validity. As discussed in Chapter 3, Section 3.2.4, the generalizability aspect of validity examines the extent to which properties and interpretations of scores on the construct of interest generalize across population groups, settings, and tasks, including validity generalization of test criterion relationships (Messick, 1995). For example, there is an evidence that self-regulation is positively related to student academic achievement (Kornell & Metcalfe, 2006; Zimmerman & Kitsantas, 2005). As self-efficacy, metacognitive self-regulation, and attributions are all constructs that underlie the phases of the self-regulation process (Zimmerman, 1989), researchers are often interested in investigating differences in these constructs across groups by gender, socioeconomic status, ethnicity, and other grouping variables.

A central question to be addressed before comparing groups on constructs is whether the constructs have the same meaning for each group. Technically, this question translates into a set of questions about (a) equivalent relationships between the latent factors and their indicators in the CFA model across groups, (b) differential items functioning, (c) changes in the origin of the scale across groups, and (d) other aspects of group equivalency related to construct validity. Such questions are usually addressed through testing for factorial invariance of targeted construct(s) across groups. In the remainder of this section, the term *groups* is used to mean samples of data collected for either different groups (e.g., gender or ethnicity) or one group across different occasions.

The invariance of a factor model over different groups is called *factorial invariance* (or *multiple-group invariance*). Although there are approaches to testing multiple-group invariance in the framework of EFA (e.g., Cliff, 1966; Meredith, 1964), they focus only on similarity of factor patterns across groups. In contrast, testing for factorial invariance of CFA models addresses the configural invariance, measurement invariance, and structural invariance of the model (e.g., Byrne, 2004; Byrne, Shavelson, & Muthén, 1989; Cheung & Rensvold, 2002; Drasgow & Kanfer, 1985; Jöreskog & Sörbom, 1979; Meredith, 1993; Meredith & Teresi, 2006). With slight inconsistency, these three aspects of multiple-group invariance are defined in the literature as described next in this section.

6.7.2 Configural Invariance

Configural invariance refers to invariance of the model configuration (the pattern of free and fixed model parameters) across groups. To test for configural invariance, it is necessary to identify a baseline model, which is estimated for each group separately. The most parsimonious, yet substantively most meaningful and best fitting, model to the data for a group is referred to as *baseline model* for this group (e.g., Byrne, 2004; Byrne et al., 1989). Configural invariance is also referred to in the literature as *form invariance*.

6.7.3 Measurement Invariance

Measurement invariance refers to (a) metric invariance—equal factor loadings across groups, (b) scalar invariance—equal item intercepts across groups, and (c) invariance of item uniquenesses—equal item error variances/covariances across groups. Typically, measurement invariance is addressed at three levels. First, weak measurement invariance requires metric invariance. At this level, the equality of factor loadings across groups indicates equivalent relationships between the latent factors and their indicators in the CFA model. When metric invariance for a latent factor is in place, (a) relations between this factor and external variables can be compared across groups because a one-unit change in one group would be equal to one-unit change in any other group, yet (b) the factor means still cannot be compared as the origin of the scale may differ across groups.

Second, strong measurement invariance requires both metric and scalar invariance—that is, equal factor loadings and equal indicator intercepts (i.e., indicator means) across groups. When strong measurement invariance is in place, the comparison of factor means across groups is permissible. The lack of invariant intercepts signals differential item functioning. For example, students from different groups that have equal verbal ability may perform differently on some items in a verbal ability test because of, say, offensive language in these items that may affect students who belong to a particular group (e.g., Holland & Wainer, 1993).

Third, strict measurement invariance requires metric invariance, scalar invariance, and uniqueness invariance—that is, equal factor loadings, equal indicator intercepts, and equal item error variances/covariance across groups. The invariance of item uniquenesses across groups provides evidence that the items were measured with the same precision in each group. When strict measurement invariance is in place, the group differences on any item are due only to group differences on the common factors.

6.7.4 Structural Invariance

Structural invariance refers to invariance of factor variances and covariances. Keep in mind, however, that group comparisons on factor variances/covariances are meaningful only when the factor loadings are invariant.

Under the classification adopted here, there are three aspects of factorial invariance—configural, measurement, and structural invariance. To avoid confusion, *factorial invariance* and *multiple-group invariance* are used synonymously here, but be aware that there are occasions in the literature where factorial invariance is used to mean only the aspect of configural invariance (or form invariance). Which aspects of factorial invariance to test would depend on the specific validation goals. For example, strong measurement invariance (equal factor loadings and equal intercepts) across groups is necessary for comparing these groups on factor means. However, if the construct validation involves testing for invariance of factor variances and/or covariances across groups, then only weak measurement invariance (equal factor loadings) is a prerequisite. In all cases, however, the first step is to test for configural invariance—that is, to fit a baseline model for each group separately. The second step is to test for metric invariance (equal factor loadings) using the data for all groups simultaneously in order to obtain more efficient parameter estimates (e.g., Bentler, 2004; Jöreskog & Sörbom, 1996). These two steps must precede testing for other aspects of multigroup invariance (if necessary).

6.8 TESTING FOR FACTORIAL INVARIANCE

6.8.1 Approaches to Testing for Factorial Invariance

There are different approaches to testing for factorial invariance. Presented here is a commonly used multistage procedure in the framework of multiple-group confirmatory factor analysis (MGCFA; e.g., Byrne, 2004; Byrne et al., 1989; Jöreskog, 1971a; Marcoulides, Emrich, & Marcoulides, 2008; Mann, Rutstein, & Hancock, 2009; Steinmetz, Schmidt, Tina-Booh, Wieczorek, & Schwartz, 2009; Taris, Bok, & Meijer, 1998; Vandenberg & Lance, 2000). This procedure is based on a chi-square square difference test ($\Delta\chi^2$) between two nested models: a constrained model, with invariance assumed, that is nested within an unconstrained model, with no invariance assumed for specific parameters (e.g., factor loadings, intercepts, and so forth). Invariance is supported when the chi-square difference ($\Delta\chi^2 = \chi^2_{\text{constr.}} - \chi^2_{\text{unconstr.}}$) is *not* statistically significant at a prespecified level of significance (e.g., $\alpha = .05$). The analysis begins with the least constrained solution (total lack of invariance), and subsequent restrictions for equality of specific parameters across groups are imposed, thus producing nested models that are tested against each other using the chi-square difference test. This approach is referred to here as *step-up constraints method* of testing for factorial invariance across groups.

The step-up constraints method is preferable to a step-down strategy (e.g., Horn & McArdle, 1992), whereby the analysis starts with a model that contains all targeted invariance constraints and then gradually relaxes these constraints in models. Two important reasons for preferring the step-up method are that (a) testing for some aspects of invariance requires that other aspects of invariance are already in place—a condition that is easier to test under the step-up constraints method, and (b) under the step-down method, it can be difficult to determine which invariance aspects do not hold in case of poor model fit, especially with relatively complex CFA models.

6.8.2 Chi-Square Difference Test for Nested Models

Chi-Square Difference of ML-Based Chi-Square Values. After configural invariance across groups is established, testing for factorial invariance is conducted using a chi-square difference ($\Delta\chi^2$) test for two nested models. If the assumption of multivariate normality of the observed variables is met, $\Delta\chi^2$ is the difference of the usual maximum-likelihood chi-square (MLχ^2) values of the nested models. Under the step-up invariance constraints method, the testing is organized in a logical sequence of nested models ordered in an increasingly restrictive fashion. At each step, $\Delta\chi^2$ is used to test for invariance of factor loadings, intercepts, residual variances/covariances, or factor variances/covariances. A sequence of CFA models and respective $\Delta\chi^2$ tests is listed in Table 6.4. The starting model, referred to here as Model 0, is a baseline model that is fit in two different groups together, with no invariance assumed (i.e., all parameters are freely estimated). Next, Model 1 is obtained from Model 0 by constraining all factor loadings to be equal across the two groups. As Model 1 is nested within Model 0, a nonsignificant chi-square difference for these two models, $\Delta\chi^2_{M1-M0}$, will indicate invariance of the factor loadings (i.e., weak measurement invariance). The other models and tests in Table 6.4 are interpreted in a similar fashion (note, however, that Model 4 is nested within Model 2, not within Model 3).

Satorra–Bentler Scaled Chi-Square Difference. As noted earlier, the usual maximum-likelihood chi-square statistic (MLχ^2) is based on the assumption of multivariate normality for the observed variables (indicators). If this assumption is not met, the chi-square difference test based on MLχ^2 estimates for the nested models can be misleading. This problem can be avoided by computing chi-square differences using the Satorra–Bentler scaled chi-square, SBχ^2, described earlier (see Section 6.6.1). It is important, however, to note that the difference of two SBχ^2 statistics (SB$\Delta\chi^2$) is *not* distributed as chi-square (e.g., Satorra, 2000). Instead, an additional scaling of SB$\Delta\chi^2$, referred to as *Satorra–Bentler scaled chi-square difference* (SBS$\Delta\chi^2$), follows the chi-square distribution (Satorra & Bentler, 1999, 2001). The computation of SBS$\Delta\chi^2$ is illustrated with Example 6.6 in Appendix 6.2. Keep in mind that in either case ($\Delta\chi^2$ or SBS$\Delta\chi^2$), the chi-square difference is sensitive to sample size.

TABLE 6.4

Steps in Testing for Measurement and Structural Invariance Across Two Groups

Baseline Model	Parameters Constrainted to Be Equal	$\Delta\chi^2$ Test	Type of Invariance[a]
Model 0	None		
Model 1	Factor loadings	$\Delta\chi^2_{M1-M0}$	Weak measurement invariance
Model 2	Factor loadings and item intercepts	$\Delta\chi^2_{M2-M1}$	Strong measurement invariance
Model 3	Factor loadings, item intercepts, and residual item variances/covariances	$\Delta\chi^2_{M3-M2}$	Strict measurement invariance
Model 4	Factor loadings, item intercepts, and factor variances/covariances	$\Delta\chi^2_{M4-M2}$	Structural invariance

Note. From "Testing for Factorial Invariance in the Context of Construct Validation," by D. M. Dimitrov, 2010, *Measurement and Evaluation in Counseling and Development, 43,* p. 126. Copyright 2010 by Sage Publications. Reprinted with permission.
[a]Invariance is indicated by nonsignificant $\Delta\chi^2$ test.

6.8.3 CFI Difference

Given that model chi-square (χ^2 or $SB\chi^2$) and modification indices are sensitive to sample size, some researchers have suggested that changes in other fit statistics that occur with imposition of parameter constraints should also be considered in testing for factorial invariance across groups (e.g., Cheung & Rensvold, 2002; Little, 1997; Vandenberg & Lance, 2000). In a Monte Carlo simulation study, Cheung and Rensvold (2002) examined changes in goodness-of-fit indices caused by invariance constraints on specific parameters (factor loadings, intercepts, and so forth) across two groups. They found that among frequently used fit indices, such as CFI, TLI, and RMSEA, only the CFI difference ($\Delta CFI = CFI_{constr.} - CFI_{unconstr.}$) was not affected by the specification accuracy in the overall model. On the basis of this finding, Cheung and Rensvold (2002) recommended that along with $\Delta\chi^2$, researchers also report ΔCFI with results on testing for invariance. Under the assumption of multivariate normality, they suggested that the hypothesized invariance of the respective parameters should not be retained when there is a decrease of 0.01 or larger in CFI. That is, a negative ΔCFI value lower than or equal to –0.01 ($\Delta CFI \leq -0.01$) would indicate a lack of invariance (e.g., $\Delta CFI = -0.02$). There is no need to worry when CFI increases ($\Delta CFI > 0$), which may occur because of changes in degrees of freedom and sample fluctuations, because larger CFIs indicate better fit.

Although the proposed rule for rejecting invariance ($\Delta CFI \leq -0.01$) needs further verification, researchers are encouraged to report ΔCFI to complement the chi-square difference test for invariance of model parameters across groups. Reporting ΔCFI, along with $\Delta\chi^2$ and some absolute indices of fit such as RMSEA, is gaining popularity in studies that involve testing for multiple-group invariance (e.g., Green-Demers, Legault, Pelletier, & Pelletier, 2008; Le, Casillas, Robbins, & Langley, 2005; Lievens, Anseel, Harris, & Eisenberg, 2007; Whitman, Van Rooy, Viswesvaran, & Kraus, 2009; A. D. Wu & Zumbo, 2007).

The reader should be alert, however, that some studies on invariance refer incorrectly to Cheung and Rensvold's (2002) rule for rejecting invariance as "ΔCFI higher than .01" (e.g., Libbrecht, Lievens, & Schollaert, 2010; Lievens et al., 2007). Under this incorrect interpretation, $\Delta CFI > .01$ should yield rejection of invariance when, in fact, a positive ΔCFI indicates fit improvement, thus providing evidence of invariance. Only $\Delta CFI \leq -0.01$ is indicative of meaningful drop in fit and, thus, should be interpreted as a signal for lack of invariance. Perhaps part of the confusion in this regard is due to a misfortunate typo in a summary statement in the original article (Cheung & Rensvold, 2002): "A value of ΔCFI smaller than or equal to –0.01 indicates that the null hypothesis of invariance should not be rejected" (p. 251). In fact, it is just the opposite, $\Delta CFI \leq -0.01$ indicates a decrease in CFI larger than 0.01, and, thus, the null hypothesis of invariance *should* be rejected. Also, keep in mind that the $\Delta CFI \leq -0.01$ rule was derived under the assumption of multivariate normality.

6.8.4 Partial Invariance

There are situations in which there is no perfect invariance for specific parameters, but neither is there evidence of their complete inequality. This situation is called *partial invariance*. As indicated in previous studies, given the stringent nature of the hypotheses for invariance, the invariance is a matter of degree estimated by the proportion of parameters that are invariant (e.g., Byrne et al., 1989).

Suppose that in testing for invariance across two groups the factor loadings are invariant (i.e., $\Delta\chi^2_{M1-M0}$ is not statistically significant), but $\Delta\chi^2_{M2-M1}$ *is* statistically significant, thus indicating that the intercepts are *not* invariant across the two groups. To determine the degree of partial measurement invariance in this case, Model 2 (see Table 6.4) must be modified by setting some intercepts free (non invariant) across the two groups. Which intercepts to start freeing depends on the values of their modification indices reported for Model 2 by the software being used (e.g., Mplus, Amos, EQS, or LISREL). As noted earlier, the MI for a parameter gives the expected drop in the model's chi-square value if this parameter is freely estimated. The MI for one parameter is statistically significant if it exceeds 3.84 (the chi-square value with $df = 1$). If there are several parameters with statistically significant MIs, they should be freed one at a time, starting with the parameter that has the largest MI. There is no strict rule as to what degree of partial invariance is acceptable. Less than 20% freed parameters seems to be an acceptable level in practical applications, but it is up to researchers to decide—just be sure to report the observed degree of invariance with the results (e.g., Byrne et al., 1989; Levine et al., 2003).

The presence of measurement invariance is critical for practical comparisons of groups on constructs. However, testing for invariant item uniquenesses (error variances/covariances) is not of practical interest in comparing group means on a construct. Moreover, key references show that testing for invariance of item uniquenesses represents an overly restrictive test of the data (e.g., Bentler, 2004; Byrne, 1988). The assumption of structural invariance (invariant factor variances and covariances) is analogous to the assumption of homogeneous variance–covariance matrices in MANOVA. As shown in Table 6.4, this assumption is met when the chi-square difference between Model 4 and Model 2 ($\Delta\chi^2_{M4-M2}$) is nonsignificant. As to testing for invariant factor means across groups, Marsh et al. (2009) noted that "models with freely estimated indicator intercepts and freely estimated latent means are not identified, so that the invariance of these parameters cannot be tested in the same model. The primary purpose of a model with invariant intercepts and latent means freely estimated is to test whether mean differences at the level of individual items can be explained in terms of differences in latent means" (pp. 442–443).

Example 6.2 The purpose of this example is to illustrate testing for invariance across two groups. Specifically, the CFA model of two related constructs, Psychosocial Distress and Successful Coping, depicted in Figure 6.2, was tested for invariance over two groups of people with multiple sclerosis. The two groups were formed based on their typical course of illness relapsing (relapsing or relapsing–remitting) or progressive (secondary progressive or primary progressive). These two groups are referred to hereafter as *relapsing illness* ($n = 669$) and *progressive illness* ($n = 359$). The data consist of 1,028 observations on the grouping variable GROUP (0 = relapsing, 1 = progressive) and seven survey items (Item 1, . . ., Item 7) used as indicators of the two constructs of interest as shown in Figure 6.2 (see also Table 6.1).

The CFA model in Figure 6.2 is used here as a baseline model and tested for data fit in each of the two groups separately using Mplus. The goodness-of-fit indices indicated a very good model fit for each group (see Table 6.5). The standardized factor loadings with the baseline model for each group are provided in Table 6.6. Thus, we can conclude that there is a configural invariance of the CFA model in Figure 6.2 over the two groups of people with multiple sclerosis (relapsing illness and progressive illness).

After configural invariance of the model is established, the testing for measurement and structural invariance is conducted by using the sequential procedures described earlier (see Table 6.4). As preliminary tests indicated multivariate normality of the seven observed variables in this example, the chi-square difference tests in these procedures were based on the usual chi-square values under the ML estimator. The results, obtained through the use of Mplus, are summarized in Table 6.7 (the Mplus code is given in Appendix 6.1).

TABLE 6.5

Goodness-of-Fit Indices for the Baseline Model in Two Groups (Relapsing and Progressive Illness)

Group	χ^2	*df*	CFI	TLI	SRMR	RMSEA	90% CI for RMSEA LL	90% CI for RMSEA UL
Relapsing	16.165[a]	13	.999	.998	.015	.019	.000	.045
Progressive	24.200[b]	13	.988	.980	.027	.049	.015	.079

Note. CFI = Comparative Fit Index; TLI = Tucker–Lewis Index; SRMR = standardized root mean square residual; RMSEA = root mean square error of approximation; CI = confidence interval; LL = lower limit; UL = upper limit. From "Testing for Factorial Invariance in the Context of Construct Validation," by D. M. Dimitrov, 2010, *Measurement and Evaluation in Counseling and Development, 43,* p. 126. Copyright 2010 by Sage Publications. Reprinted with permission.
[a]p = .240 and n = 669. [b]p = .029 and n = 359.

As can be seen, the chi-square difference between Model 1 and Model 0 ($\Delta\chi^2_{M1-M0}$) is not statistically significant, $\chi^2(5) = 3.893$, $p > .05$, thus indicating invariance of the factor loadings across the two groups. However, the chi-square difference between Model 2 and Model 1 ($\Delta\chi^2_{M2-M1}$) is statistically significant, $\chi^2(5) = 12.491$, $p < .05$, which indicates that there is *no* complete invariance of the intercepts across the two groups. Examination of the MIs in this case showed that there were two modification indices in the Mplus output with chi-square values exceeding the critical chi-square value of 3.84 for $df = 1$: namely, MI = 7.29 for Item 1, and MI = 8.47 for Item 2 (both in the relapsing illness group). Following the recommendation of freeing one parameter at a time, starting with the largest MI, Model 2 was modified by freeing the intercept for Item 2 (i.e., allowing the intercept for Item 2 to have different estimates across the two groups). With this, the chi-square value for Model 2 dropped from 56.749 to 48.201 (this modified model is labeled "Model 2P" in Table 6.7). The chi-square difference between Model 2P and Model 1 was no longer statistically significant, $\chi^2(4) = 3.943$, $p > .05$, thus indicating that there are invariant factor loadings and invariant intercepts except for the intercept of one indicator (Item 2).

Still at the level of measurement invariance, we continue with testing for invariance of item uniquenesses. As a step in this direction, Model 3 is obtained from Model 2P by im-

TABLE 6.6

Standardized Factor Loadings and Standard Errors by Groups

Construct/Indicator	Relapsing Illness SFL	Relapsing Illness *SE*	Progressive Illness SFL	Progressive Illness *SE*
Psychosocial Distress				
Item 1	.82	.02	.75	.03
Item 2	.76	.02	.75	.03
Item 3	.74	.02	.65	.04
Item 4	.65	.03	.61	.04
Successful Coping				
Item 5	.88	.02	.80	.03
Item 6	.76	.02	.76	.03
Item 7	.76	.02	.78	.03

Note. All factor loadings are statistically significant (p < .001). The correlation between the two constructs is –.51 and –.45 for the relapsing and progressive illness groups, respectively. SFL = standard factor loading; *SE* = standard error. From "Testing for Factorial Invariance in the Context of Construct Validation," by D. M. Dimitrov, 2010, *Measurement and Evaluation in Counseling and Development, 43,* p. 129. Copyright 2010 by Sage Publications. Reprinted with permission.

Note 6.3

For illustration, the Sattora–Bentler scaled chi-square differences (SBS$\Delta\chi^2$), discussed in Section 6.8.2, were also computed for the data in this example (see Appendix 6.2). The results on testing for invariance were identical under the use of the usual $\Delta\chi^2$ and SBS$\Delta\chi^2$, which was expected under multivariate normality of the data in this case.

posing equal variances and covariances of the items residuals across the two groups (note that Model 3 is nested within Model 2P). The chi-square difference between these two models ($\Delta\chi^2_{M3-M2P}$) is statistically significant, $\chi^2(7) = 32.099$, $p < .01$, thus indicating that the item uniquenesses are *not* invariant across the two groups. Examination of the MIs showed that the MIs for the residual variances of two items were greater than 3.84 (critical value for chi-square with $df = 1$): MI = 9.830 for Item 1, and MI = 18.196 for Item 5. The residual variance of Item 5, with the larger MI, was freed first, but the resulting chi-square difference was still statistically significant (not shown in Table 6.7). After the residual variances for both items were freed, the chi-square for the resulting model (denoted "Model 3P" in Table 6.7) dropped to 53.597. With this, the chi-square difference between Model 3P and Model 2P ($\Delta\chi^2_{M3P-M2P}$) was no longer statistically significant, $\chi^2(5) = 5.396$, $p > .05$. Thus, the item uniquenesses were partially invariant, with the residual variances of two items freely estimated. We can conclude that there is a partial measurement invariance, with invariance of all factor loadings, invariance of all but one intercept, and invariance of all but two item uniquenesses.

The adequate level of measurement invariance achieved with Model 2P (invariance of all factor loadings and invariance of all but one intercept) allows us to continue with testing for structural invariance. As a step in this direction, Model 4 is obtained from Model 2P by imposing invariant factor variances and covariances. Note that Model 4 and Model 3 (or Model 3P) are treated independently, with each of them being nested within Model 2P. The chi-square difference between Model 4 and Model 2P ($\Delta\chi^2_{M4-M2P}$) is not statistically significant, $\chi^2(3) = 1.707$, $p > .05$, thus indicating that structural invariance is in place.

As noted earlier, the CFI difference (ΔCFI) can provide some triangulation in testing for invariance (Cheung & Rensvold, 2002). As shown in Table 6.7, CFI decreases by a magnitude

TABLE 6.7

Testing for Measurement and Structural Invariance Across Two Groups

Model	χ^2	*df*	Comparison	$\Delta\chi^2$	Δdf	CFI	ΔCFI[a]	RMSEA
Model 0	40.365	26	—		—	.995	—	.033
Model 1	44.258	31	M1 – M0	3.893	5	.996	.001	.029
Model 2	56.749	36	M2 – M1	12.491*	5	.993	**–.003**	.033
Model 2P	48.201	35	M2P – M1	3.943	4	.996	.003	.027
Model 3	80.300	42	M3 – M2P	32.099**	7	.986	**–.010**	.042
Model 3P	53.597	40	M3P – M2P	5.396	5	.995	.008	.026
Model 4	49.908	38	M4 – M2P	1.707	3	.996	.001	.026

Note. CFI = Comparative Fit Index; RMSEA = root mean square error of approximation; Model 0 = baseline model (no invariance); Model 1 = invariant slopes; Model 2 = invariant slopes and invariant intercepts; Model 2P = invariant slopes and partially invariant intercepts (free intercept of Item 2); Model 3 = invariant slopes, partially invariant intercepts, and invariant uniqueness; Model 3P = invariant slopes, partially invariant intercepts, and partially invariant uniqueness (free error variances for Item 1 and Item 5); Model 4 = invariant slopes, partially invariant intercepts, and invariant factor variances and covariances (structural invariance). From "Testing for Factorial Invariance in the Context of Construct Validation," by D. M. Dimitrov, 2010, *Measurement and Evaluation in Counseling and Development, 43,* p. 126. Copyright 2010 by Sage Publications. Reprinted with permission.

[a]ΔCFI ≤ –0.01 and boldface signals lack of invariance (Cheung & Rensvold, 2002).

*$p < .05$. **$p < .01$.

of 0.01 or larger (ΔCFI ≤ -0.01) only when invariance is rejected by the $\Delta\chi^2$ test, thus indicating worsening of the model fit in these two cases. Based on the $\Delta\chi^2$ and ΔCFI results, the conclusion is that there is a reasonable level of partial measurement invariance and structural invariance for the tested CFA model of Psychosocial Distress and Successful Coping across two groups of people with multiple sclerosis (relapsing and progressive illness groups).

For studies that have used testing for factorial invariance to validated assessment scale data in areas related to counseling, the reader may refer, for example, to Ang, Lau, Tan, and Lim (2007); Cordon and Finney (2008); Immekus and Maller (2010); Inglés, Marzo, Hidalgo, Zhou, and Garcia-Fernandez (2008); Lopez, Morúa, and Rice (2007); Pomplun and Omar (2001); Steger (2007); and Yin & Fan (2003).

6.9 COMPARING GROUPS ON CONSTRUCTS

6.9.1 Why Compare Groups on Constructs?

Testing hypotheses about mean differences among the groups on the construct of interest is often a part of collecting evidence about the external aspect of construct validity. For example, validation of scale data that assess motivation goals (task mastery, ego, and work avoidance) of middle-school students may involve testing for gender differences on motivation goals because hypotheses about such differences have been stated in theoretical and empirical studies (e.g., Meece & Jones, 1996; Ridley & Novak, 1983).

There are two major approaches to addressing this task in the context of SEM: *structured means modeling* (SMM) and *group-code modeling* (e.g., Bollen, 1989; Dimitrov, 2008; Hancock, 2004; Kaplan, 2000; Schumacker & Lomax, 1996). Just like a *t* test, the SMM method keeps the data from the two groups separate. In contrast, the group-code modeling keeps the data from the two groups together and is based on the idea of using dummy coding in regression analysis for group comparisons. The SMM method requires invariance of factor loadings and intercepts across the groups, whereas the group-code modeling assumes invariance of factor loadings, item uniquenesses, and factor variances/covariances (unlike the SMM, the group–code modeling does not involve intercepts because all variables are scaled as deviation scores). On the other hand, the group-code modeling has an advantage over the SMM method in terms of simplicity and design flexibility. A brief presentation of the group–code modeling, with an example of its application using the CFA model described in Example 6.2, is provided next.

6.9.2 Group-Code (MIMIC) Modeling

As already noted, group-code modeling keeps the data from two groups together and is based on the idea of using dummy coding in regression analysis for group comparisons. The construct of interest is regressed on a dummy variable, X, which assumes values of 0 and 1. All subjects in one group, referred to as *reference group,* are assigned a score of 0 on X, whereas all subjects in the other group are assigned a score of 1 on X. To specify that the group comparison is within the framework of SEM, the group–code modeling is called *multiple-indicator, multiple-cause (MIMIC) modeling*. As an example, a MIMIC model for gender differences on motivation, as measured by three indicators (Y_1, Y_2, and Y_3), is depicted in Figure 6.4.

The structural part of the MIMIC model is presented by the regression of the construct, η, on the dummy variable, X, with coding values of 0 and 1 (0 = male and 1 = female):

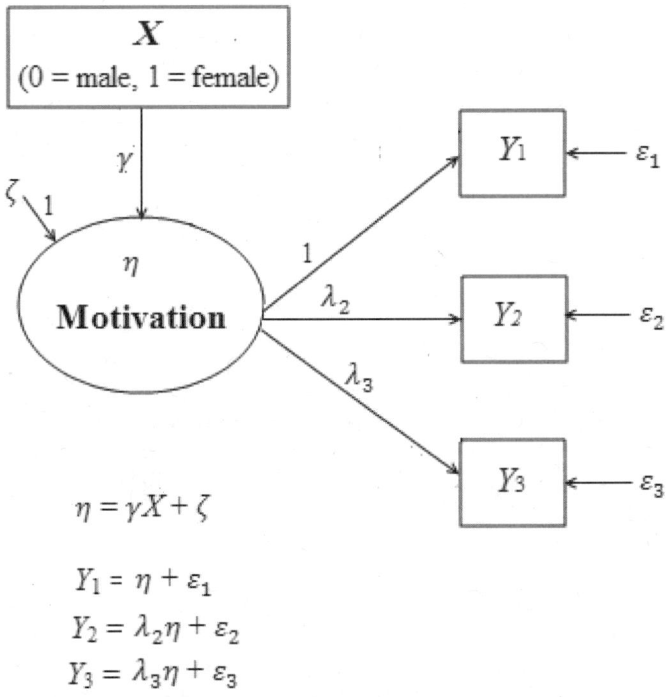

FIGURE 6.4

Multiple-Indicator, Multiple-Cause (MIMIC) Model for Gender Differences on Motivation

$$\eta = \gamma X + \zeta, \qquad (6.1)$$

where γ (*gamma*) is the regression coefficient, representing the impact of the dummy variable X on the construct η, and ζ (*dzeta*) is the residual in η (i.e., the part in η that is not explained by gender differences). The variance of this residual, VAR(ζ), is called *disturbance variance*. There is no intercept in Equation 6.1 because all variables, including the dummy variable X, are treated as if there were presented as deviation scores.

A statistically significant direct effect of the dummy code (covariate, X) on the latent factor (construct, η) indicates population heterogeneity (i.e., group differences on latent means). A statistically significant direct effect of the dummy code, X, on an indicator (item, Y_i) signals differential item functioning—that is, the item is operating differentially across the two groups. Note that such direct effect is not depicted in Figure 6.4. A direct effect from the dummy code, X, to an indicator is included in the model to test for invariance of the indicator's intercept across the two groups coded by X. This procedure is done when (a) there is a good reason to expect that the indicator may behave differentially across the groups, or (b) a preliminary testing for measurement invariance has indicated a lack of intercept invariance for the indicator (e.g., as was the case with Item 2 in Example 6.2 [see Table 6.7]) so the goal is to determine the direction and the magnitude of the effect of differential item functioning.

Clearly, the statistical significance of the structural coefficient γ and its magnitude (effect size) is of central interest in testing for between-group differences on the construct of interest. A statistically significant positive γ would indicate that the group coded 1 (females) score higher on motivation compared with the reference group (0 = males). In fact, the magnitude of γ reflects the difference between the population means for the two groups. This difference can be seen by replacing X in Equation 6.1 with its binary values ($X = 0$ and $X = 1$) and taking into account that the mean of the residual ζ is zero. The standardized effect size of the difference between the means of the two groups on the construct of interest (η) is estimated as follows (Hancock, 2001):

$$\hat{d} = \frac{|\hat{\gamma}|}{\sqrt{\widehat{VAR}(\zeta)}}, \tag{6.2}$$

where $\widehat{VAR}(\zeta)$ is the estimated variance of the residual ζ—that is, the variance in the construct (η) that is not explained by the group differences. As $\widehat{VAR}(\zeta)$ represents an estimate of a pooled within-group variance, the effect size estimate, $\hat{d}$, shows how many latent standard deviations separate the means of the two groups on the construct of interest (η). The values of $\hat{\gamma}$ and $\widehat{VAR}(\zeta)$ are provided with computer programs for SEM such as Mplus, LISREL, Amos, and EQS.

Example 6.3 The purpose of this example is to illustrate the use of group–code (MIMIC) modeling for the comparison of two groups of people with multiple sclerosis (relapsing illness group and progressive illness group) on the constructs Psychosocial Distress and Successful Coping. The MIMIC model for this group comparison is depicted in Figure 6.5. The model in Figure 6.5 is obtained by incorporating the dummy variable GROUP for course of illness (0 = relapsing, 1 = progressive) into the CFA model in Figure 6.2. The data used in Example 6.2 were also used for the MIMIC modeling in this example ($n = 699$ for the relapsing illness group, and $n = 359$ for the progressive illness group).

Based on the testing for measurement and structural invariance described in Example 6.2, we may consider that the MIMIC assumption of invariant factor loadings, item uniquenesses, and factor variances/covariances across the two groups is met. The MIMIC analysis was performed using the Mplus code provided in Table 6.8.

For the model in Figure 6.5, the goodness-of-fit indices indicated that, despite the statistically significant chi-square value, $\chi^2(17) = 31.91$, $p = .015$, there is a good model fit: CFI = .995, SRMR = .016, and RMSEA = .029, with 90% CI [.013, .045]. In Figure 6.5, the factor loadings are standardized, so their squared values indicate the proportion of the variance in the indicator accounted for by the variability in the construct. The statistically significant standardized coefficient associated with the two-way arrow connecting "Psychosocial Distress" and "Successful Coping" represents an estimate of the correlation between these two constructs ($r = -.68$, $p < .001$). The structural coefficient with the path from "GROUP" to "Psychosocial Distress" (.04) is not statistically significant, thus indicating that the two groups do *not* differ on Psychosocial Distress. However, the statistically significant direct effect of "GROUP" on Item 2 indicates that this item is operating differentially across the two groups (recall that, as shown in Example 6.2, the intercept for Item 2 was *not* invariant across the two groups in testing for measurement invariance). Given the group coding (0 = relapsing, 1 = progressive), the negative sign of this direct effect (–.07) indicates that the progressive illness group performed slightly lower than expected on Item 2 ("In the last month, how often you felt nervous and distressed?").

The standardized structural coefficient for the path from "GROUP" to "Successful Coping" ($\hat{\gamma}_2 = -.07$) is statistically significant ($p < .05$), thus indicating that the two groups differ on

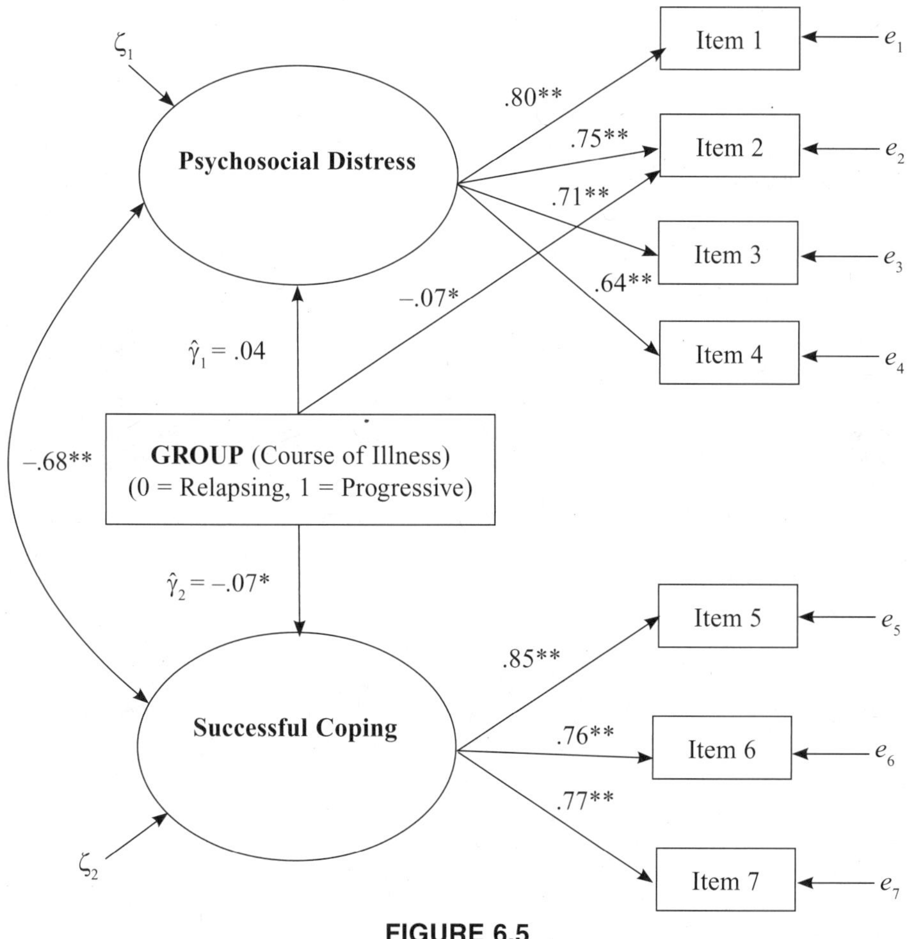

FIGURE 6.5

Multiple-Indicator, Multiple-Cause (MIMIC) Model for Group Differences on Two Latent Factors (Psychosocial Distress and Successful Coping)

$^*p < .05$. $^{**}p < .001$.

Successful Coping. Given the group coding (0 = relapsing, 1 = progressive), the negative sign of this coefficient shows that members of the progressive illness group score lower than relapsing illness group members on Successful Coping. The unstandardized estimates of the structural coefficient γ_2, and the residual variance for successful coping, $VAR(\zeta_2)$, not shown in Figure 6.5, were as follows: $\hat{\gamma}_2 = -0.12$ and $\widehat{VAR}(\zeta_2) = 0.66$. When these estimates are used with Equation 6.2, the effect size of the mean group difference on successful coping is obtained: $\hat{d} = |-0.12|/\sqrt{0.66} = 0.15$. This result indicates that there is a

TABLE 6.8

Mplus Code for the Multiple-Indicator, Multiple-Cause Model in Figure 6.5

```
     DATA:  FILE IS "C:\EXAMPLE_6_2.dat";
 VARIABLE:  NAMES ARE group X1-X7
            USEVARIABLES ARE group X1-X7;
 ANALYSIS:  TYPE IS GENERAL;
    MODEL:  DISTRESS BY X1-X4;
            COPING BY X5-X7;
            DISTRESS, COPING, X2 ON group;
   OUTPUT:  MODINDICES (3.84) STANDARDIZED;
```

Note. DISTRESS = Psychosocial Distress; COPING = Successful Coping.

small effect size ($\hat{d} = 0.15$) of the difference in successful coping between people with a progressive course versus a relapsing course of multiple sclerosis—according to Cohen's (1988) guidelines, the magnitude of the effect size of the difference between two group means is (a) small if $d = .2$, (b) medium if $d = .5$, and (c) large if $d = .8$.

6.10 HIGHER-ORDER CFA

6.10.1 What Is Higher-Order CFA?

The CFA models presented thus far are first-order measurement models, and the factors involved in such models are referred to as *first-order factors*. Typically, higher-order CFA models reflect theory-driven hypotheses about more general factors that underlie the first-order factors. A classical example in this regard is a second-order factor model of intelligence based on the Spearman's general factor (*g*) theory of intelligence. Under the *g*-model, it is hypothesized that the positive correlations between four first-order factors of intelligence (verbal ability, quantitative ability, visualspatial ability, and mechanical skills) are explained by a general (second-order) factor of intelligence (Spearman, 1927). Another classic example is the hierarchical structure of the Sixteen Personality Factor Questionnaire (or 16PF), a multiple-choice personality questionnaire in which 16 primary traits represent first-order factors and five higher order traits represent second-order factors in the 16PF model (Cattell, Cattell, & Cattell, 1993). The five second-order factors, referred to as the Big Five, represent five major dimensions of personality. Identified originally by Cattell (1946), the Big Five have had their comprehensiveness supported in research on personality traits over the past half century and have been widely adopted in other major personality tests. For example, the five-factor model (FFM; Costa & McCrae, 1990, 1991, 1992, 2003) identified the Big Five as Openness, Conscientiousness, Agreeableness, Extraversion, and Neuroticism (OCEAN). Keith, Fine, Taub, Reynolds, and Kranzler (2006) used higher order CFA for the factorial structure of the Wechsler Intelligence Scale for Children (4th ed.).

Figure 6.6 depicts a second-order CFA model of General Wellness as a dimension that underlies three primary traits—Mental Health, Social Functioning, and Vitality—each of which is measured by three items. Statistically, the second-order factor accounts for covariation among the three first-order factors. The disturbances of the first-order factors (ζ_1, ζ_2, and ζ_3) represent the variance unaccounted for by the second-order factor.

A second-order CFA model, similar in structure to that depicted in Figure 6.6, was used by Smith, Rosenstein, and Granaas (2001) in a study of the factorial structure of the Self-Rating Depression Scale (SDS; Zung, 1965). Specifically, they represented depression as a general factor underlying three specific symptoms of depression: affective, somatic, and psychological.

6.10.2 Identification and Acceptability of Higher-Order Models

In general, the rules of identification in first-order CFA apply to the higher-order part of the model. The direct effects of the higher-order factor(s) on lower-order factors and the correlations between higher-order factors (if more than one) account for covariation of the lower-order factors. Keep in mind that (a) the number of higher-order factors and higher-order factor loadings is less than the number of correlations between the lower level factors, and (b) the number of freely estimated parameters in the higher-order level of the model must not exceed the total number of factor variances and covariances in the first-order solution. The model in Figure 6.6, and in general any model that specifies three first-order

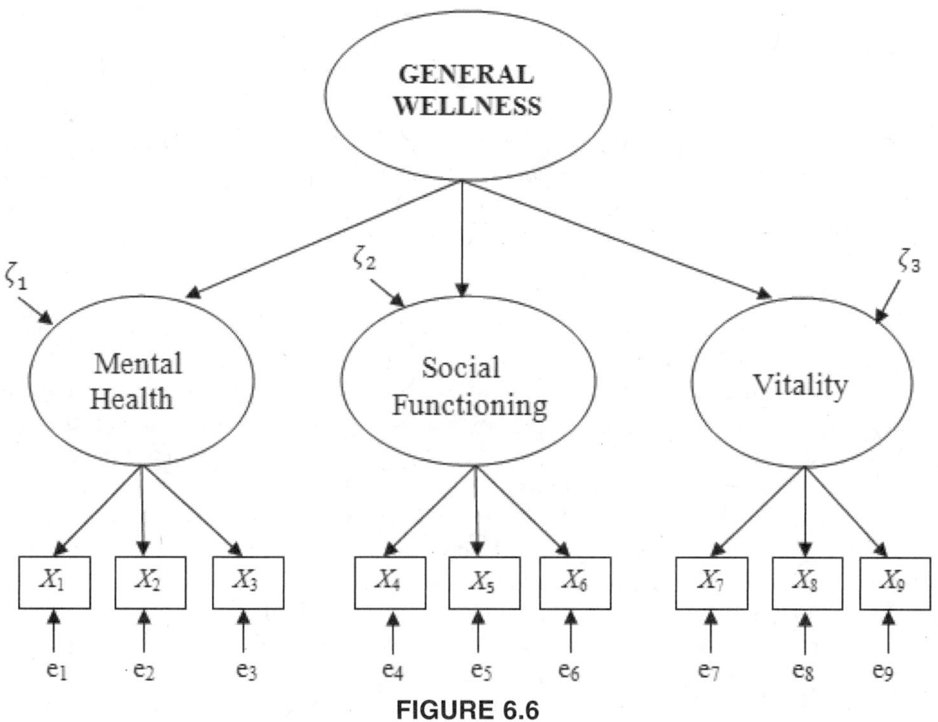

FIGURE 6.6

A Second-Order Confirmatory Factor Analysis Model for Wellness

Note. From "Testing for Factorial Invariance in the Context of Construct Validation," by D. M. Dimitrov, 2010, *Measurement and Evaluation in Counseling and Development, 43,* p. 131. Copyright 2010 by Sage Publications. Reprinted with permission.

factors and a single second-order, is a just-identified model (see the analogy of a first-order just-identified model in Figure 6.3B). Indeed, there are six freely estimated parameters in the second-order level: three second-order factor loadings and three residual variances (disturbances, ζ_1, ζ_2, and ζ_3), assuming that the variance of the second-order factor is fixed to 1.0 (or, alternatively, one of the first-order factors is used as a reference indicator of the second-order factor). At the same time, the number of known elements is also six (three variances of the first-order factors plus three covariances among them), thus indicating that the model is just-identified. Despite its limitations, a just-identified higher-order model may be substantively meaningful and can help model interpretations as it allows the researcher to examine relationships between higher-order factors and observed measures. As with first-order models, (a) underidentified second-order models are useless, (b) overidentified higher-order models are preferable, and (c) an empirical underidentification in the higher-order part of the model may occur when, because of sampling fluctuation, the estimate of a correlation between two first-order factors equals zero (see Section 6.5). Keep in mind that for higher-order CFA models, it is not enough that the degrees of freedom for the overall model are positive—the higher order structure must also be overidentified.

There are three major steps in performing higher order CFA: (a) Develop a conceptually sound and statistically fitting first-order model, (b) examine the magnitude and pattern of correlations between the first-order factors, and (c) if there are meaningful patterns of (moderate or higher magnitude) correlations between the first-order factors, fit the second-order model. To establish a metric for a higher-order factor, either fix its variance to 1.0 or specify a lower-order factor as a reference indicator for the higher-order factor (both approaches yield identical model fit indices and completely standardized parameter estimates). When the higher-order model is overidentified, its acceptability is supported by a nonsignificant chi-square difference test between the higher-order model and the first-order model (i.e., the higher-order model should not yield a significant decrease in model fit). This rule does not apply to a just-identified higher-order model because its chi-square value and other goodness-of-fit indices are equal to their counterparts produced by the first-order model, that is, $\Delta\chi^2(0) = 0$. In either case, the second-order factor loadings should be statistically significant and sizable enough to support substantive relations between lower-order and higher-order factors.

Example 6.4. The purpose of this example is to illustrate a second-order CFA using the model in Figure 6.6, where the covariation among three first-order factors (Mental Health, Social Functioning, and Vitality) is accounted for by a second-order factor (General Wellness). Each first-order factor is measured by three items of a self-rating scale. Appendix 6.3 contains the Mplus code for this analysis and the input matrix, with the sample standard deviations of nine items and correlations between them (N = 460). As noted earlier, the second-order model in Figure 6.6 is just-identified, but it is substantively meaningful. Moreover, the purpose here is only to illustrate second-order CFA using Mplus. The obtained results are then used to illustrate the Schmid–Leiman transformation, which makes it possible to examine the relationship of the observed measures to higher order factors. The illustrated approach is applicable to more complex higher order models.

As a first step, only the model with first-order factors was fit using the input matrix in Appendix 6.3. The goodness-of-fit indices indicated an excellent fit: $\chi^2(24) = 28.198$, $p = .252$; CFI = .992, TLI = .988, SRMR = .028, and RMSEA = .020, with 90% CI [.000, .044]. All first-order completely standardized factor loadings were statistically significant and varied in magnitude from .823 to .931, thus indicating dependability in the relations of the first-order factors to their indicators (see Table 6.9). Also, the intercorrelations between the first-order factors (not reported in Table 6.9) were statistically significant and moderate in magnitude.

Given the very good fit of the first-order factor model and the statistically significant moderate intercorrelations between the first-order factors, the second-order model depicted in Figure 6.6 was fit (see Appendix 6.3). The goodness-of-fit indices obtained with the second-order model were identical to their counterparts obtained with the first-order model. The reason the indices were the same was because, as noted earlier, the second-order part of the model in this example is just-identified. Keep in mind that with an overidentified model, which is the typical (and recommended) case in the practice of higher-order CFA, it would be useful to use the chi-square difference test between the first-order and second-order models (a nonsignificant chi-square difference is needed to accept the higher-order model). Completely standardized parameter estimates for both the first-order and second-order models are provided with the selected Mplus output in Table 6.9. All second-order factor loadings are statistically significant ($p < .001$) and vary in magnitude from 0.549 to 0.659. These results indicate that the second-order CFA model is acceptable and provides evidence of the structural aspect of General Wellness as a general dimension for the primary traits of Mental Health, Social Functioning, and Vitality. The completely standardized parameter estimates in Table 6.9 are used in a continuation of this analysis provided next with the illustration of the Schmid–Leiman transformation.

TABLE 6.9

Selected Mplus Output for the Second-Order Model of Wellness (Comments Added)

Mplus Item	Est.	*SE*	Est./*SE*	*p* value	Comment
MH by					
X1	0.900	0.015	61.021	.000	First-order factor loadings on Mental Health
X2	0.869	0.016	53.644	.000	
X3	0.823	0.019	44.147	.000	
SF by					
X4	0.893	0.015	58.710	.000	First-order factor loadings on Social Functioning
X5	0.861	0.017	51.400	.000	
X6	0.833	0.018	45.698	.000	
VT by					
X7	0.931	0.012	78.864	.000	First-order factor loadings on Vitality
X8	0.859	0.015	55.671	.000	
X9	0.861	0.015	56.238	.000	
GW by					
MH	0.549	0.060	9.161	.000	Second-order factor loadings on General Wellness
SF	0.562	0.061	9.275	.000	
VT	0.659	0.065	10.150	.000	
Residual Variances					
X1	0.189	0.027	7.133	.000	Residual variances (item uniquenesses) for X1, X2, . . ., X9
X2	0.245	0.028	8.719	.000	
X3	0.323	0.031	10.520	.000	
X4	0.202	0.027	7.431	.000	
X5	0.259	0.029	8.994	.000	
X6	0.307	0.030	10.101	.000	
X7	0.134	0.022	6.095	.000	
X8	0.263	0.026	9.908	.000	
X9	0.259	0.026	9.829	.000	
MH	0.698	0.066	10.595	.000	Disturbance for Mental Health
SF	0.685	0.068	10.063	.000	Disturbance for Social Functioning
VT	0.566	0.086	6.615	.000	Disturbance for Vitality

Note. Est. = Estimate of the factor loading; *SE* = standard error; Est./*SE* = critical ratio; *p* value = *p* value associated with the critical ratio (under the standard normal distribution); MH = Mental Health; SF = Social Functioning; VT = Vitality; GW = General Wellness.

6.10.3 Schmid–Leiman Transformation

Addressing problems related to interpretations of higher-order factors in EFA, Gorsuch (1983) stated that to avoid basing interpretations of higher-order factors on interpretations of first-order factors, the relationships of the original variables to higher-order factors should be determined. He also noted that "interpreting from the variables should improve the theoretical understanding of the data and produce a better identification of each higher-order factor" (Gorsuch, 1983, p. 246). Such interpretations are facilitated a great deal by using the Schmid–Leiman transformation (Schmid & Leiman, 1957). This transformation allows researchers to estimate the direct effect of each higher-order factor on individual items, hence the proportion of item variance explained by the higher-order factor as well as the unique contribution of each first-order factor to explaining item variance. Developed initially in the framework of EFA, the Schmid–Leiman transformation was translated and used in the framework of higher-order CFA (e.g., Brown, 2006; Brown, White, Forsyth, & Barlow, 2004; Campbell-Sills, Liverant, & Brown, 2004).

The Schmid–Leiman transformation is described here for the second-order model of General Wellness analyzed in Example 6.4. The procedure is outlined in Table 6.10, which shows an SPSS spreadsheet for computations based on estimates of the first-order factor

TABLE 6.10

SPSS Spreadsheet and Syntax for the Schmid–Leiman Transformation[a] of the Second-Order Confirmatory Factor Analysis Model of Wellness (Figure 6.6)

Item	FL1	FL2	SFL1	SFL2	SOE	DL	RPL	SRPL	SSOE	SumR2
X1	0.900	0.549	0.810	0.301	0.494	0.836	0.752	0.566	0.244	0.810
X2	0.869	0.549	0.755	0.301	0.477	0.836	0.726	0.528	0.228	0.755
X3	0.823	0.549	0.677	0.301	0.452	0.836	0.688	0.473	0.204	0.677
X4	0.893	0.562	0.797	0.316	0.502	0.827	0.739	0.546	0.252	0.797
X5	0.861	0.562	0.741	0.316	0.484	0.827	0.712	0.507	0.234	0.741
X6	0.833	0.562	0.694	0.316	0.468	0.827	0.689	0.475	0.219	0.694
X7	0.931	0.659	0.867	0.434	0.614	0.752	0.700	0.490	0.376	0.867
X8	0.859	0.659	0.738	0.434	0.566	0.752	0.646	0.417	0.320	0.738
X9	0.861	0.659	0.741	0.434	0.567	0.752	0.648	0.419	0.322	0.741

Note. FL1 = first-order factor loading (input data taken from Table 6.9); FL2 = second-order factor loading (input data taken from Table 6.9); SFL1 = squared first-order loading, or $(FL1)^2$; SFL2 = squared second-order loading, or $(FL2)^2$; SOE = second-order effect, or FL1*FL2; DL = disturbance loading, or $\sqrt{1 - SFL2}$; RPL = residualized primary loading, or FL1*DL; SRPL = squared residual primary loading, or $(RPL)^2$; SSOE = squared second-order effect, or $(SOE)^2$; SumR2 = total R^2, or SSOE + SRPL.
[a]SPSS syntax for Schmid–Leiman transformation is as follows:

```
COMPUTE SFL1 = FL1**2.
COMPUTE SFL2 = FL2**2.
COMPUTE SOE = FL1*FL2.
COMPUTE DL = SQRT(1 – SFL2).
COMPUTE RPL = FL1*DL.
COMPUTE SRPL = RPL**2.
COMPUTE SSOE = SOE**2.
COMPUTE SumR2 = SSOE + SRPL.
EXECUTE.
```

loadings and the second-order factor loadings (taken from Table 6.9). The note to Table 6.9 provides interpretation of the variable names used in SPSS spreadsheet and the SPSS syntax used for computations (one could also use, say, an Excel spreadsheet; e.g., see Brown, 2006, p. 336).

There are three major steps in this procedure: First, using an SPSS spreadsheet, enter the estimates of the first-order factor loadings (variable FL1) and second-factor loadings (variable FL2). Second, run the SPSS syntax (see the note to Table 6.10). Third, interpret the results using the following clarifications about the variables in the SPSS spreadsheet and their computation under the Schmid-Leiman transformation:

- Variable FL1 (first-order factor loadings): Completely standardized estimates of the first-factor loadings are provided with the Mplus output (Table 6.9).
- Variable FL2 (second-order factor loadings): Completely standardized estimates of the second-order factor loadings are provided with the Mplus output (Table 6.9).
- Variable SFL1 (squared first-order factor loading): This variable is obtained by squaring the first-order factor loadings (FL1). Thus, SFL1 indicates the proportion of item variance explained by the first-order factor related to the respective item. For item X_1, for example, SFL1 = $(FL1)^2 = 0.900^2 = 0.810$, which indicates that 81% of the variance of this item is explained by its first-order factor (i.e., mental health; see Figure 6.6).
- Variable SFL2 (squared second-order factor loading): This variable is obtained by squaring the second-order factor loading (FL2). Thus, SFL2 indicates the proportion of variance in a first-order factor explained by the second factor. For the

Mental Health factor (a first-order factor), for example, SFL2 = $(FL2)^2 = 0.549^2 = 0.301$, which indicates that 30.1% of the variance in Mental Health is explained by General Wellness. As completely standardized estimates of FL2 are used, the difference 1 – SFL2 reflects the disturbance (residual variance) in the first-order factor (i.e., ζ_1, ζ_2, or ζ_3 in Figure 6.6).

- Variable SOE (second-order effect): This variable is obtained by multiplying the first-order and the second-order factor loadings, thus obtaining the indirect effect of the second-order factor on the respective item. In fact, this number is also the total effect of the second-order factor on the item because direct effects of the second-order factor to individual items are not specified (see Figure 6.6). For example, the second-order effect on item X_1 is SOE = (FL1)(FL2) = (0.900)(0.549) = 0.494 (the squared value of this effect indicates the proportion of item variance explained by the second-order factor).
- Variable DL (disturbance loading): This variable is obtained by taking the square root of the disturbance of a first-order factor (1 – SFL2), thus obtaining the path coefficient from the disturbance term to that factor—that is, DL = $\sqrt{1 - \text{SFL2}}$ (if depicted in Figure 6.6, DL would be a path coefficient associated with the short one-way arrow from ζ_1, ζ_2, or ζ_3 to the respective first-order factor).
- Variable RPL (residual primary loading): This variable is obtained by multiplying the first-order factor loading (FL1) and the disturbance loading (DL). For item X_1, for example, RPL = (FL1)(DL) = (0.900)(0.836) = 0.752. In a multiple regression context, RPL can be viewed as a part correlation between an item and its first-order factor, controlling for the second-order factor. Thus, the squared RPL reflects the unique contribution of a first-order factor in predicting an item, controlling for the second-order factor.
- Variable SRPL (*squared residual primary loading*): This variable is obtained by squaring the residual primary loading, RPL. Thus, as already noted in the description of RPL, SPRL reflects the proportion of item variance uniquely explained by a first-order factor, while controlling for the second-order factor. For item X_1, for example, SPRL = $(RPL)^2 = 0.752^2 = 0.566$. Thus, 56.6% of the variance in item X_1 is uniquely explained by its first-order factor (Mental Health) controlling for the second-order factor (General Wellness).
- Variable SSOE (squared second-order effect): This variable is obtained by squaring the second-order effect on an item (SOE). Therefore, SSOE indicates how much variance in each item is explained by the second-order factor. For item X_1, for example, SSOE = $(SOE)^2 = 0.494^2 = 0.244$, which indicates that 24.4% of the variance in this item is explained by the second-order factor. As noted earlier, the information provided by SSOE is of primary interest in interpreting second-order factors based on their relations to observed measures (items).
- Variable SumR2 (total R^2): This variable is the sum of the squared second-order effect and the squared residual primary loading, that is: SumR2 = SSOE + SRPL. Thus, SumR2 shows the proportion of item variance that is explained by the second-order factor and the respective first-order factor together. For item X_1, for example, SumR2 = SSOE + SRPL = 0.244 + 0.566 = 0.810, which indicates that 81% of the variance in item X_1 is explained jointly by the second-order factor (General Wellness) and the first-order factor associated with the item (Mental Health). Note also that, as all estimates are completely standardized, 1.0 represents the total item variance. Therefore, the difference (1 – SumR2) represents the residual item variance (e.g., see the residual variances for items X_1, X_2, . . ., X_9 in Table 6.9).

6.10.4 Testing for Measurement Invariance of Second-Order Models

The logic of testing for measurement invariance of first-order factors, described earlier (see Section 6.8), carries over to testing for measurement invariance of second-order models, with some additional aspects: First, factor loading invariance is tested for both the first-order and second-order factors. Second, intercept invariance is tested for both the indicators and first-order factors. Third, residual invariance is tested for both the uniquenesses of indicators and disturbances of first-order factors. The first two conditions (invariance of factor loadings and intercepts) are necessary to test for group differences on a second-order factor mean. In general, specifying a lower-order factor as a reference indicator of a higher-order factor is preferred to fixing the variance of the higher-order factor to 1.0 in testing for invariance across groups in higher-order CFA models (e.g., Chen, Sousa, & West, 2005; Whitman et al., 2009).

The approach to testing for factorial invariance of first-order CFA models across groups described earlier (see Example 6.2) also carries over to second-order CFA models. Namely, starting with a baseline model without invariance, a sequence of nested models is obtained by imposing constraints for invariance of model parameters (factor loadings, intercepts, and so forth). At each step, a lack of invariance is signaled by a statistically significant chi-square difference ($\Delta\chi^2$) test for the respective pair of nested models (recall that $\Delta\text{CFI} \leq -.01$ can be used as a triangulation for lack of invariance). The choice of a sequential order for nested models in a higher order CFA model would depend on the type of invariance of interest in a particular study. In any case, the first step is to test for configural invariance; that is, a baseline model must fit the data for each group separately. After configural invariance is established, one can proceed with testing for factorial invariance. For a second-order CFA model, the step-up constraints method with the following sequence of nested models allows testing for measurement and structural aspects of factorial invariance across groups (e.g., see Chen et al., 2005):

- Model 0 (without invariance). This is the baseline model fit to the data for all groups together with no invariance assumed; that is, all models parameters (factor loadings, intercepts, and so forth) are freely estimated.
- Model 1 (invariant first-order factor loadings). Model 1 is obtained from Model 0 by imposing the constraint of equal first-order factor loadings across the groups. (Model 1 is nested within Model 0.)
- Model 2 (invariant first-order and second-order factor loadings). Model 2 is obtained from Model 1 by adding the constraint of equal second-order factor loadings across the groups. (Model 2 is nested within Model 1.)
- Model 3 (invariant first-order factor loadings, second-order factor loadings, and item intercepts). Model 3 is obtained from Model 2 by adding the constraint of equal item intercepts across the groups. (Model 3 is nested within Model 2.)
- Model 4 (invariant first-order factor loadings, second-order factor loadings, item intercepts, and first-order factor intercepts). Model 4 is obtained from Model 3 by adding the constraint of equal first-order factor intercepts across the groups. (Model 4 is nested within Model 3.)
- Model 5 (invariant first-order factor loadings, second-order factor loadings, item intercepts, first-order factor intercepts, and first-order factor disturbances). Model 5 is obtained from Model 4 by adding the constraint of equal first-order factor disturbances across the groups. (Model 5 is nested within Model 4.)

- Model 6 (invariant first-order factor loadings, second-order factor loadings, item intercepts, first-order factor intercepts, first-order factor disturbances, and item uniquenesses). Model 6 is obtained from Model 5 by adding the constraint of invariant item uniquenesses across the groups. (Model 6 is nested within Model 5.) As noted earlier, testing for invariance of item uniquenesses represents an overly restrictive test of the data (e.g., Byrne, 1988; Levine et al., 2003; Widaman & Reise, 1997).

Example 6.5. This example illustrates the described approach to testing for factorial invariance of a second-order CFA model using Mplus (the procedure can be readily applied in the framework of other computer programs, such as LISREL, Amos, and EQS). Specifically, the second-order CFA model in Figure 6.6 is tested for factorial invariance across gender: women ($n = 210$) and men ($n = 250$). As shown in Example 6.4, this model provides a very good data fit for the entire sample ($N = 460$). To test for configural invariance, the model was fit for each group separately. The goodness-of-fit indices provided in Table 6.11 indicate that, although the model fit the women's data better than the men's data, the data fit is reasonable enough to assume configural invariance of the model across gender.

After configural invariance across groups is established, testing for factorial invariance is conducted using the sequence of nested models described earlier (Model 0, . . ., Model 6). The results are summarized in Table 6.12 (the Mplus code is given in Appendix 6.4). Given the illustrative purpose of this example and the normality of the distributions of scores on each item, the usual chi-square difference test ($\Delta\chi^2$) is reported in Table 6.12 for the comparison of nested models (M1 vs. M0), (M2 vs. M1), and so forth (in case of multivariate nonnormality, the Satorra-Bentler scaled chi-square difference, SBS$\Delta\chi^2$, can be computed as described in Appendix 6.2 and Table 6.13).

The examination of the chi-square differences in Table 6.12 shows that the first five pairwise comparisons of nested models provide evidence of invariant first-order factor loadings (M1 – M0), second-order factor loadings (M2 – M1), item intercepts (M3 – M2), first-order factor intercepts (M4 – M3), and first-order factor disturbances (M5 – M4). However, the chi-square difference for the comparison of Model 6 and Model 5 is not statistically significant, $\Delta\chi^2(9) = 19.294$, $p < .05$, thus indicating that the constraint of invariant item residual variances (item uniquenesses) does not hold. This finding is also supported by the ΔCFI value (–.019), which, according to the criterion $\Delta\text{CFI} \leq -.01$, indicates lack of invariance

TABLE 6.11

Configural Invariance of the Second-Order Confirmatory Factor Analysis Model of Wellness Across Gender

								90% CI for RMSEA	
Group	χ^2	*df*	*p*	CFI	TLI	SRMR	RMSEA	LL	UL
Women	30.22	24	.177	.979	.969	.041	.035	.000	.070
Men	39.42	24	.025	.939	.909	.041	.044	.018	.078

Note. CFI = Comparative Fit Index; TLI = Tucker–Lewis Index; SRMR = standardized root mean square residual; RMSEA = root mean square error of approximation; CI = confidence interval; LL = lower limit; UL = upper limit. From "Testing for Factorial Invariance in the Context of Construct Validation," by D. M. Dimitrov, 2010, *Measurement and Evaluation in Counseling and Development, 43,* p. 134. Copyright 2010 by Sage Publications. Reprinted with permission.

TABLE 6.12

Testing for Invariance of the Second-Order Factor Model of Wellness Across Gender

Model	χ^2	*df*	Comparison	$\Delta\chi^2$	Δdf	CFI	ΔCFI[a]	RMSEA
M0	69.462	48	—	—		.961	—	.044
M1	72.498	54	M1 – M0	2.856	6	.967	.006	.039
M2	75.885	56	M2 – M1	3.387	2	.964	–.003	.039
M3	84.623	64	M3 – M2	8.738	8	.963	–.001	.037
M4	87.079	65	M4 – M3	2.456	1	.960	–.003	.038
M5	89.766	68	M5 – M4	2.687	3	.961	.001	.037
M6	109.079	77	M6 – M5	19.294*	9	.942	–.019[a]	.043
M6P	100.599	76	M6P – M5	10.833	8	.956	–.005	.038

Note. CFI = Comparative Fit Index; RMSEA = root mean square error of approximation; M0 = baseline model (no variance); M1 = first-order factor loadings invariant; M2 = first-order and second-order factor loadings invariant; M3 = first-order and second-order factor loadings and item intercepts invariant; M4 = first-order and second-order factor loadings, item intercepts, and first-order factor intercepts invariant; M5 = first-order and second-order factor loadings, indicator intercepts, first-order factor intercepts, and first-order factor disturbances invariant; M6 = first-order and second-order factor loadings, indicator intercepts, first-order factor intercepts, first-order factor disturbances, and item residual variances invariant; M6P = first-order and second-order factor loadings, indicator intercepts, first-order factor intercepts, first-order factor disturbances, and partial invariance of item residual variances (all invariant, except the residual variance of Item 6). From "Testing for factorial invariance in the context of construct validation," by D. M. Dimitrov, 2010, *Measurement and Evaluation in Counseling and Development, 43,* p. 134. Copyright 2010 by the Sage Publications. Reprinted with permission.
[a]ΔCFI ≤ -0.01 signals lack of invariance.
*$p < .05$.

(Cheung & Rensvold, 2002). Only one item was found to have a statistically significant MI for the residual variances: Item 6, with MI = 7.944. After freeing the residual variance for this item, thus obtaining the model labeled "M6P" in Table 6.12, the chi-square difference is no longer statistically significant, $\Delta\chi^2(8) = 10.833$, $p > .05$, and ΔCFI = –.005 is no longer below the cutting score of –.01 (note also the drop in RMSEA from .043 in Model 6 to .038 in Model 6P). These findings indicate that there is a high level of partial invariance for item residual variances—all item residual variances, except that of Item 6,

TABLE 6.13

SPSS Spreadsheet for the Computation of the Satorra-Bentler Scaled Chi-Square Difference (SBS$\Delta\chi^2$)

Model	T0	T1	TR0	TR1	df0	df1	C0	C1	CD	SBS_DIFF
M1 – M0	44.258	40.365	34.992	30.901	31	26	1.26	1.31	1.05	3.71
M2 – M1	56.749	44.258	46.225	34.992	36	31	1.23	1.26	1.00	12.52
M2P – M1	48.201	44.258	39.058	34.992	35	31	1.23	1.26	1.00	3.96
M3 – M2P	80.300	48.201	63.530	39.058	42	35	1.26	1.23	1.41	22.71
M3P – M2P	53.597	48.201	43.420	39.058	40	35	1.23	1.23	1.24	4.36
M4 – M2P	49.908	48.201	39.997	39.058	38	35	1.25	1.23	1.41	1.21

Note. T0 = the usual χ^2 value under the ML estimator used with model M0 (nested within model M1); T1 = the usual χ^2 value under the ML estimator used with model M1; TR0 = the SBχ^2 value under the MLM estimator used with model M0; TR1 = the SBχ^2 value under the MLM estimator used with model M1; df0 = degrees of freedom for model M0; df1 = degrees of freedom for model M1; C0 = scaling correction factor for model M0 (see Equation 6.3); C1 = scaling correction factor for model M1 (see Equation 6.3); CD = the difference test scaling correction (see Equation 6.4); SBS_DIFF = the Satorra–Bentler scaled chi-square difference (SBS$\Delta\chi^2$; see Equation 6.5). From "Testing for Factorial Invariance in the Context of Construct Validation," by D. M. Dimitrov, 2010, *Measurement and Evaluation in Counseling and Development, 43,* p. 142. Copyright 2010 by Sage Publications. Reprinted with permission.

are invariant across gender. In summary, the factorial invariance of the second-order CFA model of wellness is supported by the invariance of first- and second-order factor loadings, item intercepts, first-order factor intercepts, first-order factor disturbances, and invariance of residual variances for all items except for Item 6 (i.e., the precision of measurement for Item 6 is not the same for women and men).

For empirical studies involving testing for factorial invariance of second-order CFA models, the reader may refer to Byrne, Baron, and Balev (1998); Byrne and Campbell (1999); Chen et al. (2005); Guo, Aveyard, and Dai (2009); Le et al. (2005); and Whitman et al. (2009).

6.11 POINTS OF CAUTION IN TESTING FOR FACTORIAL INVARIANCE

6.11.1 The Role of Referent Indicators

There are two main approaches to establishing the metric of a latent factor in a CFA model. One widely used approach is to select an indicator of the latent factor as a referent indicator (RI) and to fix its factor loading to 1.0. By doing this, the RI metric becomes the metric of its latent factor. This approach is generally preferred to an alternative approach, whereby the variance of the latent factor is fixed to 1.0 (e.g., Vanderberg & Lance, 2000; Yoon & Millsap, 2007). The role of RIs in testing for measurement invariance has been investigated in previous research, yet it is not fully accounted for in published studies on measurement invariance testing (e.g., E. C. Johnson, Meade, & DuVernet, 2009; Rensvold & Cheung, 2001; Yoon & Millsap, 2007). For example, E. C. Johnson et al. (2009) found that when RIs are erroneously assumed to be invariant across two groups (i.e., differentially functionning items are selected as RIs), this is accurately detected by the measurement invariance tests at the scale-level but not for individual items. Thus, when an RI is not invariant across groups, this situation will yeld misleading results in testing for partial invariance of factor loadings (if such testing is used), because in the process of testing for partial metric invariance, each factor loading is tested independently under the assumption that the RI is invariant across the groups. Therefore, it is important that reseachers make efforts to select RIs that remain invariant across the groups of interest. This is not an easy task, but it can be based, ideally, on sound theoretical considerations or recently developed procedures for selecting RIs (e.g., Rensvold & Cheung, 2001; Yoon & Millsap, 2007); the computations in the procedure proposed by Yoon and Millsap (2007) are less complicated than those in the procedure proposed by Rensvold and Cheung (2001).

6.11.2 The Role of Item Parceling

Although combining items into parcels in CFA can improve model fit (e.g., Nasser & Wisenbaker, 2003), it may at the same time have undesired effects on tests of measurement invariance. Using simulated data with a known lack of measurement invariance, Meade and Kroustalis (2006) illustrated that CFA models using parcels as indicatiors of latent factors erroneously indicated that measurement invariance exists much more often than did models using individual items as indicators. They also found that the power of measurement invariance tests was generally very low for sample sizes of 100 and often somewhat poor for samples of 200 per group; therefore, they recommended that sample sizes of least 200 per group be available before undertaking such tests. In addition, Meade and Kroustalis (2006) suggested that item-level testing for measurement invariance be conducted even when the scale-level tests indicate its presence, because a lack of measurement invariance for a small number of items can be obscured by grouping these items with items for which it exists. They stated that "for large surveys, it is possible that nearly every item assessing a factor may show a LOI [lack of invariance]. However, if metric invariance holds for all other items in other factors, tests of the entire matrix of factor loadings could erroneously indicate that metric invariance exists" (Meade & Kroustalis, 2006, p. 399). In the context of construct validation, researchers must determine the scope and approaches to measurement invariance testing based on the purpose of validation and validity aspects being targeted.

6.11.3 Measurement Invariance, Prediction Invariance, and Selection Invariance

The conception of *fairness* (or lack of *bias*) in testing and assessment can be addressed from the perspectives of measurement invariance, prediction invariance, or selection invariance. It is important to emphasize that contrary to common misconceptions, these three perspectives on invariance are not identical; in fact, they are generally inconsistent (e.g., Borsboom, Romeijn, & Wicherts, 2008; Millsap, 1997, 2007; Millsap & Everson, 1993; Millsap & Kwok, 2004). As discussed earlier, measurement invariance across groups holds when the relation between the latent trait being measured and the test scores is the same for those groups. That is, an invariant test measures the same trait in the same way for different subpopulations (e.g., Holland & Wainer, 1993; Meredith, 1993; Millsap & Everson, 1993; Millsap & Kwok, 2004).

Prediction invariance, on the other hand, holds when the test scores predict an external criterion in the same way for different subpopulations; for example, the prediction of GPA of college freshmen from their SAT scores is the same for males and females. This perspective on invariance is based on a definition of test bias proposed by Cleary (1968), which states that "a test is biased for members of a subgroup of the population if the criterion score predicted from the common regression line is consistently too high or too low for members of the subgroup" (p. 115). This conception of test bias is adopted in the *Standards for Educational and Psychological Testing* (AERA, APA, & NCME, 1999, p. 79). Without going into technical details, it should be noted that prediction invariance does not provide evidence of measurement invariance. In fact, Millsap (1997, 2007) showed that measurement invariance is inconsistent with prediction invariance, and that with few exceptions, the presence of measurement invariance implies a lack of predictive invariance and vice versa. When it comes to a choice in defining bias, the recommendation is that researchers favor measurement invariance over prediction invariance (see Borsboom et al., 2008).

When the purpose of an assessment is to select individuals for differential treatment on the basis of their test scores, a fair selection across groups is achieved if the same number of selection errors occurs in each group. From this perspective, selection invariance holds when the probability that the classification of a person as true positive, true negative, false positive, or false negative does not depend on the group membership of that individual (e.g., Borsboom et al., 2008; Petersen & Novick, 1976).

Researchers should be aware, however, that classification invariance and measurement invariance are mutually inconsistent. For example, Borsboom et al. (2008, p. 82) reported that "under a variety of conditions, the satisfaction of measurement invariance entails the violation of selection invariance." They explained the paradoxical nature of this finding as a continuous version of Simpson's paradox (Simpson, 1951), which describes how effects that are observed in subpopulations can differ dramatically from effects observed in the aggregates of the subpopulations. Specifically, although measurement invariance assures that the probability of incorrect classification decisions is independent from group membership in all subpopulations with an equal trait score that is used as a classification cut-off, this independence is destroyed with the aggregation of different cut-off score values (see Borsboom et al., 2008, for details). Relating this finding to the conception of fairness, Borsboom et al. (2008) stated:

> On one hand, we want selection procedures to be fair in the sense that any two individuals with the same ability have an equal probability of passing the test. The conditions that best protect such fairness are provided through the requirements of measurement invariance, because measurement invariance operates at the levels of ability. On the other hand, we want selection procedures to be equally accurate for different groups. This condition applies to aggregate populations and therefore is best guaranteed by selection invariance. In one interpretation, the conditions of measurement invariance and selection invariance could be paired to conceptions of fairness that apply at the level of individual and at the group, respectively. (p. 86)

An important implication for researchers in the context of construct validation is that the decision they have to make about whether the focus should be on measurement invariance or selection invariance would depend on whether the aspect of construct validity under evaluation is treated at individual level or group level. For evaluation at the individual level, researchers should focus on measurement invariance; for the group level, the focus should be on selection invariance.

6.12 SAMPLE SIZE FOR CFA

The problems and complexity of issues related to sample size for EFA, discussed earlier in this book (Chapter 5, Section 5.8), do not go away in decisions on sample size for CFA. On the contrary, the required sample size in CFA depends on even larger number of issues that occur with operationalizing model complexity, quality of indicators (e.g., reliability and size of factor loadings), statistical power of testing hypotheses about model fit and individual parameters, and so forth (e.g., Gagné & Hancock, 2006; K. H. Kim, 2005; Marsh, Hau, Balla, & Grayson, 1998; L. K. Muthén & B. O. Muthén, 2002). There is a theme in the current literature about the inappropriateness of using rules of thumb to determine sample size in CFA—rules of thumb that were suggested in the past. Although some rules of thumb are absolute in nature, such as the recommendation for "a minimum of 100 to 200 observations" (e.g., Boomsma, 1982; Hoyle, 1995), others involve relations between sample size, n; number of indicators, p; number of factors, f; and number of free model parameters, q. Examples of such rules are (a) $n/p \geq 15$ (e.g., Stevens, 2002), (b) $n/q \geq 5$ (e.g., Bentler & Chou, 1987; Tanaka, 1987), and (c) $p/f \geq 4$ (e.g., Marsh et al., 1988).

It should be noted, however, that all recommended rules for sample size in CFA are established under specific conditions that should be taken into account in practical applications of such rules. For example, Bentler and Chou (1987) suggested that the ratio of number of cases per free model parameter be at least five ($n/q \geq 5$) under maximum likelihood estimation and multivariate normality (or $n/q \geq 10$, in case of distribution free analyses). Jackson (2003) also found support of the assertion that "the appropriate sample size should be considered in light of the number of parameters being estimated" and reported that "in conditions with higher n/q ratios, on average chi-square bias and RMSEA values were lower" (p. 139). Furthermore, Marsh et al. (1998) suggested that the ratio of number of indicators to number of factors be at least 4 ($p/f \geq 4$), but in their study all population standardized factor loadings were equal to .6 (or higher, when item parcels were used). They also reported that when the p/f ratio increased, the rate of proper convergence in CFA solutions also increased even when the sample size was held constant.

Gagné and Hancock (2006) extended Marsh et al.'s (1998) study by modeling a larger number of loading magnitudes and indicators per factor, relating the results to construct reliability. They examined seven values of *p*/*f* (2, 3, 4, 5, 6, 7, and 12), with four different loading magnitudes (.2, .4, .6, and .8), and six sample sizes (25, 50, 100, 200, 400, and 1,000). Along with supporting the finding by Marsh et al. (1998) that convergence improves with increases in *p*/*f* ratio, even when the sample size is fixed, Gagné and Hancock (2006) found an interaction of *n* with *p*/*f* and loading magnitude to affect convergence. However, as they noted, "the relation was too complex for a simple statement about a critical ratio. It seems instead that combining *p*/*f* and loading magnitudes into a measure of construct reliability is a more effective way of explaining the relation between sample size and facets of the model" (p. 79). Gagné and Hancock (2006) provided tables for the minimum sample size that is needed to achieve convergence under different conditions of factor loadings and *p*/*f* ratios (researchers can use such tables in making decisions about sample size under specific conditions of the CFA model at hand).

L. K. Muthén and B. O. Muthén (2002) demonstrated how researchers can use a Monte Carlo study to decide on sample size and to determine power in the context of a CFA model (they also studied a growth model, which is beyond the scope of this discussion). The criteria that they examined to determine sample size were as follows: (a) parameter and standard error biases do not exceed 10% for any parameter in the model, (b) the standard error bias for the parameter for which power is being assessed does not exceed 5%, and (c) the coverage (range of standard errors) remains between 0.91 and 0.98. Under these criteria, the sample size is chosen to keep power close to 0.80, which is a commonly accepted value for sufficient power. L. K. Muthén and B. O. Muthén (2002) used a CFA model with three factors and five continuous indicators for each factor, but the Mplus code that they provided for Monte Carlo simulations can be adapted to different CFA models under four scenarios of normal (vs. nonnormal) and missing (vs. no missing) data. For example, they found that to reach a power of .81 in rejecting the hypothesis that the factor correlation is zero, the needed sample size was (a) $n = 150$ for normal indicators with no missing data, (b) $n = 175$ for normal indicators with missing data, (c) $n = 265$ for nonnormal indicators with no missing data, and (d) $n = 315$ for nonnormal indicators with missing data. These results provide some guidance for sample size, but they should not be generalized beyond the conditions for the CFA model used by L. K. Muthén and B. O. Muthén (2002). Researchers may use the Monte Carlo approach to determine sample size by specifying conditions for a variety of CFA models using the Mplus code provided by L. K. Muthén and B. O. Muthén (2002, p. 609; see also Brown, 2006, pp. 420–429).

SUMMARY

1. The main conceptual difference between EFA and CFA is that EFA is a data-driven approach to discovering unknown factorial structures, whereas CFA is a theory-driven approach to confirming hypothesized factorial structures.
2. CFA model parameters are (a) all variances of independent variables, (b) all covariances between independent variables (unless the model states that some of them are equal to 0 or to a given constant), (c) all factor loadings connecting the latent variables with their indicators (unless the model states that some of them are equal to zero or to a given constant), and (d) all regression coefficients between observed or latent variables (unless the model states that some of them are equal to 0 or to a given constant).
3. The degrees of freedom (*df*) for a CFA model is determined by the difference between the number of known elements in the input variance–covariance matrix and the number of freely estimated parameters in the model. The CFA model is (a) overidentified if $df > 0$, (b) just identified if $df = 0$, and (c) underidentified if $df < 0$.

4. Testing for CFA data fit is valid under the SEM assumption of multivariate normality. Violations of this assumption can cause distortion of the goodness-of-fit statistics and inflation of the Type I error rate in testing factor loadings, correlations, and other model parameters for statistical significance.
5. Two Mardia's (1970) kappa coefficients, k_1 (for skewness) and k_2 (for kurtosis), indicate departure from multivariate normality if they are statistically significant (k_1 follows a chi-square distribution, and k_2 follows the standard normal distribution). Yet another Mardia's coefficient, known as *Mardia's normalized estimate*, should be less than 3.0 to indicate that the assumption of multivariate normality is met.
6. A commonly used rule for CFA data fit is that a reasonably good fit is supported when the following fit criteria are met: SRMR ≤ .08, RMSEA ≤ .06, CFI ≥ .95, and TLI ≥ .95 (Hu & Bentler, 1999). Less stringent cutting values that indicate a reasonable data fit and that can be used in many practical applications are as follows: SRMR ≤ .08, RMSEA ≤ .08, CFI ≥ .90, and TLI ≥ .90 (e.g., Marsh et al., 2004). It is important that researchers base their decision about the validity of a CFA model on a joint examination of overall fit indices, model complexity, adequacy and interpretability of model parameters, and other issues relevant to the goals of their study.
7. The modification index (MI) value for a parameter gives the expected drop in the model chi-square value if this parameter is freely estimated. If there are several parameters with statistically significant MIs, they should be freed one at a time, starting with the parameter that has the largest MI. Changes suggested by MIs must be made *only* if they allow for substantive interpretations in the framework of the theory behind the initial model and its possible modifications.
8. Out-of-range values of parameter estimates, referred to as *improper solutions* (or *Heywood cases*)—for example, factor correlations that exceed 1.0 in absolute value, negative factor variances, or negative variances of errors terms—can occur as a result of model identification problems, outliers, sampling fluctuations, or misspecifications in the model.
9. Researchers are strongly recommended to conduct a CFA cross-validation of the hypothesized model with an independent sample, especially when model modifications have been made or an EFA was initially used.
10. Testing for factorial invariance is conducted to check whether the constructs have the same meaning for each group—that is, to check whether there are (a) equivalent relationships between the latent factors and their indicators in the CFA model across groups, (b) cases of differential items functioning, (c) changes in the origin of the scale across groups, and (d) other aspects of group equivalency related to construct validity.
11. The factorial invariance of a CFA model includes configural invariance, measurement invariance, and structural invariance of the model.
12. *Configural invariance* refers to invariance of the model configuration (the pattern of free and fixed model parameters) across groups. To test for configural invariance, it is necessary to identify a baseline model, which is estimated for each group separately.
13. *Measurement invariance* refers to (a) metric invariance—equal factor loadings across groups, (b) scalar invariance—equal item intercepts across groups, and (c) invariance of item uniquenesses—equal item error variances/covariances across groups. Furthermore, weak measurement invariance requires metric invariance; strong measurement invariance requires both metric and scalar invariance; and strict measurement invariance requires metric invariance, scalar invariance, and invariance of item uniquenesses.

14. *Structural invariance* refers to invariance of factor variances and covariances. Keep in mind, however, that group comparisons on factor variances/covariances are meaningful only in the presence of metric invariance (i.e., when the factor loadings are invariant).
15. Under the step-up constraints method of testing for factorial invariance across groups, the analysis begins with the least constrained solution (total lack of invariance), and subsequent restrictions for equality of specific parameters across groups are imposed; thus, nested model are produced, which can be tested against each other using the chi-square difference test. If the assumption of multivariate normality is not met, the Satorra–Bentler scaled chi-square difference test must be used.
16. Testing hypotheses about mean differences among the groups on the construct of interest is often a part of collecting evidence about the external aspect of construct validity. There are two major approaches to such testing in the context of SEM: structured means modeling (SMM) and group-code (multiple-indicator, multiple-cause [MIMIC]) modeling. The SMM approach assumes invariant factor loadings and item intercepts, whereas the MIMIC modeling approach assumes invariant factor loadings, item uniquenesses, and factor variances and covariances.
17. Typically, higher-order CFA models reflect theory-driven hypotheses about more general factors that underlie the first-order factors. In general, the rules of identification in first-order CFA apply to the higher-order part of the model. Keep in mind, however, that for higher-order CFA models, it is not enough that the degrees of freedom for the overall model are positive—the higher-order structure must also be overidentified.
18. Understanding the relationships of the original variables to higher-order factors, which is critical for meaningful interpretations of higher-order models, is facilitated a great deal by the use of the Schmid–Leiman transformation (Schmid & Leiman, 1957). This transformation allows researchers to estimate the direct effect of each higher-order factor on individual items—and, hence, the proportion of item variance explained by the higher-order factor—as well as the unique contribution of each first-order factor to explaining item variance.
19. The logic of testing for measurement invariance of first-order factors carries over to testing for measurement invariance of second-order models, with the addition that (a) factor loading invariance is tested for both the first-order and second-order factors, (b) intercept invariance is tested for both the indicators and first-order factors, and (c) residual invariance is tested for both the uniquenesses of indicators and disturbances of first-order factors.
20. Points of caution in testing for factorial invariance relate to the role of referent indicators, item parceling, and fairness in assessment from perspectives of measurement invariance, prediction invariance, and selection invariance.
21. The required sample size in CFA depends on a large number of issues that occur with operationalizing model complexity: quality of indicators (e.g., reliability and size of factor loadings), statistical power of testing hypotheses about model fit and individual parameters, and so forth. Researchers are encouraged to use the Monte Carlo approach to determining sample size by specifying conditions for a variety of CFA models using, say, Mplus or other computer programs that incorporate Monte Carlo simulations within the framework of SEM.

APPENDIX 6.1

Mplus Code for Testing Factorial Invariance of a Confirmatory Factor Analysis (CFA) Model Across Two Groups: An Illustration for the CFA Model of Psychosocial Distress and Successful Coping Across Two Groups of People With Multiple Sclerosis by Course of Illness (Relapsing and Progressive)

```
TITLE:          Model 0 [Without invariance]
DATA:           FILE IS "C:\MSDATA.dat";
                VARIABLE: NAMES ARE group Y1-Y7;
                GROUPING IS group (0 = relapse, 1 = progress);
                USEVARIABLES ARE Y1-Y7;
MODEL:          DISTRESS BY Y1-Y4;
                COPING BY Y5-Y7;
                DISTRESS WITH COPING;
                [DISTRESS@0  COPING@0];  !factor variances fixed to zero
MODEL progress: DISTRESS BY Y2-Y4;
                COPING BY Y6-Y7;
                DISTRESS WITH COPING;
                [Y1-Y7];  !intercepts of Y1-Y7 freely estimated
OUTPUT:         STANDARDIZED MODINDICES(3.84);
```

```
TITLE:          Model 1 [Invariant factor loadings (FLs)—by default in Mplus]
DATA:           FILE IS "C:\MSDATA.dat";
VARIABLE:       NAMES ARE group Y1-Y7;
                GROUPING IS group (0 = relapse, 1 = progress);
                USEVARIABLES ARE Y1-Y7;
MODEL:          DISTRESS BY Y1-Y4;
                COPING BY Y5-Y7;
                DISTRESS WITH COPING;
                [DISTRESS@0 COPING@0];
MODEL progress: [Y1-Y7];
OUTPUT:         STANDARDIZED MODINDICES(3.84);
```

```
TITLE:          Model 2 [Invariant FLs + invariant intercepts, both by default in Mplus]
DATA:           FILE IS "C:\MSDATA.dat";
VARIABLE:       NAMES ARE group Y1-Y7;
                GROUPING IS group (0 = relapse, 1 = progress);
                USEVARIABLES ARE Y1-Y7;
MODEL:          DISTRESS BY Y1-Y4;
                COPING BY Y5-Y7;
                DISTRESS WITH COPING;
OUTPUT:         STANDARDIZED MODINDICES (3.84);
```

```
TITLE:          Model 2P [invariant FLs +  partially invariant intercepts]
DATA:           FILE IS "C:\MSDATA.dat";
VARIABLE:       NAMES ARE group Y1-Y7;
                GROUPING IS group (0 = relapse, 1 = progress);
                USEVARIABLES ARE Y1-Y7;
MODEL:          DISTRESS BY Y1-Y4;
                COPING BY Y5-Y7;
                DISTRESS WITH COPING;
MODEL progress: [Y2];                !the intercept of Y2 set free (noninvariant)
OUTPUT:         STANDARDIZED MODINDICES(3.84);
```

```
TITLE:          Model 3 [invariant FLs + partially invariant intercepts + invariant residual variances]
DATA:           FILE IS "C:\MSDATA.dat";
VARIABLE:       NAMES ARE group Y1-Y7;
                GROUPING IS group (0 = relapse, 1 = progress);
                USEVARIABLES ARE Y1-Y7;
MODEL:          DISTRESS BY Y1-Y4;
                COPING BY Y5-Y7;
                DISTRESS WITH COPING;
                Y1-Y7 (1-7);           ! the residual variances of Y1-Y7 set invariant
MODEL progress: [Y2];
OUTPUT:         STANDARDIZED MODINDICES (3.84);
```

(Continued on next page)

APPENDIX 6.1 (*Continued*)

Mplus Code for Testing Factorial Invariance of a Confirmatory Factor Analysis (CFA) Model Across Two Groups: An Illustration for the CFA Model of Psychosocial Distress and Successful Coping Across Two Groups of People With Multiple Sclerosis by Course of Illness (Relapsing and Progressive)

```
          TITLE: Model 3P [Invariant FLs + partially invariant intercepts + partially invariant residual
                 variances]
           DATA: FILE IS "C:\MSDATA.dat";
       VARIABLE: NAMES ARE group Y1-Y7;
                 GROUPING IS group (0 = relapse, 1 = progress);
                 USEVARIABLES ARE Y1-Y7;
          MODEL: DISTRESS BY Y1-Y4;
                 COPING BY Y5-Y7;
                 DISTRESS WITH COPING;
                 Y2-Y4  (1-3);          ! the residual variances of Y2, Y3, and Y4 set invariant
                 Y6-Y7  (5-6);          ! the residual variances of Y6 and Y7 set invariant
 MODEL progress: [Y2];
         OUTPUT: STANDARDIZED MODINDICES (3.84);
```

```
          TITLE: Model 4 [Invariant FLs + partially invar. intercepts + partially invariant residual
                 variances + invariant factor variances and covariances]
           DATA: FILE IS "C:\MSDATA.dat";
       VARIABLE: NAMES ARE group Y1-Y7;
                 GROUPING IS group (0 = relapse, 1 = progress);
                 USEVARIABLES ARE Y1-Y7;
          MODEL: DISTRESS BY Y1-Y4;
                 COPING BY Y5-Y7;
                 DISTRESS (1);                 !The variance of DISTRESS set invariant
                 COPING (2);                   !The variance of COPING set invariant
                 DISTRESS WITH COPING (3);     !Covariance (DISTRESS, COPING) set invariant
 MODEL progress: [Y2];
         OUTPUT: STANDARDIZED MODINDICES (3.84);
```

Note. In the ASCII data file (MSDATA.dat), group (0 = relapse, 1 = progress) is the grouping variable for the two groups by course of illness (relapsing and progressive) and Y1-Y7 are the seven indicators of the two latent factors (DISTRESS = Psychosocial Distress; COPING = Successful Coping). Using this data file, the provided syntax codes are for seven independent runs in Mplus for the CFA models labeled M0, M1, M2, M2P, M3, M3P, and M4, respectively. The chi-square test values for model fit of these models, provided with the Mplus outputs, are used in Table 6.7. From "Testing for Factorial Invariance in the Context of Construct Validation," by D. M. Dimitrov, 2010, *Measurement and Evaluation in Counseling and Development, 43,* p. 139. Copyright 2010 by Sage Publications. Reprinted with permission.

APPENDIX 6.2

Computation of the Satorra–Bentler Scaled Chi-Square Difference (SBS$\Delta\chi^2$)

Described is a stepwise procedure for computing the Satorra–Bentler scales chi-square difference (SBS$\Delta\chi^2$) based on a formula provided by Satorra and Bentler (1999) and illustrated on the Mplus website (http://statmodel.com/chidiff.shtml). The SBS$\Delta\chi^2$ is computed by scaling the chi-square difference between two nested models (say, model M_0 nested within model M_1). The chi-square values are denoted T as they represent values of the test statistic $T = (N-1)F_{min}$, where N is the sample size and F_{min} is the computed minimal difference between the covariance matrices **S** and Σ obtained with the actual sample data and implied for the population by the model, respectively. The computation of SBS$\Delta\chi^2$ can be carried out in steps as follows:

1. Fit each model (M_0 nested within M_1) twice to obtain the usual chi-square value (χ^2) and its Satorra–Bentler correction (SBχ^2) using the ML and MLM estimator, respectively (both available, for example, in Mplus, LISREL, and EQS).

2. The T-notations of the four chi-square values obtained in Step 1 are (a) for model M_0: $T_0 = \chi^2$ and $TR_0 = SB\chi^2$, and (b) for model M_1: $T_1 = \chi^2$ and $TR_1 = SB\chi^2$.

3. Compute the scaling correction factors for model M_0 and M_1, respectively:

$$C_0 = T_0/TR_0 \text{ and } C_1 = T_1/TR_1. \qquad (6.3)$$

4. Compute the difference test scaling correction:

$$CD = (df_0 * C_0 - df_1 * C_1)/(df_0 - df_1), \qquad (6.4)$$

where df_0 and df_1 are the degrees of freedom for model M_0 and M_1, respectively.

5. Compute the Satorra–Bentler scaled chi-square difference (SBS$\Delta\chi^2$) as follows:

$$SBS\Delta\chi^2 = (T_0 - T_1)/CD. \qquad (6.5)$$

EXAMPLE 6.6 Table 6.7 summarizes results related to testing for factorial invariance using the usual (ML) chi-square difference under multivariate normality of the data. The present example illustrates the computation of SBS$\Delta\chi^2$ for the same data, assuming that they do not meet the condition of multivariate normality. Specifically, let's illustrate the computation of SBS$\Delta\chi^2$ for the comparison of models M2 versus M1 described in Table 6.7. Under the ML estimator in Mplus, the chi-square values for M2 and M1 in Table 6.7 are $\chi^2 = 56.749$ (= T_0) and $\chi^2 = 44.258$ (= T_1), respectively. Under the MLM estimator, the Satorra–Bentler scaled chi-square values for M2 and M1 (reported by Mplus) were found to be $SB\chi^2 = 46.225$ (= TR_0) and $SB\chi^2 = 34.992$ (= TR_1), respectively. As shown in Table 6.7, the chi-square degrees of freedom were $df_0 = 36$ (for the nested model, M2) and $df_1 = 31$ (for tho roforonoc modcl, M1).

Using Equations 6.3, we have: $C_0 = T_0/TR_0 = 56.749/46.225 = 1.2277$ and $C_1 = T_1/TR_1 = 44.258/34.992 = 1.2648$. Furthermore, using Equation 6.4, we obtain the scaled correction of the chi-square difference: CD = [(36)(1.2277) – (31)(1.2648)]/(36 – 31) = 4.9884/5 = 0.9977. Finally, using Equation 6.5 with $T_0 = 56.749$, $T_1 = 44.258$, and CD = 0.9977, the Satorra–Bentler scaled chi-square difference is as follows: $SBS\Delta\chi^2 = (56.749 - 44.258)/\ 0.9977 = 12.5198$; ($SBS\Delta\chi^2 \approx 12.520$).

The computation of SBS$\Delta\chi^2$ can be easily performed using SPSS (or any spreadsheet program), as illustrated in Table 6.13 (for the model comparisons in Table 6.7). In Table 6.13, the first column indicates the model comparisons in Table 6.7, the next six columns contain input values (T0 = T_0, T1 = T_1, TR0 = TR_0, TR1 = TR_1, df0 = df_0, df1 = df_1), and the remaining columns contain values computed from these input values using Equations 6.3, 6.4, and 6.5, respectively. The last column, labeled "SBS_DIF," contains the resulting SBS$\Delta\chi^2$ values.

Note. From "Testing for Factorial Invariance in the Context of Construct Validation," by D. M. Dimitrov, 2010, *Measurement and Evaluation in Counseling and Development, 43,* p. 128. Copyright 2010 by Sage Publications. Reprinted with permission.

APPENDIX 6.3

Mplus Code and Input Data for Second-Order Confirmatory Factory Analysis of Wellness in Figure 6.6

1. Mplus Code:

```
    TITLE: SECOND-ORDER CFA MODEL OF WELLNESS
     DATA: FILE IS EX6_4.dat;
           TYPE IS STD CORR;
           NOBS ARE 460;
 VARIABLE: NAMES ARE X1-X9;
    MODEL: MH BY X1-X3;         !MH = MENTAL HEALTH
           SF  BY X4-X6;        !SF = SOCIAL FUNCTIONING
           VT BY X7-X9;         !VT = VITALITY
           GW BY  MH SF VT;     !GW = GENERAL WELLNESS
   OUTPUT: STANDARDIZED MODINDICES (3.84);
```

2. Input Data File (EX6_4.dat): Standard Deviations and Correlations Among the Observed Measures (Items X1, . . ., X9)

```
1.566 1.465 1.548 1.568 1.501 1.409 1.578 1.470 1.449
1.000
 .395 1.000
 .396  .364 1.000
 .140  .117  .232 1.000
 .127  .101  .175  .294 1.000
 .176  .228  .160  .337  .303 1.000
 .185  .133  .092  .051  .052  .084 1.000
 .136  .104  .162  .159  .106  .209  .385 1.000
 .162  .154  .129  .122  .100  .156  .301  .374 1.000
```

Note. With this type of data (standard deviations and correlations) in Mplus, the standard deviations of the observed measures (items) are provided at the first horizontal row, followed by the correlations.

APPENDIX 6.4

Mplus Code for Testing Factorial Invariance of a Second-Order Confirmatory Factor Analysis (CFA) Model Across Two Groups: An Illustration for the CFA Model of Wellness Across Gender

```
      TITLE: Model 0 [Without invariance]
       DATA: FILE IS HEALTH.dat;
   VARIABLE: NAMES ARE group X1-X9;
             GROUPING IS group (0 = female, 1 = male);
             USEVARIABLES ARE X1-X9;
      MODEL: F1 BY X1-X3;              !F1 = Mental health
             F2 BY X4-X6;              !F2 = Social functioning
             F3 BY X7-X9;              !F3 = Vitality
             SOF BY F1 F2 F3;          !Second-Order Factor (Wellness)
             [F1@0 F2@0 F3@0];         !1st-order factor means fixed at zero
             [SOF@0];                  !2nd-order factor mean fixed at zero
 MODEL male: F1 BY X2-X3;              !noninvariant loadings on F1
             F2 BY X5-X6;              !noninvariant loadings on F2
             F3 BY X8-X9;              !noninvariant loadings on F3
             [X1-X9];                  !noninvariant indicator intercepts
     OUTPUT: STANDARDIZED MODINDICES(3.84);
```

```
      TITLE: Model 1 [Invariant 1st-order factor loadings]
       DATA: FILE IS HEALTH.dat;
   VARIABLE: NAMES ARE group X1-X9;
             GROUPING IS group (0 = female, 1 = male);
             USEVARIABLES ARE X1-X9;
      MODEL: F1 BY X1-X3;
             F2 BY X4-X6;
             F3 BY X7-X9;
             SOF BY F1 F2 F3;
             [F1@0 F2@0 F3@0];
             [SOF@0];
 MODEL male: [X1-X9];
     OUTPUT: STANDARDIZED MODINDICES(3.84);
```

```
      TITLE: Model 2 [Model 1 + invariant 2nd-order factor loadings]
       DATA: FILE IS HEALTH.dat;
   VARIABLE: NAMES ARE group X1-X9;
             GROUPING IS group (0 = female, 1 = male);
             USEVARIABLES ARE X1-X9;
      MODEL: F1 BY X1-X3;
             F2 BY X4-X6;
             F3 BY X7-X9;
             SOF BY F1        !F1 serves as a reference indicator of the 2nd-order factor (SOF)
             F2 (1)           !invariant 2nd-order factor loadings for F2
             F3 (2);          !invariant 2nd-order factor loadings for F3
             [F1@0 F2@0 F3@0];
             [SOF@0];
 MODEL male: [X1-X9];
     OUTPUT: STANDARDIZED MODINDICES(3.84);
```

```
      TITLE: Model 3 [Model 2 + Invariant item intercepts]
       DATA: FILE IS HEALTH.dat;
   VARIABLE: NAMES ARE group X1-X9;
             GROUPING IS group (0 = female, 1 = male);
             USEVARIABLES ARE X1-X9;
      MODEL: F1 BY X1-X3;
             F2 BY X4-X6;
             F3 BY X7-X9;
             SOF BY F1
             F2 (1)
             F3 (2);
             [F1@0 F2@0 F3@0];
     OUTPUT: STANDARDIZED MODINDICES(3.84);
```

(Continued on next page)

APPENDIX 6.4 (*Continued*)

Mplus Code for Testing Factorial Invariance of a Second-Order Confirmatory Factor Analysis (CFA) Model Across Two Groups: An Illustration for the CFA Model of Wellness Across Gender

```
      TITLE: Model 4 [Model 3 + Invariant 1st-order factor intercepts]
       DATA: FILE IS HEALTH.dat;
   VARIABLE: NAMES ARE group X1-X9;
             GROUPING IS group (0 = female, 1 = male);
             USEVARIABLES ARE X1-X9;
      MODEL: F1 BY X1-X3;
             F2 BY X4-X6;
             F3 BY X7-X9;
             SOF BY F1
             F2 (1)
             F3 (2);
             [F1@0 F2@0 F3@0];
 MODEL male: [SOF@0];
     OUTPUT: STANDARDIZED MODINDICES(3.84);
```

```
      TITLE: Model 5 [Model 4 + Invariant 1st-order factor disturbances]
       DATA: FILE IS HEALTH.dat;
   VARIABLE: NAMES ARE group X1-X9;
             GROUPING IS group (0 = female, 1 = male);
             USEVARIABLES ARE X1-X9;
      MODEL: F1 BY X1-X3;
             F2 BY X4-X6;
             F3 BY X7-X9;
             SOF BY F1
             F2 (1)
             F3 (2);
             [F1@0 F2@0 F3@0];
             F1-F3 (3-5);            !invariant 1st-order factor disturbances
 MODEL male: [SOF@0];
     OUTPUT: STANDARDIZED MODINDICES(3.84);
```

```
      TITLE: Model 6 [Model 5 + Invariant item residual variances]
       DATA: FILE IS HEALTH.dat;
   VARIABLE: NAMES ARE group X1-X9;
             GROUPING IS group (0 = female, 1 = male);
             USEVARIABLES ARE X1-X9;
      MODEL: F1 BY X1-X3;
             F2 BY X4-X6;
             F3 BY X7-X9;
             SOF BY F1
             F2 (1)
             F3 (2);
             [F1@0 F2@0 F3@0];
             F1-F3 (3-5);
             X1-X9 (6-14);           !Invariant item residual variances
 MODEL male: [SOF@0];
     OUTPUT: STANDARDIZED MODINDICES(3.84);
```

Note. Specifying a lower order factor as a reference indicator of a higher order factor is preferred to fixing the variance of the higher-order factor to 1.0 in testing for invariance across groups in higher order CFA models (e.g., Chen, Sousa, & West, 2005; Whitman, Van Rooy, Viswesvaran, & Kraus, 2009). From "Testing for Factorial Invariance in the Context of Construct Validation," by D. M. Dimitrov, 2010, *Measurement and Evaluation in Counseling and Development, 43,* p. 142. Copyright 2010 by Sage Publications. Reprinted with permission.

Chapter 7

CFA-Based Models of Multitrait–Multimethod Data

In this chapter I describe approaches to analysis of multitrait–multimethod (MTMM) data in the framework of confirmatory factor analysis (CFA) with the purpose of collecting convergent and discriminant evidence of the external aspect of validity. After a brief review of basic concepts and terms in the conventional MTMM approach (Campbell & Fiske, 1959), I describe the following CFA-based models of MTMM data: standard CFA model, correlated uniqueness (CU) model, CU-CFA model, correlated trait–correlated method minus one [CTC(*M*–1)] model, random intercept model, hierarchical CFA (HCFA) model, and multilevel confirmatory factor analysis (ML-CFA) model. A conventional MTMM analysis using latent variable modeling is also presented. The examples of models of MTMM data are provided with computer codes in Mplus (L. K. Muthén & B. O. Muthén, 2008), but these codes can be translated into the syntax of computer programs such as LISREL, EQS, or Amos, depending on the user's preferences. In this chapter, the terms *convergent validity* and *discriminant validity* are used only when necessary to maintain consistency with referenced sources, but these terms do not stand for different *types* of validity. Rather, *convergent validity* and *discriminant validity* are treated here as short labels for convergent and discriminant evidence, respectively, of the external aspect of construct validity under the unified construct-based model of validity (Messick, 1995). For the same reason, the term *scale validation* is occasionally used in this chapter as an shorthand for "validation of assessment scale data."

7.1 CONVENTIONAL MTMM ANALYSIS

MTMM analyses can be very useful in collecting convergent and discriminant evidence of the external aspect of construct validity. The MTMM matrix was first used by Campbell and Fiske (1959) to analyze correlations between multiple traits measured by multiple methods for the purpose of scale validation. *Traits* refer to constructs such as abilities, attitudes, and personality characteristics, whereas the term *multiple methods* refers to multiple tests, multiple methods of assessment, multiple response scale rates or category labels in questionnaires, multiple raters, multiple data collection procedures, or multiple occasions. The correlations between pairs of trait–method (TM) combinations can be classified as (a) same trait–different methods—or monotrait–heteromethod (MTHM)—correlations; (b) different traits–same method—or heterotrait–monomethod (HTMM)—correlations; and (c) different traits–different methods—or heterotrait–heteromethod (HTHM)—correlations (see also Fiske, 1982).

Under Campbell and Fiske's (1959) guidelines, convergent validity is supported by high correlations between scores on the same trait measured by different methods, whereas discriminant validity is supported by low correlations between scores on different traits, especially when the same method is used. Method effect is detected when correlations between scores on different traits are higher when using the same method versus when using different methods to measure these traits (method effect indicates an undesired systematic variance that distorts correlations between different traits measured with the same method).

Example 7.1 Table 7.1 represents the MTMM matrix for student data on two traits (Motivation and Anxiety) measured by two different methods (a questionnaire and school counselor evaluations). The questionnaire scores come from student responses, and the counselor scores are derived from evaluations provided by school counselors. The correlation values of 1.00 in the main diagonal have been replaced by estimates of reliability for the scores on each trait as measured by each method. These reliability estimates must be sufficiently large to warrant confidence in the interpretations based on the MTMM validity matrix.

The correlation coefficients in Table 7.1 provide evidence of both convergent and discriminant MTMM validity. Specifically, the high correlation between scores obtained with two different methods (questionnaire and counselor) on the same trait (.80 for Motivation and .77 for Anxiety) provides convergent evidence of validity. At the same time, discriminant evidence of validity is provided by the low correlations between scores on different traits (Motivation and Anxiety) measured by the same method (.22 and .27) or different methods (.12 and .15). There is, however, a possibility of method bias, as indicated by the fact that the correlations between scores on the two different traits when measured by the same method (.22 and .27) are higher than those when the traits are measured by different methods (.12 and .15).

Compared with the conventional MTMM analysis (Campbell & Fiske, 1959), CFA-based models of MTMM data are more flexible and provide more rigorous tests for convergent and discriminant evidence of construct validity as well as for the presence of method effects (e.g., Althauser, Herberlein, & Scott, 1971; Alwin, 1974; Bong & Hocevar, 2002; Coenders & Saris, 2000; Jöreskog, 1974; Marsh, 1988, 1993; Marsh & Bailey, 1991; Marsh & Hocevar, 1983). As noted by Marsh and Hocevar (1983), the most serious problem with the Campbell–Fiske criteria is that they are based on inspection of correlations between observed variables but make inferences about underlying trait and method factors. CFA-based MTMM analyses avoid this problem, take into account differences in the reliability of measures, and allow the variance to be decomposed into trait variance, method variance, and random error variance, thus enhancing the assessment of measurement quality.

TABLE 7.1

Multitrait–Multimethod Matrix for Two Traits (Motivation and Anxiety) Measured by Two Methods (Questionnaire and Counselor Evaluations)

Variable	1	2	3	4
1. T_1M_1 (Motivation; Questionnaire)	**.82**	.22	.80	.12
2. T_2M_1 (Anxiety; Questionnaire)		**.86**	.15	.77
3. T_1M_2 (Motivation; Counselor)			**.84**	.27
4. T_2M_2 (Anxiety; Counselor)				**.80**

Note. The correlation coefficients of 1.00 on the main diagonal are replaced by estimates of reliability for the scores on each trait as measured by each method. These reliability estimates must be sufficiently large to warrant confidence in the interpretations based on the multitrait–multimethod validity matrix.

7.2 THE STANDARD CFA MODEL

The standard (first-order) CFA model of MTMM data is commonly referred to as the *CFA model of MTMM data*. Under this model, each observed variable loads on one trait factor and one method factor. The method factors represent the variation attributable to the method being used. It is usually assumed that the error terms are uncorrelated and that method factors are not correlated with trait factors. The assumption of *no* correlation between traits and methods allows the variance to be decomposed into trait variance, method variance, and random error variance. Without this assumption, the solution is almost always empirically underidentified (e.g., Jöreskog, 1971b; Widaman, 1985). In general, the CFA model for MTMM data requires that (a) there are at least three traits (T ≥ 3) and three methods (M ≥ 3), (b) there are T × M measured variables used as indicators of the (T + M) factors, (c) each measured variable loads on only one method and one trait, and (d) correlations are permissible between method factors and between trait factors but not between trait and method factors (e.g., Jöreskog, 1974; Marsh & Hocevar, 1983). In case of, say, three traits and two methods, appropriate restrictions must be imposed to assure identification of the model.

Widaman (1985) developed a taxonomy of hierarchically nested CFA models for MTMM data that allows for possible combinations of four trait structures and four method structures. The options for the trait structure are (1) no trait factors, (2) one general trait factor defined by all measured variables, (3) T uncorrelated trait factors, and (4) T correlated trait factors. The *method structure* allows for (A) no method factors, (B) one general method factor defined by all measured variables, (C) M uncorrelated method factors, and (D) M correlated method factors. The combination 4D (Option 4 for trait and Option D for method), referred to as the *general CFA model for MTMM data*, allows for correlated trait factors and correlated method factors (as noted earlier, correlations between traits and methods are not assumed with MTMM models). Another combination, 4C (Option 4 for trait and Option C for method), defines an MTMM model with correlated traits and uncorrelated methods.

A CFA model of MTMM data with three traits (T = 3) and three methods (M = 3) is depicted in Figure 7.1. Specifically, the traits (Ts, in ovals) are T_1 = Anxiety, T_2 = Motivation, and T_3 = Extraversion, whereas the methods (Ms, in ovals) are M_1 = Self-rating, M_2 = Teachers, and M_3 = Parents. There are nine trait–method combinations ($T_1M_1, \ldots, T_3M_3$), each of which is from a single indicator (in boxes). The analytic expression of this model is

$$T_iM_j = \lambda_{T_i}T_i + \lambda_{M_j}M_j + \delta_{ij}\,, \qquad (7.1)$$

where λ_{T_i} and λ_{M_j} are the loadings of the measure (T_iM_j) on trait T_i and method M_j, respectively, and δ_{ij} is a residual term (the part of T_iM_j unexplained by its related factors, T_i and M_j). The residual δ_{ij}, referred to also as *disturbance* (or *uniqueness*), is an aggregation of a specific systematic effect, s_{ij}, and random error, e_{ij}. That is,

$$\delta_{ij} = s_{ij} + e_{ij}\,. \qquad (7.2)$$

In the CFA of MTMM, convergent evidence of validity is indicated by (a) statistically significant and substantial loadings on the trait factors, and (b) statistically significant decrement in fit when trait factors are deleted from model specification (e.g., Gardner, Cummings, Dunham, & Pierce, 1998; Marsh & Hocevar, 1988). Also, as suggested by Campbell and Fiske (1959), convergent evidence requires that monotrait–heteromethod correlation coefficients be significant and substantial in magnitude and be higher than heterotrait–monomethod or heterotrait–heteromethod coefficients. In fact, because correlations between CFA

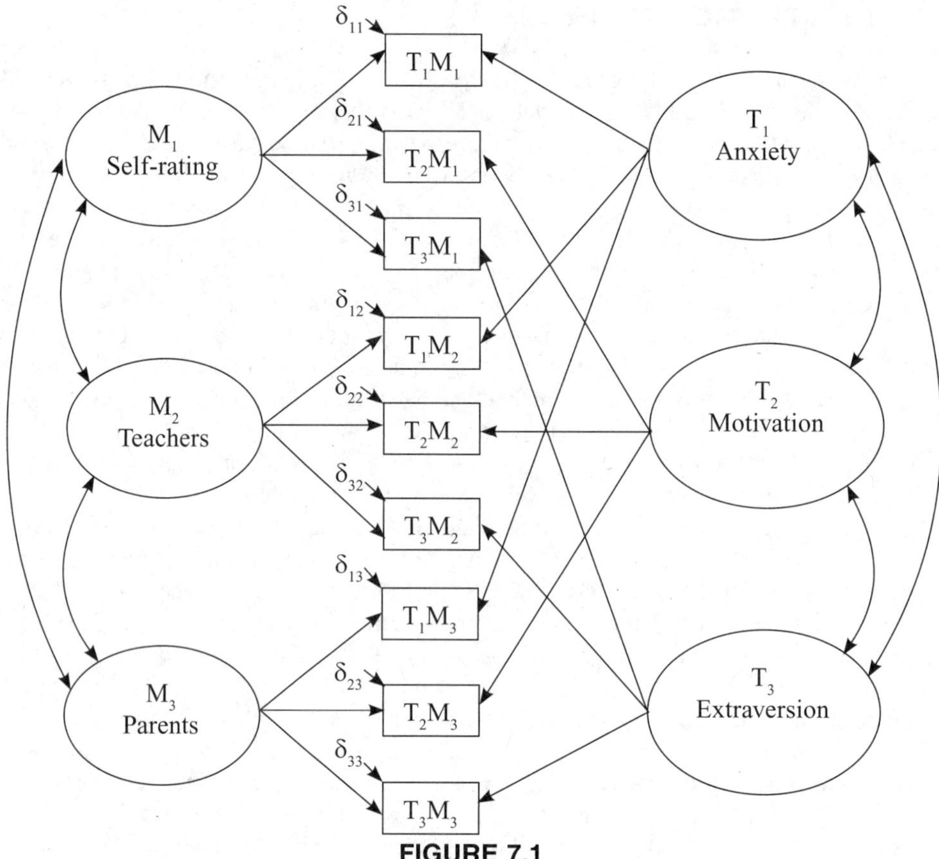

FIGURE 7.1

A Confirmatory Factor Analysis Model of Multitrait–Multimethod Data With Three Traits (T) and Three Methods (M)

factors essentially represent correlations between true (error-free) scale scores, Campbell and Fiske's criteria of determining convergent and discriminant correlation patterns can be readily and even more accurately applied (e.g., Marsh & Hocevar, 1988).

Although there are no universally accepted criteria for discriminant evidence of validity in CFA of MTMM data, there is an overall agreement that high trait correlations indicate lack of discriminant evidence, whereas low correlations between trait factors support discriminant evidence of validity. Based on this, discriminant evidence can be tested by setting the correlation between trait factors to 1.0, which is the equivalent of a single-factor model, to see whether this model fits better than the initial model where the trait factor correlations are freely estimated (note that the former model is nested within the latter). If the chi-square difference test for these two models is statistically significant (i.e., the trait factors are not perfectly correlated), discriminant evidence of validity would be supported (e.g., Kenny, 1979; Marsh et al., 1988; Stacy, Widaman, Hayes, & DiMateo, 1985).

Method effect in a CFA of MTMM is indicated by a statistically significant decrement in fit when the method factors are deleted from the model specifications (e.g., Gardner et al., 1998; Marsh & Hocevar, 1988). As the trait-only model, obtained after deleting the method factors, is nested within the initial (trait and method) model, a statistically significant chi-square difference test between the two models would indicate the presence of a method effect.

In general, the methods effects can be additive or multiplicative. When method effects are additive, they do not vary in size across traits. Additive effects can be expected when the methods consist of category labels or scale lengths in questionnaires. People may differ in their way of using a certain response scale, but the use of such a scale by a single person is about the same across traits (Andrews, 1984; Kumar & Dillon, 1992). In contrast, when method effects are multiplicative, the method correlation would be proportional to the correlations between the traits (e.g., Campbell & O'Connell, 1967; Cudeck, 1988). Multiplicative effects may occur when (a) raters are used as methods (e.g., Bagozzi & Yi, 1991); (b) ordinal measurements are used, and, thus, categorization errors of closely related variables can be correlated (e.g., Coenders, Satorra, & Saris, 1997); and (c) there is differential augmentation and differential attenuation (Campbell & O'Connell, 1967, 1982). Multiplicative effects can be analyzed by using the direct product (DP) model (Browne, 1984) or the correlated uniqueness (CU) model (Kenny, 1976; Marsh, 1988, 1989). The CU model, which handles both additive and multiplicative effects under certain constraints on correlated errors, is discussed next.

7.3 THE CU MODEL

In a study on standard CFA models of MTMM data, Marsh (1989) showed that such models often lead to ill-defined solutions. As an alternative, he used a CFA-based model, referred to as the CU model, in which there are no method factors; instead, method effects are represented as correlated errors. The CU approach to MTMM data was first demonstrated by Kenny (1979) for the restricted case of two trait factors, and then it was extended by Marsh (1989) for the general case of three or more trait factors. Marsh and Bailey (1991) showed that the CU model almost always leads to proper solutions and rarely leads to problems of empirical underidentification, failure to converge, or inadmissible estimates (i.e., Heywood cases—e.g., negative estimates of variances and/or correlation estimates greater than 1.00 in absolute values).

When the number of trait factors is three ($T = 3$), the CU model is equivalent to the CFA model in which the correlations between method factors are not assumed. When the number of traits is greater than three ($T > 3$), the CFA model is nested within the CU model (Marsh & Bailey, 1991; Corten et al., 2002). The CU model in Figure 7.2 contains trait factors but does not contain method factors—instead, methods effects are represented as correlated uniquenesses.

Under the CU model of MTMM data, the correlated uniquenesses are, in fact, covariances between the residual terms of the observed variables associated with the same method. For example, the correlated uniquenesses associated with the first method (M_1) in Figure 7.2 are the following covariances: $\text{Cov}(\delta_{11}, \delta_{21})$, $\text{Cov}(\delta_{11}, \delta_{31})$, and $\text{Cov}(\delta_{21}, \delta_{31})$. Thus, although nonzero values of the covariances indicate that the uniquenesses are correlated, the terminology may be misleading because the "correlated uniquenesses" are covariances—*not* correlations.

Under CFA models of MTMM data, the effects of a particular method are implicitly assumed to be unidimensional, and the sizes of the method factor loadings provide an estimate of its influence on each measured variable (e.g., see Figure 7.1). Under the CU model, there is no assumption of unidimensionality of effects associated with a particular method. Instead, method effects are represented as correlated uniquenesses, that is, correlations between pairs of variables measured with the same method after removing trait effects. If these correlations are statistically significant and sufficiently large, there is evidence for method effects (Marsh & Bailey, 1991).

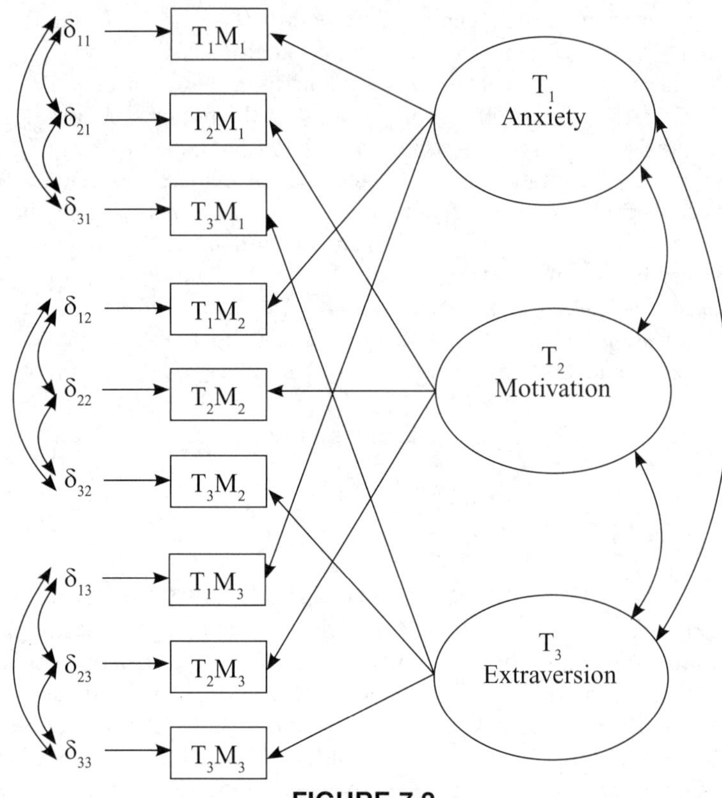

FIGURE 7.2

A Correlated Uniqueness Model With Three Traits (T)

Coenders and Saris (2000) showed that CFA models of MTMM data can be equivalently represented by a CU model with additive constraints on the correlated errors (e.g., the CU model in Figure 7.2 is equivalent to the CFA model in Figure 7.1 if the correlations between the method factors are fixed to zero). They also showed that, for MTMM designs with three methods (M = 3), a CU model with multiplicative constraints is equivalent to the DP model which is designed to detect multiplicative effects (Browne, 1984). For a detailed discussion on data fit of different MTMM models, the reader may refer to Corten et al. (2002).

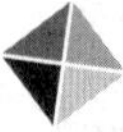

Example 7.2 This example provides a path diagram and brief discussion of results for the CU model used by Kenny (1979) in a case of two traits and four methods. In Figure 7.3, the traits denoted ACS and ACP represent attitude toward cigarette smoking and attitude toward capital punishment, respectively. Each trait is measured by four methods of scaling, denoted here by A, B, C, and D. Specifically, A = semantic differential, B = Likert scale, C = Thurstone scale, and D = Guilford scale (Kenny, 1979, p. 189). In fact, Kenny (1979) employed this CU model using correlation data provided by Jaccard, Weber, and Lundmark (1975). As the general CFA model of MTMM data requires at least three traits and three methods ($T \geq 3$ and $M \geq 3$), which is not the case here, Kenny (1979) introduced a CU model by associating a unique factor to each variable and then allowing the unique factors of the variables that are related to the same method to correlate.

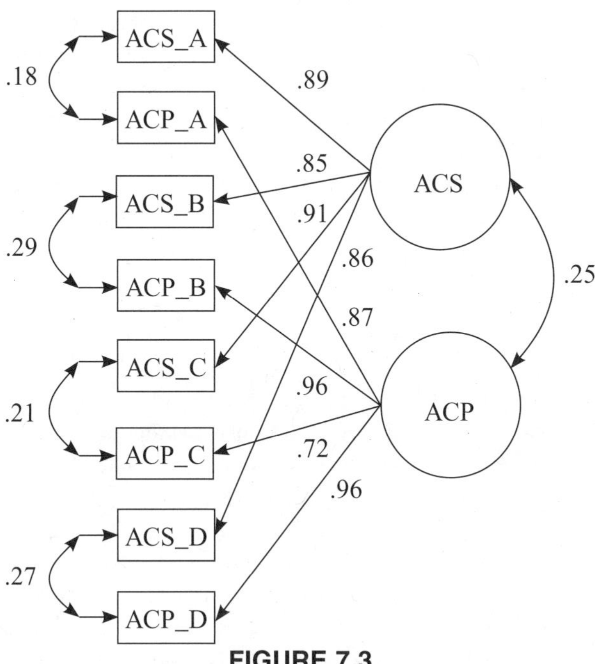

FIGURE 7.3

A Correlated Uniqueness Model of Multitrait–Multimethod Data in a Case With Two Traits (ACS and ACP) and Four Methods (A, B, C, and D)

Note. ACS = attitude toward cigarette smoking; ACP = attitude toward capital punishment. A = semantic differential; B = Likert scale; C = Thurstone scale; D = Guilford scale.

The chi-square test statistic reported by Kenny (1979, p. 190) was not statistically significant, $\chi^2(15) = 10.35, p > .05$, thus indicating a reasonable data fit for the CU model in Figure 7.3. Also, a strong convergent evidence of validity is indicated by the high values of the factor loadings for both the ACS trait (from .85 to .91) and the ACP trait (from .72 to .96).

To test for discriminant evidence, Kenny (1979, p. 190) fixed the correlation between the two trait factors to 1.00. Under this constraint, the chi-square test statistic for the resulting model is $\chi^2(16) = 120.75$. The chi-square difference between this model and the initial model is $\Delta\chi^2 = 120.75 - 10.35 = 110.40$; ($\Delta df = 16 - 15 = 1$). As the chi-square difference is statistically significant, $\Delta\chi^2(1) = 110.40, p < .001$, the conclusion is that the correlation between the two traits is *not* equal to 1.0 (i.e., the traits are not perfectly correlated). Thus, although the two traits are somewhat correlated ($r = .25$), the data indicate a reasonable level of discrimination between them. This conclusion is based on the argument that significant correlations between trait factors should only be interpreted as a lack of discriminant evidence when such correlations approach 1.0 or are inconsistent with the substantive nature of the data (Marsh & Hocevar, 1983). Furthermore, as the correlations between the unique factors for variables measured by the same method are relatively low (from .18 to .29), there is *no* evidence of method effect.

Correlated uniquenesses may stem, for example, from relative answers in a test battery or as a consequence of acquiescence bias. Relative answers typically occur when it is likely that respondents compare answers on questions that are placed in a battery. The acquiescence bias occurs when respondents tend to agree with statements regardless of their content—typically, when scales such as agree/disagree, true/false, or yes/no are used. Different models for relative answers and acquiescence bias have been defined and tested by Saris and Aalberts (2003).

A major drawback of the CU model is that the method effects are not modeled explicitly. Rather, method effects are relegated to the uniqueness terms of the trait–method measurements. Under the CU model (e.g., Figure 7.2), the uniqueness term, δ_{ij}, for a trait–method measurement (T_iM_j) is an aggregation of systematic specific effect, random error, and method effect. Unlike the CFA model (e.g., Figure 7.1), where the uniqueness term consists of systematic specific effect and random error, $\delta_{ij} = s_{ij} + e_{ij}$, the uniqueness term of the CU model is $\delta_{ij} = s_{ij} + e_{ij} + \lambda_{M_j}M_j$ (see Equations 7.1 and 7.2 for the CFA model).

7.4 THE CU-CFA MODEL

Although the CU model renders convergent and proper solutions far more often than the standard CFA model (e.g., Conway, 1996; Marsh, 1990; Marsh & Bailey, 1991), there are problems with the CU model that may lead to incomplete and inaccurate inferences regarding construct validity. Three things are of particular concern under the CU model: (a) There is a potential bias in estimated trait factor correlations and trait factor loadings (Lance, Noble, & Scullen, 2002); (b) it is assumed that the methods are uncorrelated, yet research indicates that methods routinely *are* correlated (e.g., Becker & Cote, 1994; Kenny & Kashy, 1992; Marsh, 1989); and (c) variance components are not directly estimable, which is an issue because information about the method variance is important in determining its effects on construct validity (e.g., Doty & Glick, 1998).

Conway (1998) proposed an estimation of the average proportion of method variance under the CU model by averaging the CUs. A general explanation of this averaging method was provided by Scullen (1999), who noted that the method is based on the fact that, as noted earlier, the CUs under the CU model are covariances (not correlations) and they directly estimate the method variance of the observed variables. The average method variance can be useful in evaluating the average method effect, but it does not provide information about how specific measures are affected by a particular method. To address this problem, Scullen (1999) proposed a method for partitioning observed variance into trait- and method-related components. This method, referred to as the *CU-CFA method*, consists of two steps. First, a CU analysis is conducted to partition the variance in each observed variable into a trait component and a unique component. Second, follow-up CFAs are conducted to partition the unique variance component of each variable into method variance and error variance (specifically, a standard CFA of the correlated uniquenesses is conducted separately for each method).

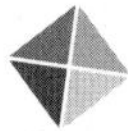

Example 7.3 This example illustrates the CU-CFA of MTMM data using Mplus. The MTMM data shown in Table 7.2 are correlations between TM measures on three traits and three methods. These correlations were reported by Conway (1998, p. 217, Table 2) in a study that assessed job applicants on Motivation, Job Knowledge, and Apprehensiveness, with the assessments being made by three raters in an employment interview panel.

The same data were used by Scullen (1999) to illustrate the CU-CFA method using the PROC CALIS procedure in the statistical package SAS (SAS syntax code is not provided in Scullen, 1999). Although the reader is encouraged to examine previous studies using these data (Conway, 1998; Scullen, 1999), this example describes how to conduct the two-step CU-CFA analysis using Mplus.

Step 1. In the first step, a CU analysis of the MTMM data is conducted. The MTMM data listed in Table 7.2 are correlations between TM measures for three traits (T_1 = Motivation, T_2 = Job Knowledge, T_3 = Apprehensiveness) and their associated methods (M_1 = Rater 1, M_2 = Rater 2, and M_3 = Rater 3). The CU model is depicted in Figure 7.4.

TABLE 7.2

Multitrait–Multimethod Matrix for Assessment of Job Applicants on Three Traits by Three Methods

Variable	1	2	3	4	5	6	7	8	9
1. T_1M_1	1.00								
2. T_2M_1	0.60	1.00							
3. T_3M_1	0.51	0.64	1.00						
4. T_1M_2	0.51	0.54	0.40	1.00					
5. T_2M_2	0.22	0.58	0.34	0.50	1.00				
6. T_3M_2	0.32	0.44	0.59	0.54	0.60	1.00			
7. T_1M_3	0.54	0.32	0.34	0.53	0.15	0.26	1.00		
8. T_2M_3	0.35	0.60	0.40	0.41	0.62	0.41	0.43	1.00	
9. T_3M_3	0.37	0.43	0.63	0.37	0.31	0.58	0.51	0.56	1.00

Note. N = 102. T_1 = Motivation; T_2 = Job Knowledge; T_3 = Apprehensiveness; M_1 = Rater 1; M_2 = Rater 2; and M_3 = Rater 3. From "Estimation and Uses of the Proportion of Method Variance for Multitrait–Multimethod Data," by J. M. Conway, 1998, *Organizational Research Methods, 1,* p. 216. Copyright 1998 by Sage Publications. Reprinted with permission.

The Mplus code for the CU model in Figure 7.4 is provided in Table 7.3. In the Mplus output, the chi-square test for model fit was not statistically significant, $\chi^2(15) = 22.34$, $p = .099$, thus indicating a reasonable data fit. Other goodness-of-fit indices also supported data fit of the CU model: CFI = .985, TLI = .965, RMSEA = .069, and SRMR = .058. As a side note, using Mplus with the data in Table 7.2 to conduct a standard CFA with three traits and three methods (see Figure 7.1) led to estimation problems (because of a large negative estimate of the variance for the T_1M_3 measure). This problem is not a surprise because, as noted earlier, the standard CFA of MTMM data often yields poorly defined results (e.g., Marsh & Bailey, 1991).

Table 7.4 provides a selected output (with added comments) from the execution of the Mplus code in Table 7.3. The top panel in Table 7.4 contains the unstandardized factor loadings of the three trait factors on their respective TM measures. The squared values of these loadings show what proportion of the variance in each TM measure is attributed to the respective trait factor. The next panel provides the correlations between the trait factors. The next panel shows the correlated uniquenesses (covariances between residual terms) for the TM measures of methods M_1, M_2, and M_3, respectively. Finally, the last panel shows the residual variances (uniquenesses) of the TM measures of methods M_1, M_2, and M_3, respectively. The matrix of residual variances and covariances of the TM measures for each method is used as input data in separate CFAs in Step 2 of the CU-CFA.

Step 2. In this step, separate CFAs on the residual variances and covariances of the TM measures of methods M1, M2, and M3, respectively, are conducted. Table 7.5 shows the Mplus code and selected results for method M1 (i.e., Rater 1). The results from CFAs on CUs for methods M2 and M3 (i.e., Raters 2 and 3) were obtained in a similar fashion. They are shown in Table 7.6, along with other results from both Step 1 and Step 2 in the CU-CFA of the MTMM matrix in this example.

For proper interpretation of the results in Table 7.6, some clarifications need to be made. First, Step 1 in the CU-CFA yields the proportion of the variance in each TM measure that is trait-related, *not* an estimate of the trait variance per se. Also, as noted in the discussion of CU models, the uniqueness term, δ_{ij}, for a TM measurement (T_iM_j) is an aggregation of systematic specific effect, random error, and method effect. For example, in Table 7.6 the trait-related estimate of .392 for the variance in the TM measurement T_1M_1 (T_1 = Motiva-

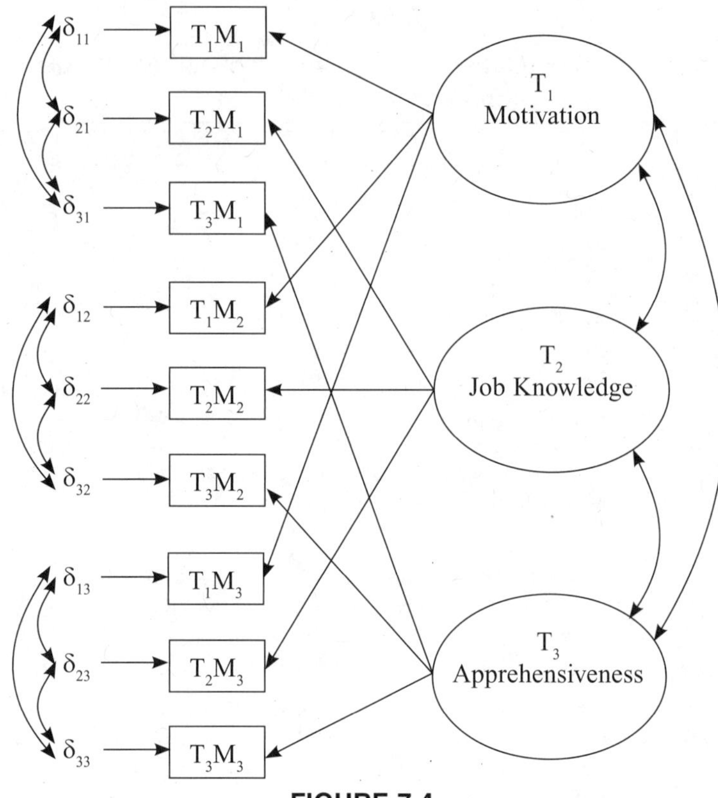

FIGURE 7.4

A Correlated Uniqueness–Confirmatory Factor Analysis Model of Multitrait–Multimethod Data for Three Traits (T_1, T_2, and T_3) and Three Raters as Methods (M_1, M_2, and M_3)

tion, M_1 = Rater 1) indicates that 39.2% of the variance in scores on motivation provided by the first rater are attributed to Motivation. The remaining 59.8% of this variance represents an aggregation of specific systematic effect, random error, and effect of the first rater (method M1).

Furthermore, Step 2 in the CU-CFA yields the proportion of variance in each TM measure that is method-related, *not* an estimate of the method variance per se. To illustrate, again for the T_1M_1 measure in Table 7.6, the method-related variance of .165 indicates that 16.5% of the variance in scores on motivation provided by the first rater is attributed to that rater. The average method-related variance of .217 for Rater 1 shows that this rater accounts for 21.7% of the variance in all three traits (Motivation, Job Knowledge, and Apprehensiveness).

7.5 THE CORRELATED TRAIT–CORRELATED METHOD MINUS ONE [CTC(*M*–1)] MODEL

As noted earlier, major disadvantages of the standard CFA model of MTMM data, referred to also as the *correlated trait–correlated method* (CTCM) model, are that this model is prone to identification and/or convergence problems and often renders solutions that contain out-of-range parameters (e.g., improper solutions with negative estimates of variances).

TABLE 7.3

Mplus Code for Correlated Uniqueness Multitrait–Multimethod (MTMM) Model—Step 1 in Correlated Uniqueness–Confirmatory Factor Analysis Model of MTMM Data

```
     DATA:  FILE IS CUCFA.DAT;        ! Correlations in Table 7.2, Conway (1998)
            TYPE IS CORRELATION;
            NOBS ARE 102;
 VARIABLE:  NAMES ARE T1M1 T2M1 T3M1 T1M2 T2M2 T3M2 T1M3 T2M3 T3M3;
 ANALYSIS:  ESTIMATOR=ML;
    MODEL:  T1 BY T1M1* T1M2 T1M3;
            T2 BY T2M1* T2M2 T2M3;
            T3 BY T3M1* T3M2 T3M3;
            T1@1.0; T2@1.0; T3@1.0;
            T1M1 T2M1 WITH T3M1; T1M1 WITH T2M1;
            T1M2 T2M2 WITH T3M2; T1M2 WITH T2M2;
            T1M3 T2M3 WITH T3M3; T1M3 WITH T2M3;
            T1 T2 WITH T3; T1 WITH T2;
   OUTPUT:  SAMPSTAT MODINDICES(3.84) STAND RESIDUAL;
```

Furthermore, the interpretation of the trait and method factors in the CTCM model is ambiguous when all method factors are correlated because it is unclear whether the method factors represent method effects or, rather, general trait effects. To avoid problems with the CTCM model, Eid (2000) proposed a model that allows a satisfactory determination of the variance components attributable to trait and method effects. His model, referred to as the *correlated trait–correlated method minus one* [*CTC(M–1)*] *model*, is a variant of the CTCM model that contains one method factor less—hence, the name of the model. Specifically, the method factors in the CTC(*M*–1) model are defined by restricting the number of method factors to one fewer than the number of methods included in the design. One method is chosen as the comparison standard, and all other methods are contrasted with this standard.

In the CTC(*M*–1) model, the standard method, referred to also as the *reference method*, is either a gold standard measure (when such measure exists) or is chosen because it provides a convenient interpretation of the results. There is no method factor for the reference method, but there is a method factor for each nonreference method. That is, there are measures for all methods, but method factors are used only for the nonreference methods. As there is no method factor for the reference method, the trait factors represent the common factors measured with the reference method. The method factors can be interpreted as method-specific deviations from the reference method. They reflect the over- or underestimation of a trait score by a nonreference method with respect to the trait-score prediction based on the reference method (Eid, 2000; Eid, Lischetzke, Nussbeck, & Trierweiler, 2003).

Figure 7.5 depicts a CTC(*M*–1) model obtained from the CTCM model in Figure 7.1 by selecting method M_1 (self-rating) as the reference method (the residual terms of the TM measures for M_1 in Figure 7.1 are not equal to their counterparts in Figure 7.5). The method factors for the parent and teacher reports represent deviations of the parent and teacher ratings from the self-report ratings of students on a specific trait (Anxiety, Motivation, or Extraversion).

Gaudron and Vautier (2007) used the CTC(*M*–1) model to assess to what extent interindividual variability in vocational interests accounts for interindividual variability in leisure and family interests, respectively. Specifically, the vocational domain was the standard method against which the two other domains (leisure and family life) were contrasted on three activities (traits), separately for each Holland's type: Realistic, Investigative, Artistic, Social, Enterprising, and Conventional (Holland, 1959, 1997). For example, the three activities

TABLE 7.4

Selected Mplus Output From the Correlated Uniqueness Multitrait–Multimethod Data on Assessment of Job Applicants on Three Traits by Three Methods (Comments Added)

	Unstandardized Model Results				
Mplus Item	**Est.**	***SE***	**Est./*SE***	***p* value**	**Comment**
T1 by					
T1M1	**0.626**	0.092	6.812	.000	Factor loadings of the trait factor T1 on its TM measures
T1M2	**0.777**	0.097	8.043	.000	
T1M3	**0.730**	0.096	7.564	.000	
T2 by					
T2M1	**0.742**	0.085	8.718	.000	Factor loadings of the trait factor T2 on its TM measures
T2M2	**0.738**	0.086	8.556	.000	
T2M3	**0.834**	0.090	9.256	.000	
T3 by					
T3M1	**0.739**	0.085	8.680	.000	Factor loadings of the trait factor T3 on its TM measures
T3M2	**0.765**	0.088	8.696	.000	
T3M3	**0.811**	0.089	9.101	.000	
T1 with					
T3	**0.611**	0.083	7.390	.000	Correlations between the trait factors
T2	**0.597**	0.084	7.078	.000	
T2 with					
T3	**0.644**	0.073	8.836	.000	
T1M1 with					
T3M1	**0.158**	0.063	2.509	.012	Correlated uniquenesses for method M1 (Rater 1): covariances between the residual terms of the TM measures of method M1 (used as off-diagonal elements in the covariance matrix in Step 2—CFA of the correlated uniquenesses for method M1).
T2M1	**0.238**	0.067	3.564	.000	
T2M1 with					
T3M1	**0.226**	0.063	3.560	.000	
T1M2 with					
T3M2	**0.199**	0.069	2.897	.004	Correlated uniquenesses for method M2 (Rater 2): covariances between the residual terms of the TM measures of method M2 (used as off-diagonal elements in the covariance matrix in Step 2—CFA of the correlated uniquenesses for method M2).
T2M2	**0.167**	0.066	2.508	.012	
T2M2 with					
T3M2	**0.253**	0.067	3.778	.000	
T1M3 with					
T3M3	**0.179**	0.067	2.676	.007	Correlated uniquenesses for method M3 (Rater 3): covariances between the residual terms of the TM measures of method M3 (used as off-diagonal elements in the covariance matrix in Step 2—CFA of the correlated uniquenesses for method M3).
T2M3	**0.153**	0.067	2.297	.002	
T2M3 with					
T3M3	**0.154**	0.064	2.393	.017	
Residual Variances					
T1M1	**0.530**	0.096	5.542	.000	Residual variances (uniquenesses) of the TM measures of method M1 (used as diagonal elements in the covariance matrix in Step 2—CFA of the correlated uniquenesses for method M1).
T2M1	**0.420**	0.084	5.026	.000	
T3M1	**0.394**	0.081	4.883	.000	
T1M2	**0.427**	0.106	4.041	.000	Residual variances (uniquenesses) of the TM measures of method M2 (used as diagonal elements in the covariance matrix in Step 2—CFA of the correlated uniquenesses for method M2).
T2M2	**0.423**	0.084	5.050	.000	
T3M2	**0.436**	0.088	4.972	.000	
T1M3	**0.468**	0.102	4.573	.000	Residual variances (uniquenesses) of the TM measures of method M3 (used as diagonal elements in the covariance matrix in Step 2—CFA of the correlated uniquenesses for method M3).
T2M3	**0.343**	0.088	3.874	.000	
T3M3	**0.357**	0.087	4.120	.000	

Note. Est. = Estimate of the factor loading; *SE* = standard error; Est./*SE* = critical ratio; *p* value = *p* value associated with the critical ratio (under the standard normal distribution); TM = trait–method; T1 = Motivation; T2 = Job Knowledge; T3 = Apprehensiveness; M1 = Rater 1; M2 = Rater 2; and M3 = Rater 3. All parameter estimates (in boldface) are significant ($p < .001$).

TABLE 7.5

Mplus Code and Selected Output for the Confirmatory Factor Analysis (CFA) of Correlated Uniqueness (CU) of the Trait–Method (TM) Measures of Method 1—Step 2 in CU–CFA Model of Multitrait–Multimethod Data

```
               DATA:  FILE IS COV_M1.DAT;        ! Residual variances and covariances of the trait–
                                                   method measures of method M1
TYPE IS COVARIANCE:   NOBS ARE 102;              ! N = 102 (sample size)
           VARIABLE:  NAMES ARE T1M1 T2M1 T3M1;
           ANALYSIS:  ESTIMATOR=ML;
              MODEL:  M1 BY T1M1* T2M1 T3M1;     ! All TM indicators of M1 are freely estimated
                      M1@1.0;                    ! The variance of the method factor M1set to 1.0
             OUTPUT:  SAMPSTAT MODINDICES(3.84) STAND RESIDUAL;
```

Selected Output:

Covariances/Correlations/Residual Correlations[a]

	T1M1	**T2M1**	**T3M1**
T1M1	0.530		
T2M1	0.238	0.420	
T3M1	0.158	0.226	0.394

MODEL RESULTS

	Estimate	***SE***	**Est./*SE***	***p* value**
M1 by				
T1M1	**0.406**	0.078	5.184	0.000
T2M1	**0.581**	0.078	7.436	0.000
T3M1	**0.385**	0.069	5.614	0.000
Residual Variances				
T1M1	**0.360**	0.061	5.899	0.000
T2M1	**0.079**	0.071	1.107	0.268
T3M1	**0.242**	0.046	5.264	0.000

Note. The Mplus code was used for the CFA of the CUs of the TM measures of methods M2 and M3 by replacing the M1 input data (residual variances and covariances) in the command line DATA and the M1 notations in the command lines VARIABLE and MODEL with those for M2 and M3, respectively.

[a]This matrix represents the input data (COV_M1.DAT) in the Mplus code—it contains the residual variances and covariances (CUs) for the TM measures of M1 that are reported with the Mplus output in Step 1 (see Table 7.4).

for the Artistic type were as follows: to act in a play, to play a musical instrument, and to create a drawing. Use of the CTC(*M*–1) model, for each Holland's type separately, allowed for estimating the correlations between the activities of Holland's type on the one hand, and the correlation between the standard measure (vocational interest) and the contextualized measure (leisure/family interest) on the other (Gaudron & Vautier, 2007).

A readable discussion on the meaning of the latent variables in the CTC(*M*–1) model and how to interpret results obtained through the use of this model is provided in an article by Geiser, Eid, and Nussbeck (2008). This article also addresses concerns about potential problems with the CTC(*M*–1) model raised in previous research (Maydeu-Olivares & Coffman, 2006). A major point of concern is the asymmetry of the CTC(*M*–1) model in the sense that the goodness-of-fit and the parameter estimates in this model depend on the selection of the reference method. To address this issue, Geiser et al. (2008) proposed a restricted CTC(*M*–1) model. They used different versions of the proposed model in validating the trait Optimism (and its relation to the trait Pessimism), as measured by positively and negatively worded items in the Life Orientation Test (LOT; Scheier & Carver, 1985). Figure 7.6 depicts a CTC(*M*–1) model used in both studies (Geiser et al., 2008; Maydeu-Olivares & Coffman, 2006), whereas Figure 7.7 depicts a restricted version of this model proposed by Geiser et al. (2008). The items are numbered as in the original LOT questionnaire. The

TABLE 7.6

Results From the Correlated Uniqueness-Confirmatory Factor Analysis of the Multitrait–Multimethod Data Matrix in Table 7.2

	Trait-Related Estimates[a]		Method-Related Estimates[b]		
Method–Trait	**FL**	**Var.**[c]	**FL**	**Var.**[d]	**Ave. Var.**[e]
M1 (Rater 1)					.217
T1 (Motivation)	.626	.392	.406	.165	
T2 (Job Knowledge)	.742	.551	.581	.338	
T3 (Apprehensiveness)	.739	.546	.385	.148	
M2 (Rater 2)					.213
T1 (Motivation)	.777	.604	.361	.130	
T2 (Job Knowledge)	.738	.545	.459	.211	
T3 (Apprehensiveness)	.765	.585	.546	.298	
M3 (Rater 3)					.161
T1 (Motivation)	.730	.533	.420	.176	
T2 (Job Knowledge)	.834	.696	.361	.130	
T3 (Apprehensiveness)	.811	.658	.422	.178	

Note. $N = 102$. FL = factor loading; Var. = variance; Ave. Var. = average variance.
[a]Unstandardized estimates obtained at Step 1. [b]Unstandardized estimates obtained at Step 2. [c]Squared trait-factor loading (proportion of the variance in the Trait–Method measure of the trait). [d]Squared method-factor loading (proportion of the variance in the Trait–Method measure of the method). [e]Average proportion of method-related variance for each measurement method.

positively worded items (i1, i4, and i5) are chosen as the reference method and negatively worded items as the nonreference method. In Figure 7.6, the CTC(M–1) model has one trait factor (Optimism) and one method factor (negatively worded items). The other method factor (positively worded items) is chosen as reference method.

As stated by Geiser et al. (2008), the restricted CTC(M–1) model presented in Figure 7.7 assumes that there are two common factors: one factor for the reference method (the positively worded items) and one factor for the nonreference method (the negatively worded items). The common factor pertaining to the negatively worded items is regressed on the common factor underlying the positively worded items. The residual associated with the nonreference factor captures the common deviation of the negative items from the positive items (i.e., method effect). Convergent evidence of validity is supported if the variance explained by the method factor is small in comparison with the variance accounted for by the trait factor. In contrast, a lack of convergent evidence is indicated by a large amount of method-specific variance after statistically controlling for the trait factor. In other words, a relatively large amount of the error-free variance associated with the negatively worded items cannot be explained by the trait optimism as measured by positively worded items (Geiser et al., 2008).

7.6 THE RANDOM INTERCEPT FACTOR MODEL

The random intercept model was proposed by Maydeu-Olivares and Coffman (2006). Basically, this is a common factor model in which the intercept is decomposed into fixed and random parts. The fixed part of the intercept is the same for all individuals but may differ across items, whereas the random part may vary across respondents but remains the same across all items (observed measures). That is, the variance of each item can be decomposed into parts related to the common latent factor (trait), random intercept, and random error (the variance of the fixed part is zero). The random intercept captures individual differences in scale usage that are common across items—for example, response style of acquiescence and social desirability.

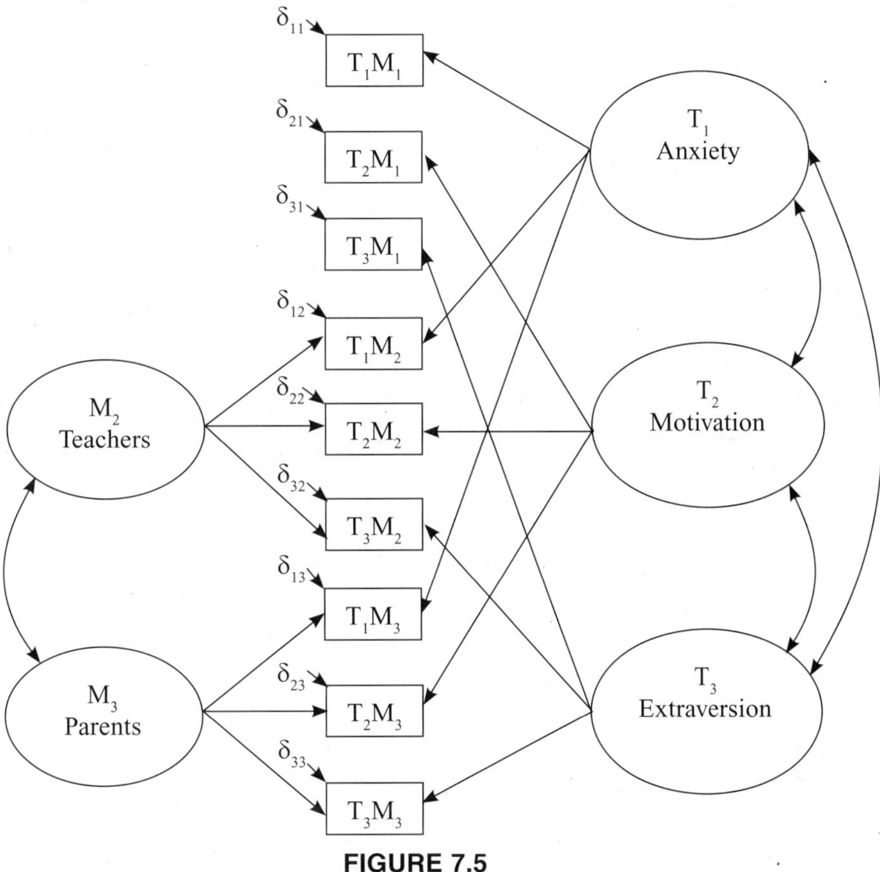

FIGURE 7.5

A Correlated Trait–Correlated Method Minus One Model Obtained From the Correlated Trait–Correlated Method Model in Figure 7.1 by Using the First Method (M_1) as a Reference Method

Figure 7.8 depicts the random intercept model used by Maydeu-Olivares and Coffman (2006). They compared results obtained through the use of this model with those obtained via the CTC(*M*–1) model depicted in Figure 7.6 for the same data on seven positively and negatively worded items from LOT. This model has two factors: for one of them, the factor loadings are all fixed to 1 and the variance of the random intercepts is estimated.

In response to concerns that Maydeu-Olivares and Coffman (2006) raised about the CTC(*M*–1) model, Geiser et al. (2008) argued that these concerns rest on an improper interpretation of the meaning of the latent factors in the CTC(*M*–1) model. As noted in the previous section, Geiser et al. (2008) introduced the restricted CTC(*M*–1) model to avoid the asymmetry problem with the CTC(*M*–1) and illustrated this by using the restricted CTC(*M*–1) model in Figure 7.7. They clarified that under the CTC(*M*–1) model, the correlations between the nonreference factor and external variables are semipartial correlations. Thus, if the positively worded items are taken as the reference method, this would provide information about whether adding the negatively worded items adds to predicting external variables. Geiser et al. (2008) used this interpretation to explain why the trait factor scores obtained from the CTC(*M*–1) model showed considerably lower correlations with external criteria (hopelessness, avoidance,

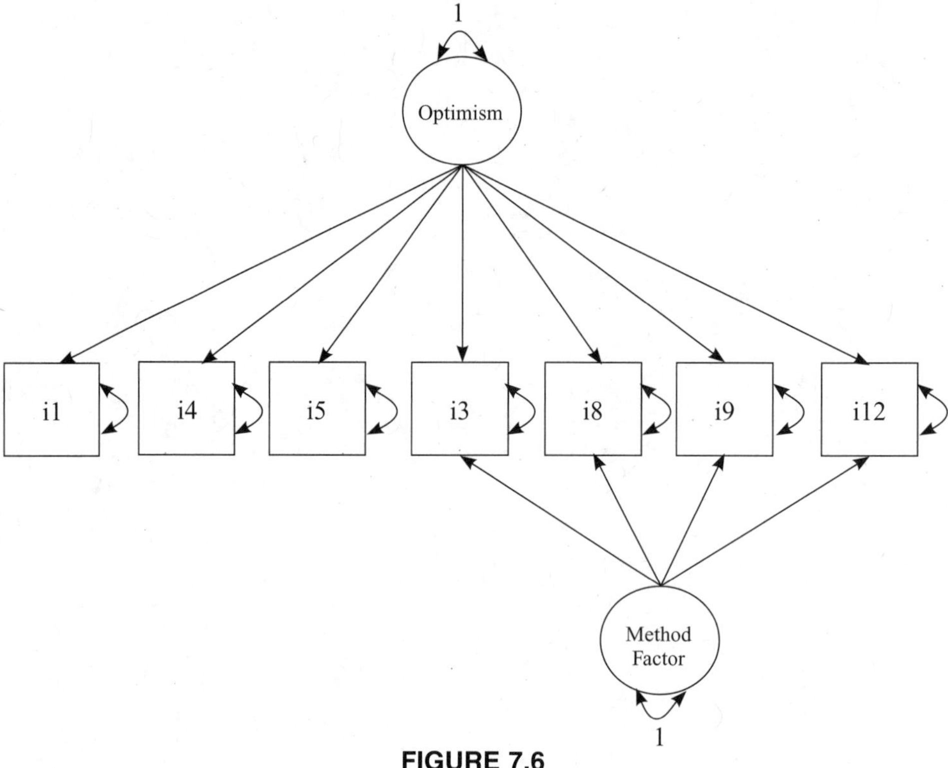

FIGURE 7.6

A Correlated Trait–Correlated Method Minus One Model Fitted to the Life Orientation Test Data (Chang et al., 1994)

Note. Items 1, 4, and 5 are positively worded, whereas Items 3, 8, 9, and 12 are negatively worded. Variances are depicted with double-headed arrows from a variable to itself. The variances of the factors are fixed to 1 for identification. From "Random Intercept Item Factor Analysis," by A. Maydeu-Olivares and D. L. Coffman, 2006, *Psychological Methods, 11,* p. 346. Copyright 2006 by the American Psychological Association. Reprinted with permission.

and negative problem orientation) than did both the trait factor scores based on the random intercept factor model and a simple sum score of the LOT items.

Geiser et al. (2008) also suggested that (a) the random intercept model of Maydeu-Olivares and Coffman (2006) is appropriate "if there is good reason to assume that a consistent response style characterizes the entire set of items" (p. 50), and (b) the CTC(M–1) model (or its restricted variant) is a good choice "if one has applied structurally different methods to measure the same attribute or attributes, and one wishes to determine the degree of convergent validity of the different methods" (p. 56). To clarify, methods are called *structurally different* when they are not interchangeable—that is, they differ from each other with respect to important aspects (e.g., in assessing anxiety, the methods of self-report, counselors, and parents are not interchangeable).

7.7 THE HIERARCHICAL CFA (HCFA) MODEL

An HCFA model of MTMM data is a two-level CFA in which the trait–method measures are first-order factors measured by multiple indicators, whereas the trait and method fac-

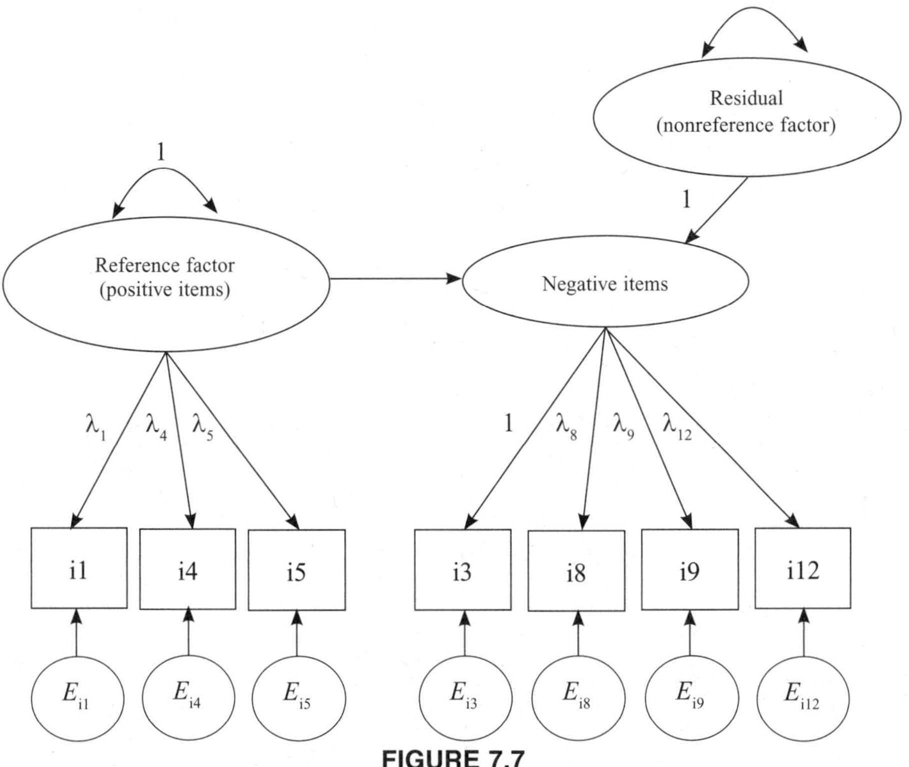

FIGURE 7.7

Path Diagram of a Restricted Correlated Trait–Correlated Method Minus One Model

Note. The common factor of the nonreference method (negative items) is regressed on the common factor of the reference method (positive items). The residual associated with the nonreference factor captures the common deviation of the negative items from the positive items (i.e., method effect). From "On the Meaning of the Latent Variables in the CT-C(*M*-1) Model: A Comment on Maydeu-Olivares and Coffman (2006)," by C. Geiser, M. Eid, and F. W. Nussbeck, 2008, *Psychological Methods, 13,* p. 54. Copyright 2008 by the American Psychological Association. Reprinted with permission.

tors represent second-order factors. Figure 7.9 depicts an HCFA model for correlated trait factors and correlated method factors. There are three second-order trait factors (T_1, T_2, and T_3), two second-order method factors (M_1 and M_2), and six first-order factors for all TM combinations (T_1M_1, . . ., T_3M_2). Each first-order factor is measured by three indicators, so there are nine *X*-indicators for the TM measures related to method M_1 and nine *Y*-indicators for the TM measures related to method M_2. For example, if methods M_1 and M_2 are two different occasions of administering a 9-item test, X_1, . . ., X_9 would represent the item measures on the first occasion, whereas Y_1, . . ., Y_9 would be measures for the same items on the second occasion.

Whereas each TM combination in a standard (first-order) CFA is measured by a single observable variable (e.g., Figure 7.1), such a combination in HCFA is inferred from a set of multiple indicators (e.g., Figure 7.9). The HCFA was proposed to address drawbacks of the standard CFA of MTMM data (Marsh, 1987; Marsh & Hocevar, 1985, 1988). Specifically, Marsh and Hocevar (1988) reported the failure of CFA models to (a) correct appropriately for measurement error in scale scores, (b) separate error attributable to low internal consistency from uniqueness attributable to weak trait or method effects, (c) test whether items or

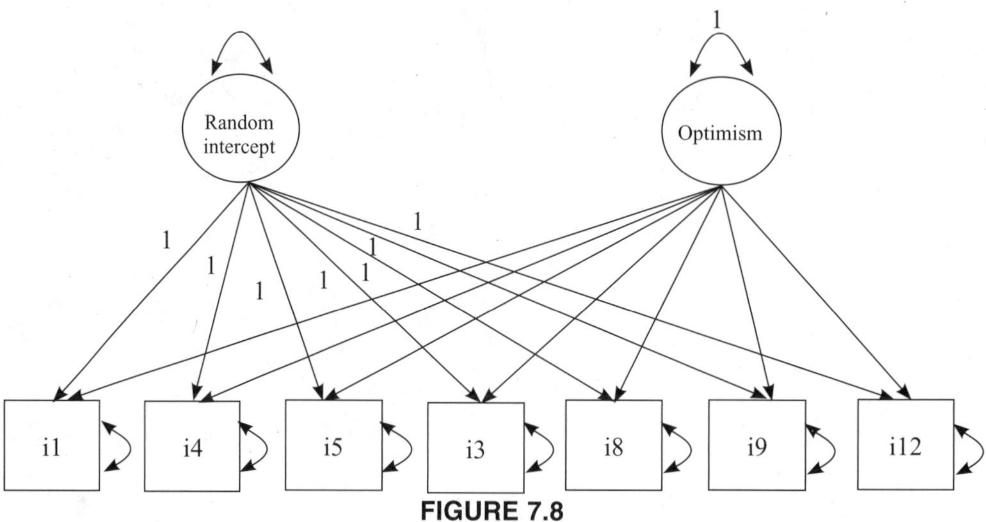

FIGURE 7.8

A Random Intercept Model for the Life Orientation Test (LOT)

Note. The items are numbered as in the original LOT questionnaire. Items 1, 4, and 5 are positively worded, whereas Items 3, 8, 9, and 12 are negatively worded. Variances are depicted with double-headed arrows from a variable to itself and factor loadings are single-headed arrows. The variances of factors are fixed to 1 for identification. The factor loadings for one of the two factors are all fixed to 1, and its variance (the variance of random intercepts) is estimated. From "Random Intercept Item Factor Analysis," by A. Maydeu-Olivares and D. L. Coffman, 2006, *Psychological Methods, 11,* p. 349. Copyright 2006 by the American Psychological Association. Reprinted with permission.

subscales accurately reflect the intended factor structure, and (d) test for correlated uniquenesses. Each of these problems can be addressed using HCFA modeling of MTMM data.

As depicted in Figure 7.9, random errors inferred from low correlations between multiple indicators of the same scale (e.g., e_{X1}, e_{X2}, and e_{X3} for the T_1M_1 scale) are separated from the specific residual component for this scale—that is, a systematic source of variation in the scale unexplained by the trait and method factors (e.g., s_{11} for the T_1M_1 scale). For the standard CFA depicted in Figure 7.1, however, the residual term for a TM unit (T_i, M_j), denoted δ_{ij}, is an aggregation of random error, e_{ij}, and systematic specific effect, s_{ij}.

Before conducting HCFA of MTMM data, it is important to test the first-order model for data fit, because unless the parameter estimates support the a priori factor structure and the fit is reasonable, subsequent interpretations of trait and method factors may be unjustified. A well-defined factor structure is indicated by the high loadings of the indicators on the first-order factors. Campbell and Fiske's (1959) criteria for convergent and discriminant evidence can be readily and more accurately applied using correlations between first-order factors as the scores on such factors are true (error-free) because of their multiple indicators.

Studies on HCFA of MTMM data suggest that (a) strong convergent evidence is provided by high loadings on the second-order trait factors, substantial variances of these second-order factors, and substantial decrement in fit produced by eliminating the trait factors in the HCFA model; (b) weak method effects are indicated by low loadings on second-order method factors, small variances of these second-order factors, and small decrement in fit produced by eliminating the method factors in the HCFA model; and (c) significant correlations between trait factors imply true trait correlations and should be interpreted only as a lack of discriminant evidence unless such correlations approach 1.0 or are inconsistent with

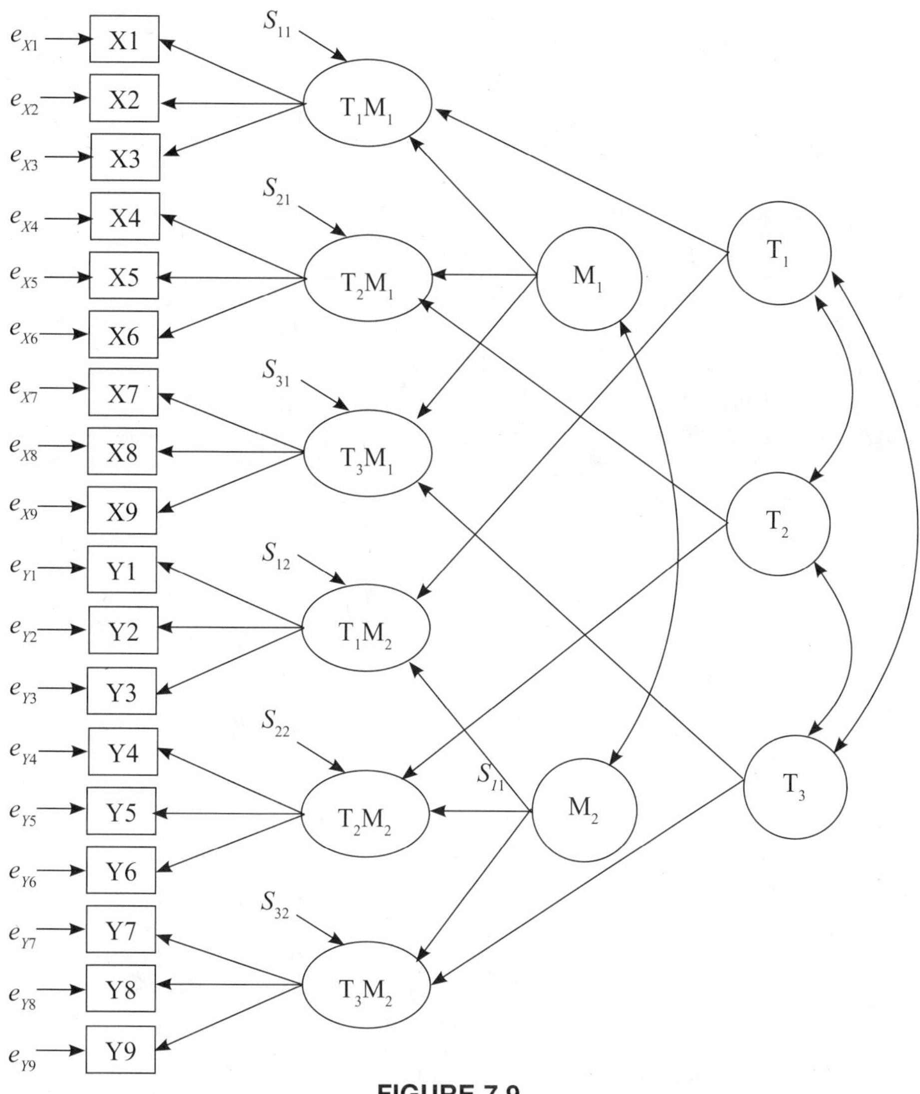

FIGURE 7.9

A Hierarchical Confirmatory Factor Analysis Model of Multitrait–Multimethod Data for Three Correlated Traits and Two Uncorrelated Methods

the substantive nature of the data (e.g., Marsh & Hocevar, 1985, 1988). Previous research provides various applications of HCFA models in counseling, education, psychology, and other areas (e.g., Bong, 2001; Bong & Hocevar, 2002; Kumar & Dillon, 1990; Lance et al., 2002; Lance, Teachout, & Donnelly, 1992; Marsh, 1993; Marsh & Grayson, 1995; Marsh & Hocevar, 1988).

7.8 THE MULTILEVEL CFA (ML-CFA) METHOD

The multilevel confirmatory factor analysis (ML-CFA) model of MTMM data is most appropriate for interchangeable methods (Eid et al., 2008; Hox & Kleiboer, 2007). An example of interchangeable methods are raters that are randomly selected from a pool of potential raters say, students who evaluate their teachers on teaching quality. Recall that methods that are not interchangeable are referred to as *structurally different methods*—for example, when methods of measuring competence are (a) self-rating, (b) teacher reports/ratings, and (c) parent reports/ratings. Eid et al. (2008) addressed the situation in which interchangeable raters are characterized by using a nested multilevel structure within the framework of ML-CFA (e.g., Brown, 2006; Hox, 2002; F. Li, Duncan, Harmer, Acock, & Stoolmiller, 1998; B. O. Muthén, 1994; L. K. Muthén & B. O. Muthén, 2008). Specifically, they used the ML-CFA model depicted in Figure 7.10 to analyze the effects of interchangeable raters (Level-1 units; e.g., students) who are nested within targets (Level-2 units, e.g., teachers) in validating three different traits (e.g., facets of teacher quality).

In Figure 7.10, the ML-CFA model is illustrated for the assessment of three traits (k = 1, 2, 3) using three indicators (i = 1, 2, 3). For example, if the traits are facets of teacher quality assessed by students, there are three items (indicators) for each facet. That is, each student (rater, r) rates his or her teacher (target, t) on each facet of teacher quality using three indicators of that facet (note that students are "nested" within teachers). The variable notations in Figure 7.10 are as follows: Y_{rtik} = observed variable (the rating proved by rater r for target t using indicator i of trait k); M_{rtk} = method factor, T_{tik} = latent trait variable, and E_{rtik} = error variable. Specifically, T_{tik} is an indicator-specific centered trait variable. That is, the value of T_{tik} for a specific teacher t, for example, represents the teacher's deviation from μ_{ik}—the mean on indicator i of trait k across all teachers (thus, $\mu_{ik} + T_{tik}$ renders the true k-trait value of teacher t on indicator i).

The method factor M_{rtk} is trait-specific—it is assumed that the method effects do not vary across the indicators of a given trait (i.e., rater-specific effects are unidimensional within each trait). That is why there is one method factor for each trait in the Level-1 part of the ML-CFA model (M_{rtk} does not have an index i because this factor is common to all indicators i of the same trait k; see the right panel in Figure 7.10). That is, it is assumed that any rater is either consistently severe or consistently lenient across all indicators of a given trait but not so across traits (i.e., the rater may overestimate one trait but underestimate another trait).

The analytic presentation of the ML-CFA model in Figure 7.10 is as follows:

$$Y_{rtik} = \mu_{ik} + T_{tik} + \lambda_{Mtk} + E_{rtik}. \tag{7.3}$$

The separation of measurement error from method effects in this model is made possible by the use of multiple indicators per trait. This allows the researcher to test whether systematic method effects exist and whether these method effects are homogeneous across traits and within traits (Eid et al., 2003). Some important points of interpretation provided by Eid et al. (2008) are as follows:

- A positive value on the method factor, M_{rtk}, for a specific rater indicates that the rater overestimates the trait value of the target, whereas a negative value means that the target's trait is underestimated.
- A high correlation between two method factors indicates that raters who overestimate a target's trait value with respect to one trait have the tendency to overestimate the target's trait value also with respect to the other trait.
- Large variances of the method factors show that the raters differ strongly from each other, indicating a lack of convergent evidence of validity. Small variances of method factors and error variables reflect high convergence on the level of observed ratings.

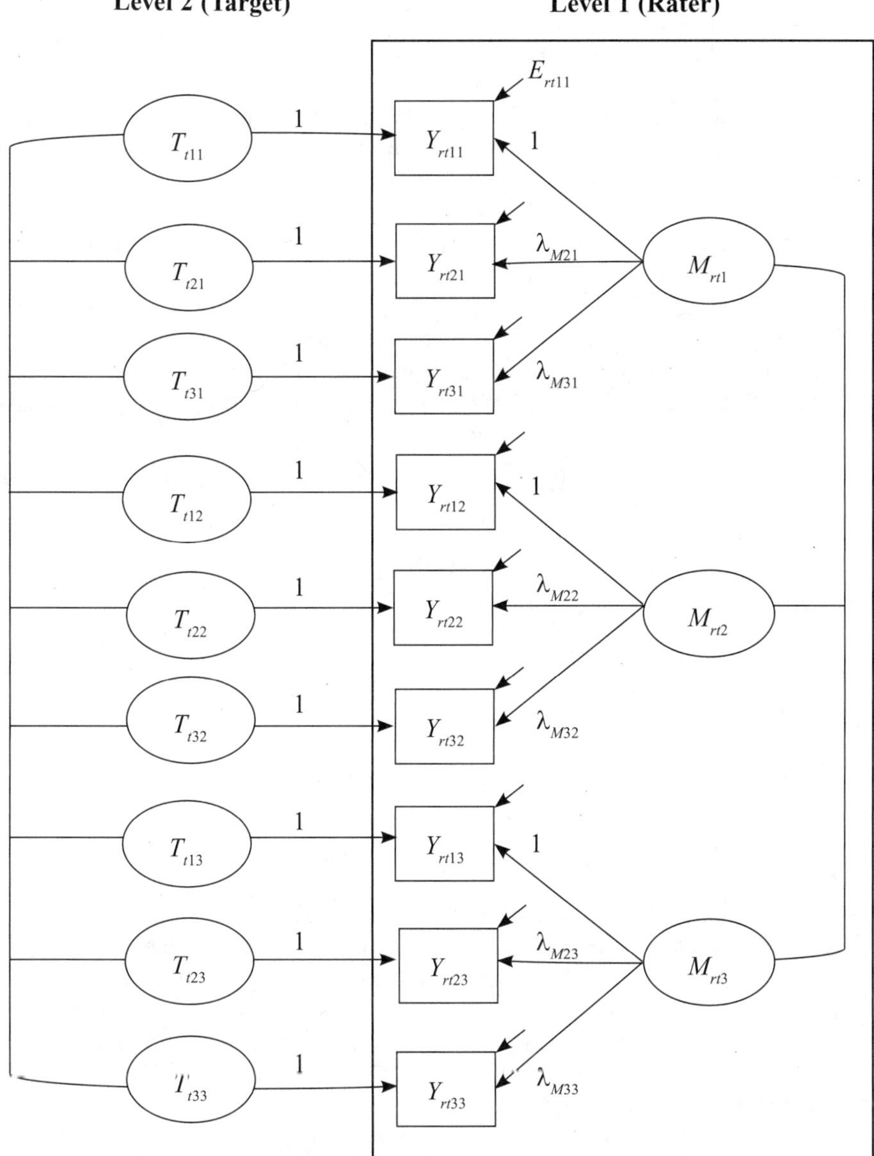

FIGURE 7.10

A Multilevel Confirmatory Factor Analysis—Multitrait–Multimethod Model for Interchangeable Raters

Note. All trait-loading parameters are fixed to 1. The first method factor loading is fixed to 1. Y_{rtik} = observed variable, T_{tik} = latent trait variables, M_{rtk} = method factors, E_{rtik} = error variables; r = rater; t = target; i = indicator; k = trait. All trait-loading parameters are fixed to 1. The first method factor loading is fixed to 1. λ_{Mik} indicates method factor loadings that are estimated. The curved lines between the constructs indicate that all of the linked constructs can be correlated. From "Structural Equation Modeling of Multitrait–Multimethod Data: Different Models for Different Types of Methods," by M. Eid, F. W. Nussbeck, C. Geiser, D. A. Cole, M. Gollwitzer, and T. Lischetzke, 2008, *Psychological Methods, 13,* p. 234. Copyright 2008 by the American Psychological Association. Reprinted with permission.

- The variances of the trait variables T_{tik} reflect interindividual differences between the targets (e.g., teachers) in their trait scores.
- The correlations between the trait variables T_{tik} that belong to *different* traits indicate discriminant validity of the traits at the target (e.g., teacher) level. The correlations between the variables T_{tik} belonging to the *same* trait indicate the homogeneity of indicators that are supposed to measure the same trait.

Eid et al. (2008) also suggested the use of coefficients of reliability, consistency, and specificity in collecting evidence of validity. As known, the coefficient of reliability represents the proportion of the total variance of the observed measures, Y_{rtik}, that is not related to measurement error. The evaluation of scale reliability for multilevel data by means of SEM is addressed, for example, by Raykov and Marcoulides (2006b). The ML-CFA model provides variance estimates for the observed scores, Y_{rtik}, latent trait variables, T_{tik}, method factors, M_{rtk}, and residuals, E_{rtik}, as well as estimates of the factor loading, λ_{Mik}, thus making possible the computation of the following:

- reliability coefficient:

$$Rel(Y_{rtik}) = 1 - Var(E_{rtik})/Var(Y_{rtik}) \tag{7.4}$$

- consistency coefficient:

$$CO(Y_{rtik}) = Var(T_{tik})/[Var(T_{tik}) + \lambda^2_{Mik}\,Var(M_{rtk})], \text{ and} \tag{7.5}$$

- specificity coefficient:

$$MS(Y_{rtik}) = \frac{\lambda^2_{Mik}\,Var(M_{rtk})}{[Var(T_{tik}) + \lambda^2_{Mik}\,Var(M_{rtk})]}. \tag{7.6}$$

Theoretically, all thee coefficients can take on values from 0 to 1. The consistency coefficient indicates the proportion of true variance of the ratings that is due to differences between targets, whereas the specificity coefficient shows the proportion of true variance of the ratings that is due to differences between raters. If the consistency coefficient exceeds the specificity coefficient $[CO(Y_{rtik}) > MS(Y_{rtik})]$, this shows that the variability in the observed ratings is due primarily to differences between targets (across raters) rather than to differences between raters (within targets). A higher consistency coefficient provides stronger convergent evidence of validity.

For the case of structurally different raters (e.g., anxiety ratings by self-reports, teachers, and parents), Eid et al. (2008) recommended the CMC(M–1) model and illustrated this model in an example of multiple indicators. They also proposed a model combining both structurally different and interchangeable raters and illustrated the simplest case of such a combination—two interchangeable raters and one rater who is structurally different from them—using an example with two interchangeable peer reports and one self-report (as a structurally different method).

Hox and Kleiboer (2007) used ML-CFA modeling of MTMM data in a comparison between retrospective questions and daily diaries inquiring about positive and negative support in spousal interactions. They used an MTMM matrix for which the trait factors consisted of positive and negative support and the method factors consisted of retrospective questions and questions asked daily. The data were multilevel, with daily measurement occasions nested within subjects. The authors concluded that "at the daily level both positive and negative support should be viewed as transient events that do not indicate an underlying latent variable, but that could be modeled as a formative construct" (p. 311).

Eid et al. (2008) pointed out limitations of the ML-CFA models, particularly the strong assumption that the method factors are unidimensional. Moreover, it is not possible to test this assumption when the trait indicators represent item parcels. Given this problem, Eid et al. (2008) suggested that (a) during the planning of an MTMM study researchers should make an effort to identify homogeneous indicators for all TM units, and (b) before creating item parcels (if deciding to do so), researchers should test whether there is measurement invariance across raters for each trait separately.

7.9 CONVENTIONAL MTMM ANALYSIS USING LATENT VARIABLE MODELING

As described in Section 7.1, the conventional MTMM analysis (Campbell & Fiske, 1959) uses estimates of correlations between observed TM measures to make judgments about convergent validity and discriminant validity—conventional terms for convergent evidence and discriminant evidence of the external aspect of validity under the unified construct-based model of validity (Messick, 1995). As described in Section 7.1, convergent evidence is demonstrated by high MTHM correlations, discriminant evidence is demonstrated by low HTMM correlations, and method effect is signaled when the correlations between measures for different traits are higher when the same method is used to measure both traits than when different methods are used to measure the traits. That is, method bias is demonstrated when HTMM correlations exceed HTHM correlations (e.g., Allen & Yen, 1979, p. 110).

Judgments about convergence, discrimination, and method bias can be made (a) individually, by pairs of TM measures; and (b) collectively, by comparing the average values of convergent and discriminant correlations reported for the respective pairs of TM measures in the MTMM matrix. However, in most studies using conventional MTMM analysis, the sampling error affecting the correlation estimates has not been taken into account, thus allowing for incorrect conclusions about validity of the measures under consideration. To address this issue, Raykov (2011) proposed a latent variable modeling (LVM) approach to interval estimation of convergent and discriminant validity coefficients, as well as differences between them, at the population level. Specifically, as depicted in Figure 7.11 for the case of two traits and two methods, a dummy latent variable, F_{ij}, with variance 1.0, is assumed to underlie each TM_{ij} measure under the assumptions of *no* measurement error ($E_{ij} = 0$; $i = 1, 2$; $j = 1, 2, 3$). That is,

$$TM_{ij} = \lambda_{ij} F_{ij}. \tag{7.7}$$

Parameters estimated under the model depicted in Figure 7.11 are the loadings, λ_{ij}, and the covariances between the latent variables. As there are no restrictions imposed within this model, it provides a perfect fit of the covariance matrix at both the sample and population levels. Also, the loadings equal the standard deviation of the respective observed measure (i.e., $\lambda_{ij} = \sigma_{TM_{ij}}$), and the covariance between any two latent variables equals the correlation between them [$Cov(F_{11}, F_{12}) = Corr(F_{11}, F_{12})$, . . . and so forth] (B. O. Muthén, 2002; Raykov, 2011).

Fitting the model defined in Equation 7.7 renders estimates for each of the convergent (MTHM) and discriminant (HTMM and HTHM) correlation coefficients and their standard

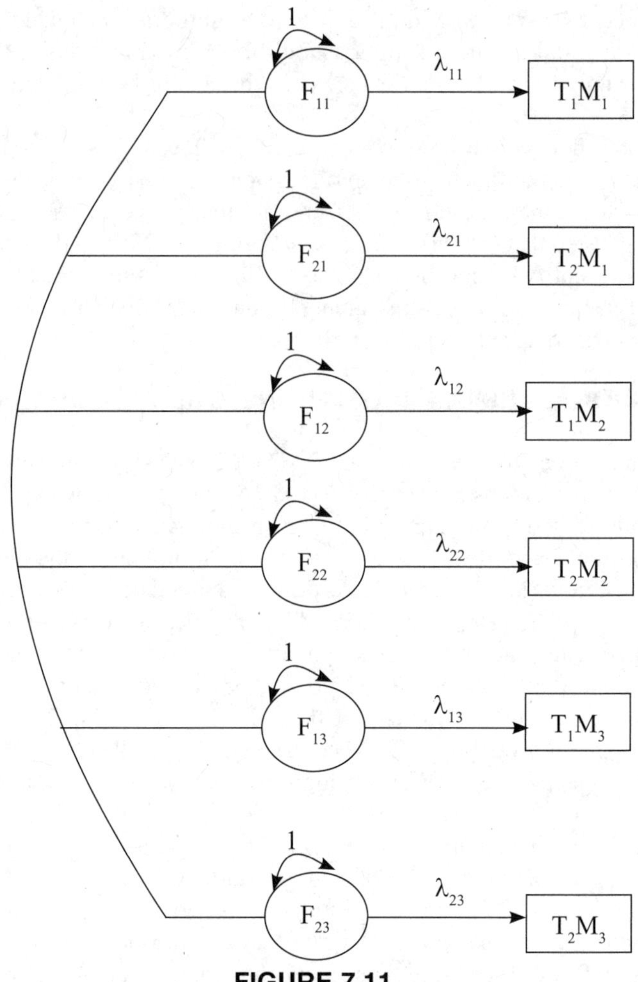

FIGURE 7.11

Latent Variable Model for Conventional Multitrait–Multimethod Analysis of the Trait–Method Correlations in Table 7.7

Note. The two-way small arrow attached to each latent variable, F_{ij} (where i = 1, 2; and j = 1, 2, 3), depicts its variance (fixed to 1.0). All latent variables are allowed to correlate.

errors. When maximum likelihood estimation is used, these estimates are the same as the observed sample correlations in the MTMM matrix, so the main benefit remains in the estimation of their standard errors. The standard errors of the correlations in the MTMM matrix play an instrumental role in the computation of confidence intervals for these correlations and differences among them or their average values, thus facilitating judgments about MTMM-based evidence of validity (see Raykov, 2011).

Example 7.4 This example uses the MTMM matrix in Table 7.7 to illustrate the model depicted in Figure 7.11 using Mplus. Raykov (2011) provided a description of this model and Mplus code for the computation of confidence intervals of (a) MTMM correlations, (b) the difference between two correlations, and (c) the difference between the

average convergent correlations (MTHM) and the average of all (HTMM and HTHM) discriminant correlations. This example illustrates the estimation for the last case, with two additional comparisons to investigate for possible method bias. Specifically, as noted by Raykov (2011), if the difference between the average MTHM convergence correlations and the average of all (HTMM + HTHM) discriminant correlations is a positive numeric value, this provides validity evidence. This type of validity evidence is referred to here as *overall validity evidence* (OVE). That is, OVE = Average (MTHM) – Average (HTMM + HTHM). In addition, introduced in this example are the following differences: (a) Average (MTHM) – Average (HTMM): if positive, this difference provides validity evidence referred to here as *strong validity evidence* (SVE); and (b) Average (HTMM) – Average (HTHM): if positive, this difference provides evidence of method bias.

The Mplus source code for confidence intervals of the average correlation differences targeted in this example is provided in Appendix 7.1. As the results show, the estimate of the OVE difference is positive (. 406), with a 95% confidence interval (CI) [.343, .468], thus providing overall validity evidence. Furthermore, the estimate of the SVE difference is also positive (.333), with a 95% CI [.266, .400], thus providing strong validity evidence. There is, however, an evidence of method bias, as indicated by the positive value of the difference for method bias (.108), with a 95% CI [.084, .132]. Estimates of the standard errors of the MTMM sample correlations are also provided with the Mplus output, but they are not presented here becausc of space considerations.

7.10 BRIEF GUIDELINES FOR SELECTING MODELS OF MTMM DATA

The most general rule for selecting models of MTMM data is simple—different models for different types of methods (Eid et al., 2008). Of course, how to operationalize this rule would depend on the context of the study, the nature and focus of the research questions, the structure of the data (e.g., availability of multiple indicators, hierarchy, and so forth), sample size, software availability, and other possible factors. Provided

TABLE 7.7

Multitrait–Multimethod Correlations for Two Traits Measured by Three Methods in Self-Report Inventories

Trait–Method Measure	1	2	3	4	5	6
1. T_1M_1	1.00					
2. T_2M_1	0.45	1.00				
3. T_1M_2	0.85	0.40	1.00			
4. T_2M_2	0.35	0.80	0.30	1.00		
5. T_1M_3	0.65	0.15	0.70	0.25	1.00	
6. T_2M_3	0.20	0.55	0.20	0.65	0.35	1.00

Note. N = 435. The means and standard deviations of the six Trait–Method measures reported in the source (Raykov, 2011) are not necessary for the computations with the Mplus source code given in Appendix 7.1. T_1 = hostility guilt; T_2 = morality conscience; M_1 = true-false; M_2 = forced choice; and M_3 = incomplete sentences. From "Evaluation of Convergent and Discriminant Validity with Multitrait–Multimethod Correlations," by T. Raykov, 2011, *British Journal of Mathematical and Statistical Psychology, 64,* p. 46. Copyright 2011 by The British Psychological Society. Reprinted with permission.

below is a short list of practical suggestions that can help the reader in selecting models of MTMM data:

1. Start with a preliminary conventional analysis of the MTMM matrix (e.g., Campbell & Fiske, 1959; Lubinski, Tellegen, & Butcher, 1983; Reichardt & Coleman, 1995; Steger, Frazier, Oishi, & Kaler, 2006; Taylor, Ptacek, Carithers, Griffin, & Coyne, 1972; Ward, 1982). This analysis might be particularly useful in the piloting stages of instrument development. To avoid problems related to sampling error with the conventional MTMM approach, consider using the LVM approach illustrated in the previous section (Raykov, 2011).
2. More refined information on trait and method effects can then be obtained using appropriate CFA-based models, with the following guidelines applicable to such models:
    a. Use multiple indicators (when available) for the TM combinations, thus making possible the use of HCFA or ML-CFA models for refined information on trait and method effects (e.g., Anderson, 1985; Bong, 2001; Eid et al., 2008; Kumar & Dillon, 1990; Lance et al., 1992; Marsh, 1993; Marsh & Hocevar, 1988). If necessary, use item parceling, keeping in mind the pros and cons of this process (e.g., Eid et al., 2008; Little, Cunningham, Shahar, & Widaman, 2002).
    b. With MTMM designs that use interchangeable raters, characterized by a nested data structure (e.g., students nested within teachers), use the ML-CFA model (Eid et al., 2008).
    c. With MTMM designs that use structurally different methods, appropriate models are as follows:
        (1) the CU model or its CU-CFA modification (e.g., Coenders & Saris, 2000; Conway, 1998; Conway, Lievens, Scullen, & Lance, 2004; Corten et al., 2002; Kenny, 1979; Marsh & Bailey, 1991; Saris & Aalberts, 2003; Scullen, 1999; Scullen, Mount, & Goff, 2000),
        (2) the CTM(M–1) model, especially if one method is a gold standard against which other methods are contrasted (e.g., Eid et al., 2003, 2008; Gaudron & Vautier, 2007; Geiser et al., 2008),
        (3) the random intercept model, if there is an indication of consistent response style across the entire set of items (Maydeu-Olivares & Coffman, 2006), or
        (4) the standard CFA model (e.g., Bagozzi & Yi, 1991; Lance & Sloan, 1993; Marsh, 1989; Plucker, 1996; Windle & Dumenci, 1999).
    d. With MTMM designs that use both interchangeable and structurally different methods, with multiple indictors for each combination of TM measures available, it would be appropriate to use a model that combines the ML-CFA and CTM(M–1) models (e.g., Eid et al., 2008).

Using the above guidelines, by taking into account the context and goals of the study, researchers can reach dependable MTMM-based evidence of the external aspect of validity. For additional reading on MTMM data analysis in the context of construct validation, the reader may refer to Aldridge, Dorman, and Fraser (2004); Barbaranelli and Caprara (2000); Bartle-Haring, Kenny, and Gavazzi (1999); Chan (2001); Cole, Truglio, and Peeke (1997); Lowe and Ryan-Wenger (1992); Courvoisier, Nussbeck, Eid, Geiser, and Cole (2008); Fitzpatrick and Irannejad (2008); Dumenci (2000); Saris, Satorra, and Coenders (2004); Stowe (1985); and Williams and Anderson (1994).

SUMMARY

1. The multitrait–multimethod (MTMM) matrix was first used by Campbell and Fiske (1959) to analyze correlations between multiple traits measured by multiple methods with the purpose of scale validation. *Traits* refer to constructs such as abilities, attitudes, and personality characteristics, whereas the term *multiple methods* refers to multiple tests, multiple methods of assessment, multiple response scale rates or category labels in questionnaires, multiple raters, multiple data collection procedures, or multiple occasions.
2. Under Campbell and Fiske's (1959) guidelines, convergent validity is supported by high correlations between scores on the same trait measured by different methods, whereas discriminant validity is supported by low correlations between scores on different traits, especially when the same method is used. Method effect is detected when correlations between scores on different traits are higher when using the same method versus when using different methods to measure these traits (method effect indicates an undesired systematic variance that distorts correlations between different traits measured with the same method).
3. The most serious problem with the Campbell–Fiske criteria is that they are based on inspection of correlations between observed variables but make inferences about underlying trait and method factors. CFA-based MTMM analyses avoid this problem, take into account differences in the reliability of measures, and allow the variance to be decomposed into trait variance, method variance, and random error variance.
4. Under the standard (first-order) CFA model of MTMM data, commonly referred to as the *CFA model of MTMM data*, each observed variable loads on one trait factor and one method factor. Convergent evidence of validity is indicated by (a) statistically significant and substantial loadings on the trait factors, and (b) statistically significant decrement in fit when trait factors are deleted from model specification. Discriminant evidence of validity is supported by low correlations between trait factors. Method effect is indicated by a statistically significant decrement in fit when the method factors are deleted from the model specifications.
5. The correlated uniqueness (CU) model—in which there are no method factors, but, instead, method effects are represented as correlated errors—is designed to avoid ill-defined solutions that often occur under the standard CFA models of MTMM data. Method effects are indicated by statistical significance of correlated uniquenesses—that is, the correlations between pairs of variables measured with the same method after removing trait effects.
6. The CU-CFA method consists of two steps. First, a CU analysis is conducted to partition the variance in each observed variable into a trait component and a unique component. Second, follow-up CFAs are conducted to partition the unique variance component of each variable into method variance and error variance (a standard CFA of the correlated uniquenesses is conducted separately for each method). The purpose is to avoid problems with the CU model under which method effects are not modeled explicitly—a drawback that may lead to incomplete and inaccurate inferences regarding construct validity.
7. To avoid major disadvantages of the standard CFA model of MTMM data, referred to also as the *correlated trait-correlated method* (CTCM) model, Eid (2000) proposed a model that allows a satisfactory determination of the variance components

attributable to trait and method effects. This model, called the *correlated trait–correlated method minus one* [*CTC(M–1)*] *model*, is a variant of the CTCM model that contains one method factor less, hence the name of the model.

8. The random intercept model (Maydeu-Olivares & Coffman, 2006) is a common factor model in which the intercept is decomposed into fixed and random parts. The fixed part of the intercept is the same for all individuals but may differ across items, whereas the random part may vary across respondents but remains the same across all items (observed measures). The random intercept captures individual differences in scale usage that are common across items—for example, response style of acquiescence and social desirability.
9. A hierarchical confirmatory factor analysis (HCFA) model of MTMM data is a two-level CFA in which the trait–method measures are first-order factors measured by multiple indicators, whereas the trait and method factors represent second-order factors. The HCFA was proposed to address drawbacks of the standard CFA of MTMM data related to its failure to (a) correct appropriately for measurement error in scale scores, (b) separate error attributable to low internal consistency from uniqueness attributable to weak trait or method effects, (c) test whether items or subscales accurately reflect the intended factor structure, and (d) test for CUs.
10. The multilevel confirmatory factor analysis (ML-CFA) model of MTMM data is most appropriate for interchangeable methods (e.g., raters who are randomly selected from a pool of potential raters). The assumption is that the method factors are unidimensional.
11. Under conventional MTMM analyses, the sampling error affecting the correlation estimates is usually not taken into account, which allows for incorrect conclusions about validity of measures. To address this issue, Raykov (2011) proposed a latent variable modeling (LVM) approach to interval estimation of convergent and discriminant validity coefficients, as well as differences between them, at the population level.
12. The most general rule for selecting models of MTMM data is that different models should be used for different types of methods. How to operationalize this rule depends on the context of the study, the nature and focus of the research questions, the structure of the data (e.g., availability of multiple indicators, hierarchy, and so forth), sample size, software availability, and other relevant factors.

APPENDIX 7.1

Mplus Source Code and Selected Output for Interval Estimation of Relationships Between Convergent and Discriminant Validity Coefficients

```
          TITLE:  MTMM Based Evaluation of Overall Validity, Strong Validity, and Method Bias
           DATA:  FILE = TABLE7_7.DAT;       ! see Table 7.7
          TYPE =  CORRELATION;
  NOBSERVATIONS = 435;
       VARIABLE:  NAMES = T1M1 T2M1 T1M2 T2M2 T1M3 T2M3;
          MODEL:  F11 BY T1M1*1; T1M1@0;
                  F21 BY T2M1*1; T2M1@0;
                  F12 BY T1M2*1; T1M2@0;
                  F22 BY T2M2*1; T2M2@0;
                  F13 BY T1M3*1; T1M3@0;
                  F23 BY T2M3*1; T2M3@0;
                    F11-F23@1;
                  F11 WITH F12(C1);           !monotrait–heteromethod (MTHM) correlations
                  F11 WITH F13(C2);
                  F12 WITH F13(C3);
                  F21 WITH F22(C4);
                  F21 WITH F23(C5);
                  F22 WITH F23(C6);
                  F11 WITH F21(D1);           !heterotrait–monomethod (HTMM) correlations
                  F12 WITH F22(D2);
                  F13 WITH F23(D3);
                  F11 WITH F22(B1);           !heterotrait–heteromethod (HTHM) correlations
                  F11 WITH F23(B2);
                  F21 WITH F12(B3);
                  F21 WITH F13(B4);
                  F12 WITH F23(B5);
                  F22 WITH F13(B6);
  MODEL CONSTRAINT:
    NEW(OVE  SVE  MB);
    OVE = (C1+C2+C3+C4+C5+C6)/6 – (D1+D2+D3+ B1+B2+B3+B4+B5+B6)/9;
    SVE = (C1+C2+C3+C4+C5+C6)/6 – (D1+D2+D3)/3;
    MB = (D1+D2+D3)/3 – (B1+B2+B3+B4+B5+B6)/6;
  OUTPUT: CINTERVAL;
```

Selected Output:

Confidence Intervals of Model Results

	Lower .5%	Lower 2.5%	Estimate	Upper 2.5%	Upper .5%
OVE	0.323	0.343	**0.406**	0.468	0.488
SVE	0.245	0.266	**0.333**	0.400	0.421
MB	0.077	0.084	**0.108**	0.132	0.140

Note. OVE = MTHM – (HTMM + HTHM): Overall validity evidence (if positive difference); SVE = MTHM – HTMM: Strong validity evidence (if positive difference); MB = HTMM – HTHM: Method bias (if positive difference). From "Evaluation of Convergent and Discriminant Validity with Multitrait–Multimethod Correlations," by T. Raykov, 2011, *British Journal of Mathematical and Statistical Psychology, 64,* p. 52. Copyright 2011 by The British Psychological Society. Modified with permission.

Part III

Psychometric Scale Analysis

Chapter 8
Conventional Scale Analysis

In this chapter I describe some basic concepts and procedures related to conventional analysis of binary and rating scales. Such analysis, conducted in the framework of classical test theory and survey development, can be very useful in initial (pilot) stages of the development of assessment instruments. More refined scale analyses, which require relatively large samples, are typically performed within the framework of item response theory (IRT) or Rasch modeling (e.g., as discussed in Chapter 9). To facilitate understanding of the sections that follow, the reader may review Chapter 1, Section 1.4, for basic properties of binary and rating scales.

8.1 ANALYSIS OF BINARY SCALES

As described in Chapter 1, a binary scale is obtained by adding (or averaging) binary scores (1/0) assigned to a person's responses on individual items (e.g., 1 = true, 0 = false) in an assessment instrument. An examinee's total score on a binary scale is referred to as the *scale score* of that individual. That is, if $X_1, X_2, \ldots, X_k$ are the item scores in a test of k items, the scale score is $X = X_1 + X_2 + \ldots + X_k$. In this section, the focus is on the analysis of individual binary items and the distribution of scale scores.

8.1.1 Analysis of Binary Items

The analysis of binary items is intended to provide information about their measurement properties in terms of difficulty, discrimination, and probability of correct response across levels of the ability (trait) being measured by the test. The terminology used in this section is suitable for ability or achievement tests, but the logic holds for items that measure "traits" in personality or psychological tests. For example, the expression that "an examinee at a given ability level has provided a correct item response" is suitable terminology for an achievement test, whereas in a personality test the expression may be that "a respondent at a given trait level has endorsed the item."

Item Difficulty. The difficulty of an item is defined as the proportion of examinees who get that item correct. Thus, with the notation p_i for difficulty of item i, we have $0 \leq p_i \leq 1$. If p_i is close (or equal) to 0 or 1, the item should be revised or discarded because it does not provide any information about differences among examinees on the scale of ability (or trait) being measured. Indeed, $p_i = 0$ indicates that no one got the item right; that is, the item is too difficult. Conversely, $p_i = 1$ indicates that everyone got the item right; in this case, the item is too easy. In either case, the item is not useful. Given that p_i is the proportion of correct responses on a binary item, the variance of that item is $s^2_i = p_i(1 - p_i)$. As known in statistics, this variance is maximized when $p_i = .5$. Thus, an item with average difficulty ($p_i = .5$) provides the maximum information about differences among examinees. However, it is not advisable to have all items with $p_i = .5$, as this may produce undesirable effects under certain intercorrelations among items. For example, in the case of perfect intercorrelations among items, all with $p_i = .5$, half of the examinees would receive a total test score of 0 and the other half would receive a perfect total test score (e.g., Allen & Yen, 1979, p. 121).

In general, it is recommended that researchers choose items with a range of difficulties that average about .5; for example, item difficulties of about .3 to .7 are considered optimal in differentiating examinees in the ability (or trait) being measured by the test. However, when a cutting scale score is used for selection purposes, the best item selection contains items that are passed by about 50% of the examinees whose scale score on the test equals the cutting score (Lord, 1953). Thus, if a performance test is used to select the top 20% of the applicants for a program (or a job position), the test should contain difficult items. Conversely, if a test is used to identify students "at risk" in a given subject area, the test should contain easy items. In both cases, there will be a high discrimination among examinees near the cutting scale score and low discrimination among examinees not near the cutting score.

Item Discrimination. The item discrimination shows to what degree an item discriminates between high-performing and low-performing examinees on the test as a whole. An item discrimination index, d_i, for item i is computed as the difference $d_i = U_i/n_U - L_i/n_L$, where U_i and L_i indicate the number of examinees in the upper and low range, respectively, of the total test scores who got item i correct; n_U and n_L indicate the number of examinees in the upper and lower range of the total test scores, regardless of their responses on item i. If the total test scores are normally distributed, the best estimate of d_i is obtained when the lower range group consists of the examinees in the bottom 27% and the upper range group consists of those in the top 27% of the distribution of total test scores (Kelley, 1939). If the distribution of the total scores is flatter than the normal curve, then the lowest 33% and the highest 33% should be taken for the lower range and upper range groups, respectively. In most cases, any choice between 25% and 33% will yield similar estimates of d_i (e.g., Allen & Yen, 1979, p. 122).

Theoretically, the item discrimination index, d_i, can take on values from –1.00 to 1.00. A positive d_i means that more examinees from the upper-range group answered the item correctly than the lower-range group, thus indicating that this item discriminates the examinees from the two groups. The closer d_i is to 1.00, the stronger the discrimination. If d_i is equal (or close) to zero, the item does not differentiate the two groups and should be revised or discarded. If d_i for an item is negative ($d_i < 0$), this item should be discarded as it is not logical that the lower range group examinees perform better on the item than the upper-range group examinees.

Item-Total Test Score Correlation. Another measure of item discrimination is the correlation between the item score (1/0) and the total test score, X, denoted here r_{iX}. As the item score is a binary variable and the total test score is a continuous variable, the correlation between them is estimated by the *point-biserial correlation coefficient* using the following formula:

$$r_{iX} = \left(\frac{\bar{X}_1 - \bar{X}}{s_X}\right)\sqrt{\frac{p_i}{1 - p_i}}\,, \tag{8.1}$$

where p_i is the item difficulty; $\bar{X}$ and s_X are the mean and standard deviation, respectively, of the total test scores of all examinees; and $\bar{X}_1$ is the mean total test score of the examinees who have answered the item correctly. Sometimes r_{iX} is converted to a biserial correlation as the variable of item performance is continuous in nature, but it is artificially dichotomized by using the 1/0 item scoring (e.g., see Allen & Yen, 1979, p. 39). In either case (point-biserial or biserial), the item-total test score correlation behaves similarly to the item discrimination index, d_i.

The item-total test score correlation, r_{iX}, is somewhat inflated as the item score is also a part of the total score. To eliminate this effect, a corrected item-total test score correlation can be computed by excluding the item score from the total test score (e.g., "corrected item-total correlation" is reported with the SPSS output for reliability analysis of scale scores).

Analysis of Multiple-Choice Items. Along with examining item difficulty, p_i, discrimination, d_i, and item-total test score correlation, r_{iX}, researchers should also analyze item distractors in the case of multiple-choice items (MCI; the incorrect answer choices in a MCI are called *distractors*). Specifically, if the examinees are classified into upper, middle, and lower groups based on their total test scores, it is useful to examine the proportion of examinees in each group who have selected each (correct and distractor) answer choice in each item. In general, good distractors should be selected (a) at about equal rate by examinees who do not know the correct answer, and (b) at higher rate by examinees in the lower group compared with the examinees in the middle group and, particularly, with those in the upper group. Also, a good distractor should not be too appealing, especially for examinees in the upper scoring group. The joint examination of item difficulty, item discrimination, item-total test score correlation, and proportion of selected answer choices by (upper, middle, and lower) groups provides valuable information about the measurement characteristics of test items. It is convenient to present the data for item analysis as illustrated in Table 8.1 for two hypothetical items. As can be seen, the first item (Item 1) is a very good item, with a moderate difficulty (p_i = .43), good discrimination power (d_i = .60), sizable item-total score correlation (r_{iX} = .58), and well functioning distractors—specifically, (a) the proportion of selection of each distractor decreases for examinees from the lower, middle, and upper range of total test score, and (b) each distractor is equally attractive to examinees who do not know the correct answer within each range (lower, middle, and upper) of total test score. Item 2, however, is not a good item because it is very difficult—only 10% of all examinees answered this item correctly (p_i = .10)—and it does not differentiate well between examinees with low and high test performance (d_i = .20). The distractors of this item serve no function either—for example, Distractor B is too appealing to examinees in the upper range of total test score, Distractor A is not attractive to examinees in the lower range of total test score, and Distractor D is selected at higher rate by examinees in the upper range compared with those in the lower range of total test score. Clearly, Item 2 should be revised or discarded.

TABLE 8.1

Data for Analysis of Multiple-Choice Items Using Their Indices p_i, d_i, and r_{iX} and the Proportion of Examinees Choosing Each Answer Option

	Group Range on Total Test Score					
Item and Answer Option	Lower	Middle	Upper	p_i	d_i	r_{iX}
1				.43	.60	.58
A*	**.10**	**.40**	**.70**			
B	.35	.25	.10			
C	.25	.15	.08			
D	.30	.20	.12			
2				.10	.20	.12
A	.10	.05	.00			
B	.80	.60	.50			
C*	**.00**	**.10**	**.20**			
D	.10	.25	.30			

Note. Correct answers are noted by asterisks, and their proportions are boldface. p_i = item difficulty; d_i = discrimination; r_{iX} = item-total test score correlation.

Item-Reliability Index. As the item difficulty, p_i, is a proportion of a binary outcome (correct item response), the standard deviation of p_i is computed as $s_i = \sqrt{p_i(1 - p_i)}$. Theoretically, the item score reliability, ρ_{ii}, is the ratio of true item variance to observed item variance, that is: $\rho_{ii} = \sigma^2_{T_i} / \sigma^2_{X_i}$ (see Chapter 2). A sample-based estimate of ρ_{ii} is typically provided by the item-reliability index $r_{ii} = s_i r_{iX}$, where s_i is the standard deviation of the item and r_{iX} is the point-biserial item-total test score correlation (see Equation 8.1). Given an initial pool of items, one can develop a test with a maximized internal consistency reliability by selecting items as shown in Figure 8.1: Each item is depicted as a dot using as its coordinates the reliability index, r_{ii}, on the horizontal axis and the standard deviation, s_i, on the vertical axis. The items located along the right-hand edge of the plot yield a maximized internal consistency (e.g., Allen & Yen, 1979).

Item Characteristic Curve. An item characteristic curve (*ICC*) is a graphical display of the relationship between the probability of correct item response and the examinee's location on the scale of the underlying ability (trait) measured by the test. In the framework of classical test theory, an examinee's test ability is typically estimated by his or her total test score. The *ICC* of an item is represented by a plot with total test scores, X, on the horizontal axis and the proportion of examinees who answered the item correctly, p_X, on the vertical axis. Figure 8.2 depicts the *ICC*s of two items from a test composed of 20 binary items. Clearly, Item 1 discriminates well among examinees across the range of total test score. The *ICC* of Item 2, however, is not steep enough, which indicates that this item is a poor discriminator. Therefore, Item 2 should be revised or deleted from the test, especially if the test is designed for norm-referenced interpretations where the goal is to spread the examinees over the range of total test scores (Item 1 does a better job in this regard). However, Item 2 may be kept for the sake of content representation and if, say, the test is designed to differentiate high performances on the test—for example, examinees with a total test score above 17 (note that Item 2 differentiates relatively well among examinees with $X > 17$).

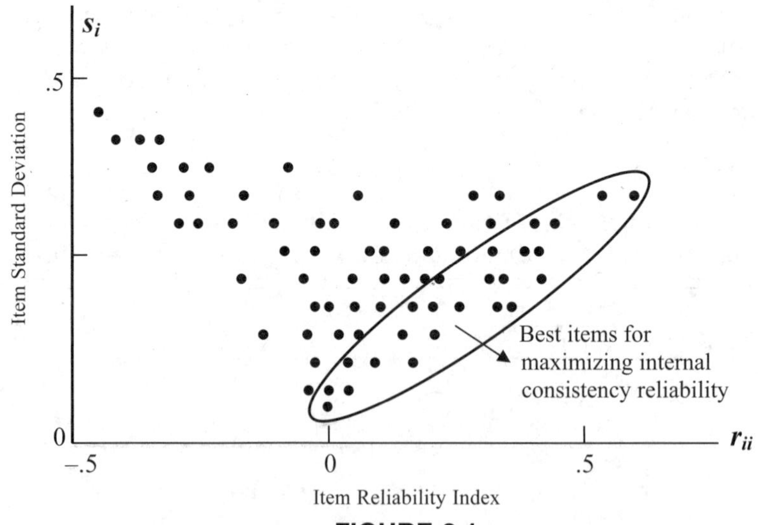

FIGURE 8.1

Selection of Items to Produce Maximized Internal Consistency Reliability

Note. From *Introduction to Measurement Theory* (1st ed., p. 126), by M. J. Allen and W. M. Yen, 1979, Pacific Grove, CA: Brooks/Cole Publishing. Copyright 1979 by Wadsworth, a part of Centage Learning, Inc. Reproduced with permission, www.centage.com/permissions.

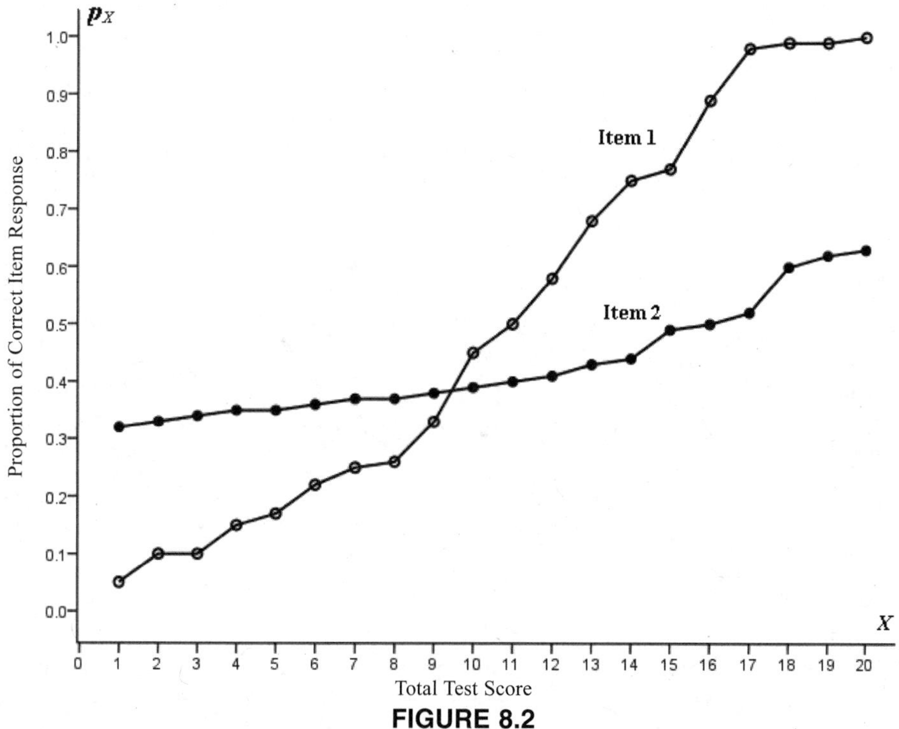

FIGURE 8.2

Item Characteristic Curves of Two Items (Classical Test Theory Estimation)

Whereas the steepness of the *ICC* relates to item discrimination, an *ICC*-based item difficulty index, b_i, can be defined by the total test score that corresponds to a proportion of .50 for correct item response (i.e., 50% chance of passing the item). In Figure 8.2, the total test score that corresponds to $p_X = .50$ for Item 1 is $X = 11$; thus, the *ICC*-based difficulty index of this item is $b_1 = 11$. On the other hand, the total test score that corresponds to $p_X = .50$ for Item 2 is $X = 16$, thus indicating that $b_2 = 16$. As $b_1 < b_2$, we can say that, on the average, Item 2 is more difficult than Item 1. However, we cannot say that Item 2 is consistently more difficult than Item 1. Indeed, the *ICC*s of the two items cross approximately at $X = 9$, and for examinees with a total test score below 9 ($X < 9$), Item 1 is more difficult, whereas for those with $X > 9$, Item 2 is more difficult.

*ICC*s can also be very useful in detecting differential item functioning (DIF) in pilot stages of test development. For example, if test developers are concerned that a given item might be functioning differentially against a minority group (e.g., because of an inappropriate wording of the item for this group), they can develop *ICC*s for this item separately for each (minority and majority) group. In the presence of item bias, the *ICC*s for the two groups will differ over the range of total test scores—that is, examinees with the same total test score will have different chances of correct item response because they belong to different groups. This situation is illustrated in Figure 8.3, where the *ICC* of an item for a minority group is consistently below the *ICC* of the same item for the majority group, thus indicating item bias against the minority group. It should be noted that although item difficulty, p_i, item discrimination, d_i, and item-total test score correlation, r_{iX}, provide useful information for moderate sample sizes, the *ICC*s requires relatively large sample sizes so that there are enough examinees to estimate the proportion of correct item response for each total test score.

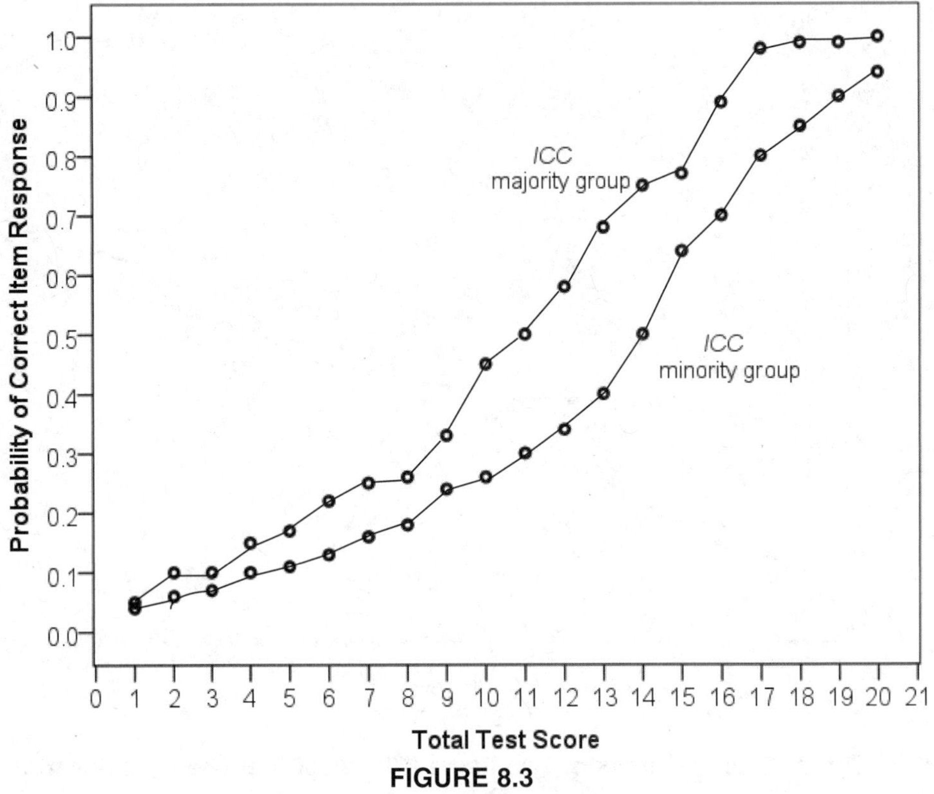

FIGURE 8.3

Using the Item Charateristic Curve (ICC) of an Item to Detect Item Bias Against a Minority Group

Recall that in the framework of confirmatory factor analysis (CFA), DIF is signaled by the lack of measurement invariance across groups (see Chapter 6, Section 6.7.3). Rigorous approaches to testing for DIF exist also in the framework of IRT (e.g., Embretson & Reise, 2000; Hambleton, Swaminathan, & Rogers, 1991). It should be noted that both CFA-based and IRT-based estimates of the examinees' location on the underlying ability (trait) are more accurate compared with the total test score. *ICC*s are further discussed in Chapter 9, Section 9.1.2.

8.1.2 Distribution of Total Test Scores

Examining the distribution of total test scores is also useful in classical scale analysis at pilot stages of test development. For many tests in counseling, psychology, and education, the underlying ability (trait) is normal, but the distribution of observed total test scores may deviate from normality in different ways. For example, if the test is too easy, the result is a ceiling effect for the distribution of total test scores, although the underlying trait might be normally distributed. An illustration of ceiling effect is provided in Figure 8.4, where the examinees that are crowded into the upper range of total test scores would belong to the upper tail of the underlying normal distribution of the trait if the test were of average difficulty. In this case, a greater number of difficult items should be added to the test to eliminate the ceiling effect. However, it might be not necessary to change the test if the underlying trait is negatively skewed for the

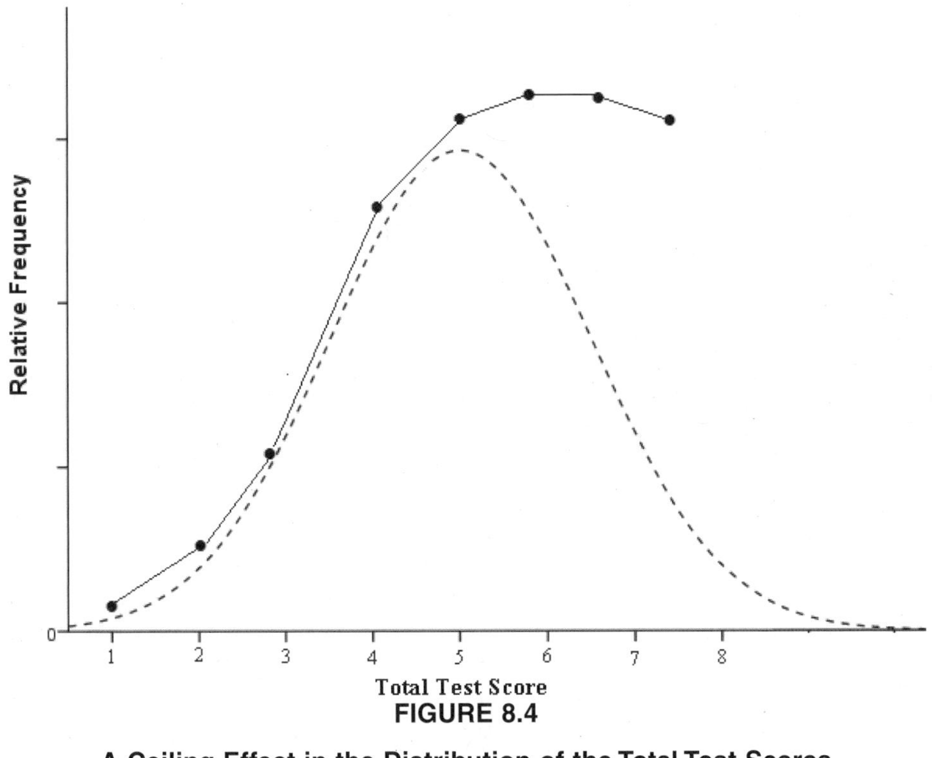

FIGURE 8.4

A Ceiling Effect in the Distribution of the Total Test Scores

Note. The dashed line indicates the underlying trait distribution.

population of interest or the test does not target discrimination among examinees at the ceiling of total scores.

If the test is too difficult, the result is a floor effect; for example, see Figure 8.5, where the largest proportion of examinees fall into the lower range of total test scores (these examinees would belong to the lower tail of the underlying normal distribution of the trait if the test were of average difficulty). In this case, a greater number of easy items should be added to the test to eliminate the floor effect. However, it might not be necessary to change the test if the underlying trait is positively skewed for the population of interest or the test does not target discrimination among examinees at the floor of total scores.

8.2 ANALYSIS OF RATING SCALES

A rating scale is represented by a set of ordered-category statements that express attitude, satisfaction, or perception about something (e.g., how often a specific behavior occurs). The nature of rating scales and different types of rating scales—Likert scales, Likert-type scales, frequency rating scales, and so forth—are described in Chapter 1, Section 1.4.2. The development of a Likert (or Likert-type) scale is a process of unidimensional scaling. After generating a pool of potential Likert items—preferably 80–100 items rated on a 1-to-5 (or 1-to-7) *disagree–agree* response scale—test developers are advised to have a group of judges rate the items on how favorable the items are to the construct, using a 1-to-5 scale: 1 = *strongly unfavorable*, 2 = *somewhat unfavorable*, 3 = *undecided*, 4 = *somewhat favorable*, 5 = *strongly favorable*.

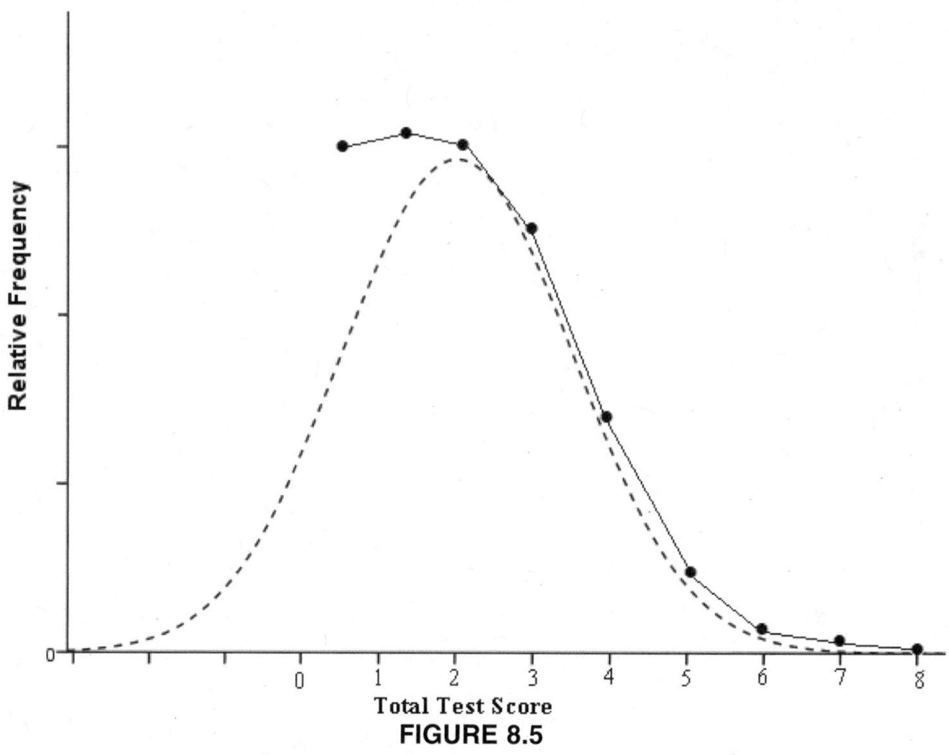

FIGURE 8.5

A Floor Effect in the Distribution of the Total Test Scores

Note. The dashed line indicates the underlying trait distribution.

8.2.1 Item Selection

To select the items that are most favorable to the construct, the test developer can sort all items in descending order by the mean score of the judges for each item (for items with the same mean, sort by the standard deviation of the judges' scores). If, say, 40 items are to be selected for subsequent piloting, the test developer should choose the items with the top 40 highest means. Based on the analysis of item ratings provided by the judges and their interrater agreement, some items may be excluded from the initial pool of items.

The remaining items are used in a pilot stage of instrument development, using an adequate sample of respondents from the target population, to make judgments about which items to retain for the final scale. This step involves procedures for evaluating the internal consistency of the scale under development and psychometric quality of its items. Specifically, test developers should (a) compute the intercorrelatons between all pairs of items based on the ratings of the judges; (b) throw out items that have a low correlation with the total score across all items; (c) for each item, do a *t* test of the differences between the mean values for the item using for the top quarter and the bottom quarter of ranking numbers for the item provided by the judges—items with higher *t* values are better discriminators; and (d) prefer items with high corrected item-total correlation and high discrimination, but their substantive merit and some practical considerations must also be taken into account in making decisions about which items to retain in the scale. If there are not enough judges, these first four steps can be conducted in a piloting stage of instrument development using an adequate sample of respondents from the target population. Prior to that, researchers should carefully examine the wording of the items. If there are negatively worded items, they must be reverse scored. For each item, a high item score should represent a high level of the underlying trait, and a low item score should represent a low level of the trait. Some additional comments related to classical analysis of rating scale items, suitable primarily in piloting stages of instrument development, are discussed next.

8.2.2 Joining Adjacent Response Categories

The analysis of rating scales often involves judgments about the necessity of joining adjacent response categories for scale items. For example, as noted in Chapter 1, Likert scales may be distorted because of (a) central tendency bias—respondents avoid using extreme response categories, (b) acquiescence bias—respondents agree with the statements as presented, and/or (c) social desirability bias—respondents try to portray themselves or their organization in a more favorable light. Designing a scale with an equal number of positively and negatively worded statements can avert the problem of acquiescence bias, but central tendency and social desirability are somewhat more problematic and require careful examination, including the necessity of joining adjacent categories.

In a rigorous manner, the analysis of response categories is typically performed within the framework of Rasch rating scale models (e.g., Andrich, 1978a, 1978b, 1988; Linacre, 1999a, 1999b, 2002; E. V. Smith et al., 2003; Wright & Masters, 1982); this approach is discussed in Chapter 9. Provided next are only empirical suggestions on joining adjacent response categories that can be useful in piloting stages of instrument development:

- Joining response categories of rating scales should make sense. That is, it should be reasonable to expect that the joined categories signify the same level of the underlying variable.
- As the original number of modal (most frequent) response categories brings out the number of meaningful segments on the continuum of the underlying variable perceived by the respondents, joining response categories should *not* result in additional (artificially generated) modal categories.
- Joining response categories should result in a distribution of category frequencies that matches the profile in the histogram of the scale score distribution. In Figure 8.6, for example, the original six categories for a scale item are reduced to three categories after joining (a) Categories 1 and 2 and (b) Categories 3, 4, and 5. The resulting frequency distribution across the new categories follows the symmetrical profile of the scale score distribution—the distribution of total scores in the top panel of Figure 8.6. Likewise, the original six categories for a scale item in Figure 8.7 are reduced to three categories, but this time by joining (a) Categories 2, 3, and 4 and (b) Categories 5 and 6, so that the resulting distribution of category frequencies follows the negatively skewed profile of the scale score distribution.

It is important to note that, along with statistical considerations, researchers should decide whether joining categories of rating scales makes sense. For example, E. V. Smith et al. (2003) noted that "in a traditional Likert scale with labels of *strongly agree*, *agree*, *undecided*, *disagree*, and *strongly disagree*, it would make sense to combine *strongly agree* and *agree* or *strongly disagree* and *disagree*, but not to join *agree* and *undecided* or *disagree* and *undecided*. In the latter situation, one would be better suited in treating responses to undecided as missing" (p. 376).

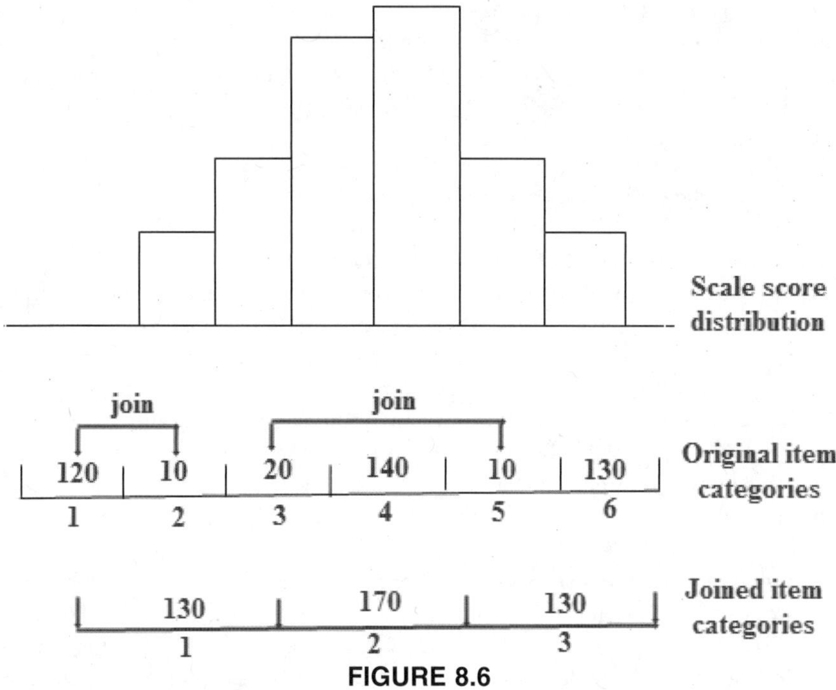

FIGURE 8.6

Joining Adjacent Categories of a Scale Item to Match the Symmetrical Profile of the Scale Score Distribution

8.2.3 Probability Tests for Likert-Type Scales

Previous research provides probability tests for use with Likert (or Likert-type) scale items when the purpose is to determine whether the population of respondents does, or does not, hold a particular belief or attitude measured by the item (e.g., Cooper, 1976; Whitney, 1978). Specifically, if S is the total score for all respondents in the sample for a given item and $E(S)$ is its expected (theoretical) value for the population, assuming that all response categories of that item have equal chances of being selected, the null hypothesis H_0: $E(S) = S$ is tested against the alternative H_1: $E(S) \neq S$. If H_0 is rejected, at a prespecified level of significance (say, $\alpha = .05$), one can conclude that the population responses are different from random selection of response categories—that is, they tend to depart from the middle category—thus either endorsing or failing to endorse (e.g., *agree* or *disagree*) the belief or attitude statement of the Likert-type item.

Under the assumptions that (a) the response categories are equally spaced and (b) all categories have an equal probability of being marked by a randomly selected subject from the population, Cooper (1976) derived the following z statistic for testing the null hypothesis, H_0: $E(S) = S$, against the alternative H_1: $E(S) \neq S$:

$$z = \frac{S - N(r+1)/2}{\sqrt{\frac{N(r^2-1)}{12}}}, \qquad (8.2)$$

where S is the total score of the sample on the item of interest, N is the sample size, and r is the number of item response categories. Equation 8.2 assumes sufficiently large samples

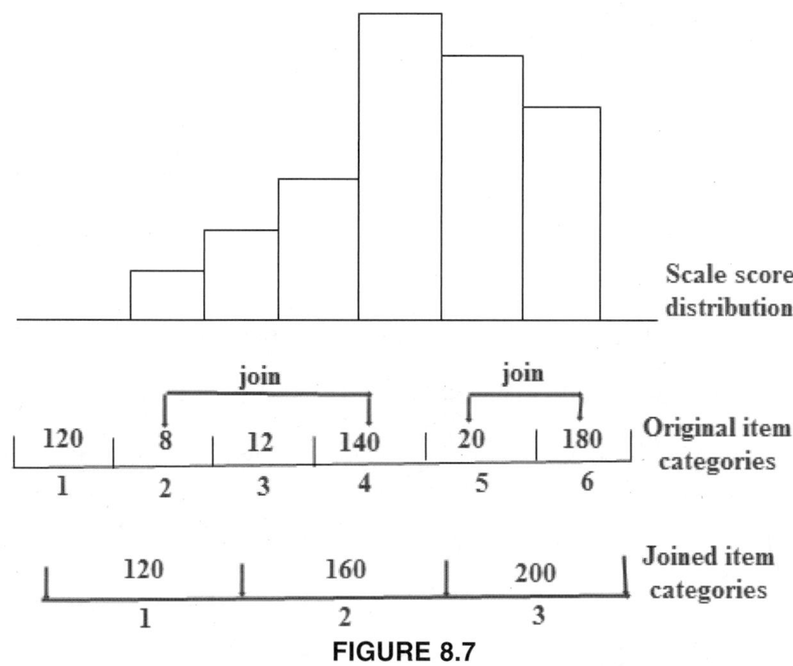

FIGURE 8.7

Joining Adjacent Categories of a Scale Item to Match the Negatively Skewed Profile of the Scale Score Distribution

($N > 100$). As z follows (approximately) the standard normal distribution, z greater than 1.96 in absolute value would suggest rejection of H_0 at the .05 level of significance.

An alternative test was proposed by Whitney (1978) to accommodate for cases of smaller samples and to drop the assumption of uniform frequency distribution across the item response categories. He proposed the following t test statistic (with degrees of freedom $df = N - 1$) for testing the null hypothesis of interest, H_0: $E(S) = S$,

$$t = \frac{S - N(r+1)/2}{\sqrt{\frac{\Sigma^{r}_{k=1} f_k(kN - S)^2}{N(N-1)}}}, \qquad (8.3)$$

where k is the weight of the kth category of an item with r response categories ($k = 1, 2, \ldots, r$).

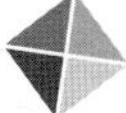

Example 8.1. This example illustrates the use of Equation 8.3 in testing H_0 for a Likert scale item (1 = *strongly disagree*, 2 = *disagree*, 3 = *neither agree nor disagree*, 4 = *agree*, and 5 = *strongly agree*) measuring attitude toward school for a population of middle school students. The frequency distribution of the responses of 25 students ($N = 25$) across these five response categories ($r = 5$) is presented in Table 8.2. The total score on this item for the sample of 25 students is as follows: $S = \Sigma^5_{k=1} kf_k = (1)(2) + (2)(2) + (3)(8) + (4)(10) + (5)(6) = 100$. Also, as shown in Table 8.2 for convenience, the sum under the square root in the denominator of the t statistic in Formula 7.2 equals 25,000. Thus, using Equation 8.3 with $\Sigma^{r}_{k=1} f_k(kN - S)^2 = (1)(2) = 25{,}000$, $S = 100$, $N = 25$, and $r = 5$, we obtain the following:

$$t = \frac{100 - (25)(5+1)/2}{\sqrt{\dfrac{25{,}000}{25(25-1)}}} = 3.873. \tag{8.4}$$

As the t statistic (3.873) exceeds the t critical value (2.064), for $df = N - 1 = 24$, at the .05 level of significance, we can reject the null hypothesis, H_0. Thus, the students' responses depart from the middle (neutral) category. Specifically, given that the t statistic (3.873) is on the positive side of the t distribution, we can expect that on average the students hold a positive attitude toward school, as measured by the item of interest (it is assumed that higher scores on the item scale indicate higher level of positive attitude toward school).

8.3 ESTIMATION OF RELIABILITY FOR CONGENERIC MEASURES

A key procedure in the process of unidimensional scaling is the evaluation of internal consistency reliability of the scale scores and the contribution of individual items in this regard. As noted earlier, the commonly used Cronbach's coefficient alpha can be a biased estimate of the scale reliability if the item measures are not essentially tau-equivalent and/or there are correlated errors (see Chapter 2, Section 2.3.1). Keep in mind, however, that high intercorrelations between items may produce high internal consistency, but this does not necessarily guarantee that the items measure a single underlying construct. For example, if two scales represent two correlated yet distinct constructs, the items of the two scales together might yield high internal consistency even though they do not reflect a single construct.

In pilot phases of scale development, when relatively small samples are used, Cronbach's coefficient alpha can be useful, but in final stages of scale validation estimates of scale reliability based on latent variable modeling (LVM) are preferable (e.g., Bollen, 1989; Raykov, 2009; Raykov & Shrout, 2002). As Cronbach's alpha and classical estimation of the standard error of measurement (*SEM*) were already discussed in Chapter 2, an LVM approach to estimating internal consistency reliability, $\rho_{XX'}$, and *SEM* is described and illustrated next (a simple Mplus code for related computations is also provided).

For simplicity, consider again the test model depicted in Figure 2.1 (Chapter 2, Section 2.2.2), where a single latent variable, η (eta), is measured by three observed variables, X_1, X_2, and X_3 (the observed scale score is $X = X_1 + X_2 + X_3$). In fact, this is a CFA-based congeneric model of a latent factor with three indicators. Under this model, the LVM translation of scale reliability, defined as the ratio of true score variance to observed variance ($\rho_{XX} = \sigma^2_T / \sigma^2_X$), is provided by the following equation (e.g., Bollen, 1989):

TABLE 8.2

Frequency Distribution Across Likert Response Categories and Computation of the Summation Term in Equation 8.3

Category k	Frequency f_k	$kN - S$	$f_k(kN - S)^2$
1	2	(1)(25) – 100 = –75	(2)(–75)² = 11,250
2	2	(2)(25) – 100 = –50	(2)(–50)² = 5,000
3	8	(3)(25) – 100 = –25	(8)(–25)² = 5,000
4	10	(4)(25) – 100 = 0	(10)(0)² = 0
5	6	(5)(25) – 100 = 25	(6)(25)² = 3,750
			Sum = 25,000

$$\rho_{XX} = \frac{(\lambda_1 + \lambda_2 + \lambda_3)^2}{(\lambda_1 + \lambda_2, + \lambda_3)^2 + VAR(E_1) + VAR(E_2) + VAR(E_3)}, \quad (8.5)$$

where λ_1, λ_2, and λ_3 are the factor loadings and $VAR(E_1)$, $VAR(E_2)$, and $VAR(E_3)$ are the error variances in the model. It should be noted that the estimation of ρ_{XX} under Equation 8.5 assumes *no* correlation among the error terms (E_1, E_2, and E_3). With correlated errors, assuming model identification, the right-hand side of Equation 8.5 needs to be extended by adding twice the sum of error covariances in the denominator (e.g., Bollen, 1989, p. 220). This assumes that the model with the added error covariances is identified (the concept of identified latent variable models is discussed in Chapter 6, Section 6.5). Of course, Equation 8.5 can be readily extended for the case of more than three observable variables.

A readable discussion of the LVM approach to evaluating reliability through the use of Equation 8.5 is provided by Raykov (2009). Unlike Cronbach's alpha, which assumes tau-equivalency, the LVM estimation of internal consistency reliability through the use of Equation 8.5 works in the general case of congeneric measures (see Chapter 2, Section 2.2.2). Related computations can be easily performed in the framework of computer programs such as Mplus, EQS, and LISREL.

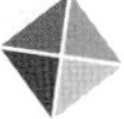

Example 8.2. This example illustrates the use of Mplus for the estimation of scale reliability, ρ_{XX}, for congeneric measures using Equation 8.5. Based on this, the estimation of *SEM* is also provided (see Equation 2.8 in Chapter 2). The data consist of simulated scores of 2,000 examinees on five test items, $X_1, \ldots, X_5$. Each item was on a scale from 0 to 10, so the scale score for the five items varied from 0 to 50 (the sample mean and variance for the scale scores were $\bar{X} = 25.7$ and $s^2_X = 23.287$, respectively).

Prior to using Equation 8.5, extended here to five measures, it is necessary to test the assumption of unidimensionality (i.e., to make sure that $X_1, \ldots, X_5$ are congeneric measures). Therefore, a one-factor CFA model with five indicators ($X_1, \ldots, X_5$) was tested for data fit first using Mplus. The goodness-of-fit test indicated an excellent data fit. Specifically, the chi-square goodness-of-fit test statistic was not statistically significant, $\chi^2(5) = 1.64$, $p = .897$, and the following indices indicated an excellent data fit: CFI = 1.00, TLI = 1.00, RMSEA = 0.00, with a 90% CI [0.00, 0.014], and SRMR = 0.004 (see Chapter 6, Section 6.6.2). The excellent data ft in this case is not surprising given that the simulated measures were generated as related to a single underlying construct. Nevertheless, testing for unidimensionality is presented here to illustrate the first step in the LVM approach to estimating score reliability.

Next, the Mplus code in Table 8.3 was used for the estimation of scale reliability, ρ_{XX}, using Equation 8.5 extended to the case of five indicators ($X_1, \ldots, X_5$). The estimation of the *SEM* is also provided with the Mplus code. The computation of point estimates of ρ_{XX} and *SEM*, and their 90%, 95%, and 99% CIs, was performed by using the bootstrap procedure in Mplus. The selected Mplus output (lower panel in Table 8.3) provides the estimate of the scale reliability, $\hat{\rho}_{XX} = .769$, with three CIs: 90% CI [.755, .781], 95% [.753, .783], and 99% [.748, .788]. As can be seen, the estimate of standard error of measurement is $\widehat{SEM} = 2.319$, with 90% CI [2.292, 2.351], 95% CI [2.286, 2.356], and 99% CI [2.274, 2.368]. As noted in Chapter 2, Section 2.2.5, *SEM* relates directly to the meaning of the test's scale of measurement and is, therefore, very useful for score interpretations.

TABLE 8.3

Mplus Code and Selected Output for Latent Variable Modeling Estimation of Scale Reliability and Standard Error of Measurement (*SEM*): An Illustration for the Case of Five Indicators (X1, X2, X3, X4, X5)

```
            DATA:  FILE IS "C:\X2000.dat";           !Input data file
                   FORMAT IS 5F4.0;
        VARIABLE:  NAMES ARE X1-X5;                  !Variable names
                   USEVARIABLES ARE X1-X5;
           MODEL:  ETA BY X1*(B1)                    !Model specification
                   X2-X5(B2-B5);
                   ETA@1;
                   X1-X5 (EV1-EV5);
MODEL CONSTRAINT:                                    !Computation of Reliability and SEM
                   NEW(REL SEM TVAR EVAR XVAR);
                   TVAR = (B1+B2+B3+B4+B5)**2;       !True-score variance
                   EVAR = EV1+EV2+EV3+EV4+EV5;       !Error variance
                   REL = TVAR/(TVAR+EVAR);           !Scale Reliability
                   XVAR = TVAR+EVAR;                 !Observed variance
                   SEM = SQRT(XVAR*(1-REL));         !SEM
        ANALYSIS:  BOOTSTRAP = 5000;
          OUTPUT:  CINTERVAL(BCBOOTSTRAP);
```

Selected Output

	Lower .5%	**Lower 2.5%**	**Lower 5%**	**Estimate**	**Upper 5%**	**Upper 2.5%**	**Upper .5%**
REL	0.748	0.753	0.755	**0.769**	0.781	0.783	0.788
SEM	2.274	2.286	2.292	**2.319**	2.351	2.356	2.368

Note. If the number of indicators is different from five, this should be reflected in the Mplus code. Along with estimates of scale reliability (REL) and standard error of measurement (*SEM*), this Mplus code renders estimates of the true score variance (TVAR), error variance (EVAR), and observed variance (XVAR), not shown in the selected output, which can be useful in some additional analyses, if necessary.

SUMMARY

1. The classical analysis of binary items is intended to provide information about their measurement properties in terms of difficulty, discrimination, and probability of correct response across levels of the ability (trait) being measured by the test.
2. The difficulty of an item is defined as the proportion of examinees who get that item correct. In general, it is advisable to choose items with a range of difficulties that average about .5; for example, item difficulties of about .3 to .7 are considered optimal in differentiating examinees in the ability (or trait) being measured by the test.
3. The item discrimination shows to what degree an item discriminates between high-performing and low-performing examinees on the test as a whole. Theoretically, the item discrimination index can take on values from –1.00 to 1.00. A positive value means that more examinees from the upper range group (e.g., top 27%) answered the item correctly compared with the lower range group (e.g., bottom 27%), thus indicating that this item provides a proper discrimination of examinees from the two groups.
4. The item-total test score correlation, estimated by the point-biserial correlation coefficient between the binary item score and the total test score, represents another measure of item discrimination.
5. The incorrect answer choices in a multiple-choice item are called *distractors*. In general, good distractors should be selected (a) at about an equal rate by examinees who do not know the correct answer, and (b) at a higher rate by examinees in the lower test performing group compared with the examinees in the middle group and, particularly, those in the upper group.

6. A sample-based estimate of item reliability is typically provided by the item-reliability index, which equals the product of the item standard deviation and the point-biserial item-total test score correlation.
7. An item characteristic curve (*ICC*) is a graphical display of the relationship between the probability of correct item response and the examinee's location on the scale of the underlying ability (trait) measured by the test. In conventional item analysis, the *ICC* of a binary item is represented by a plot with total test scores on the horizontal axis and the proportion of examinees who answered the item correctly on the vertical axis.
8. Along with providing information about item difficulty and discrimination, the *ICC*s can also be very useful in providing information about differential item functioning (DIF). Typically, test developers analyze DIF by comparing the *ICC*s developed separately for the two (majority and minority) groups of interest.
9. If the test is too easy (or too difficult), this will result in a ceiling effect (or floor effect) for the distribution of total test scores, although the underlying trait might be normally distributed.
10. After generating an initial pool of rating scale (e.g., Likert) items, test developers continue the process of item selection by having judges rate items on how favorable they are to the construct and then evaluating the psychometric quality of the items. Typically, items with high corrected item-total correlation, high discrimination, substantive merit, and practical utility are preferred.
11. The analysis of rating scales often involves judgments about the necessity of joining adjacent response categories for scale items. Rating (e.g., Likert) scales may be distorted because of (a) central tendency bias—respondents avoid using extreme response categories, (b) acquiescence bias—respondents agree with the statements as presented, and/or (c) social desirability bias—respondents try to portray themselves or their organization in a more favorable light.
12. Joining response categories of rating scales should make sense; it should *not* result in additional (artificially generated) modal categories. Furthermore, the distribution of category frequencies should match the profile in the histogram of the scale score distribution.
13. Probability tests for use with Likert (or Likert-type) scale are conducted to determine whether the population of respondents does, or does not, hold a particular belief or attitude measured by the item. A z test (Cooper, 1976) or a t test (Whitney, 1978) can be used to test whether the responses are different from random selection of response categories—that is, they tend to depart from the middle category (see Equations 8.2 and 8.3, respectively).
14. A key procedure in the process of unidimensional scaling is the evaluation of internal consistency reliability of the scale scores and the contribution of individual items in this regard. Keep in mind, however, that high intercorrelations between items may produce high internal consistency, but this does not necessarily guarantee that the items measure a single underlying construct.
15. The commonly used Cronbach's coefficient alpha can be a biased estimate of the scale reliability if the item measures are not essentially tau-equivalent and/or there are correlated errors. In pilot phases of scale development, when relatively small samples are used, Cronbach's coefficient alpha can be useful, but in final stages of scale validation estimates of scale reliability based on latent variable modeling are preferable.

Chapter 9
Rasch-Based Scale Analysis

Concepts and procedures of conventional scale analysis discussed in Chapter 8 are elaborated at a more rigorous level in the framework of item response theory (IRT) or Rasch measurement in this chapter. Because a comprehensive presentation of IRT models is beyond the scope of this book, I discuss only concepts and procedures related to Rasch models for scale analysis. Besides space consideration, an important reason for this choice is that Rasch-based analysis is frequently used in published studies on the development of assessment instruments and validation of related data.

Methodological issues and practical applications of relevant Rasch models are almost regularly published in professional journal such as *Journal of Applied Measurement*, *Educational and Psychological Measurement*, and *Measurement and Evaluation in Counseling and Development*. Numerous books that provide readable treatment of Rasch measurement are also available (e.g., Andrich, 1988; Bond & Fox, 2001; E. V. Smith & R. M. Smith, 2007; E. V. Smith & Stone, 2009; Wright & Stone, 1979; Wright & Masters, 1982). Widely used computer programs for Rasch-based scale analysis are WINSTEPS (Linacre & Wright, 1999), FACETS (Linacre, 1994, 2006), BIGSTEPS (Linacre & Wright, 1998), ConQuest (M. L. Wu, Adams, & Wilson, 1998), and RUMM (Andrich, Lyne, Sheridan, & Luo, 1997, 2003). Rasch analysis is gaining popularity in studies examining psychometric properties of assessment instruments in counseling, psychology, education, and other fields (e.g., Bradley, Sampson, & Royal, 2006; Clark, 2004; Cunningham, Bradley, & Gilman, 2006; Green & Frantom, 2002; Hardigan & Carvajal, 2008; Hong & Wong, 2005; B. S. K. Kim & Hong, 2004; Ludlow, Enterline, & Cochran-Smith, 2008; Ludlow & Haley, 1992; Searing, 2008; E. V. Smith, 2005; E. V. Smith & Johnson, 2000; E. V. Smith et al., 2003; Wolfe & Nogle, 2002; Wolfe, Ray, & Harris, 2004; and P.-C. Wu & Chang, 2008; Yamaguchi, 1997).

In this chapter I address procedures and methodological issues related to Rasch-based analysis of binary scales and rating (e.g., Likert) scales. Under Rasch modeling of binary data, the discussion taps on the concepts of item characteristic curves, test characteristic curves, item information function, test information function, fit analysis, and person–item distribution map. Rasch analysis of rating scales deals with issues of threshold (step) disordering, category disordering, optimizing rating scale category effectiveness, person–item distribution map, and testing for multidimensionality.

9.1 RASCH MODEL FOR BINARY DATA

9.1.1 Rasch Model and Logit Scale

The Rasch modeling approach to measurement was developed by the Danish mathematician Georg Rasch (1960, 1966). A key conception of the Rasch model is that the test developer should first identify a particular construct (trait, ability) for assessment and then prepare observable indicators (items) of that construct that fit into the model. That is, the goal in Rasch measurement is to select items that fit the model, whereas in IRT the goal is to assess whether the respective IRT model fits the data at hand (e.g., Hambleton et al., 1991).

In this chapter I consider only unidimensional measures. With unidimensional measures, a single dominating dimension (construct) is presumed to explain the examinees' performance on the test. The underlying dimension is referred to as *ability* (or *trait*). The location of a person on the continuum of the ability being measured is the *ability level* of that person. Under the Rasch model for binary responses (1 = correct, 0 = incorrect), referred to as *dichotomous Rasch model*, the chances of a person giving a correct response on an item are governed solely by the person's ability and the item difficulty. Specifically, the probability of correct item response for person n on item i is given by the equation

$$P_i(\theta_n) = \frac{exp(\theta_n - \delta_i)}{1 + exp(\theta_n - \delta_i)}, \qquad (9.1)$$

where θ_n is the person's ability, δ_i is the item difficulty, and $exp(.)$is the exponential function; that is, $exp(\theta_n - \delta_i) = e^{\theta_n - \delta_i}$, where e is a constant: $e = 2.718$ (rounded to three decimals).

For simplicity, let's denote $P_{ni} = P_i(\theta_n)$. Given that P_{ni} is the probability for success, the ratio $P_{ni}/(1 - P_{ni})$ represents the odds for success on item i for a person with ability θ_n. With simple algebra, Equation 9.1 can be represented as

$$ln[P_{ni}/(1 - P_{ni})] = \theta_n - \delta_i, \qquad (9.2)$$

where the expression on the left-hand side is the natural logarithm of the odds for success on item i, with difficulty δ_i, for a person with ability θ_n.

Equation 9.1 shows that the probability of success on an item depends on the difference between a person's ability and the item difficulty ($\theta_n - \delta_i$). When the ability equals the item difficulty ($\theta_n = \delta_i$), the probability of correct item response is 0.5. At the same time, Equation 9.2 shows that the difference $\theta_n - \delta_i$ is represented as the natural logarithm of the odds of the person's success on the item. On the basis of this equation, the measurement unit of the scale for person ability and item difficulty is referred to as *logit* (a contraction of *log odds unit*). Note that if one adds the same constant to both θ_n and δ_i, their difference ($\theta_n - \delta_i$) does not change. Thus, the logit scale only determines relative differences between ability and item difficulty, between person abilities, or between item difficulties. In other words, the logit scale is an interval scale because it maintains the differences, but its origin may change across different tests that measure the same ability (or trait). Therefore, the comparison of (person and/or item) parameters across different test calibrations would be appropriate only after equating these parameters (i.e., putting them on a common scale).

To illustrate a fundamental property of the Rasch model, let P_1 and P_2 be the probabilities of success on an item with difficulty δ for two persons with ability θ_1 and θ_2, respectively. Then the difference between the logits of success on the item for the two persons is given by

$$ln\left(\frac{P_1}{1 - P_1}\right) - ln\left(\frac{P_2}{1\ \ P_2}\right) = \theta_1 - \delta - (\theta_2 - \delta) = \theta_1 - \theta_2.$$

Thus, the difference between the logits (log odds) of success for two persons on any item does not depend on the difficulty of that item. That is, the comparison of two persons on the ability being measured is "item free." Similarly, it can be demonstrated that the comparison of two items in terms of difficulty is "person free." This unique Rasch property of item free estimation of person ability and person free estimation of item difficulty is called *specific objectivity*.

9.1.2 Item Characteristic Curve

The graph of the relationship between the ability score of a person and the probability that this person will answer an item correctly is called the *item characteristic curve* (*ICC*). The *ICC*s of three items calibrated under the Rasch model for binary items are depicted in Figure 9.1. The *ICC*s of these three items are parallel as under the Rasch model all items have the same discrimination power (specifically, the item discrimination indices are equal and fixed to 1.0).

As noted earlier, the difficulty parameter, δ_i, for an item is the location on the ability scale where the probability for correct response on that item is 0.5 (i.e., 50% chance of correct response). This parameter is referred to also as a *location parameter* as it indicates the position of the *ICC* of the item on the ability scale. As illustrated in Figure 9.1, the difficulty of Item 1 is one and a half units below the origin of the logit scale ($\delta_1 = -1.5$)—the location on the ability scale where the probability for correct response on Item 1 is 0.5. Likewise, the difficulty of Item 2 is exactly at the origin of the scale ($\delta_2 = 0$), and the difficulty of Item 3 is one and a

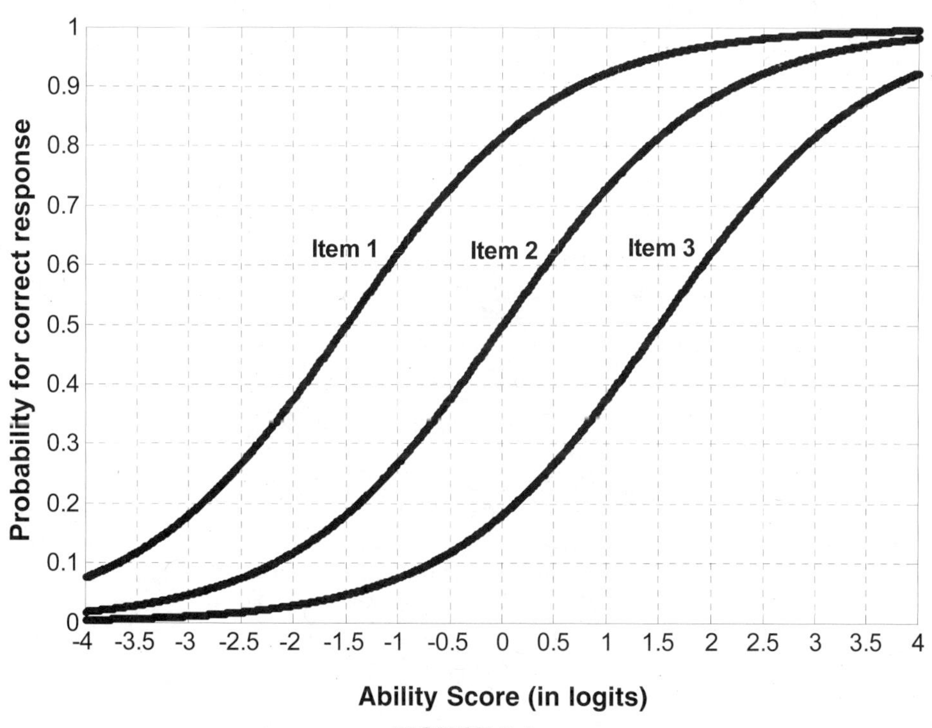

FIGURE 9.1

Item Characteristic Curves of Three Items Calibrated Under the Dichotomous Rasch Model

Note. Item 1 ($b_1 = -1.5$), Item 2 ($b_2 = 0$), and Item 3 ($b_3 = 1.5$).

half units above the origin of the logit scale ($\delta_3 = 1.5$). Clearly, the most difficult item is Item 3, followed by Item 2 and by Item 1 (the easiest item). For a person located at the origin of the scale ($\theta = 0$), Figure 9.1 shows that the probability for correct response is about .80 on Item 1, .50 on Item 2, and .20 on Item 3. More accurate estimates of these probabilities are obtained using Equation 9.1 with $\theta = 0$ and (a) $\delta_1 = 1.5$ for Item 1, which yields $P_1 = .8176$; (b) $\delta_2 = 0$ for Item 2, which yields $P_2 = .50$; and (c) $\delta_3 = 1.5$ for Item 3, which yields $P_3 = .1824$.

9.1.3 Test Characteristic Curve

Given the ability score of a person on the logit scale, the classical true score for this person on a test can be obtained by adding the person's probabilities for correct response on each test item (e.g., Hambleton et al., 1991, p. 85). If, for example, a test consists of the three binary items in Figure 9.1, the number-right score that a person may obtain on this test is 0, 1, 2, or 3; (in any case, some measurement error will be a part of this score). As described earlier, for a person at the origin of the logit scale ($\theta = 0$), the probability for success on Items 1, 2, and 3 is $P_1 = .8176$, $P_2 = .50$, and $P_3 = .1824$, respectively. The true number-right score for this person is then the sum $P_1 + P_2 + P_3 = .8176 + .50 + .1824 = 1.50$ (i.e., not necessarily 0, 1, 2, or 3). The domain score (true proportion correct) for the same person is obtained by dividing the true score to the number of items: 1.5/3 = 0.5 (i.e., 50% correct responses). Similarly, one can obtain the true number-right score and domain score for a person on a test with more than three items. The graphical depiction of the relationship between ability scores (on the horizontal axis) and their true-score equivalents (on the vertical axis) is called the *test characteristic curve*. That is, the test characteristic curve is the sum of all item characteristic curves across the θ values on the logit scale. As noted by Hambleton et al. (1991, p. 85), transforming (Rasch or other IRT-based) ability scores to true scores or domain scores has important implications, such as (a) negative scores on the IRT logit scale are converted into positive true scores, and (b) the true (or domain) scores are readily interpretable because for a test of n binary items, the true score scale ranges from 0 to n (or from 0% to 100% if domain scores are used). For example, pass–fail cutting scores are often set on the domain-score scale (e.g., 80% mastery). Then, with the domain scores plotted against the logit scores, the cutting score on the logit scale is identified by the logit value that corresponds to the prespecified domain cutting score. It is useful to provide test characteristic curves with boundaries (e.g., one standard deviation) about the true score to delineate the interval in which the true number-right score for a person with a given ability score (in logits) is expected to fall.

9.1.4 Item Information Function

The information function of item i at location θ on the logit scale, denoted $I_i(\theta)$, provides information about the contribution of the item to the ability estimation at θ. Under the dichotomous Rasch model, $I_i(\theta)$ equals the product of the probability for success, $P_i(\theta)$, and the probability for failure, $1 - P_i(\theta)$, on item i for a person located at θ on the logit scale. That is,

$$I_i(\theta) = P_i(\theta)[1 - P_i(\theta)] \,. \tag{9.3}$$

It has also been shown that when $I_i(\theta)$ is graphed across all values of $\theta(-\infty, \infty)$, the area under the resulting information function curve equals 1.0, regardless of the item's difficulty (e.g., Penfield, 2005). Figure 9.2 presents the information functions of the three binary items depicted in Figure 9.1. In the previous section I showed, for example, that the probabilities for correct response on these three items at $\theta = 0$ were $P_1(0) = 0.8176$, $P_2(0) = 0.50$, and

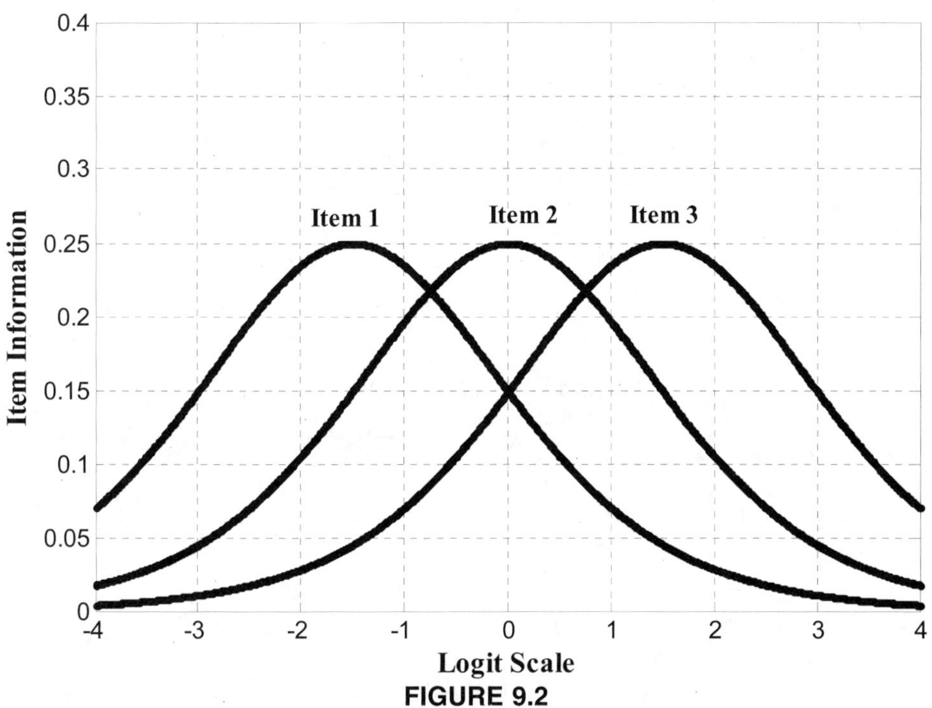

FIGURE 9.2

Item Information Functions for Three Items Under the Dichotomous Rasch Model

Note. Item 1 ($b_1 = -1.5$), Item 2 ($b_2 = 0$), and Item 3 ($b_3 = 1.5$).

$P_3(0) = 0.1824$. Thus, the magnitudes of the item information functions of the three items at $\theta = 0$ are as follows: $I_1(0) = P_1(0)[1 - P_1(0)] = (0.8176)(1 - 0.8176) = 0.1491$; $I_2(0) = P_2(0)[1 - P_2(0)] = (0.50)(1 - 0.50) = 0.25$; and $I_3(0) = P_3(0)[1 - P_3(0)] = (0.1824)(1 - 0.1824) = 0.1491$. Note that $I_1(0) = I_3(0) = 0.1491$ because the difficulties of Item 1 and Item 3 are symmetrically located around the origin (zero) of the logit scale: –1.50 and 1.50, respectively.

9.1.5 Test Information Function

The test information function at θ for a test of m binary items is defined as the sum of the item information functions for the test items, that is, $I_T(\theta) = \Sigma I_i(\theta)$; $(i = 1, \ldots, m)$. For example, the sum of the three item information functions in Figure 9.2 produces the test information function depicted in Figure 9.3. To illustrate, using the $I_i(\theta)$ values of these three items at $\theta = 0$, computed in the previous section, the magnitude of their test information function at $\theta = 0$ is: $I_T(0) = I_1(0) + I_2(0) + I_1(0) = 0.1491 + 0.25 + 0.1491 = 0.5482$. The test information function plays an instrumental role in determining the error in the ability score estimate, $\hat{\theta}$. Specifically, the standard error of $\hat{\theta}$ is the inverse of the square root of the test information function. That is,

$$SE(\hat{\theta}) = 1/\sqrt{I_T(\theta)}\,. \tag{9.4}$$

For example, given that the magnitude of the test information function in Figure 9.3 at $\theta = 0$ is $I_T(0) = 0.5482$, the standard error of the estimate of the ability of a person located at

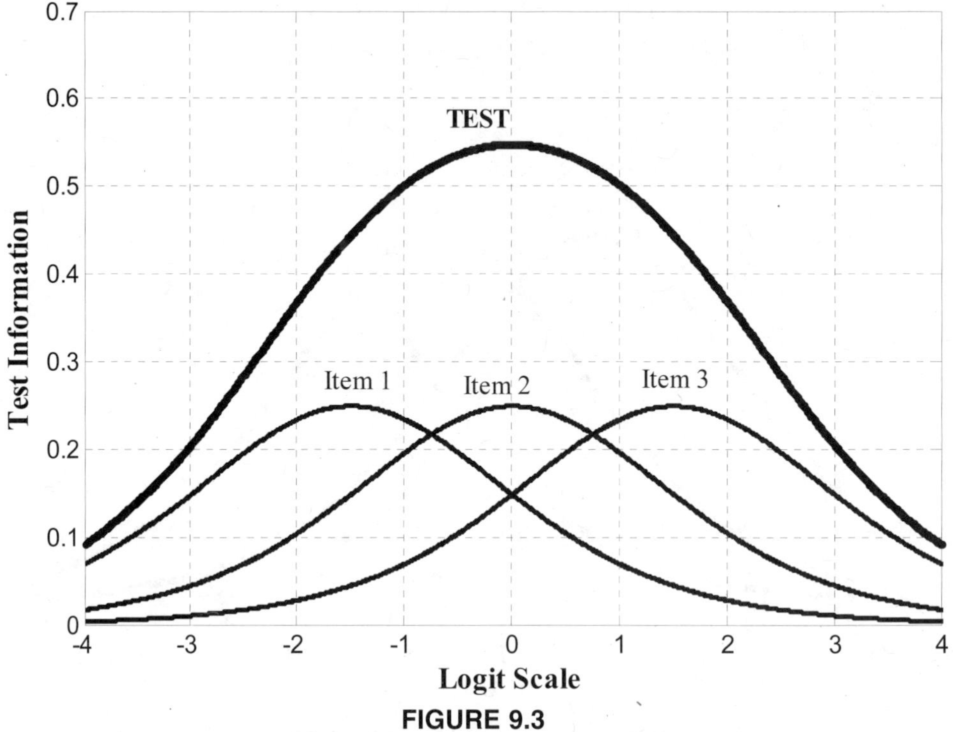

FIGURE 9.3

Test information Function as a Sum of the Information Functions of Three Items Under the Dichotomous Rasch Model

$\theta = 0$ is $SE(\hat{\theta}) = 1/\sqrt{0.5482} = 1.3506$. As one may notice, the largest information function value in this case is at $\theta = 0$, thus indicating that the smallest standard error (1.3506) occurs at $\theta = 0$. At the same time, however, this error is quite large because the test consists of only three items. By increasing the number of items that fit the Rasch model, $SE(\hat{\theta})$ will become smaller, thus yielding more accurate ability estimates.

As the test information function is the sum of the information functions of the test items, the contribution of each item to the test information function is additive and independent from the contribution of all other items. Unlike other IRT models, the information functions of items that fit the Rasch model have a unique property in the sense that, as already noted, the area under the information function of any such item is a constant (equal to 1.0). This property, referred to as *item information constancy*, implies that under the Rasch model all items contribute equally to the magnitude of the test information function across the entire continuum of θ (e.g., Penfield, 2005). Test developers can use this property to build tests with desired test information functions.

In general, when a test is designed to measure broad-range abilities (e.g., for norm-referenced interpretation), the test information function should be relatively flat, thus indicating that the precision of ability estimates, $\hat{\theta}$s, is about the same over the logit scale. For a criterion-referenced test, the graphical curve of the test information function should be highly peaked near the location of the cut-off ability score that is used for the respective classification decision (e.g., mastery/nonmastery, pass/fail, and so forth). Also, if there is preliminary information about the ability range for the study population of examinees, it would be useful to select items that maximize the test information over that particular range on the logit scale.

9.1.6 Fit Analysis

The Rasch model puts both person ability and item difficulty on a common interval scale, referred to as the *logit scale*, if the data fit the Rasch model requirements. Also, according to the separation of item and person parameters in Rasch measurement, estimates of people's abilities do not depend on the item difficulties, and vice versa: Estimates of item difficulties do not depend on people's abilities (again, under the assumption that the data fit the Rasch model requirements). This unique property of the Rasch measurement allows for rigorous assessment of the fit of person responses to the Rasch model. Given that a comprehensive treatment of this topic is beyond the scope of this book, in this section I provide only some basic concepts and fit statistics that relate to Rasch-based scale analysis addressed in this chapter. For details on Rasch fit analysis, the reader may refer to Dimitrov and Smith (2006); R. M. Smith (1991, 2004); R. M. Smith, Schumacker, and Bush (1998); and Wright and Linacre (1994).

Briefly presented next are some fit statistics that are frequently reported in studies using Rasch analysis and related software (e.g., WINSTEPS, FACETS, ConQuest, and RUMM). These statistics are based on the concept of standardized residuals, $Z = (X - E)/\sqrt{\text{VAR}(X)}$, where X is the observed score, E is its expected value under the Rasch model (e.g., see Equation 9.1), and VAR(X) is the variance of the observed scores. The sum of the squared standardized residuals is a chi-square (χ^2) statistic. For example, if N persons responded to item i, the chi-square statistic for this item is the sum of the squared standardized residuals for all N scores on the item; that is,

$$\chi^2_i = \Sigma^N_{n=1} Z^2_{ni}. \tag{9.5}$$

The following item fit statistics are based on the chi-square statistic in Equation 9.5:

- *Outfit mean-square*: This statistic is obtained by dividing the chi-square statistic by its degrees of freedom (χ^2_i/N). The outfit mean-square (Outfit MnSq) is sensitive to outliers, hence the name "outfit." More specifically, when describing Outfit MnSq, it is more accurate to say that this statistic is more sensitive to unexpected (rather than misfitting) responses by persons on items that are relatively very easy or very hard for them. The expected value of Outfit MnSq is close to 1.0 (Wright & Panchapakesan, 1969). Values less than 1.0 (termed *overfit*) indicate that the model predicts the data too well, thus causing inflation of summary statistics for the sample at hand (e.g., score reliability). Values greater than 1.0 (termed *underfit*) indicate so-called noise in the data, which degrades measurement. Such data noise is viewed as the more immediate threat to the measurement system. A widely used rule of thumb for binary items is that Outfit MnSq values in the range from 0.7 to 1.3 are acceptable (e.g., Wright & Linacre, 1994). However, more accurate estimates of reasonable lower and upper limits for acceptable Outfit MnSq values for a given measurement situation can be obtained via bootstrap procedures (e.g., Su, Sheu, & Wang, 2007; Wolfe, 2008).
- *Infit mean-square*: This statistic, denoted Infit MnSq, is developed to diminish the off-target outlier effect of the Outfit MnSq in order to signal unexpected response patterns for in-target measures, hence the name "infit." The Infit MnSq weighs the squared standardized residuals, Z^2_{ni}, by their individual variances, W_{ni}. That is, $\Sigma^N_{n=1} W_{ni} Z^2_{ni} / \Sigma^N_{n=1} W_{ni}$ is the Infit MnSq statistic for item i. As the expected value of Infit MnSq is close to 1.0, the above notes on the meaning

of overfit, underfit, and acceptable range (0.7 to 1.3) for Outfit MnSq apply to Infit MnSq as well.

- *Standardized fit statistic*: A more general cutoff for determining outfit (or infit) disturbances in data–model fit is obtained through a transformation of the Outfit MnSq (or Infit MnSq) statistic into a *t* statistic for outfit (or infit) irregularities (Wright & Masters, 1982). This *t* statistic, called the *standardized mean square statistic*, follows an approximate standard normal distribution. For this reason, it is also called the *standardized Z-statistic* (*Zstd*). When obtained from transforming Outfit MnSq, the standardized fit statistic is called *standardized unweighted mean square* (Z_{UMS}), or *Outfit Zstd*. When obtained from transforming Infit MnSq, it is called *standardized weighted mean square* (Z_{WMS}), or *Infit Zstd*; (Wright & Masters, 1982). Problems in data-model fit are flagged by standardized values greater than +2.0 (underfit) or values smaller than –2.0 (redundancy, data overfit the model; e.g., see R. M. Smith, 1991).

Table 9.1 shows an output table from WINSTEPS for Rasch analysis of 10 binary items. This table was provided by Karabatsos (2001), who examined some drawbacks of Rasch misfit residual statistics, but the table's purpose here is purely illustrative. As can be seen, a misfit is flagged for five items. Specifically, the Infit Zstd and Outfit Zstd values for two items (7 and 9) exceed +2.0, thus indicating underfit for these items. On the other hand, Items 4, 8, and 10 fit the model better than expected (overfit, flagged by Infit Zstd and Outfit Zstd smaller than –2.0). There are no misfit problems for the remaining items (1, 2, 3, 5, and 6) as their Infit Zstd and Outfit Zstd values are within the acceptable range (from –2.0 to +2.0).

TABLE 9.1

A WINSTEPS Output Table for Item Statistics Under the Dichotomous Rasch Model Based on the Scores of 459 Examinees on 10 Binary Items

ITEM STATISTICS: ENTRY ORDER

ITEM	RAW SCORE	COUNT	MEASURE	ERROR	INFIT MNSQ	INFIT ZSTD	OUTFIT MNSQ	OUTFIT ZSTD
1	121	459	1.52	.12	1.09	1.5	1.29	1.9
2	350	459	-1.48	.13	1.01	.2	1.03	.2
3	366	459	-1.75	.13	.89	-1.6	.79	-1.3
4	123	459	1.49	.12	.74	-4.8	.55	-3.9
5	270	459	-.37	.11	1.08	1.6	1.13	1.4
6	290	459	-.63	.11	.91	-1.8	.85	-1.6
7	212	459	.33	.11	1.30	5.7	1.43	4.6
8	224	459	.19	.11	.83	-3.8	.74	-3.6
9	267	459	-.34	.11	1.25	4.7	1.51	5.1
10	156	459	1.03	.11	.79	-4.1	.68	-3.3
MEAN	238	459	.00	.12	.99	-.2	1.00	.0
S.D.	82	0	1.08	.01	.18	3.5	.31	3.1

Note. MEASURE is the item difficulty estimate, $\hat{\delta}$, and ERROR is its standard error: *SE*($\hat{\delta}$). From "The Rasch Model, Additive Conjoint Measurement, and New Models of Probabilistic Measurement Theory," by G. Karabatsos, 2001, *Journal of Applied Measurement, 2,* p. 418. Copyright 2001 by Richard M. Smith, Editor. Reprinted with permission.

9.1.7 Person–Item Distribution Map for Binary Scales

The person–item distribution map (PIDM) is a visual representation of the distributions of people's abilities and item difficulties (e.g., Wright & Stone, 1979). This map shows how well the range of item difficulties covers the range of people's abilities, thus providing feedback on the adequacy of measurement. For example, Figure 9.4 shows a PIDM reported by Clark (2004) in a Rasch-based study of the Academic Listening Test (ALT), which is used by the University of Hawaii at Manoa for placing incoming students into listening classes. A higher score on the ALT indicates higher level of listening ability. The PIDM in Figure 9.4 reveals an adequate overlap between levels of person ability and item

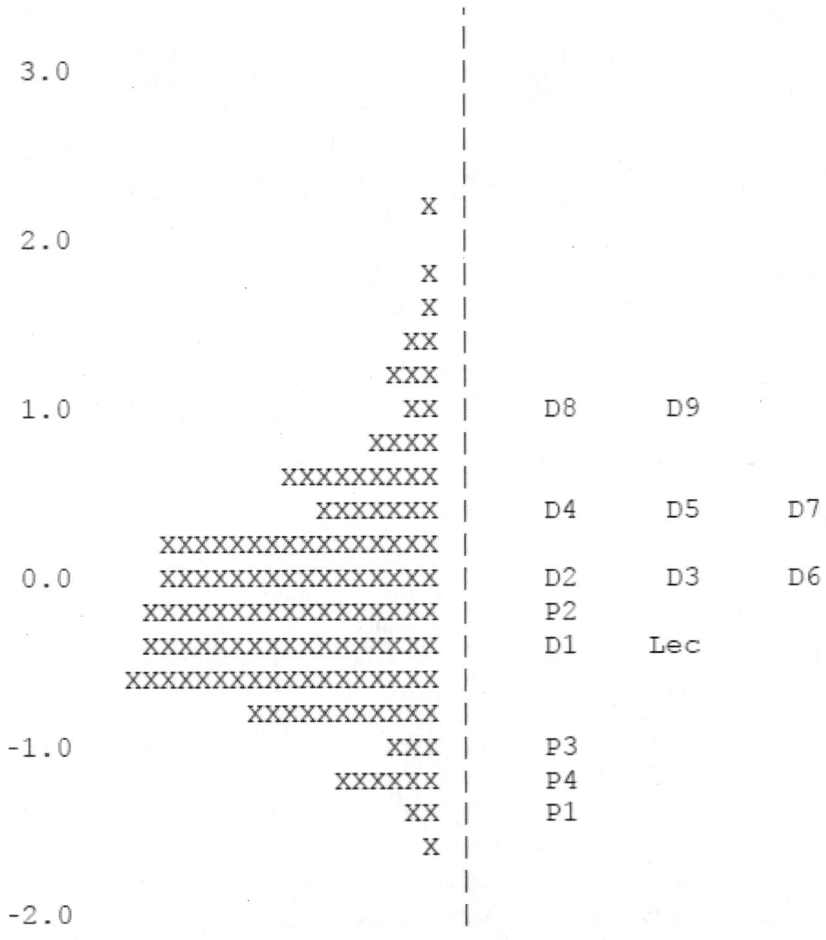

FIGURE 9.4

Person–Item Distribution Map for the Location of Examinees on the Rasch Logit Scale

Note. N = 685. Rasch Logit Scale is 14 items. The item coding (D1, . . ., Lec) relates to targeted tasks measured by test items; "X" on the map counts for 5 persons. From "By the Numbers: The Rational for a Rasch Analysis in Placement Testing," by M. Clark, 2004, *Second Language Studies, 22,* p. 88 (a collection of working papers from the University of Hawaii, Department of Second Language Studies). Copyright 2004 by the author, M. Clark. Reprinted with permission.

difficulty over the range from –2.0 to +2.0 on the logit scale. This finding indicates that the ALT is adequate to assess examinees from the study population within a reasonable range of academic listening ability.

9.2 RATING SCALE MODEL (RSM)

9.2.1 Basic RSM Concepts

Particularly relevant to assessment in counseling and other social sciences are rating scales—Likert (or Likert-type) scales whereby people are asked to respond to an item using a set of responses that are the same for all items, for example, ranging from 1 (*strongly disagree*) to 5 (*strongly agree*). The RSM is a special case of polytomous response models developed in the framework of IRT (e.g., Samejima, 1969) and Rasch modeling (e.g., Andrich, 1978a; Andersen, 1997; Masters, 1982, 1988; Rost, 1988). I discuss only the Rasch-based approach to RSM here (Andrich, 1978a). An important assumption of the RSM that makes it different from other polytomous models is that the response format is intended to function in the same way across all items (using the same number of response categories with the same set of labels for each item). If a test contains items that have different numbers of scale categories or if the categories have different labels, these items can be grouped into separate RSM scales.

The mathematical form of the RSM, as a special case in the family of Rasch polytomous models (e.g., Linacre, 2002), can be presented as

$$\ln(P_{nik}/P_{ni(k-1)}) = \theta_n - (\delta_i + \tau_k), \tag{9.6}$$

where

- ln(.) denotes the natural logarithm,
- P_{nik} is the probability that person n would respond in category k when answering item i,
- $P_{ni(k-1)}$ is the probability that person n would respond in category $k - 1$ of item i,
- θ_n is the trait score of person n (e.g., attitude score on the logit scale),
- δ_i is the difficulty (or scale value) of item i, and
- τ_k is a threshold indicating the impediment to being observed in category k relative to its preceding category $(k - 1)$; that is, τ_k is the kth step calibration $(k = 1, \ldots, m)$.

The mathematical form of the RSM in Equation 9.6 is preferred here for its relative simplicity, but it can be represented under different equivalent forms (e.g., see Andrich, 1978a; Andersen, 1997; Ostini & Nering, 2006, pp. 34–41; Wright & Masters, 1982, pp. 48–49). In RSM, the item difficulty, δ_i, is the location on the trait scale at which a respondent has an equal chance of choosing the two extreme categories (e.g., 1 = *strongly disagree* or 5 = *strongly agree*). On the other hand, $\delta_i + \tau_k$ is the location on the trait scale where the respondents have equal probability of responding in category k or its preceding category, $k - 1$. In the Rasch literature, $\delta_i + \tau_k$ is referred to as *Rasch–Andrich threshold* (or *structure measure*) for category k of item i.

It should be also noted that replacing the sum in parentheses on the right-hand side of Equation 9.6 $(\delta_i + \tau_k)$ with a parameter, δ_{ik}, results in a more general Rasch model referred to as *partial credit model* (PCM; Masters, 1982, 1988). The PCM allows the number of categories to vary across test items. For more details on the PCM and its relation to the RSM, the reader may refer to Masters (1982, 1988), Wright and Masters (1982, pp. 40–48), or Ostini and Nering (2006, pp. 25–33).

Figure 9.5 depicts the *category probability curves* (CPCs) for a three-category item in a questionnaire for attitude toward learning science (i.e., the trait being measured is attitude toward learning science). The rating scale categories are 1 (*dislike*), 2 (*uncertain*), and 3 (*like*). The vertical axis indicates the probability that a person with a trait score θ will respond in category k ($k = 1, 2, 3$). The item difficulty in this case is $\delta = 2$. Thus, a respondent located two logits above the origin of the trait scale has an equal chance of choosing each of the two extreme categories: 1 = *dislike* or 3 = *like*; note, however, that, this respondent: is most likely to choose category 2 (*uncertain*). The thresholds are $\tau_1 = -1$ and $\tau_2 = 1$. As noted earlier, the Rasch–Andrich threshold for category k ($\delta_i + \tau_k$) is the location on the trait scale where a person has an equal chance of responding in category k or its preceding category, $k - 1$, for item i. In Figure 9.5, $\delta + \tau_1 = 2 + (-1) = 1$ is the location on the logit scale for persons who have an equal chance of selecting the second category (*uncertain*) or its preceding category (*dislike*). At the same time, $\delta + \tau_2 = 2 + 1 = 3$ is the location on the logit scale for persons who have equal chances of selecting the third category (*like*) or its preceding category (*uncertain*). That is, the item difficulty is 2.0 and the Rasch–Andrich thresholds are 1.0 and 3.0 on the logit scale. Clearly, people with a trait score lower than 1 ($\theta < 1$) are most likely to respond *dislike*, those with a trait score between 1 and 3 ($1 < \theta < 3$) are most likely to respond *uncertain*, and people with a trait score greater than 3 ($\theta > 3$) are most likely to respond *like* to the item with CPCs depicted in Figure 9.5.

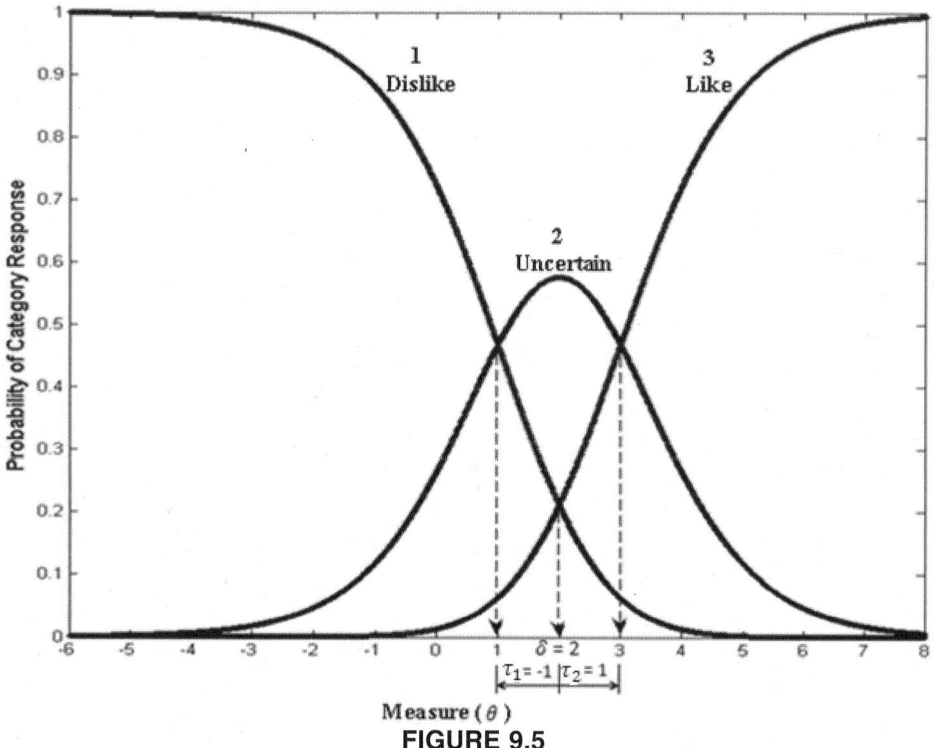

FIGURE 9.5

Category Probability Curves for a Polytomous Item on a Three-Point Scale Measuring Attitude Toward Learning Science

Note. Three-point scale: 1 = *dislike*, 2 = *uncertain*, 3 = *like*. The item difficulty is at two logits above the origin of the scale ($\delta = 2$), and the thresholds are $\tau_1 = -1$ and $\tau_2 = 1$.

Under the RSM, different items may have different difficulty, δ, but the set of thresholds, τ_1, τ_2, . . ., τ_m, is the same for all items (with m thresholds, there are $m + 1$ response categories for each item). This allows us to present the CPCs as centered around the origin (zero) of the logit scale by using the difference ($\theta - \delta$) on the horizontal axis, referred to as *measure relative to item difficulty*. For example, the CPCs in Figure 9.5 can be presented as shown in Figure 9.6.

9.2.2 Threshold (or Step) Disordering

An essential property of the RSM is that the probabilities of responding in higher categories of the rating scale increase with the increase of the respondents' scores on the trait being measured. This property holds true not only for the entire rating scale, but for individual categories as well (Andrich, 1996). It follows then that the category thresholds, τ_1, τ_2, . . ., τ_m, (in RSM items with $m + 1$ categories), should advance monotonically with the categories. This case is illustrated in Figure 9.7, which depicts the CPCs for an item on a five-category Likert scale. The small arrows point to the intersections of the CPCs for two adjacent categories (k, $k + 1$). There are four points of intersection, with the locations of these points on the

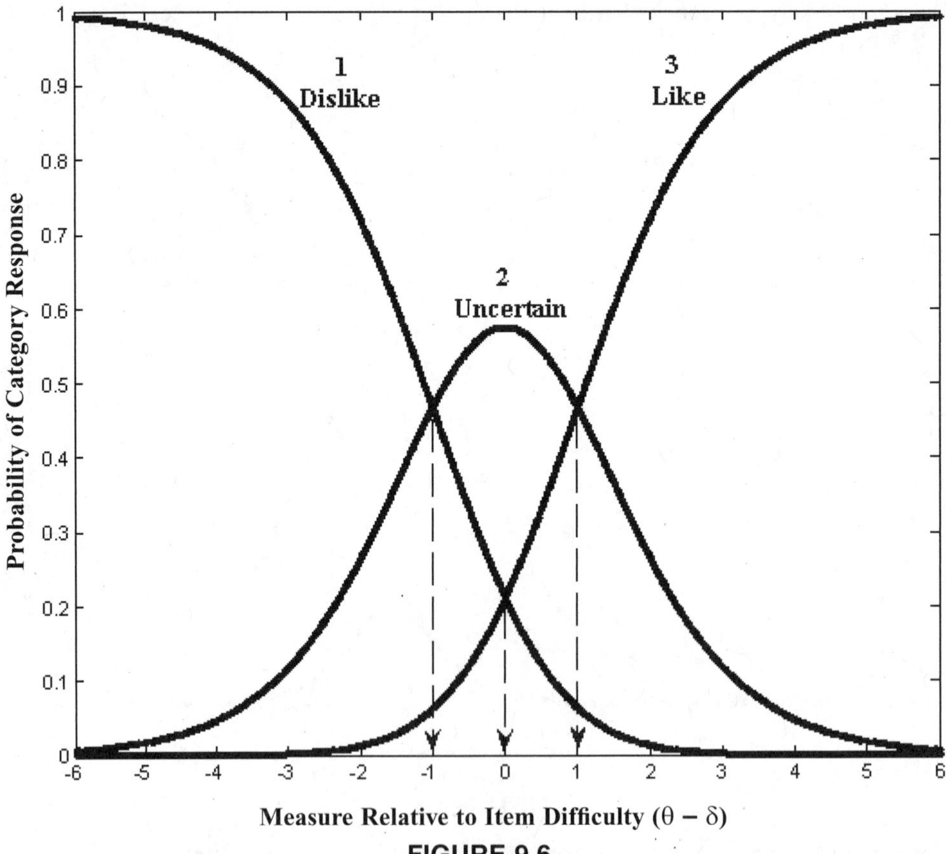

FIGURE 9.6

Category Probability Curves in Figure 9.5 Presented as Centered Around Origin (Zero) of the Logit Scale Using the Difference Measure Relative to Item Difficulty ($\theta - \delta$)

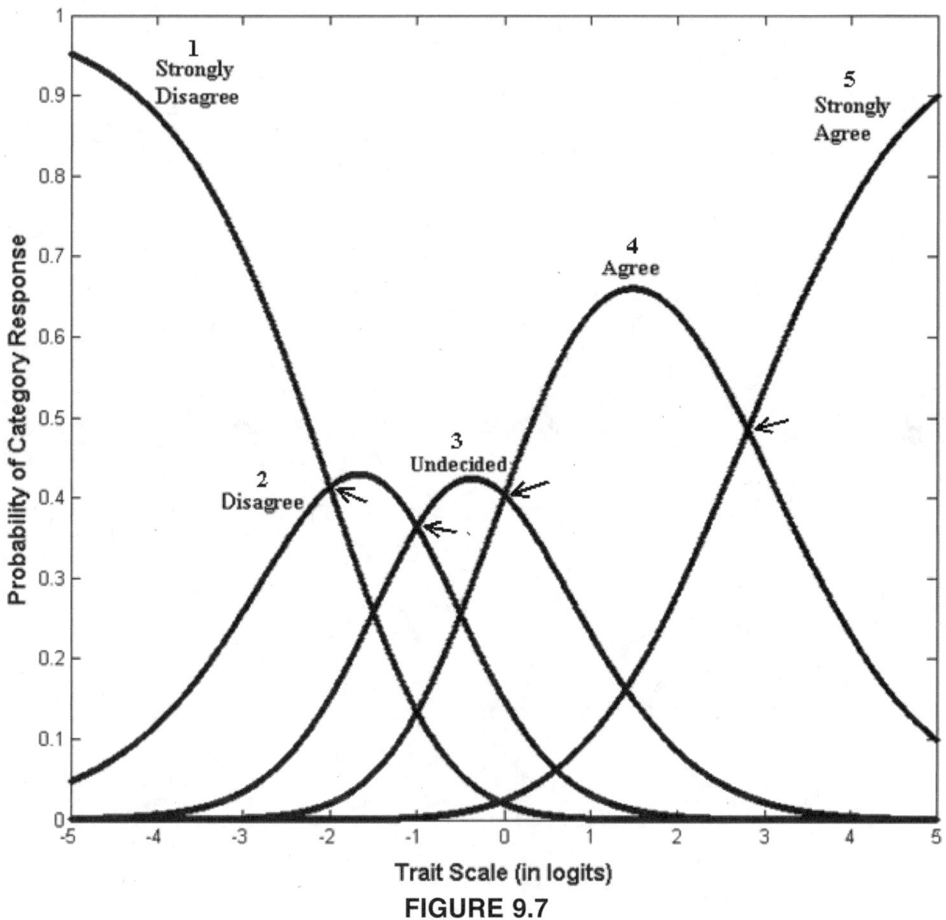

FIGURE 9.7

Category Probability Curves for a Five-Category Likert Item, Without Threshold Disordering

Note. The order of the thresholds here is τ_1, τ_2, τ_3, τ_4—the scale coordinates of intersection points of the category probability curves for adjacent categories that appear, from left to right, in the sequence (1, 2) → (2, 3) → (3, 4) → (4, 5).

trait scale representing the four thresholds, τ_1, τ_2, τ_3, and τ_4 for the five-category item. The thresholds advance monotonically across the trait scale with the advancement of the points of intersection for the CPCs of adjacent categories, from left to right: (1, 2) → (2, 3) → (3, 4) → (4, 5).

The lack of monotonic advancement of thresholds for the CPCs of adjacent categories is referred to as *threshold disordering*. The term *disordering in step calibrations* (or, briefly, *step disordering*) is also used in this regard (e.g., see Linacre, 1999a, 2002). Step disordering is illustrated in Figure 9.8, where the order of thresholds is τ_2, τ_1, τ_3, τ_4 (i.e., different from the theoretically expected "natural" order: τ_1, τ_2, τ_3, τ_4).

Step disordering may occur, for example, when a higher category is not selected by the respondents as often as expected or a lower category is selected too often by respondents with higher trait scores—typically, when the response formats include a middle category labeled *undecided* (or *neutral*), when intermediate categories are not labeled, or when too many category options have been provided. Linacre (2002) noted that "step disordering

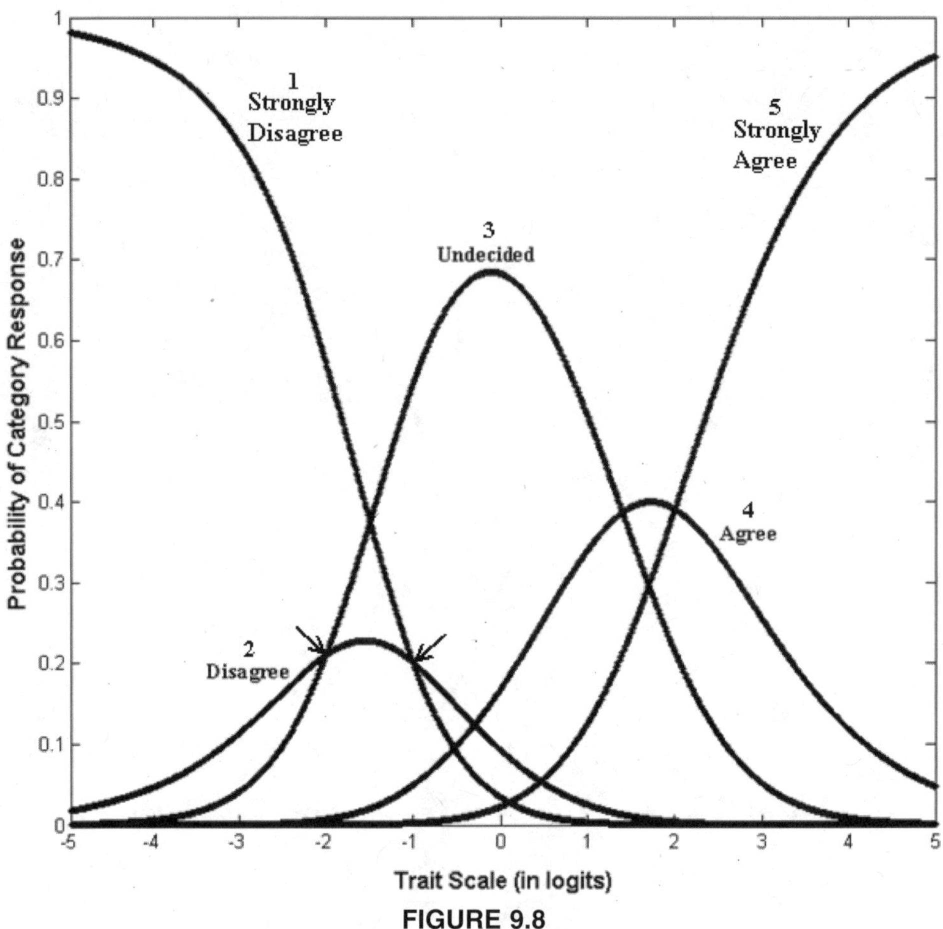

FIGURE 9.8

Category Probability Curves for a Five-Category Likert Item, With Threshold Disordering

Note. The order of the thresholds here is τ_2, τ_1, τ_3, τ_4—the scale coordinates of intersection points of the category probability curves for adjacent categories that appear, from left to right, in the sequence (2, 3) → (1, 2) → (3, 4) → (4, 5). The two short arrows point at the intersection points for the two disordered thresholds: (2, 3) → (1, 2).

degrades the interpretability of the resulting measures. It can indicate that a category represents too narrow a segment of the latent variable [the trait being measured] or corresponds to a concept that is poorly defined in the mind of the respondents" (p. 94).

Andrich, de Jong, and Sheridan (1997) pointed out that there are many possible causes of threshold disordering, "but descriptively violation of the order may result from multidimensional rather than unidimensional responses, from different discriminations at the thresholds, from the lack of capacity to use all of the assigned number of categories, or from a genuine empirical disordering of the categories" (p. 70). They argued that "if the thresholds are not ordered, or if other fit statistics reveal misfit between the data and the model, then some collapsing may reveal the effective number and ordering of categories *post-hoc* (Wright, 1994), which ideally would be checked with a follow-up study using the new format" (p. 70). E. V. Smith et al. (2003) specified that "in a traditional Likert scale with labels of *strongly agree*, *agree*, *undecided*, *disagree*, and *strongly disagree*, it would make sense to combine *strongly agree* and *agree* or *strongly disagree* and *disagree*, but not to join *agree* and *undecided* or *disagree* and *undecided*. In the later situation, one would be better suited in treating responses to *undecided* as missing" (p. 376).

9.2.3 Category Disordering

Under the RSM, respondents with higher levels on the trait scale are expected to reach higher scale categories. That is, a higher category number should relate to higher level of category functioning. Category disordering occurs when the categories are substantively disordered—that is, a higher category number corresponds to a lower level of category functioning. Category disordering is different from step disordering because step disordering relates to irregularity in the frequencies of selected categories, *not* to the substantive order of achievement of the categories. That is, step disordering indicates that a category is less likely to be selected, *not* that it is easier to perform by the respondents (e.g., Linacre, 2002). Some researchers argue that the threshold disordering is also a substantive issue as it indicates that there is something wrong with the scoring model. This position is in line with Andrich's (2005) view that threshold disordering signals that the empirical ordering of the categories is *not* consistent with their intended ordering.

Whether substantive category disordering is due to a misspecification of the rating scale or to idiosyncrasies found only in the sample requires further investigation by the researcher (Linacre, 1999a, 2002). The concept of *average measure* plays a key role in detecting category disordering. Specifically, the average measure of a given category is the mean of the differences ($\theta_n - \delta_i$) across all observations in that category. As described earlier, θ_n is the measure of person *n* (the location of the person on the logit scale for the trait being measured), and δ_i is the difficulty of the item. The difference between the person's measure and item difficulty ($\theta_n - \delta_i$) is referred to as *measure relative to item difficulty*. In consistency with the substantive ordering of categories under the RSM, higher category numbers imply higher average measures across successive categories. Failure of the average measure values to advance across successive scale categories would signal substantive disordering in the categories (e.g., Linacre, 1999a, 2002).

Along with average measure values, the Outfit MnSq is also used in detecting category disordering (e.g., Linacre, 2002). As described in Section 9.1.6, Outfit MnSq values less than 1.0 (overfit) indicate that the model predicts the data too well, thus causing inflation of summary statistics for the sample at hand. On the other hand, Outfit MnSq values greater than 1.0 (underfit) indicate noise in the data, which degrades measurement.

Other mean-square statistics are also available in the framework of Rasch modeling, but the Outfit MnSq is seen as more appropriate for assessing category disordering. For example, the Infit MnSq, which is regularly reported along with the Outfit MnSq in the assessment of aberrant responses, signals aberrant response patterns (e.g., R. M. Smith, 1996b, 2000; Wright & Masters, 1982). Infit and outfit mean-square statistics are reported in the output of computer programs for Rasch analysis such as WINSTEPS (Linacre & Wright, 2000), FACETS (Linacre, 1989), BIGSTEPS (Linacre & Wright, 1998), ConQuest (M. L. Wu et al., 1998), and RUMM (Andrich et al., 2003). Computer programs for bootstrap procedures that provide more accurate estimates of mean-square statistics, with their upper and lower limits, are also available (e.g., Su et al., 2007; Wolfe, 2008).

Example 9.1. The comments on threshold and category disordering in this example are based on results from a study by B. S. K. Kim and Hong (2004) on a psychometric revision of the Asian Values Scale (AVS) using the Rasch model for rating scales. For an initial seven-category scale of the 36-item AVS, B. S. K. Kim and Hong (2004) found that the average measure values increased with the category labels, thus suggesting the lack of category disordering (see average measures in Table 9.2, second column from the left). That is, the RSM premise that a higher category number relates to higher level of category functioning is in place. At the same time, however, there was a step disordering indicated by a disorder in the step calibrations (thresholds). The step calibrations in Table 9.2 (third column from the left) indicate threshold disordering at Category 4. Thus, the probabilities of responding in higher categories of the rating scale do *not* consistently increase with the increase of the respondents' measures on the trait under consideration (here, Asian cultural values).

Because of this threshold disordering, B. S. K. Kim and Hong (2004) conducted a follow-up Rasch analysis to identify the optimal categorization. First they changed the original seven-category scoring, denoted 1234567, by using the rescoring method 1234456. That is, they collapsed the original Categories 4 and 5 into one category (Category 4 in the new sequence of categories) and rescored the original Categories 6 and 7 as Categories 5 and 6, respectively. They also tried other rescoring methods (e.g., 1233456 and 1233345), but they all produced threshold disordering. Then B. S. K. Kim and Hong (2004) concluded that the neutral category might be poorly defined in the minds of the participants and decided to omit this category by treating it as missing data. The resulting rating scale 123 × 456 is a 6-category scale, where "×" indicates that the neutral category is treated as a missing-data category. This scoring scheme eliminated the threshold disordering, but it was still not satisfactory because the segment on the continuum of the trait (Asian cultural values) for each category was too narrow. Finally, by using the scoring method 122 × 334 (i.e., collapsing Categories 2 and 3 as well as Categories 4 and 5), the resulting four-category scale (1 = *strongly disagree*, 2 = *disagree*, 3 = *agree*, and 4 = *strongly agree*) was viewed as acceptable by the authors (B. S. K. Kim & Hong, 2004). The results for this scale, shown in Table 9.2 (right two columns), indicate that (a) there is *no* category disordering, (b) there is *no* step calibrations (threshold) disordering, and (c) the step calibrations advance with acceptable increments of 1.63 and 2.20 (from –1.82 to –0.19, and from –0.19 to 2.01, respectively)—that is, increments larger than 1.4 and smaller than 5.0, as recommended in RSM guidelines (e.g., Linacre, 2002). B. S. K. Kim and Hong (2004) also noted that in further support of this scoring method, the category probability curves exhibited the desired appearance of a range of hills (see Figure 9.9).

TABLE 9.2

Analysis of the Asian Values Scale (AVS) Data: Initial and Final Categories for the AVS Rating Scale (B. S. K. Kim & Hong, 2004)

	Initial 7 Categories of AVS Items		Final 4 Categories of AVS Items	
Category Label	Average Measure	Step Calibration	Average Measure	Step Calibration
1	–0.39	—	–0.90	—
2	–0.25	–0.68	–0.40	–1.82
3	–0.13	–0.41	0.51	–0.19
4	0.14	0.07*	1.14	2.01
5	0.19	–0.20*		
6	0.32	0.34		
7	0.52	0.87		

Note. Asterisks indicate disordered steps (thresholds).

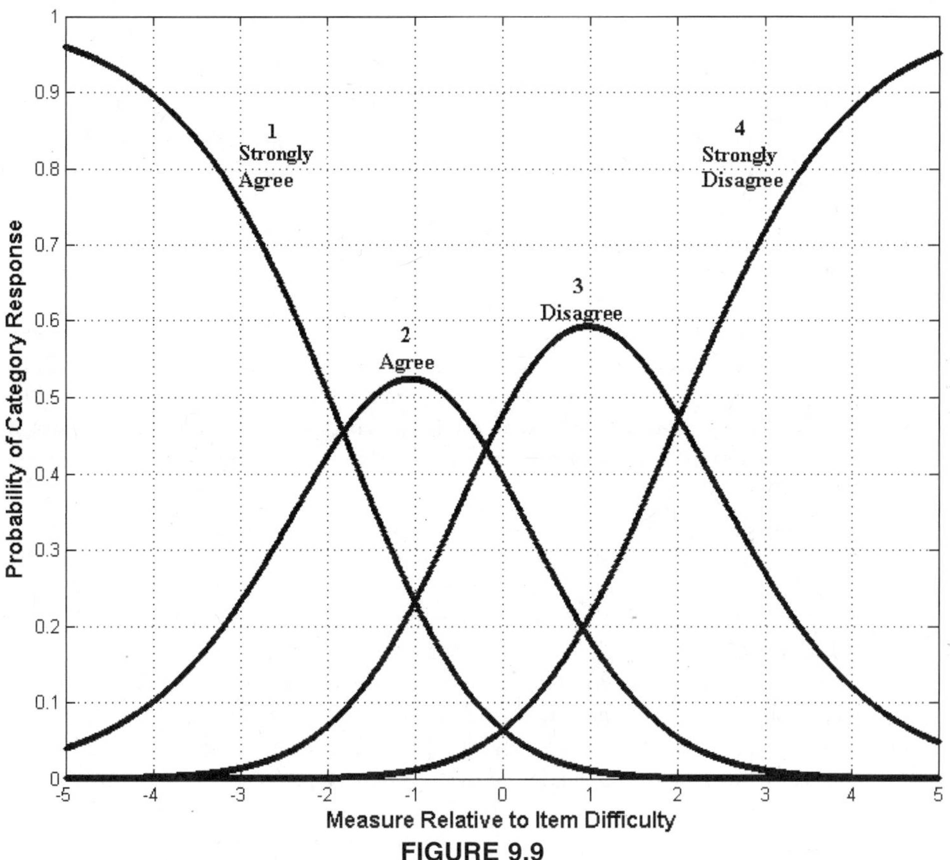

FIGURE 9.9

Category Probability Curves for a Four-Category Likert Item, Without Threshold Disordering

Note. These were obtained from its original 7-category format using the scoring method 122 × 334, that is, omitting first the neutral category and then collapsing the resulting new Categories 2 and 3, as well as Categories 4 and 5. From "A Psychometric Revision of the Asian Values Scale Using the Rasch Model," by B. S. K. Kim and S. Hong, 2004, *Measurement and Evaluation in Counseling and Development, 37,* p. 21. Copyright 2004 by the American Counseling Association.

9.2.4 Optimizing Rating Scale Category Effectiveness

The guidelines for optimizing rating scale category effectiveness in this section are based on recommendations provided in previous research on rating scales (e.g., Andrich, 1978a, 1988, 1996; Linacre, 2002; E. V. Smith et al., 2003; Wright & Masters, 1982). In a summary of such recommendations, Linacre (2002) outlined the following guidelines for optimizing the category effectiveness of rating scales:

1. *At least 10 observations in each category*. This guideline takes into account that when the category frequency is low, the thresholds are poorly estimated and potentially unstable.
2. *Regular distribution of observations.* Regular distribution of observations refers both to a uniform distribution of responses and to either unimodal distributions that peak in central or extreme categories or bimodal distributions that peak in ex-

treme categories. There are situations, however, when highly skewed distributions are produced by phenomena that could be of main interest to the assessment (e.g., severe depression or giftedness).

3. *Average measures advance monotonically with categories.* This guideline implies that the average measures are expected to advance monotonically with category (recall that the average measure of a category is the mean of the measures relative to item difficulty, $\theta_n - \delta_i$, across all observations in the category). As indicated in Section 9.2.3, this condition is necessary to guard against category disordering.
4. *Outfit MnSqs less than 2.0.* As noted in section 9.2.3, the expected value of the Outfit MnSq is close to 1.0. However, Linacre (2002) indicated that category disordering in rating scales is signaled when the average of the Outfit MnSqs associated with the responses in a given category exceeds 2.0. Specifically, the Outfit MnSq assesses the degree to which the category is being used in an idiosyncratic fashion (e.g., because of ambiguous terminology or excessive category options), so Outfit MnSq ≤ 2.0 indicates *no* problem in this regard.
5. *Thresholds advance monotonically with categories.* As noted in section 9.2.2, an essential property of the RSM is that the probabilities of responding in higher categories of the rating scale increase with the increase of the respondents' scores on the trait being measured (Andrich, 1996). This condition implies that the category thresholds should advance monotonically with the categories.
6. *Coherence between measures and category observations.* The RSM implies an expected relationship between measures (locations of persons on the logit scale) and category ratings. Coherence in both directions for this relationship is assessed by (a) M→C (Measure implies Category) index, which shows what percentage of the measures that were expected to produce observations in this category actually did; and (b) C→M (Category implies Measure) index, which shows what percentage of the observations in this category were produced by measures corresponding to the category. Linacre (2002) suggested that 40% coherence (M→C or C→M) is empirically useful. The higher the level of coherence, the stronger the evidence of a valid functioning of the Rasch model for the rating scale under consideration. The reader may refer to Linacre (2002) for technical details on the computation of M→C and C→M using the computer programs WINSTEPS and FACETS.
7. *Category width between 1.4 and 5.0 logits.* Assuming ordered thresholds $\tau_1, \tau_2, \ldots, \tau_m$ for a rating scale with $m + 1$ categories, the width of an intermediate category k ($k = 2, 3, \ldots, m$) is defined as the distance between the end thresholds for that category (τ_{k-1}, τ_k) on the logit scale (the two extreme categories, 1 and $m + 1$, are infinitely wide). The interval (τ_{k-1}, τ_k) defines the modal interval of category k—that is, the interval on the logit scale where category k is more probable to be observed than any other category. Based on previous research (Huynh, 1994), Linacre showed that for a three-category scale, the width of the intermediate category (τ_1, τ_2) must be at least 1.4 logits, whereas for a five-category scale, the category widths must be least 1.0 logits (Linacre, 2002). On the other hand, when a category is too wide, the measurement loses its precision in a middle zone of that category. Addressing this problem, Linacre (2002) noted that "when the distance between step calibrations [adjacent thresholds] is more than 5 logits, the information provided at the item's center is less than half that provided by a simple dichotomy" (p. 103).

In general, the above seven guidelines provide useful information about the functioning of rating scales. However, Linacre (2002) also warned that not all guidelines are relevant to just any analysis of rating scales. A review of applied studies involving Rasch-based rating scale analysis suggests that the following guidelines are essential to most situations:

- at least 10 observations in each category,
- regular distribution of observations,
- average measures advance with categories,
- average Outfit MnSqs less than 2.0, and
- thresholds (step calibrations) advance monotonically with categories.

It is important to reiterate, however, that researchers should rely on both statistical criteria and substantive considerations in using guidelines for optimizing the category effectiveness of rating scales. Also, as E. V. Smith et al. (2003) noted, "given that the process of optimizing a rating scale may be sample dependent and somewhat subjective, it is always required to test the revised scale with a new sample from the same population (or at least conduct a cross-validation study with one large sample)" (p. 376).

Example 9.2. This example illustrates results and interpretations related to the guidelines for optimizing the effectiveness of rating scale categories. The functioning of rating scale categories is examined based on results in WINSTEPS output tables reported by Cunningham et al. (2006) in a study on psychometric characteristics of the Multidimensional Students' Life Satisfaction Scale (MSLSS; Huebner, 1994). The MSLSS is a 40-item self-report instrument that assesses satisfaction across five specific life domains: Family, Friends, School, Living Environment, and Self. All questions have possible responses on a six-point Likert-type scale format (1 = *strongly disagree*, 2 = *moderately disagree*, 3 = *mildly disagree*, 4 = *mildly agree*, 5 = *moderately agree*, and 6 = *strongly agree*). For the purpose of this example, only the WINSTEPS output table for results related to the domain of Friends is used (see Table 9.3).

The results in Table 9.3 provide information about quality aspects of the rating scale categories of the MSLSS. This information is interpreted here in light of the aforementioned seven guidelines for optimizing rating scale category effectiveness.

1. The category frequencies range from 222 to 3,420, thus satisfying the recommendation for "at least 10 observations in each category."
2. The count distribution across the six scale categories is unimodal and does not contain irregularities (e.g., a "rollercoaster" pattern), thus indicating that the guideline for a "regular distribution of observations" is met.
3. The guideline for "average measures advance monotonically with categories" is also met, as indicated by the monotonic increase of both observed and expected measures from the lowest to the highest category—see the columns labeled "OBSVD AVRGE" and "SAMPLE EXPECT" in Table 9.3 (upper panel).
4. The infit and outfit mean-squares are close to their expected values of 1.0, with the exception of the Outfit MnSq of 2.03 for the lowest (*strongly disagree*) category—see the columns "INFIT MNSQ" and "OUTFIT MNSQ" in Table 9.3 (upper panel). However, taking into account that the Outfit MnSq statistic is sensitive to extreme unexpected responses, we can conclude that the guideline "Outfit MnSq ≤ 2.0" is also met.

TABLE 9.3

Scale Output Table in WINSTEPS for Rasch-Based Rating Scale Model Analysis of the Multidimensional Students' Life Satisfaction Scale (MSLSS; Huebner, 1994)

SUMMARY OF CATEGORY STRUCTURE. Model="R"

CATEGORY LABEL	SCORE	OBSERVED COUNT	%	OBSVD AVRGE	SAMPLE EXPECT	INFIT MNSQ	OUTFIT MNSQ	STRUCTURE CALIBRATN	CATEGORY MEASURE	
1	1	267	4	-.02	-.24	1.35	2.03	NONE	(-1.71)	1 Stronglydisagree
2	2	222	3	.15	.06	1.12	1.37	.10	-.81	2 ModeratelyDisagree
3	3	428	6	.28	.31	.93	.93	-.47	-.32	3 MildlyDisagree
4	4	995	13	.46	.58	.79	.74	-.40	.10	4 MildyAgree
5	5	2208	29	.92	.96	.86	.83	-.04	.75	5 ModeratelyAgree
6	6	3420	45	1.62	1.58	1.03	1.03	.81	(2.16)	6 StronglyAgree
MISSING		2	0	1.20						

OBSERVED AVERAGE is mean of measures in category. It is not a parameter estimate.

CATEGORY LABEL	STRUCTURE MEASURE	S.E.	SCORE-TO-MEASURE AT CAT.	----ZONE----		50% CUM. PROBABLTY	COHERENCE M->C	C->M	ESTIM DISCR	
1	NONE		(-1.71)	-INF	-1.25		80%	6%		1 Stronglydisagree
2	.10	.07	-.81	-1.25	-.54	-.80	20%	8%	-.17	2 ModeratelyDisagree
3	-.47	.05	-.32	-.54	-.12	-.46	19%	16%	.55	3 MildlyDisagree
4	-.40	.04	.10	-.12	.37	-.18	32%	39%	.84	4 MildyAgree
5	-.04	.03	.75	.37	1.45	.23	39%	66%	1.07	5 ModeratelyAgree
6	.81	.03	(2.16)	1.45	+INF	1.14	80%	50%	1.17	6 StronglyAgree

M->C = Does Measure imply Category?
C->M = Does Category imply Measure?

Note. From *Employing the Many-Facet Model to Investigate the Domains of MSLSS*, by J. D. Cunningham, K. D. Bradley, and R. Gilman, 2006 (April), Paper presented at the meeting of the American Educational Research Assoiciation, San Francisco, CA. Reprinted with permission of the authors.

5. The thresholds, reported in the column labeled "STRUCTURE CALIBRATN" (Table 9.3, upper panel) are as follows: 0.10, –0.47, –0.40, –0.04, and 0.81. Clearly, these thresholds do *not* advance monotonically with categories, thus indicating (undesirable) threshold disordering. Indeed, with $\tau_1 = 0.10$, $\tau_2 = -0.47$, $\tau_3 = -0.40$, $\tau_4 = -0.04$, and $\tau_5 = 0.81$, the order of the thresholds is: $\tau_2, \tau_3, \tau_4, \tau_1, \tau_5$. Graphically, this is reflected in irregularities of the category probability curves (see Figure 9.10). For example, the threshold disordering results in the fact that Categories 2 and 3 do not peak. Optimally, each rating scale category should peak; that is, each rating scale category should be most probable within its modal interval on the logit scale (e.g., see Figures 9.8 and 9.9).
6. The indices M $\rightarrow$ C and C $\rightarrow$ M, used to check for the guideline of "coherence between measures and category observations," are reported in the columns labeled "COHERENCE M $\rightarrow$ C" and "COHERENCE C $\rightarrow$ M" (Table 9.3, lower panel). Clearly, this guideline is not met for the most part. For example, the value of M $\rightarrow$ C for the second category (*moderately disagree*) indicates that only 20% of the measures (persons' trait scores) expected to produce the observations in this category actually did. For the same category, the C $\rightarrow$ M value indicates that only 8% of the observations in this category were produced by measures corresponding to the category (as noted earlier, at least 40% coherence is considered useful; Linacre, 2002). The values of M $\rightarrow$ C and C$\rightarrow$ M for the other categories are interpreted in a similar fashion.

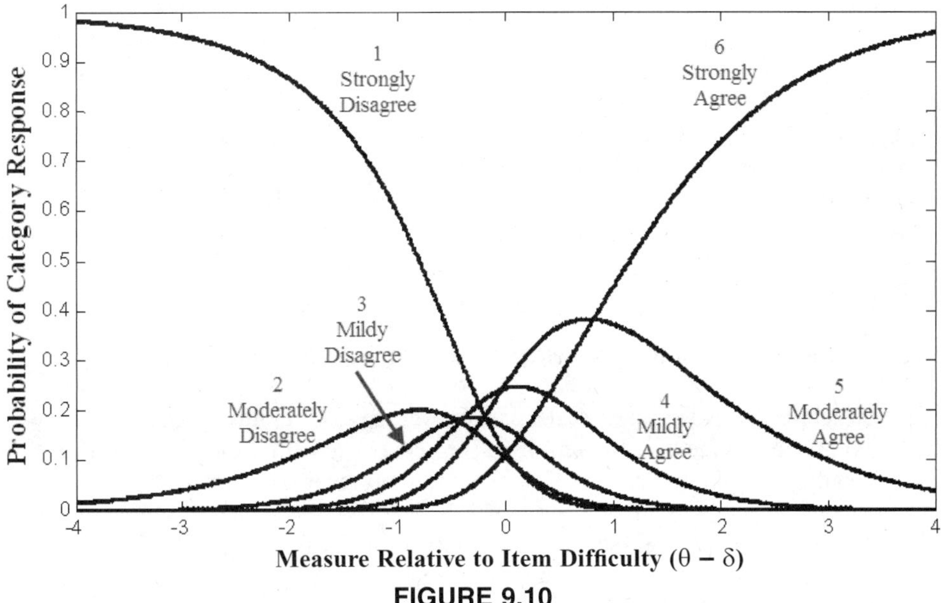

FIGURE 9.10

Category Probability Curves for a Six-Category Likert-Type Item, With Threshold Disordering

Note. The order of the thresholds here is τ_2, τ_3, τ_4, τ_1, τ_5. τ_1 = 0.10, τ_2 = –0.47, τ_3 = –0.40, τ_4 = –0.04, and τ_5 = 0.81.

7. Given the thresholds in this example (.10, –0.47, –0.40, –0.04, and 0.81), the category widths that they imply do not meet the guideline for "category width between 1.4 and 5.0 logits." In fact, excluding the two extreme categories, the width of any other category is smaller than 1.0. The finding that the categories are "too narrow" is supported also by the examination of the category "zones" in the "SCORE-TO-MEASURE" column (Table 9.3, lower panel). For details on category zones, the reader may refer to Linacre (2002).
8. The column representing estimated discrimination (labeled "ESTIM DISCR"; Table 9.3, lower panel) indicates how well the rating scale category discriminates between respondents of high and low endorsability more than expected by the model based on the difficulty estimate. A value greater than 1.0 in this column indicates that the rating scale category discriminates more than expected, whereas a value less than 1.0 indicates the opposite. As one can see, the values of estimated discrimination are greater than 1.0 for Categories 5 and 6, and smaller than 1.0 for Categories 2, 3, and 4 (there is no value assigned to Category 1).

The overall implication of the results provided in Table 9.3 and Figure 9.10 is that the rating scale categories in this example are not functioning as expected, and, therefore, revising or collapsing scale categories is warranted. As noted earlier, not all seven guidelines are relevant to just any analysis of rating scales (essential for most situations are Guidelines 1, 2, 3, 4, and 5). Researchers can use such guidelines to optimize the quality (fit and targeted functioning) of rating scale categories for valid interpretations of results.

It should be noted also that examining the effectiveness of rating scale categories is just one aspect of evaluating the adequacy of polytomous measures. In general, evaluating the adequacy of (binary or polytomous) measures produced in a particular application of Rasch-based assessments includes procedures such as testing for dimensionality, item fit, person fit, mapping of item difficulties to people's trait levels, item bias, and so forth. Testing for differential item functioning (DIF) was addressed with testing for measurement invariance in Chapter 6, Section 6.8. Testing for DIF under Rasch (or other IRT) models is beyond the scope of this book, but the reader may refer to abundant literature for theoretical and practical presentations on this topic (e.g., Baker, Caison, & Meade, 2007; H.-H. Chang, Mazzeo, & Roussos, 1996; Embretson & Reise, 2000; Hambleton & Swaminathan, 1985; Holland & Wainer, 1993; R. M. Smith, 1994; Welch & Hoover, 1993; Zwick, Donoghue, & Grima, 1993).

9.2.5 Person–Item Distribution Map for Rating Scales

The logic behind PIDM for binary scales carries over the case of rating scales. In both cases, the PIDM juxtaposes the distributions of person scores and item difficulties along the trait scale (usually in logits). In the case of rating scales, however, category thresholds are also mapped along the scale to provide additional feedback on the adequacy of measurement. Keep in mind that, as noted in Section 9.2.1, item difficulty in rating scales is the location on the trait scale at which a respondent has an equal chance of choosing the two extreme categories (e.g., 1 = *strongly disagree* or 5 = *strongly agree*).

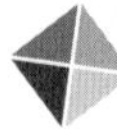

Example 9.3. This example illustrates a PIDM for a rating scale using Figure 9.11, which was presented by Ludlow et al. (2008) in a study on attitudes about teaching for social justice. Specifically, this PIDM is based on a Rasch analysis of 268 graduating teacher candidates' responses on 12 Likert items (1 = *strongly disagree,* 2 = *disagree,* 3 = *uncertain,* 4 = *agree,* and 5 = *strongly agree*) of the Learning to Teach for Social Justice–Beliefs Scale (Ludlow et al., 2008). Five of the 12 social justice (SJ) items were positively worded (SJI, SJ2, SJ4, SJ7, and SJ8), and the remaining seven items were negatively worded. As Ludlow et al. (2008) noted, the negatively worded items were intended to address concepts and experiences that only an experienced teacher candidate would have encountered.

As shown in Figure 9.11, the PIDM juxtaposes the distributions of teacher candidates' attitude scores, item difficulty (mean item estimate), and the distributions of the first and fourth thresholds for the Likert scale categories (recall that with five categories, there are four thresholds: τ_1, τ_2, τ_3, and τ_4). In line with the notations in Section 9.2.1, if δ_i denotes the difficulty of item *i*, then $\delta_i + \tau_1$ is the location on the logit scale at which a person has an equal chance of selecting the first or second categories (in this case, *strongly disagree* or *disagree*). The $\delta_i + \tau_1$ values are provided in the PIDM column labeled "1st threshold for Items." Furthermore, the PIDM column labeled "4th threshold for Items" provides the values for $\delta_i + \tau_4$—that is, the location on the logit scale at which a person has an equal chance of selecting the fourth or fifth categories (in this case, *agree* or *strongly disagree*). As can be seen, there is a substantial overlap between the range of candidates' attitude levels and item difficulties, which provides an important piece of evidence about the adequacy of measurement. For illustration, item SJ12R is the most difficult to endorse, whereas item SJ4 is the easiest to endorse by the teacher candidates. For detailed analysis and interpretations of results from Rasch modeling of the Learning to Teach for Social Justice–Beliefs Scale, the reader is encouraged to refer to Ludlow et al. (2008). In general, the PIDM (e.g., Figure 9.11) provides helpful, yet limited, visual information regarding the targeting of the

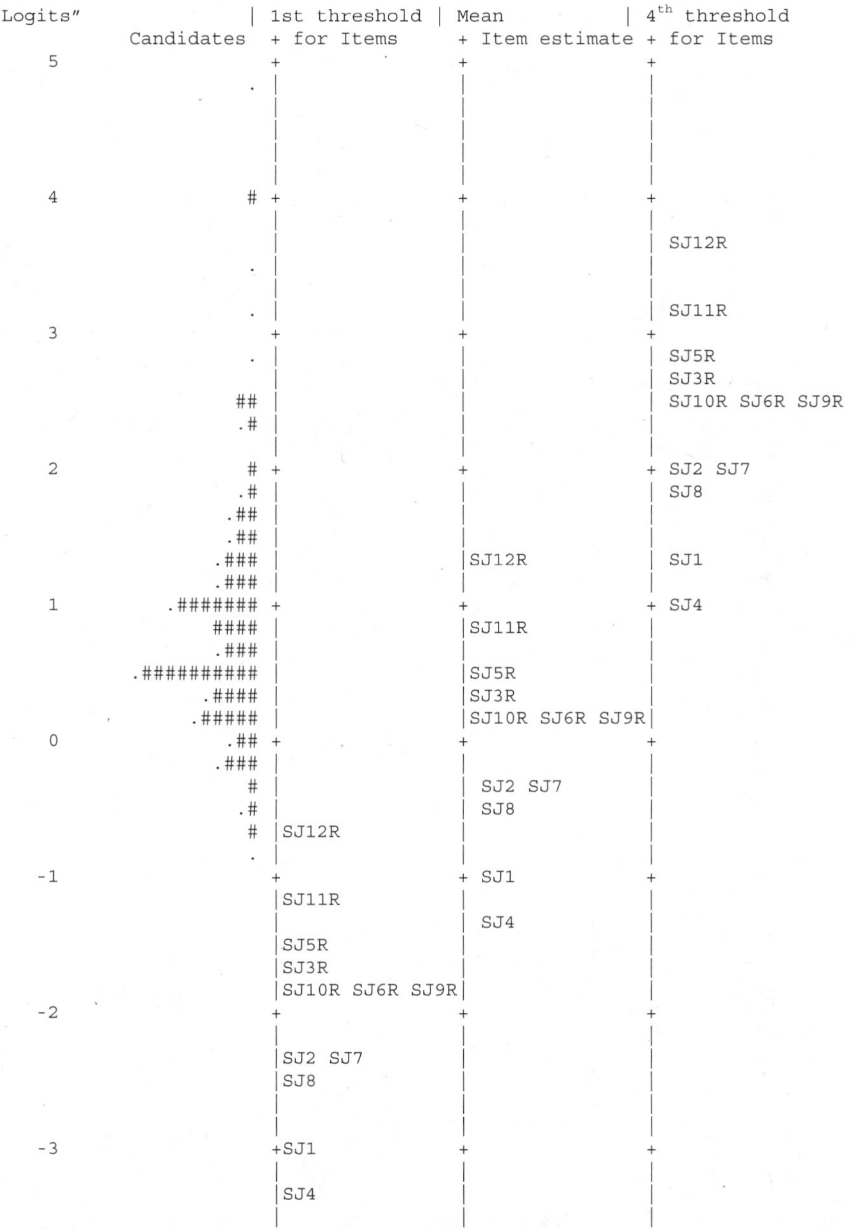

FIGURE 9.11

Person–Item Distribution Map for 268 Graduating Teacher Candidates and 12 Items Scored on a Five-Point Likert Scale (Learning to Teach for Social Justice–Beliefs)

Note. From "Learning to Teach for Social Justice–Beliefs Scale: An Application of Rasch Measurement Principles," by L. H. Ludlow, S. E. Enterline, and M. Cochran-Smith, 2008, *Measurement and Evaluation in Counseling and Development, 40,* p. 205. Copyright 2008 by the American Counseling Association.

thresholds to the person distribution (a joint examination of PIDM with other sources of information, such as those in Table 9.3 and expected score maps, will enhance the evaluation of targeting thresholds to person distribution in RSM).

9.2.6 Testing for Multidimensionality

The Rasch model discussed here assumes that the measures are unidimensional. This means that there is one dominating dimension (construct, trait) that underlies the person's responses on the test items. Of course, besides the targeted dominating dimension, there are always other cognitive, personality, and test-taking elements that also influence the assessment measures. The question is whether such elements form some secondary dimension(s) or just represent random "noise," which does not cause bias in item and person estimates.

Earlier in this book, testing for dimensionality was addressed in the framework of factor analysis—EFA and/or CFA, depending on the validation design being adopted (see Chapters 5 and 6). In Rasch modeling, infit and outfit statistics are traditionally used in making judgments about whether the assumption of unidimensionality holds. Previous studies suggest also that infit and outfit statistics and results from an appropriate factor analysis should be jointly examined in testing for multidimensionality. For example, R. M. Smith (1996a) showed that fit statistics in the Rasch rating scale model are insensitive to multidimensionality when approximately equal numbers of items load on each dimension. He recommended the combined use of principal components analysis (PCA) with Rasch fit statistics to validate scales. Specifically, the conventional PCA is conducted on standardized residuals (the *standardized residual* for a person's score is the standardized difference between the observed score and the Rasch estimate for that person—see Section 9.1.6). This approach, referred to as *principal component analysis on residuals* (PCAR), is gaining popularity in Rasch analysis of scales in counseling, education, psychology, and other fields (e.g., Chou & Wang, 2010; Hong & Wong, 2005; E. V. Smith, 2002; P.-C. Wu & Chang, 2008).

It is important to emphasize that the PCAR is not the usual factor analysis. As discussed in Chapter 5, the usual factor analysis is based on the original observed scores and rotated factor solutions. In contrast, the PCAR is conducted on residuals—that is, after the targeted Rasch dimension has been removed—and the search for secondary dimensions is based on the initial (unrotated) solutions. The reason for this procedure is because the goal with the PCAR is to identify the contrast in the residuals that explains the most variance. This goal is achieved by examining the unrotated solutions of the PCA on the standardized residuals. Also, whereas interpretations of emerging dimensions (factors) in the usual factor analysis are based only on positive loadings, interpretations in PCAR are based on the contrast between positive and negative loadings. For this purpose, a contrast plot is developed with item measures (item difficulty estimates) on the horizontal axis and the PCAR eigenvalues on the vertical axis. The contrast plot is examined to identify a cluster of items at the top or bottom of the plot that may form some secondary dimension, that is, a substantive dimension different from the Rasch-dimension trait.

The PCAR contrast plot in Figure 9.12 was reported by E. V. Smith (2002) in a study that included testing for dimensionality of the Adult Behavior Checklist—Revised (ABCR; E. V. Smith & Johnson, 2000). The ABCR is a 24-item self-report instrument designed to screen for attention deficit hyperactivity disorder (ADHD). Clearly, the seventeen ABCR items at the bottom of the plot (negative loadings: ATTN1, . . ., ATTN17) and the seven items at the top (positive loadings: HYP18, . . ., HYP24) form two distinct dimensions. This finding is not a surprise, given that the ABCR was designed to capture both the attentive aspect of ADHD, measured by seventeen items (ATTN1, . . ., ATTN17), and

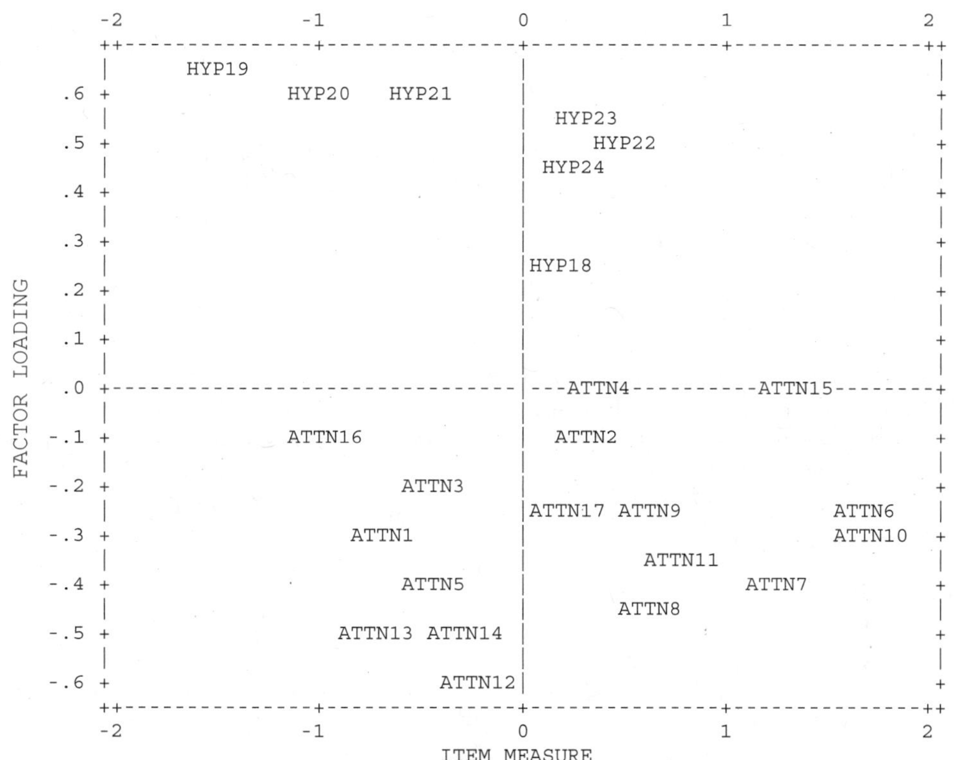

FIGURE 9.12

Principal Component Analysis on Residuals Contrast Plot for Dimensionality of the Adult Behavior Checklist—Revised (ABC–R; E. V. Smith & Johnson, 2000)

Note. From "Detecting and Evaluating Multidimensionality Using Fit Statistics and Principal Component Analysis of Residuals," by E. V. Smith, Jr., 2002, *Journal of Applied Measurement, 3,* p. 223. Copyright 2002 by Richard M. Smith, Editor. Reprinted with permission.

the hyperactivity/impulsivity aspect, measured by seven items (HYP18, . . ., HYP24). R. M. Smith (2000) reported that the eigenvalue of the hyperactive/impulsive dimension was 3.9. That is, this dimension explains 3.9 of 24 residual variance units. In other words, the ratio of eigenvalue/total number of items (3.9/24 = 0.1625) indicates that the hyperactive/impulsive dimension accounts for 16.25% of the residual variance (which, based on simulation results, was estimated as being more than just random variation; R. M. Smith, 2000). In addition to PCA, R. M. Smith (2000) examined both the standardized infit and outfit statistics for data fit as well as the impact of multidimensionality on person–measure interpretation. Based on a joint evaluation of all results (not discussed here), he concluded that the 24 items on the ABCR appear to be measuring two aspects of ADHD and suggested that the attention items (all with negative loadings) and hyperactive/impulsive items (all with positive loadings) should be calibrated separately to obtain two measures for each person. The reader may refer to E. V. Smith (2002) for details on simulation procedures to determine salient structure coefficients (factor loadings) under PCA, to compare Rasch fit statistics with PCAR results, and to generate a series of independent *t* tests to test for multidimensionality (the *t* test approach is incorporated into the RUMM2020 and RUMM2030 software; Andrich et al., 2003).

Based on a simulation study of PCAR under the Rasch model, R. M. Smith and Miao (1994) suggested that, after the first component (Rasch dimension) is taken into account, eigenvalues greater than 1.4 for the second component signal the presence of a secondary dimension. In another simulation study, Raîche (2005) showed that the mean of the critical eigenvalues for a secondary dimension varied from 1.46 to 2.00 for test lengths in the range from 20 to 60 items. For extensions of these results to tests with up to 1,000 items, the reader may refer to Linacre and Tennant (2009).

As noted earlier, computer programs such as WINSTEPS and RUMM provide fit indices and PCAR contrast plots for identification of secondary dimension(s) under the Rasch model. Prior to that, however, it is advisable to perform an EFA, with parallel analysis and/or Velicer's MAP Test, to obtain early indications on the number of proper dimensions that underlie the test measures (see Chapter 5, Section 5.6). This process is recommended because, as reported by R. M. Smith (1996a), Rasch fit statistics tend to mask the presence of two distinct dimensions when about the same number of items load on each dimension. However, if the EFA shows that most items load on the first dimension, and it is then found that the data fit the Rasch model, the joint examination of Rasch fit statistics and PCAR results (eigenvalues, factor loadings, and contrast plot) should provide clues to secondary dimensions.

SUMMARY

1. Under the Rasch model for binary responses (1 = correct, 0 = incorrect), referred to as *dichotomous Rasch model*, the chances of a person giving a correct response on any given item are governed solely by the person's ability and the item difficulty (see Equation 9.1).
2. Under the dichotomous Rasch model, both the person's ability and item difficulty are measured on the same scale, and the difference between them is represented as the natural logarithm of the odds of success of the person on the item. The measurement unit of this scale is referred to as *logit* (a contraction of *log odds unit*).
3. The graph of the relationship between the ability score of a person and the probability that this person will answer an item correctly is called the *item characteristic curve* (*ICC*).
4. The difficulty parameter for an item is the location on the ability scale where the probability for correct response on that item is 0.5 (50% chance of correct response).
5. Given the ability score of a person on the logit scale, the classical true score for this person on a test can be obtained by adding the person's probabilities for correct response on each test item. The graphical depiction of the relationship between ability scores (on the horizontal axis) and their true-score equivalents (on the vertical axis) is called the *test characteristic curve*.
6. The information function of an item at a particular location on the logit scale provides information about the contribution of the item to the ability estimation at that location (see Equation 9.3).
7. The test information function at a particular location on the logit scale, for a test of binary items, is defined as the sum of the item information functions for the test items.
8. The test information function plays an instrumental role in determining the error in the ability score estimate. Specifically, the standard error of the ability score at a particular location on the logit scale is the inverse of the square root of the test information function at that location (see Equation 9.4).
9. Unlike any IRT model, the Rasch model possesses the property of item information constancy according to which all items contribute equally to the magnitude of the

test information function across the entire continuum of the trait being measured on the logit scale.

10. According to the separation of item and person parameters in Rasch measurement, the estimates of a person's abilities do not depend on the item difficulties and vice versa, the estimates of item difficulties do not depend on the person's abilities (assuming that the data fit the Rasch model requirements). This unique property of the Rasch measurement allows for rigorous assessment of the fit of person responses to the Rasch model.
11. The outfit mean-square (Outfit MnSq) statistic is sensitive to unexpected responses by persons on items that are relatively very easy or very hard for them. The expected value of Outfit MnSq is close to 1.0. Values less than 1.0 (called *overfit*) indicate that the model predicts the data too well, thus causing inflation of summary statistics for the sample at hand. Values greater than 1.0 (called *underfit*) indicate noise in the data, which degrades measurement (typically, values in the range from 0.7 to 1.3 are considered acceptable).
12. The infit mean-square (Infit MnSq) statistic was developed to diminish the off-target outlier effect of the Outfit MnSq in order to signal unexpected response patterns for in-target measures. The expected value of Outfit MnSq is close to 1.0 (typically, values from 0.7 to 1.3 are considered acceptable).
13. The standardized mean square statistic is obtained through a transformation of the Outfit MnSq (or Infit MnSq*)* statistic into a *t* statistic for outfit (or infit) irregularities. As it follows an approximate standard normal distribution, it is also called the *standardized Z-statistic* (*Zstd*). Problems in data–model fit are flagged by standardized values greater than +2.0 (underfit) or values smaller than –2.0 (redundancy, data overfit the model).
14. The person–item distribution map (PIDM) for binary scales is a visual representation of the distributions of person abilities and item difficulties. It shows how well the range of item difficulties covers the range of person abilities.
15. The rating scale model (RSM) assumes that the response format is intended to function in the same way across all items (using the same number of response categories with the same set of labels for each item). The Rasch-based RSM is presented in Equation 9.6.
16. Under RSM, the item difficulty, δ_i, is the location on the trait scale at which a respondent has an equal chance of choosing the two extreme categories. The threshold τ_k indicates the impediment to being observed in category *k* relative to its preceding category (*k* – 1). The items may have different difficulty, but the set of thresholds is the same for all items.
17. The Rasch–Andrich threshold ($\delta_i + \tau_k$) for category *k* of item *i* is the location on the logit scale where the respondents have equal probability of responding in category *k* or its preceding category, *k* – 1.
18. The lack of monotonic advancement of thresholds for the CPCs of adjacent categories is referred to as *threshold* (or *step*) *disordering*. Threshold disordering degrades the interpretability of the resulting measures. It may occur, for example, when a higher category is not selected by the respondents as often as expected or a lower category is selected too often by respondents with higher trait scores.
19. Category disordering occurs when the categories are substantively disordered—that is, a higher category number corresponds to a lower level of category functioning. Thus, category disordering violates the RSM logic that respondents with higher level on the trait scale are expected to reach high scale categories.

20. Typically, average measure values and the Outfit MnSq statistic are used in detecting category disordering (*average measure* of a given category is the mean of the differences $\theta_n - \delta_i$ across all observations in that category).
21. Essential to most situations are the following guidelines for optimizing rating scale categories: (a) at least 10 observations in each category; (b) regular distribution of observations; (c) average measures advance with categories; (d) average Outfit MnSqs less than 2.0, and (e) thresholds advance monotonically with categories.
22. In Rasch modeling, judgments about whether the assumption of unidimensionality holds are typically based on a joint examination of infit and outfit statistics and the unrotated solutions from principal component analysis on residuals (PCAR)—the conventional PCA conducted on the standardized residuals of a person's scores (i.e., the standardized differences between the person's observed scores and Rasch-estimated scores).

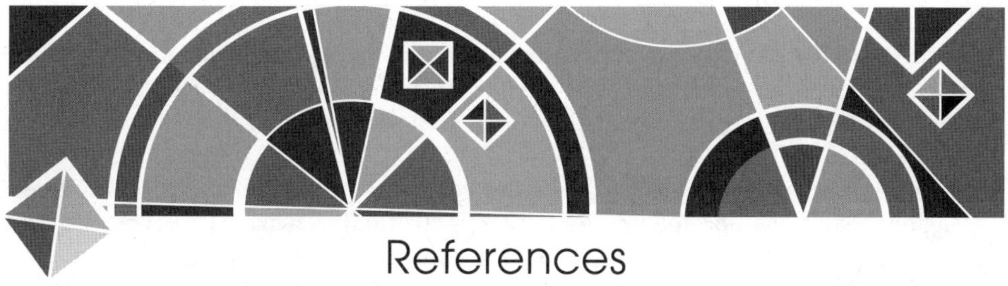

References

Abedi, J. (2006). Language issues in item development. In S. M. Downing & T. M. Haladyna (Eds.), *Handbook of test development* (pp. 377–398). Mahwah, NJ: Erlbaum.

Ackerman, T. A. (1992). A didactic explanation of item bias, item impact, and item validity from a multidimensional perspective. *Journal of Educational Measurement, 29,* 67–91.

Adams, E., & Messick, S. (1958). An axiomatic formulation and generalization of successive interval scaling. *Psychometrika, 23*, 355–368.

Ahlawat, K. S. (1985). On the negative valence items in self-report measures. *Journal of General Psychology, 112*(1), 89–99.

Aiken, L. R. (1983). Number of response categories and statistics on a teacher rating scale. *Educational and Psychological Measurement, 43,* 397–401.

Ajzen, I. (1991). The theory of planned behavior. *Organizational Behavior and Human Decision Processes, 50,* 179–211.

Akaike, H. (1987). Factor analysis and AIC. *Psychometrika, 52,* 317–332.

Aldridge, J. M., Dorman, J. P., & Fraser, B. J. (2004). Use of multitrait–multimethod modeling to validate actual and preferred forms of the Technology-Rich Outcomes-Focused Learning Environment Inventory (Troflei). *Australian Journal of Educational & Developmental Psychology, 4,* 110–125.

Allen, M. J., & Yen, W. M. (1979). *Introduction to measurement theory*. Monterey, CA: Brooks/Cole.

Althauser, R. P., Herberlein, T. A., & Scott, R. A. (1971). A causal assessment of validity: The augmented multitrait–multimethod matrix. In H. M. Blalock, Jr. (Ed.), *Causal models in the social sciences* (pp. 151–169). Chicago, IL: Aldine.

Alwin, D. (1974). An analytic comparison of four approaches to the interpretation of relationships in the multitrait–multimethod matrix. In H. L. Costner (Ed.), *Sociological methodology 1973–1974* (pp. 79–105). San Francisco, CA: Jossey-Bass.

American Educational Research Association, American Psychological Association, & National Council on Measurement in Education. (1999). *Standards for educational and psychological testing*. Washington, DC: American Educational Research Association.

American Psychiatric Association. (2000). *Diagnostic and statistical manual of mental disorders* (4th ed., text rev.). Washington, DC: Author.

Anastasi, A., & Urbina, S. (1997). *Psychological testing* (4th ed.). Upper Saddle River, NJ: Prentice Hall.

Andersen, E. (1997). The rating scale model. In W. J. van der Linden & R. K. Hambleton (Eds.), *Handbook of modern item response theory* (pp. 67–84). New York, NY: Springer.

Anderson, J. C. (1985). A measurement model to assess measure-specific factors in multiple-informant research. *Journal of Marketing Research, 22,* 86–92.

Andrews, F. M. (1984). Construct validity and error components of survey measures: A structural modeling approach. *Public Opinion Quarterly*, *48,* 409–442.

Andrich, D. (1978a). Application of psychometric rating model to ordered categories which are scored with successive integers. *Applied Psychological Measurement, 2,* 581–594.

Andrich, D. (1978b). A rating formulation for ordered response categories. *Psychometrika, 43,* 561–573.

Andrich, D. (1988). *Rasch models for measurement* (Sage University Paper on Quantitative Applications in the Social Sciences, Series No. 07-068). Newbury Park, CA: Sage.

Andrich, D. (1996). Measurement criteria for choosing among models for graded responses. In A. von Eye & C. C. Clog (Eds.), *Analysis of categorical variables in developmental research* (pp. 3–35). Orlando, FL: Academic Press.

Andrich, D. (2005). The Rasch model explained. In S. Alagumalai, D. D. Durtis, and N. Hungi (Eds.), *Applied Rasch measurement: A book of exemplars* (pp. 308–328). New York, NY: Springer-Kluwer.

Andrich, D., de Jong, J. H. A. L., & Sheridan, B. E. (1997). Diagnostic opportunities with the Rasch model for ordered response categories. In J. Rost & R. Langeheine (Ed.), *Applications of latent trait and latent class models in the social sciences* (pp. 58–70). New York, NY: Waxmann Verlag.

Andrich, D. A., Lyne, A., Sheridan, B., & Luo, G. (1997). *RUMM: Rasch unidimensional measurement models*. Perth, Australia: RUMM Laboratory.

Andrich, D., Lyne, A., Sheridan, B., & Luo, G. (2003). *RUMM 2020* [Computer software]. Perth, Australia: RUMM Laboratory.

Ang, R., Lau, S., Tan, A. G., & Lim, K. M. (2007). Refining attitudes toward seeking professional help scale: Factorial invariance across two Asian samples. *Measurement and Evaluation in Counseling and Development, 40*, 130–141.

Arbuckle, J. L., & Wothke, W. (1999). *Amos4.0 user's guide*. Chicago, IL: Smallwaters.

Asparouhov, T., & Muthén, B. O. (2009). Exploratory structural equation modeling. *Structural Equation Modeling, 16,* 397–438.

Bagozzi, R. P., & Yi, Y. (1991). Multitrait–multimethod matrices in consumer research. *Journal of Consumer Research, 17,* 426–439.

Baker, B. A., Caison, A. L., & Meade, A. W. (2007). Assessing gender-related differential item functioning and predictive validity with the Institutional Integration Scale. *Educational and Psychological Measurement, 67,* 545–559.

Baldwin, K. A., Grinslade, M. S., Baer, L. C., Watts, P., Dinger, M. K., & McCubbin, J. (2005). Higher-order factor analysis of an instrument with dichotomous data. *Research in Nursing & Health, 28,* 431–440.

Bandura, A. (1997). *Self-efficacy: The exercise of control*. New York, NY: Freeman.

Barbaranelli, C., & Caprara, G. V. (2000). Measuring the Big Five in self-report and other ratings: A multitrait–multimethod study. *European Journal of Psychological Assessment, 16,* 31–43.

Barnette, J. J. (2000). Effects of stem and Likert response option reversals on survey internal consistency: If you feel the need, there is a better alternative to using those negatively worded stems. *Educational and Psychological Measurement, 60,* 361–370.

Barrett-Lennard, G. T. (1998). *Carl Rogers' helping system: Journey and substance.* London, England: Sage.

Bartholomew, D. J. (1996). *The statistical approach to social measurement*. London, England: Academic Press.

Bartle-Haring, S., Kenny, D. A., & Gavazzi, S. M. (1999). Multiple perspectives on family differentiation: Analyses by multitrait–multimethod matrix and triadic social relations model. *Journal of Marriage and the Family, 61,* 491–503.

Bartlett, M. S. (1950).Tests of significance in factor analysis. *British Journal of Psychology, 3,* 77–85.

Basham. A., & Erford, B. T. (2007). Validity. In B. T. Erford (Ed.), *Assessment for counselors* (pp. 123–158). Boston, MA: Lahaska Press.

Beck, A. T., Steer, R. A., & Brown, G. K. (1996). *Manual for the Beck Depression Inventory—Second Edition.* San Antonio, TX: Psychological Corporation.

Becker, T. E., & Cote, J. A. (1994). Additive and multiplicative method effects in applied psychological research: Models and issues. *Journal of Management, 20,* 625–641.

Bentler, P. M. (1990). Comparative fit indexes in structural models. *Psychological Bulletin, 107,* 238–246.

Bentler, P. M. (2004). *EQS 6: Structural equation program manual.* Encino, CA: Multivariate Software.

Bentler, P. M., & Bonnett, D. (1980). Significance tests and goodness of fit in the analysis of covariance structures. *Psychological Bulletin, 88,* 588–606.

Bentler, P. M., & Chou, C. (1987). Practical issues in structural modeling. *Sociological Methods & Research, 16,* 78–117.

Bentler, P. M., Jackson, D. N., & Messick, S. (1971). Identification of content and style: A two-dimensional interpretation of acquiescence. *Psychological Bulletin, 76,* 186–204.

Bentler, P. M., & Kano, Y. (1990). On the equivalence of factors and components. *Multivariate Behavioral Research, 25*, 67–74.

Bentler, P. M., & Wu, E. J. C. (2002). *EQS for Windows user's guide*. Encino, CA. Multivariate Software.

Berk, R. A. (1980). A consumer's guide to criterion-referenced test reliability. *Journal of Educational Measurement, 17,* 323–349; errata in *Journal of Educational Measurement, 18,* 131.

Berk, R. A. (2000). *Ask mister assessment person: How do you estimate the reliability of teacher licensure/certification tests?* Retrieved from National Evaluation Systems, Inc., website: http://www.nesinc.com/PDFs/2000_11Berk.pdf

Billiet, J. B., & McClendon, M. J. (2000). Modeling acquiescence in measurement models for balanced sets of items. *Structural Equation Modeling, 7,* 608–628.

Bishop, G. F. (1987). Experiments with the middle response alternative in survey questions. *Public Opinion Quarterly, 51,* 220–232.

Blischke, W. R., Bush, J. W., & Kaplan, R. M. (1975). Successive intervals analysis of preference measures in a health status index. *Health Services Research, 10,* 181–198.

Bodenhorn, N., & Skaggs, G. (2005). Development of the School Counselor Self-Efficacy Scale. *Measurement and Evaluation in Counseling and Development, 38,* 14–28.

Bogardus, E. (1925). Measuring social distances. *Journal of Applied Sociology, 9*, 372–381.

Bollen, K. A. (1987). Outliers and improper solutions: A confirmatory factor analysis example. *Sociological Methods and Research, 15,* 375–384.

Bollen, K. A. (1989). *Structural equations with latent variables*. New York, NY: Wiley.

Bollen, K. A., & Stine, R. A. (1992). Bootstrapping goodness-of-fit measures in structural equation models. *Sociological Methods & Research, 21,* 205–229.

Bond, T. G., & Fox C. M. (2001). *Applying the Rasch model: Fundamental measurement in the human sciences*. Mahwah, NJ: Erlbaum.

Bong, M. (2001). Between- and within-domain relations of academic motivation among middle and high school students: Self-efficacy, task-value, and achievement goals. *Journal of Educational Psychology, 93,* 23–34

Bong, M., & Hocevar, D. (2002). Measuring self-efficacy: Multitrait–multimethod comparison of scaling procedures. *Applied Measurement in Education, 15,* 143–171.

Boomsma, A. (1982). The robustness of LISREL against small sample sizes in factor analysis models. In K. G. Jöreskog & H. Wold (Eds.), *Systems under indirect observation* (Part I, pp. 149–174). Amsterdam, The Netherlands: North–Holland.

Boomsma, A. (1986). On the use of bootstrap and jackknife in covariance structure analysis. *Compstat, 7,* 205–210.

Borgatta, E. F., Kercher, K., & Stull, D. E. (1986). A cautionary note on the use of principal components analysis. *Sociological Methods and Research, 15,* 160–168.

Borsboom, D., Mellenbergh, G. J., & van Heerden, J. (2004). The concept of validity. *Psychological Review, 111,* 1061–1071.

Borsboom, D., Romeijn, J.-W., & Wicherts. M. (2008). Measurement invariance versus selection invariance: Is fair selection possible? *Psychological Methods, 13,* 75–98.

Bozdogan, H. (1987). Model selection and Akaike's information criterion (AIC): The general theory and its analytical extensions. *Psychometrika, 52,* 345–370.

Bradley, K., Sampson, S., & Royal, K. (2006). Applying the Rasch rating scale model to gain insights into students' conceptualization of quality mathematics instruction. *Mathematics Education Research Journal, 18,* 11–26.

Brennan, R. L. (2004). *Generalizability theory*. New York, NY: Springer.

Brosseau-Liard, P. É., Rhemtulla, M., & Savalei, V. (2010, May). *How many categories are sufficient to use continuous data methods in structural equation modeling?* Poster presented at the meeting of the Association for Psychological Science, Boston, MA.

Brown, T. A. (2006). *Confirmatory factor analysis for applied research*. New York, NY: Guilford Press.

Brown, T. A., White, K. S., Forsyth, J. P., & Barlow, D. H. (2004). The structure of perceived emotional control: Psychometric properties of a revised Anxiety Control Questionnaire. *Behavior Therapy, 35,* 75–99.

Browne, M. W. (1984). The decomposition of multitrait–multimethod matrices. *British Journal of Mathematical and Statistical Psychology, 37,* 1–21.

Browne, M. W. (2001). An overview of analytic rotation in exploratory factor analysis. *Multivariate Behavioral Research, 36,* 111–150.

Browne, M. W., & Cudeck, R. (1993). Alternative ways of assessing model fit. In K. A. Bollen & J. S. Long (Eds.), *Testing structural equation models* (pp. 136–162). Newbury Park, CA: Sage.

Buja, A., & Eyuboglu, N. (1992). Remarks on parallel analysis. *Multivariate Behavioral Research, 27,* 509–540.

Burke, M. J. (1986). An empirical comparison of the results of five validity generalization procedures. *Journal of Applied Psychology, 71,* 349–353.

Butcher, J. N., Graham, J. R., Ben-Porath, Y. S., Tellegen, A., Dahlstrom, W. G., & Kaemmer, B. (1989). *The Minnesota Multiphasic Personality Inventory—Second Edition (MMPI–2)*. Minneapolis: University of Minnesota Press.

Byrne, B. M. (1988). The Self Description Questionnaire III: Testing for equivalent factorial validity across ability. *Educational and Psychological Measurement, 48,* 397–406.

Byrne, B. M. (2001). *Structural equation modeling with AMOS: Basic concepts, applications and programming*. Mahwah, NJ: Erlbaum.

Byrne, B. M. (2004). Testing for multigroup invariance using AMOS graphics: A road less traveled. *Structural Equation Modeling, 11,* 272–300.

Byrne, B. M., Baron, P., & Balev, J. (1998). The Beck Depression Inventory: A cross-validated test of second-order factorial structure for Bulgarian adolescents. *Educational and Psychological Measurement, 58,* 241–251.

Byrne, B. M., & Campbell, T. L. (1999). Cross-cultural comparisons and the presumption of equivalent measurement and theoretical structure: A look beneath the surface. *Journal of Cross-Cultural Psychology, 30,* 555–574.

Byrne, B. M., Shavelson, R. J., & Muthén, B. (1989). Testing for the equivalence of factor covariance and mean structures: The issue of partial measurement invariance. *Psychological Bulletin, 105,* 456–466.

Campbell, D. T., & Fiske, D. W. (1959). Convergent and discriminant validation by multitrait–multimethod matrix. *Psychological Bulletin, 56,* 81–105.

Campbell, D. T., & O'Connell, E. J. (1967). Method factors in multitrait–multimethod matrices: Multiplicative rather than additive? *Multivariate Behavioral Research, 2,* 409–426.

Campbell, D. T., & O'Connell, E. J. (1982). Methods as diluting trait relationships rather than adding irrelevant systematic variance. In D. Brinberg & L. Kidder (Eds.), *Forms of validity in research* (pp. 93–111). San Francisco, CA: Jossey-Bass.

Campbell-Sills, L. A., Liverant, G., & Brown, T. A. (2004). Psychometric evaluation of the Behavioral Inhibition/Behavioral Activation Scales (BIS/BAS) in large clinical samples. *Psychological Assessment, 16,* 244–254.

Carmines, E. G., & Zeller, R. A. (1979). *Reliability and validity assessment.* Beverly Hills, CA: Sage.

Carpenter, P. A., Just, M. A., & Shell, P. (1990). What one intelligence test measures: A theoretical account of the processing in the Raven's Progressive Matrices Test. *Psychological Review, 97,* 404–431.

Cattell, R. B. (1946). *The description and measurement of personality.* New York, NY: World Book.

Cattell, R. B. (1966). The scree test for the number of factors. *Multivariate Behavioral Research, 1,* 245–276.

Cattell, R. B. (1978). *The scientific use of factor analysis in behavioral and life sciences.* New York, NY: Plenum Press.

Cattell, R. B., Cattell, A. K. S., & Cattell, H. E. P. (1993). *16PF* (5th ed.). Champaign, IL: Institute for Personality and Ability Testing.

Chan, D. (2001). Method effects of positive affectivity, negative affectivity, and impression management in self-reports of work attitudes. *Human Performance, 14,* 77–96.

Chang, E. C., D'Zurilla, T. J., & Maydeu-Olivares, A. (1994). Assessing the dimensionality of optimism and pessimism using a multimeasure approach. *Cognitive Therapy and Research, 18,* 143–160.

Chang, H.-H., Mazzeo, J., & Roussos, L. (1996). Detecting DIF for polytomously scored items: An adaptation of the SIBTEST procedure. *Journal of Educational Measurement, 33,* 333–353.

Chang, L. (1995). Connotatively inconsistent test items. *Applied Measurement in Education, 8,* 199–209.

Chapman, B. P., & Hayslip, B., Jr. (2005). Incremental validity of a measure of emotional intelligence. *Journal of Personality Assessment, 85,* 154–169.

Charter, R. A. (2001). It is time to bury the Spearman–Brown "prophecy" formula for some common applications. *Educational and Psychological Measurement, 61,* 690–696.

Chen, F., Curran, P. J., Bollen, K. A., Kirby, J., & Paxton, P. (2008). An empirical evaluation of fixed cutoff points in RMSEA test statistic in structural equation models. *Sociological Methods & Research, 36,* 462–494.

Chen, F. F., Sousa, K. H., & West, S. G. (2005). Testing measurement invariance of second-order factor models. *Structural Equation Modeling, 12,* 471–492.

Cheung, G. W., & Rensvold, R. B. (2002). Evaluating goodness-of-fit indexes for testing measurement invariance. *Structural Equation Modeling, 9,* 233–255.

Chou, Y.-T., & Wang, W-C. (2010). Checking dimensionality in item response models with principal component analysis on standardized residuals. *Educational and Psychological Measurement, 70,* 717–731.

Cizek, G. J., Bowen, D., & Church, K. (2010). Sources of validity evidence for educational and psychological tests: A follow-up study. *Educational and Psychological Measurement, 70,* 732–743.

Cizek, G. J., Rosenberg, S. L., & Koons, H. H. (2008). Sources of validity evidence for educational and psychological tests. *Educational and Psychological Measurement, 68,* 397–412.

Clark, M. (2004). By the numbers: The rational for a Rasch analysis in placement testing. *Second Language Studies, 22,* 61–90.

Clauser, B. E. (2000). Recurrent issues and recent advances in scoring performance assessments. *Applied Psychological Measurement, 24,* 310–324.

Cleary, T. A. (1968). Test bias: Prediction of grades of Negro and White students in integrated colleges. *Journal of Educational Measurement, 5*, 115–124.

Cliff, N. (1966). Orthogonal rotation to congruence. *Psychometrika, 31*, 33–42.

Cliff, N., & Hamburger, C. D. (1967). The study of sampling errors in factor analysis by means of artificial experiments. *Psychological Bulletin, 68,* 430–445.

Coenders, G., & Saris, W. E. (2000). Testing nested additive, multiplicative and general multitrait–multimethod models. *Structural Equation Modeling, 7,* 219–250.

Coenders, G., Satorra, A., & Saris, W. E. (1997). Alternative approaches to structural modeling of ordinal data. A Monte Carlo study. *Structural Equation Modeling, 4,* 261–282.

Cohen, J. (1960). A coefficient of agreement for nominal scales. *Educational and Psychological Measurement, 20*, 37–46.

Cohen, J. (1988). *Statistical power analysis for the behavioral sciences* (2nd ed.). Hillsdale, NJ: Erlbaum.

Cohen, R. J., & Swerdlik, M. E. (1999). *Psychological testing and assessment: An introduction to tests and measurements* (4th ed.). Mountain View, CA: Mayfield.

Cole, D. A., Truglio, R., & Peeke, L. (1997). Relation between symptoms of anxiety and depression in children: A multitrait–multimethod–multigroup assessment. *Journal of Consulting and Clinical Psychology, 65,* 110–119.

Comrey, A. L., & Lee, H. B. (1992). *A first course in factor analysis* (2nd ed.). Hillsdale, NJ: Erlbaum.

Conger, A. (1980). Maximally reliable composites for multidimensional measures. *Educational and Psychological Measurement, 40,* 367–375.

Conners, C. K. (1997). *Manual for the Conners' Rating Scales—Revised*. North Tonawanda, NY: Multi-Health Systems.

Conroy, D. E. (2002). Progress in the development of a multidimensional measure of fear of failure: The Performance Fear Appraisal Inventory (PFAI). *Anxiety, Stress, and Coping, 14,* 431–452.

Conway, J. M. (1996). Analysis and design of multitrait–multirater performance appraisal studies. *Journal of Management, 22,* 139–162.

Conway, J. M. (1998). Estimation and uses of the proportion of method variance for multitrait–multimethod data. *Organizational Research Methods*, *1,* 209–222.

Conway, J. M., Lievens, F., Scullen, S. E., & Lance, C. E. (2004). Bias in the correlated uniqueness model for MTMM data. *Structural Equation Modeling, 11,* 535–559.

Cook, C., Heath, F., Thompson, R. L., & Thompson, B. (2001). Score reliability in Web- or Internet-based surveys: Unnumbered graphic rating scales versus Likert-type scales. *Educational and Psychological Measurement, 61,* 697–706.

Cooper, M. (1976). An exact test for use with Likert-type scales. *Educational and Psychological Measurement, 36,* 647–655.

Cordon, S. L. & Finney, S. J. (2008). Measurement invariance of the Mindful Attention Awareness Scale across adult attachment style. *Measurement and Evaluation in Counseling and Development, 40,* 228–245.

Corten, I. W., Saris, W. E., Coenders, G., van der Veld, W., Aalberts, C. E., & Kornelis, C. (2002). Fit of different models for multitrait–multimethod experiments. *Structural Equation Modeling, 9,* 213–232.

Corwyn, R. F. (2000). The factor structure of global self-esteem among adolescents and adults. *Journal of Research in Personality, 34,* 357–379.

Costa, P. T., Jr., & McCrae, R. R. (1990). Personality disorders and the Five-Factor Model. *Journal of Personality Disorders, 4,* 362–371.

Costa, P. T., Jr., & McCrae, R. R. (1991). *NEO Five-Factor Inventory (NEO–FFI)*, Form S (Adult). Lutz, FL: Psychological Assessment Resources.

Costa, P. T., Jr., & McCrae, R. R. (1992). Personality disorders and the Five-Factor Model. *Journal of Personality Disorders, 4,* 362–371.

Costa, P. T., Jr., & McCrae, R. R. (2003). *NEO Five-Factor Inventory (NEO–FFI)*, Form S (College Age). Lutz, FL: Psychological Assessment Resources.

Courvoisier, D. S., Nussbeck, F. W., Eid, M., Geiser, C., & Cole, D. A. (2008). Analyzing the convergent and discriminant validity of states and traits: Development and applications of multimethod latent state–trait models. *Psychological Assessment, 20,* 270–280.

Crocker, L., & Algina, J. (1986). *Introduction to classical and modern test theory.* New York, NY: Holt, Rinehart & Winston.

Cronbach, L. J. (1951). Coefficient alpha and the internal structure of tests. *Psychometrika, 16,* 297–334.

Cronbach, L. J. (1971). Test validation. In R. L. Thorndike (Ed.), *Educational measurement* (2nd ed., pp. 443–507). Washington, DC: American Council on Education.

Cronbach, L. J., & Gleser, G. C. (1965). *Psychological tests and personnel decisions* (2nd ed.). Urbana: University of Illinois Press.

Cronbach, L. J., & Meehl, P. E. (1955). Construct validity in psychological tests. *Psychological Bulletin, 52,* 281–302.

Cronbach, L. J., Schönemann, P., & McKie, D. (1965). Alpha coefficients for stratified parallel tests. *Educational and Psychological Measurement, 25,* 291–312.

Crowne, D., & Marlowe, D. (1964). *The approval motive.* New York, NY: Wiley.

CTB/McGraw-Hill. (2001). *TerraNova—Second Edition* (*TerraNova 2*). Monterey, CA: Author.

Cudeck, R. (1988). Multiplicative models and MTMM matrices. *Journal of Educational Statistics, 13,* 131–147.

Cudeck, R., & O'Dell, L. L. (1994). Applications of standard error estimates in unrestricted factor analysis: Significance tests for factor loadings and correlations. *Psychological Bulletin, 115,* 475–487.

Cunningham, J. D., Bradley, K. D., & Gilman, R. (2006, April). *Employing the many-facet model to investigate the domains of the MSLSS.* Paper presented at the meeting of the American Educational Research Association, San Francisco, CA.

Cureton, E. E. (1950). Validity. In E. F. Lindquist (Ed.), *Educational measurement* (pp. 621–695). Washington, DC: American Council on Education.

Curran, P. J., West, S. G., & Finch, J. F. (1996). The robustness of test statistics to nonnormality and specification error in confirmatory factor analysis. *Psychological Methods, 1,* 16–29.

David, H. A. (1988). *The method of paired comparisons*. New York, NY: Oxford University Press.

Davidson, R. J. (1998). Affective style and affective disorders: Perspectives from affective neuroscience. *Cognition and Emotion, 12,* 307–330.

DeCarlo, L. T. (1997). On the meaning and use of kurtosis. *Psychological Methods, 2,* 292–307.

De La Torre, J., & Douglas, J. A. (2004). Higher-order trait models for cognitive diagnosis. *Psychometrika, 69,* 333–353.

Derby, D. C., & Smith, T. J. (2008). Exploring the factorial structure for behavioral consequences of college student drinking. *Measurement and Evaluation in Counseling and Development, 41,* 32–41.

Derogatis, L. R. (1992). *Manual for the Symptom Checklist–90—Revised*. Minneapolis, MN: NCS Pearson.

DeVellis, B. M., & DeVellis, R. F. (2000). Self-efficacy and health. In A. Baum, T. A. Revenson, & J. E. Singer (Eds.), *Handbook of health psychology* (pp. 235–247). Mahwah, NJ: Erlbaum.

DeVellis, R. F. (1991). *Scale development: Theory and applications.* Newbury Park, CA: Sage.

DiBello, L. V., Stout, W. F., & Roussos, L. A. (1995). Unified cognitive/psychometric diagnostic assessment likelihood-based classification techniques. In P. Nichol, S. Chipman, & R. Brennan (Eds.), *Cognitively diagnostic assessment* (pp. 361–389). Hillsdale, NJ: Erlbaum.

Dillon, W. R., Kumar, A., & Mulani, N. (1987). Offending estimates in covariance structure analysis: Comments on the causes of and solutions to Heywood cases. *Psychological Bulletin, 101,* 126–135.

Dimitrov, D. M. (2006). Comparing groups on latent variables: A structural equation modeling approach. *WORK: A Journal of Prevention, Assessment & Rehabilitation, 26,* 429–436.

Dimitrov, D. M. (2007). Least squares distance method of cognitive validation and analysis for binary items using their item response theory parameters. *Applied Psychological Measurement, 31,* 367–387.

Dimitrov, D. M. (2008). *Quantitative research in education: Intermediate & advanced methods*. Oceanside, NY: Whittier Publications.

Dimitrov, D. M. (2010). Testing for factorial invariance in the context of construct validation. *Measurement and Evaluation in Counseling and Development, 43,* 121–149.

Dimitrov, D. M., & Raykov, T. (2003). Validation of cognitive structures: A structural equation modeling approach. *Multivariate Behavioral Research, 38,* 1–23.

Dimitrov, D. M., & Smith, R. D. (2006). Adjusted Rasch–person fit statistics. *Journal of Applied Measurement, 7,* 170–183.

DiStefano, C. (2002). The impact of categorization with confirmatory factor analysis. *Structural Equation Modeling, 9,* 327–346.

DiStefano, C., & Motl, R. W. (2002). Personality correlates of method effects due to negatively worded items on the Rosenberg Self-Esteem Scale. *Personality and Individual Differences*, *46,* 259–388.

Doggett, R. A., Sheperis, C. J., Eaves, S., Mong, M. D, & Erford, B. T. (2007). Selecting, administering, scoring, and interpreting assessment instruments and techniques. In B. T. Erford (Ed.), *Assessment for counselors* (pp. 159–188). Boston, MA: Lahaska Press.

Donnellan, M. B. (2008). A psychometric evaluation of two achievement goal inventories. *Educational and Psychological Measurement, 68,* 643–658.

Doty, D. H., & Glick, W. H. (1998). Common methods bias: Does common methods variance really bias results? *Organizational Research Methods, 1,* 374–406.

Downing, S. M., & Haladyna, T. M. (1997). Test item development: Validity evidence from quality assurance procedures. *Applied Measurement in Education, 10,* 61–82.

Downing, S. M., & Haladyna, T. M. (Eds.). (2006). *Handbook of test development.* Mahwah, NJ: Erlbaum.

Drasgow, F., & Kanfer, R. (1985). Equivalent of psychological measurement in heterogeneous populations. *Journal of Applied Psychology, 70,* 662–680.

Dumenci, L. (2000). Multitrait–multimethod analysis. In S. D. Brown & H. E. A. Tinsley (Eds.), *Handbook of applied multivariate statistics and mathematical modeling* (pp. 583–611). San Diego, CA: Academic Press.

Educational Testing Service (Ed.). (2002). *GRE: Preparing for the verbal and quantitative sections of the GRE general test.* Princeton, NJ: Author.

Eid, M. (2000). A multitrait–multimethod model with minimal assumptions. *Psychometrika, 65,* 241–261.

Eid, M., Lischetzke, T., Nussbeck, F. W., & Trierweiler, L. I. (2003). Separating trait effects from trait-specific method effects in multitrait–multimethod models: A multiple indicator CTC(*M*–1) model. *Psychological Methods, 8,* 38–60.

Eid, M., Nussbeck, F. W., Geiser, C., Cole, D. A., Gollwitzer, M., & Lischetzke, T. (2008). Structural equation modeling of multitrait–multimethod data: Different models for different types of methods. *Psychological Methods, 13,* 230–253.

Embretson, S. E. (1983). Construct validity: Construct representation versus nomothetic span. *Psychological Bulletin, 93,* 179–197.

Embretson, S. E. (1994). Application of cognitive design systems to test development. In C. R. Reynolds (Ed.), *Cognitive assessment: A multidisciplinary perspective* (pp. 107–135). New York, NY: Plenum Press.

Embretson, S. E. (1995). A measurement model for linking individual learning to process and knowledge: Application to mathematical reasoning. *Journal of Educational Measurement, 32,* 277–294.

Embretson, S. E., & Reise, S. P. (2000). *Item response theory for psychologists.* Mahwah, NJ: Erlbaum.

Embretson, S. E., & Wetzel, C. D. (1987). Component latent trait models for paragraph comprehension tests. *Applied Psychological Measurement, 11,* 175–193.

Erford, B. T. (1993). *Manual for the Disruptive Behavior Rating Scale.* East Aurora, NY: Slosson Educational Publications.

Erford, B. T. (Ed.). (2007). *Assessment for counselors.* Boston, MA: Houghton Mifflin.

Erford, B. T., Klein, L., & McNinch, K. (2007). Assessment of intelligence. In B. T. Erford (Ed.), *Assessment for counselors* (pp. 319–355). Boston, MA: Houghton Mifflin.

Everitt, B. S. (1975). Multivariate analysis: The need for data, and other problems. *British Journal of Psychiatry.* 126, 237240.

Fabrigar, L. R., Wegener, D. T., MacCallum, R. C., & Strahan, E. J. (1999). Evaluating the use of exploratory factor analysis in psychological research. *Psychological Methods, 4,* 272–299.

Fan, X., Thompson, B., & Wang, L. (1999). Effects of sample size, estimation method, and model specification on structural equation modeling fit indexes. *Structural Equation Modeling, 6,* 56–83.

Fava, J. L., & Velicer, W. F. (1992a). The effects of overextraction on factor and component analysis. *Multivariate Behavioral Research, 27,* 387–415.

Fava, J. L., & Velicer, W. F. (1992b). An empirical comparison of factor, image, component, and scale scores. *Multivariate Behavioral Research, 27*, 301–322.

Feldt, L. S., & Brennan, R. L. (1989). Reliability. In R. L. Linn (Ed.), *Educational measurement* (3rd ed., pp. 105–146). New York, NY: Macmillan.

Finney, S. J., & DiStefano, C. (2006). Non-normal and categorical data in structural equation modeling. In G. R. Hancock & R. O. Mueller (Eds.), *Structural equation modeling: A second course* (pp. 269–314). Greenwich, CT: Information Age Publishing.

Fiske, D. W. (1982). Convergent–discriminant validity in measurements and research strategies. In D. Binberg, & I. Kidder (Eds.), *New directions for methodology of social and behavioral science: Forms of validity in research* (No. 12, pp. 77–92). San Francisco, CA: Jossey-Bass.

Fitts, W. H., & Warren, W. L. (1996). *Manual for the Tennessee Self-Concept Scale—Second Edition*. Los Angeles, CA: Western Psychological Services.

Fitzpatrick, M. R., & Irannejad, S. (2008). Adolescent readiness for change and the working alliance in counseling. *Journal of Counseling & Development, 86,* 438–445.

Flora, D. B., & Curran, P. J. (2004). An empirical evaluation of alternative methods of estimation for confirmatory factor analysis with ordinal data. *Psychological Methods, 9,* 466–491.

Floyd, F. J., & Widaman, K. F. (1995). Factor analysis in the development and refinement of clinical assessment instruments. *Psychological Assessment, 7,* 286–299.

Gagné, P., & Hancock, G. R. (2006). Measurement model quality, sample size, and solution propriety in confirmatory factor models. *Multivariate Behavioral Research, 41,* 65–83.

Gardner, D. G., Cummings, L. L., Dunham, R. B., & Pierce, J. L. (1998). Single-item versus multiple-item measurement scales: An empirical comparison. *Educational and Psychological Measurement, 58,* 898–915.

Gaudron, J. P., & Vautier, S. (2007). Analyzing individual differences in vocational, leisure, and family interests: A multitrait–multimethod approach. *Journal of Vocational Behavior, 70,* 561–573.

Geiser, C., Eid, M., & Nussbeck, F. W. (2008). On the meaning of the latent variables in the CT-C(*M*–1) model: A comment on Maydeu-Olivares and Coffman (2006). *Psychological Methods, 13,* 49–57.

Gerbing, D. W., & Anderson, J. C. (1987). Improper solutions in the analysis of covariance structures: Their interpretability and a comparison of alternate respecifications. *Psychometrika, 52,* 99–111.

Gerich, J. (2007). Visual analog scales for mode-independent measurement in self-administered questionnaires. *Behavior Research Methods, 39,* 985–992.

Gilmer, J. S., & Feldt, L. S. (1983). Reliability estimation for a test with parts of unknown lengths. *Psychometrika, 48,* 99–111.

Gitomer, D. H., & Rock, D. (1993). Addressing process variables in test analysis. In N. Frederiksen, R. J. Mislevy, & I. Bejar (Eds.), *Test theory for a new generation of tests* (pp. 243–268). Hillsdale, NJ: Erlbaum.

Glass, G. V., & Hopkins, K. D. (1996). *Statistical methods in education and psychology* (3rd ed.). Needham Heights, MA: Allyn & Bacon.

Glorfeld, L. W. (1995). An improvement on Horn's parallel analysis methodology for selecting the correct number of factors to retain. *Educational and Psychological Measurement, 55,* 377–393.

Gorin, J. S. (2006). Test design with cognition in mind. *Educational Measurement: Issues and Practice, 25,* 21–35.

Gorsuch, R. L. (1983). *Factor analysis*. Hillsdale, NJ: Erlbaum.

Gorsuch, R. L. (1990). Common factor analysis versus component analysis: Some well and little known facts. *Multivariate Behavioral Research, 25*, 33–39.

Green, K. E., & Frantom, C. G. (2002, November). *Survey development and validation with the Rasch model*. Paper presented at the International Conference on Questionnaire Development, Evaluation, and Testing, Charleston, SC.

Green-Demers, I., Legault, L., Pelletier, D., & Pelletier, L. G. (2008). Factorial invariance of the Academic Amotivation Inventory (AAI) across gender and grade in a sample of Canadian high school students. *Educational and Psychological Measurement, 68,* 862–880.

Guadagnoli, E., & Velicer, W. (1988). Relation of sample size to the stability of component patterns. *Psychological Bulletin, 103,* 265–275.

Guiffre, M. (1983). *Validation of a visual analogue scale for pain measurement in childbirth* (Unpublished doctoral dissertation). University of Rochester, New York, NY.

Guo, B., Aveyard, P., & Dai, X. (2009). The Chinese Intelligence Scale for Young Children: Testing factor structure and measurement invariance using the framework of the Wechsler Intelligence Tests. *Educational and Psychological Measurement, 69,* 459–474.

Guttman, L. A. (1944). A basis for scaling qualitative data. *American Sociological Review, 9,* 139–150.

Guttman, L. A. (1950). The basis for scalogram analysis. In S. A. Stouffer, L. A. Guttman, F. A. Suchman, P. F. Lazarsfeld, S. A. Star, & J. A. Clause (Eds.), *Studies in social psychology in World War II: Measurement and prediction* (Vol. 4, pp. 60–90). Princeton, NJ: Princeton University Press.

Hair, J. F., Anderson, R. E., Tatham, R. L., & Black, W. C. (1998). *Multivariate data analysis with readings*. Englewood Cliffs, NJ: Prentice Hall.

Haladyna, T. M. (1996). *Writing test items to evaluate higher order thinking*. New York, NY: Pearson Education.

Haladyna, T. M. (1999). *Developing and validating multiple-choice items* (2nd ed.). Mahwah, NJ: Erlbaum.

Haladyna, T. M., Downing, S. M., & Rodriguez, M. C. (2002). A review of multiple-choice item writing guidelines for classroom assessment. *Applied Measurement in Education, 15,* 309–334.

Hambleton, R. K., & Swaminathan, H. (1985). *Item response theory: Principles and applications*. Boston, MA: Kluwer-Nijhoff.

Hambleton, R. K., Swaminathan, H., & Rogers, H. J. (1991). *Fundamentals of item response theory*. Newbury Park, CA: Sage.

Hamilton, M. (1960). A rating scale for depression. *Journal of Neurology, Neurosurgery and Psychiatry, 23,* 56–62.

Hancock, G. R. (2001). Effect size, power, and sample size determination for structured means modeling and MIMIC approaches to between-groups hypothesized testing of means on a single latent construct. *Psychometrika, 66,* 373–388.

Hancock, G. R. (2004). Experimental, quasi-experimental, and nonexperimental design and analysis with latent variables. In D. Kaplan (Ed.), *The SAGE handbook of quantitative methodology for the social sciences* (pp. 317–334). Thousand Oaks, CA: Sage.

Hardigan, P. C., & Carvajal, M. J. (2008). Application of Rasch rating scale model to analysis of job satisfaction among practicing pharmacists. *Journal of American Pharmacists Association, 48,* 522–529.

Harmon, L. W., Hansen, J. C., Borgen, F. H., & Hammer, A. L. (1994). *Strong Interest Inventory applications and technical guide*. Stanford, CA: Stanford University Press.

Harris, A. (1980). Response class: A Guttman Scale analysis. *Journal of Abnormal Child Psychology, 8,* 213–220.

Harter, S. (1988). *Self-perception profile for adolescents*. Denver, CO: University of Denver Press.

Hays, R. D., & Ellickson, P. L. (1990–1991). Guttman scale analysis of longitudinal data: A methodology and drug use applications. *International Journal of the Addictions, 25,* 1341–1352.

Heise, D. E. (1970). The semantic differential and attitude research. In G. F. Summers (Ed.), *Attitude measurement* (pp. 235–253). Chicago, IL: Rand McNally.

Helmreich, R. L., Sawin, L. L., & Carsrud, A. L. (1986). The honeymoon effect in job performance: Temporal increases in the predictive power of achievement motivation. *Journal of Applied Psychology, 71,* 185–188.

Henson, R., & Douglas, J. (2005). Test construction for cognitive diagnosis. *Applied Psychological Measurement, 29,* 262–277.

Henson, R. K., & Roberts, J. K. (2006). Use of exploratory factor analysis in published research: Common errors and some comments on improved practice. *Educational and Psychological Measurement, 66,* 393–416.

Hofmann, R. J. (1979). On testing a Guttman Scale for significance. *Educational and Psychological Measurement, 39,* 297–301.

Hogarty, K. Y., Hines, C. V., Kromrey, J. D., Ferron, J. M., & Mumford, K. R. (2005). The quality of factor solutions in exploratory factor analysis: The influence of sample size, communality, and overdetermination. *Educational and Psychological Measurement, 65,* 202–226.

Holland, J. L. (1959). A theory of vocational choice. *Journal of Counseling Psychology, 6,* 35–45.

Holland, J. L. (1997). *Making vocational choices: A theory of vocational personalities and work environment* (3rd ed.). Odessa, FL: Psychological Assessment Resources.

Holland, P. W., & Wainer, H. (1993). *Differential item functioning*. Hillsdale, NJ: Erlbaum.

Hong, S., & Wong, E. C. (2005). Rasch rating scale modeling of the Korean version of the Beck Depression Inventory. *Educational and Psychological Measurement, 65,* 124–139.

Hood, A. B., & Johnson, R. W. (2007). *Assessment in counseling. A guide to the use of psychological assessment procedures* (4th ed.). Alexandria, VA: American Counseling Association.

Horn, J. L. (1965). A rationale and test for the number of factors in factor analysis. *Psychometrika, 30,* 179–185.

Horn, J. L., & McArdle, J. J. (1992). A practical and theoretical guide to measurement invariance in aging research. *Experimental Aging Research, 18,* 117–144.

Hox, J. J. (2002). *Multilevel analysis techniques and applications.* Mahwah, NJ: Erlbaum.

Hox, J. J., & Kleiboer, A. M. (2007). Retrospective questions or a diary method? A two-level multitrait–multimethod analysis. *Structural Equation Modeling, 14,* 311–325.

Hoyle, R. H. (1995). *Structural equation modeling: Concepts, issues, and applications*. Thousand Oaks, CA: Sage.

Hsu, P. C. (2005). The Multidimensional Chinese Acculturation Measure (MCAM): A validation study. *Dissertation Abstracts International, 66,* 207.

Hu, L., & Bentler, P. M. (1998). Fit indices in covariance structure modeling: Sensitivity to underparameterized model misspecification. *Psychological Methods, 3*, 424–453.

Hu, L.T., & Bentler, P. M. (1999). Cutoff criteria for fit indexes in covariance structure analysis: Conventional criteria versus new alternatives. *Structural Equation Modeling, 6,* 1–55.

Hu, L. T., Bentler, P. M., & Kano, Y. (1992). Can test statistics in covariance structure analysis be trusted? *Psychological Bulletin, 112,* 351–362.

Huebner, E. S. (1994). Preliminary development and validation of a multidimensional life satisfaction scale for children. *Psychological Assessment, 6*, 149–158.

Humphreys, L. G. (1986). An analysis and evaluation of test and item bias in the prediction context. *Journal of Applied Psychology, 71,* 327–333.

Hutchinson, S. R., & Olmos, A. (1998). Behavior of descriptive fit indices on confirmatory factor analysis using ordered categorical data. *Structural Equation Modeling, 5,* 344–364.

Huynh, H. (1994). On equivalence between a partial credit item and a set of independent Rasch binary items. *Psychometrika, 59,* 111–119.

Immekus, J. C., & Imbrie, P. K. (2010). A test and cross-validation of the Revised Two-Factor Study Process Questionnaire factor structure among Western university students. *Educational and Psychological Measurement, 70,* 495–510.

Immekus, J. C., & Maller, S. J. (2010). Factor structure invariance of the Kaufman Adolescent and Adult Intelligence Test across male and female samples. *Educational and Psychological Measurement, 70,* 91–104.

Inglés, C. J., Marzo, J. C., Hidalgo, M. D., Zhou, X., & Garcia-Fernandez, J. M. (2008). Factorial invariance of the Questionnaire About Interpersonal Difficulties for Adolescents across Spanish and Chinese adolescent samples. *Measurement and Evaluation in Counseling and Development, 41,* 89–103.

Irvine, S. H., & Kyllonen, P. C. (2002). *Item generation for test development.* Mahwah, NJ: Erlbaum.

Jaccard, J., Weber, J., & Lundmark, J. (1975). A multitrait–multimethod analysis of four attitude assessment procedures. *Journal of Experimental Social Psychology, 11,* 149–154.

Jackson, D. L. (2003). Revisiting sample size and number of parameter estimates: Some support for the *N:q* hypothesis. *Structural Equation Modeling, 10,* 128–141.

Jackson, D. N. (1997). *Manual for the Jackson Personality Inventory—Revised.* Port Huron, MI: Sigma Assessment Systems.

James, L. R., Demaree, R. G., & Mulaik, S. A. (1986). A note on validity generalization procedures. *Journal of Applied Psychology, 71,* 440–450.

Janda, L. H. (1998). *Psychological testing: Theory and applications.* Boston, MA: Allyn & Bacon.

Johnson, D. R., & Creech, J. C. (1983). Ordinal measures in multiple indicator models: A simulation study of categorization error. *American Sociological Review, 48,* 398–407.

Johnson, E. C., Meade, A. W., & DuVernet, A. M. (2009). The role of referent indicators in tests of measurement invariance. *Structural Equation Modeling, 16,* 642–657.

Johnson, W. L. & Johnson, A. M. (1995). Using SAS/PC for higher order factoring. *Educational and Psychological Measurement, 55,* 429–434.

Johnson, W. L., & Johnson, A. M. (2000). Using SPSS/PC for higher order factoring. *Educational and Psychological Measurement, 60,* 648.

Johnson, W. L., Johnson, A. M., & Heimberg, F. (1999). A primary- and second-order component analysis of the organizational identification questionnaire. *Educational and Psychological Measurement, 59,* 159–170.

Jöreskog, K. G. (1969). A general approach to confirmatory maximum likelihood factor analysis. *Psychometrika, 34,* 183–202.

Jöreskog, K. G. (1971a). Simultaneous factor analysis in several populations. *Psychometrika, 36,* 409–426.

Jöreskog, K. G. (1971b). Statistical analysis of sets of congeneric measures. *Psychometrika, 36,* 109–133.

Jöreskog, K. G. (1974). Analyzing psychological data by structural analysis of covariance matrices. In R. C. Atkinson, D. H. Krantz, R. D. Luce, & P. Suppes (Eds.), *Contemporary developments in mathematical psychology* (Vol. 2, pp. 1–56). San Francisco, CA: Freeman.

Jöreskog, K. G, & Sörbom, D. (1979). *Advances in factor analysis and structural equation models*. Cambridge, MA: Abt Books.

Jöreskog, K. G., & Sörbom, D. (1996). *LISREL 8: User's reference guide*. Chicago, IL: Scientific Software International.

Kaiser, H. F. (1974). An index of factorial simplicity. *Psychometrika, 39,* 31–36.

Kalton, G., Roberts, J., & Holt, D. (1980). The effects of offering a middle response option with opinion questions. *The Statistician, 29,* 65–78.

Kamata, A., Turhan, A., & Darandari, E. (2003, April). *Estimating reliability for multidimensional composite scale scores*. Paper presented at the meeting of American Educational Research Association, Chicago, IL.

Kane, M. T. (2001). Current concerns in validity theory. *Journal of Educational Measurement, 38,* 319–342.

Kane, M. T., & Case, S. M. (2004). The reliability and validity of weighted composite scores. *Applied Measurement in Education, 17,* 221–240.

Kaplan, D. (2000). *Structural equation modeling: Foundations and extensions.* Thousand Oaks, CA: Sage.

Karabatsos, G. (2001). The Rasch model, additive conjoint measurement, and new models of probabilistic measurement theory. *Journal of Applied Measurement, 2,* 389–423.

Keith, T. Z., Fine, J. G., Taub, G. E., Reynolds, M. R., & Kranzler, J. H. (2006). Higher-order, multisample, confirmatory factor analysis of the Wechsler Intelligence Scale for Children Fourth Edition: What does it measure? *School Psychology Review, 35,* 108–127.

Kelley, T. L. (1939). The selection of upper and lower groups for the validation of test items. *Journal of Educational Psychology, 30,* 17–24.

Kenny, D. A. (1976). An empirical application of confirmatory factor analysis to the multitrait–multimethod matrix. *Journal of Experimental Social Psychology, 12,* 247–252.

Kenny, D. A. (1979). *Correlation and causality*. New York, NY: Wiley.

Kenny, D. A., & Kashy, D. A. (1992). Analysis of the multitrait–multimethod matrix by confirmatory factor analysis. *Psychological Bulletin, 112,* 165–172.

Kerlinger, F. N. (1986). *Foundations of behavioral research*. New York, NY: Holt.

Khazaal, Y., Chatton, A., Prezzemolo, R., Hoch, A., Cornuz, J., & Zullino, D. (2008). A game for smokers: A preliminary naturalistic trial in a psychiatric hospital. *Patient Education and Counseling, 70,* 205–208.

Kim, B. S. K., & Hong, S. (2004). A psychometric revision of the Asian Values Scale using the Rasch model. *Measurement and Evaluation in Counseling and Development, 37,* 15–27.

Kim, J., & Mueller, C. W. (1985). *An introduction to factor analysis: What it is and how to do it.* Sage University Paper Series on Quantitative Applications in the Social Sciences, Series No. 07-013. Beverly Hills, CA: Sage.

Kim, K. H. (2005). The relation among fit indexes, power, and sample size in structural equation modeling. *Structural Equation Modeling, 12,* 368–390.

Kirk-Brown, A., & Wallace, D. (2004). Predicting burnout and job-satisfaction in workplace counselors: The influence of role stressors, job challenge, and organizational knowledge. *Journal of Employment Counseling, 41,* 29–37

Kline, R. B. (1998). *Principles and practice of structural equation modeling.* New York, NY: Guildwood.

Klockars, A. J., & Yamagishi, M. (1988). The influence of labels and positions in rating scales. *Journal of Educational Measurement, 25,* 85–96.

Komaroff, E. (1997). Effect of simultaneous violations of essential tau-equivalence and uncorrelated error on coefficient alpha. *Applied Psychological Measurement, 21,* 337–348.

Kornell, N., & Metcalfe, J. (2006). Study efficacy and the region of proximal learning framework. *Journal of Experimental Psychology: Learning, Memory, and Cognition, 32,* 609–622.

Koth, C. W., Bradshaw, C. P., & Leaf, P. J. (2009). Teacher Observation of Classroom Adaptation—Checklist: Development and factor structure. *Measurement and Evaluation in Counseling and Development, 42,* 15–30.

Krumboltz, J. D. (1997). *Manual for the Career Beliefs Inventory*. Palo Alto, CA: Consulting Psychologists Press.

Kumar, A., & Dillon, W. R. (1990). On the use of confirmatory measurement models in the analysis of multiple-informant reports. *Journal of Marketing Research, 27,* 102–111.

Kumar, A., & Dillon, W. R. (1992). An integrative look at the use of additive and multiplicative covariance models in the analysis of MTMM data. *Journal of Marketing Research, 29,* 51–64.

Lam, T. C. M., & Klockars, A. J. (1982). Anchor point effects on the equivalence of questionnaire items. *Journal of Educational Measurement, 19,* 317–322.

Lam, T. C. M., & Stevens, J. J. (1994). Effects of content polarization, item wording, and rating scale width on rating response. *Applied Measurement in Education, 7,* 141–158.

Lance, C. E., Noble, C. L., & Scullen, S. E. (2002). A critique of the correlated trait-correlated method and correlated uniqueness models for multitrait–multimethod data. *Psychological Methods, 7,* 228–244.

Lance, C. E., & Sloan, C. (1993). Relationships between overall and life facet satisfaction: A multitrait–multimethod (MTMM) study. *Social Indicators Research, 30,* 1–15.

Lance, C. E., Teachout, M. S., & Donnelly, T. M. (1992). Specification of the criterion construct space: An application of hierarchical confirmatory factor analysis. *Journal of Applied Psychology, 77,* 437–452.

Le, H., Casillas, A., Robbins, S. B., & Langley, R. (2005). Motivational and skills, social, self-management predictors of college outcomes: Constructing the Student Readiness Inventory. *Educational and Psychological Measurement, 65,* 482–508.

Lee, S. M., Baker, C. R., Cho, S. H., Heckathorn, D. E., Holland, M. W., Newgent, R. A., . . . Yu, K. (2007). Development and initial psychometrics of the Counselor Burnout Inventory. *Measurement and Evaluation in Counseling and Development, 40,* 142–154.

Lee, S.-Y., & Tang, N.-S. (2006). Bayesian analysis of structural equation models with mixed exponential family and ordered categorical data. *British Journal of Mathematical and Statistical Psychology, 59,* 151–172.

Leighton, J. P. (2004). Avoiding misconception, misuse, and missed opportunities: The collection of verbal reports in educational achievement testing. *Educational Measurement: Issues and Practice, 23,* 6–15.

Lennon, R. T. (1956). Assumptions underlying the use of content validity. *Educational and Psychological Measurement, 16,* 294–304.

Levine, D. W., Kaplan, R. M., Kripke, D. F., Bowen, D. J., Naughton, M. J., & Shumaker, S. A. (2003). Factor structure and measurement invariance of the Women's Health Initiative Insomnia Rating Scale, *Psychological Assessment, 15,* 123–136.

Li, F., Duncan, T. E.; Harmer, P., Acock, A., & Stoolmiller, M. (1998). Analyzing measurement models of latent variables through multilevel confirmatory factor analysis and hierarchical linear modeling approaches. *Structural Equation Modeling, 5,* 294–306.

Li, H. (1997). A unifying expression for the maximal reliability of a linear composite. *Psychometrika, 62,* 245–249.

Li, H., Rosenthal, R., & Rubin, D. B. (1996). Reliability of measurement in psychology: From Spearman–Brown to maximal reliability. *Psychological Methods, 1,* 98–107.

Libbrecht, N., Lievens, F., & Schollaert, E. (2010). Measurement equivalence of the Wong and Law Emotional Intelligence Scale across self and other ratings. *Educational and Psychological Measurement, 70,* 1007–1020.

Lievens, F., Anseel, F., Harris, M. M., & Eisenberg, J. (2007). Measurement invariance of the Pay Satisfaction Questionnaire across three countries. *Educational and Psychological Measurement, 67,* 1042–1051.

Linacre, J. M. (1989). *Facets computer program for many-facet Rasch measurement*. Chicago, IL: MESA Press.

Linacre, J. M. (1994). *Many-facet Rasch measurement*. Chicago, IL: MESA Press.

Linacre, J. M. (1999a). Category disordering versus step (threshold) disordering. *Rasch Measurement Transactions, 13,* 675.

Linacre, J. M. (1999b). Investigating rating scale category utility. *Journal of Outcome Measurement, 3,* 103–122.

Linacre, J. M. (2002). Optimizing rating scale category effectiveness. *Journal of Applied Measurement, 3,* 85–106.

Linacre, J. M. (2006). *FACETS Rasch measurement computer program* (Version 3.6). Chicago, IL: Winsteps.com.

Linacre J. M., & Tennant A. (2009). More about critical eigenvalue sizes in standardized-residual principal components analysis (PCA). *Rasch Measurement Transactions, 23,* 12–28.

Linacre, J. M., & Wright, B. D. (1998). *A user's guide to BIGSTEPS*. Chicago, IL: MESA Press.

Linacre, J. M., & Wright, B. D. (1999). *A user's guide to Winsteps/Ministep: Rasch model computer programs*. Chicago, IL: MESA Press.

Linacre, J. M., & Wright, B. D. (2000). *WINSTEPS computer program for Rasch measurement*. Chicago, IL: MESA Press.

Little, T. D. (1997). Mean and covariance structures (MACS) analyses of cross-cultural data: Practical and theoretical issues. *Multivariate Behavioral Research, 32,* 53–76.

Little, T. D., Cunningham, W. A., Shahar, G., & Widaman, K. F. (2002). To parcel or not to parcel: Exploring the question, weighing the merits. *Structural Equation Modeling, 9,* 151–173.

Liu, O. L., & Rijmen, F. (2008). A modified procedure for parallel analysis of ordered categorical data. *Behavior Research Methods, 40,* 556–562.

Loevinger, J. (1957). Objective tests as instruments of psychological theory. *Psychological Reports, 3*(Monograph Supplement 9), 635–694.

Lopez, F. G., Morúa, W., & Rice, K. G. (2007). Factor structure, stability, and predictive validity of college students' Relationship Self-Efficacy Scale. *Measurement and Evaluation in Counseling and Development, 40,* 80–96.

Lord, F. M. (1953). An application of confidence intervals and of maximum likelihood to the estimation of an examinee's ability. *Psychometrika, 18,* 57–76.

Lorenzo-Seva, U., & Ferrando, P. J. (2006). FACTOR: A computer program to fit the exploratory factor analysis model. *Behavior Research Methods, Instruments, and Computers, 38,* 88–91.

Lowe, N. K., & Ryan-Wenger, N. M. (1992). Beyond Campbell and Fiske: Assessment of convergent and discriminant validity. *Research in Nursing & Health, 15,* 67–75.

Lubinski, D., Tellegen, A., & Butcher, J. N. (1983). Masculinity, femininity, and androgyny viewed and assessed as distinct concepts. *Journal of Personality and Social Psychology, 44,* 428–439.

Ludlow, L. H., Enterline, S. E., & Cochran-Smith, M. (2008). Learning to Teach for Social Justice–Beliefs scale: An application of Rasch measurement principles. *Measurement and Evaluation in Counseling and Development, 40,* 194–214.

Ludlow, L. H., & Haley, S. M. (1992). Polytomous Rasch models for behavioral assessment: The Tufts Assessment of Motor Performance. In M. Wilson (Ed.), *Objective measurement I: Theory and practice* (pp. 121–137). Norwood, NJ: Ablex.

MacCallum, R. C. (1986). Specification searches in covariance structure modeling. *Psychological Bulletin, 100,* 107–120.

MacCallum, R. C., Roznowski, M., Necowitz, L. B. (1992). Model modifications in covariance structure analysis: The problem of capitalization on chance. *Psychological Bulletin, 111,* 490–504.

MacCallum, R. C., Wegener, D. T., Uchino, B. N., & Fabrigar, L. R. (1993). The problem of equivalent models in application of covariance structure analysis. *Psychological Bulletin, 114,* 185–199.

MacCallum, R. C., Widaman, K. F., Zhang, S., & Hong S. (1999). Sample size in factor analysis. *Psychological Methods, 4,* 84–99.

Mann, H. M., Rutstein, D. W., & Hancock, G. R. (2009). The potential for differential findings among invariance testing strategies for multisample measured variable path models. *Educational and Psychological Measurement, 69,* 603–612.

Marcoulides, G. A., Emrich, C., & Marcoulides, L. D. (2008). Testing for multigroup invariance of the Computer Anxiety Scale. *Educational and Psychological Measurement, 68,* 325–334.

Mardia, K. V. (1970). Measures of multivariate skewness and kurtosis with applications. *Biometrika, 36,* 519–530.

Mardia, K. V. (1974). Applications of some measures of multivariate skewness and kurtosis in testing normality and robustness studies. *Sankhyā, 36*(B, Pt. 2), 115–128.

Mardia, K. V. (1980). Tests of univariate and multivariate normality. In P. R. Krishnaiah, (Ed.), *Handbook of statistics* (Vol. 1, pp. 279–320). Amsterdam, The Netherlands: Wiley.

Mardia, K. V., Kent, J. T., & Bibby, J. M. (1979). *Multivariate analysis.* London, England: Academic Press.

Marsh, H. W. (1987). The hierarchical structure of self-concept and the application of hierarchical confirmatory factor analysis. *Journal of Educational Measurement, 24,* 17–39.

Marsh, H. W. (1988). Multitrait–multimethod analyses. In J. P. Keeves (Ed.), *Educational research methodology, measurement and evaluation: An international handbook* (pp. 570–580). Oxford, England: Pergamon.

Marsh, H. W. (1989). Confirmatory factor analyses of multitrait–multimethod data: Many problems and a few solutions. *Applied Psychological Measurement, 13,* 335–361.

Marsh, H. W. (1990). Confirmatory factor analysis of multitrait–multimethod data: The construct validation of multidimensional self-concept responses. *Journal of Personality, 58,* 661–692.

Marsh, H. W. (1993). Multitrait–multimethod analyses: Inferring each trait–method combination with multiple indicators. *Applied Measurement in Education, 6,* 49–81.

Marsh, H. W. (1996). Positive and negative global self-esteem: A substantively meaningful distinction or artifactors? *Journal of Personality and Social Psychology, 70,* 810–819.

Marsh, H. W., & Bailey, M. (1991). Confirmatory factor analyses of multitrait–multimethod data: A comparison of the behavior of alternative models. *Applied Psychological Measurement, 15,* 47–70.

Marsh, H. W., Balla, J. R., & McDonald, R. P. (1988). Goodness-of-fit indexes in confirmatory factor analysis: The effect of sample size. *Psychological Bulletin, 103,* 391–410.

Marsh, H. W., & Grayson, D. (1995). Latent variable models of multitrait–multimethod data. In R. H. Hoyle (Ed.), *Structural equation modeling: Concepts, issues, and applications* (pp. 177–198). Thousand Oaks, CA: Sage.

Marsh, H. W., Hau, K.-T., Balla, J. R., & Grayson, D. (1998). Is more ever too much? The number of indicators per factor in confirmatory factor analysis. *Multivariate Behavioral Research, 33,* 181–220.

Marsh, H.W., Hau, K. T., & Wen, Z. (2004). In search of golden rules: Comment on hypothesis testing approaches to setting cutoff values for fit indexes and dangers in overgeneralizing findings. *Structural Equation Modeling, 11,* 320–341.

Marsh, H. W., & Hocevar, D. (1983). Confirmatory factor analysis of multitrait–multimethod matrices. *Journal of Educational Measurement, 20,* 231–248.

Marsh, H. W., & Hocevar, D. (1985). The application of confirmatory factor analysis to the study of self-concept: First- and higher order factor structures and their invariance across age groups. *Psychological Bulletin, 97,* 562–582.

Marsh, H. W., & Hocevar, D. (1988). A new more powerful approach to multitrait–multimethod analyses: Application of second-order confirmatory factor analysis. *Journal of Applied Psychology, 73,* 107–117.

Marsh, H. W., Muthén, B., Asparouhov, T., Lüdtke, O., Robitzsch, A., Morin, A. J. S., & Trautwein, U. (2009). Exploratory structural equation modeling, integrating CFA and EFA: Application to student's evaluations of university teaching. *Structural Equation Modeling, 16,* 439–476.

Masters, G. N. (1982). A Rasch model for partial credit scoring. *Psychometrika, 47,* 149–174.

Masters, G. N. (1988).The analysis of partial credit scoring. *Applied Measurement in Education, 1,* 279–297.

Masters, J. R. (1974). The relationship between number of response categories and reliability of Likert-type questionnaires. *Journal of Educational Measurement, 11,* 49–53.

Maydeu-Olivares, A., & Coffman, D. L. (2006). Random intercept item factor analysis. *Psychological Methods, 11,* 344–362.

McCarney, S. B., & Arthaud, T. J. (2004a). *Attention Deficit Disorders Evaluation Scale—Third Edition—Home Version technical manual*. Columbia, MO: Hawthorne Educational Services.

McCarney, S. B., & Arthaud, T. J. (2004b). *Attention Deficit Disorders Evaluation Scale—Third Edition—School Version technical manual*. Columbia, MO: Hawthorne Educational Services.

McGraw, K. O., & Wong, S. P. (1996). Forming inferences about some intraclass correlation coefficients. *Psychological Methods, 1,* 30–46 [Correction in *1*(4), 390].

Meade, A. W., & Kroustalis, C. M. (2006). Problems with item parceling for confirmatory factor analytic tests of measurement invariance. *Organizational Research Methods, 9,* 369–403.

Medical Outcomes Trust Scientific Advisory Committee. (1995). Instrument review criteria. *Medical Outcomes Trust Bulletin*, 1–4.

Meece, J. L., & Jones, M. G. (1996). Gender differences in motivation and strategy use in science: Are girls rote learners? *Journal of Research in Science Teaching, 33,* 393–406.

Merbitz, C., Morris J., & Grip, J. C. (1989). Ordinal scales and foundations of misinference. *Archives of Physical Medicine and Rehabilitation, 70,* 308–332.

Meredith, W. (1964). Rotation to achieve factorial invariance. *Psychometrika, 29,* 187–206.

Meredith, W. (1993). Measurement invariance, factor analysis, and factorial invariance. *Psychometrika, 58*, 525–543.

Meredith, W., & Teresi, J. (2006). An essay on measurement and factorial invariance. *Medical Care* (Suppl. 3), S69–S77.

Messick, S. (1989). Validity. In R. L. Linn (Ed.), *Educational measurement* (3rd ed., pp. 13–103). New York, NY: Macmillan.

Messick, S. (1995). Validity of psychological assessment: Validation of inferences from persons' responses and performances as scientific inquiry into score meaning. *American Psychologist, 50,* 741–749.

Miller, G. A., & Lazowski, M. (1999). *Manual for the SASSI–3*. Springville, IN: SASSI Institute.

Millsap, R. E. (1997). Invariance in measurement and prediction: Their relationship in the single-factor case. *Psychological Methods, 2,* 248–260.

Millsap, R. E. (1998). Group differences in regression intercepts: Implications for factorial invariance. *Multivariate Behavioral Research*, *33,* 403–424.

Millsap, R. E. (2007). Invariance in measurement and prediction revisited. *Psychometrika, 72,* 461–473.

Millsap, R. E., & Everson, H. T. (1991). Confirmatory measurement model comparisons using latent means. *Multivariate Behavioral Research, 26,* 479–497.

Millsap, R. E., & Everson, H. T. (1993). Methodology review: Statistical approaches for assessing bias. *Applied Psychological Measurement, 17,* 297–334.

Millsap, R. E., & Kwok, O.-M. (2004). Evaluating the impact of partial factorial invariance on selection in two populations. *Psychological Methods, 9,* 93–115.

Mislevy, R. J. (1986). Recent development in the factor analysis of categorical variables. *Journal of Educational Statistics, 11,* 3–31.

Mislevy, R. J. (1993). Foundations of a new theory. In N. Frederiksen, R. J. Mislevy, & I. Bejar (Eds.), *Test theory for a new generation of tests* (pp. 19–39). Hillsdale, NJ: Erlbaum.

Mislevy, R. J. (1994). Evidence and inference in educational assessment. *Psychometrika, 59,* 439–468.

Mislevy, R. J. (1995). Probability-based inference in cognitive diagnosis. In P. D. Nichols, S. F. Chipman, & R. L. Brennan (Eds.), *Cognitively Diagnostic Assessment* (pp. 43–71). Hillsdale, NJ: Erlbaum.

Motl, R. W., Conroy, D. E., & Horan, P. M. (2000). The Social Physique Anxiety Scale: An example of the potential consequences of negatively worded items in factorial validity studies. *Journal of Applied Measurement, 1,* 327–345.

Motl, R. W., & DiStefano, C. (2002). Longitudinal invariance of self-esteem and method effects associated with negatively worded items. *Structural Equation Modeling, 9,* 562–578.

Mulaik, S. A. (1990). Blurring the distinction between component analysis and common factor analysis. *Multivariate Behavioral Research, 25*, 53–59.

Muthén, B. O. (1984). A general structural equation model with dichotomous, ordered categorical, and continuous latent variables indicators. *Psychometrika*, *49,* 115–132.

Muthén, B. O. (1994). Multilevel covariance structure analysis. *Sociological Methods and Research, 22,* 376–398.

Muthén, B. O. (2002). Beyond SEM: General latent variable modeling. *Behaviormetrika, 29,* 87–117.

Muthén, B. O., & Kaplan, D. (1992). A comparison of some methodologies for the factor analysis of non-normal Likert variables: A note on the size of the model. *British Journal of Mathematical and Statistical Psychology, 45,* 19–30.

Muthén, L. K., & Muthén, B. O. (2002). How to use a Monte Carlo study to decide on sample size and determine power. *Structural Equation Modeling, 9,* 599–620.

Muthén, L. K., & Muthén, B. O. (2008). *Mplus user's guide*. Los Angeles, CA: Muthén & Muthén.

Narayan, S., & Krosnick, J. A. (1996). Education moderates some response effects in attitude measurement. *Public Opinion Quarterly, 60,* 58–88.

Nasser, F., & Wisenbaker, J. (2003). A Monte Carlo study investigating the impact of item parceling on measures of fit in confirmatory factor analysis. *Educational and Psychological Measurement*, *63,* 729–757.

Nelson, J. M., Canivez, G. L., Lindstrom, W., & Hatt, C. V. (2007). Higher-order exploratory factor analysis of the Reynolds Intellectual Assessment Scales with a referred sample. *Journal of School Psychology, 45,* 439–456.

Nevitt, J., & Hancock, G. R. (2001). Performance of bootstrapping approaches to model test statistics and parameter standard error estimation in structural equation modeling. *Structural Equation Modeling, 8*, 353–377.

Nunnally, J. C. (1978). *Psychometric theory*. New York, NY: McGraw-Hill.

Nunnally, J. C., & Bernstein, I. H. (1994). *Psychometric theory* (3rd ed.). New York, NY: McGraw-Hill.

O'Connor, B. P. (2000). SPSS and SAS programs for determining the number of components using parallel analysis and Velicer's MAP test. *Behavior Research Methods, Instrumentation, and Computers, 32,* 396–402.

Osborn, C. J. (2004). Seven salutary suggestions for counselor stamina. *Journal of Counseling & Development, 82,* 319–328.

Osborn, H. G. (2000). Coefficient alpha and related internal consistency reliability coefficients. *Psychological Methods, 5,* 343–355.

Osgood, C. E. (1962). Studies of the generality of affective meaning systems. *American Psychologist, 17,* 10–28.

Osgood, C. E., May, W. H., & Miron, M. S. (1975). *Cross-cultural universals of affective meaning.* Urbana: University of Illinois Press.

Osgood, C. E., Tannenbaum, P. H., & Suci, G. J. (1957). *The measurement of meaning*. Urbana: University of Illinois Press.

Ostini, R., & Nering, M. L. (2006). *Polytomous item response theory models*. Thousand Oaks, CA: Sage.

Otis, A. S., & Lennon, R. T. (2004). *Manual for the Otis–Lennon School Ability Test–Eighth Edition* (*OLSAT–8*). San Antonio, TX: Psychological Corporation.

Payne, S. L. (1951). *The art of asking questions*. Princeton, NJ: Princeton University Press.

Penfield, R. D. (2005). Unique properties of Rasch model item information functions. *Journal of Applied Measurement, 6,* 355–362.

Petersen, N. S., & Novick, M. R. (1976). An evaluation of some models for culture-fair selection. *Journal of Educational Measurement, 13,* 3–29.

Pett, M. A., Lackey, N. R., & Sullivan, J. J. (2003). *Making sense of factor analysis: The use of factor analysis for instrument development in health care research.* Thousand Oaks, CA: Sage.

Piers, E. V., & Herzberg, D. S. (2002). *Manual for the Piers–Harris Children's Self-Concept Scale—Second Edition*. Los Angeles, CA: Western Psychological Services.

Pistole, M. C., & Roberts, A. (2011). Measuring long-distance romantic relationships: A validity study. *Measurement and Evaluation in Counseling and Development, 44,* 63–76.

Plucker, J. A. (1996). Construct validity evidence for the Student Aspirations Survey. *Journal of Research in Rural Education, 12,* 161–170.

Pomplun, M., & Omar, M. H. (2001). The factorial invariance of a test of reading comprehension across groups of limited English proficiency students. *Applied Measurement in Education, 14,* 261–283.

Preacher, K. J., & MacCallum, R. C. (2003). Repairing Tom Swift's electric factor analysis machine. *Understanding Statistics*, *2*, 13–32.

Presser, S., & Schuman, H. (1980). The measurement of a middle position in attitude surveys. *Public Opinion Quarterly, 44,* 70–86.

Prochaska, J. O., Norcross, J. C., Fowler, J., Follick, M. J., & Abrams, D. B. (1992). Attendance and outcome in a worksite weight control program: Processes and stages of change as process and predictor variables. *Addictive Behaviors, 17,* 35–45.

Rae, G. (2008). A note on using stratified alpha to estimate the composite reliability of a test composed of interrelated nonhomogeneous items. *British Journal of Mathematical and Statistical Psychology, 61,* 515–525.

Raîche, G. (2005). Critical eigenvalue sizes in standardized residual principal component analysis. *Rasch Measurement Transactions, 19,* 1012.

Raju, N. S., & Burke, M. J. (1983). Two new procedures for studying validity generalization. *Journal of Applied Psychology, 68,* 382–395.

Rasch, G. (1960). *Probabilistic models for some intelligence and attainment tests.* Copenhagen, Denmark: Danish Institute for Educational Research. (Expanded edition published in 1980, Chicago, IL: University of Chicago Press)

Rasch, G. (1966). An item analysis which takes individual differences into account. *British Journal of Mathematical and Statistical Psychology, 19,* 49–57.

Raven, J., Raven, J. C., & Court, J. H. (2003). *Manual for Raven's Progressive Matrices and Vocabulary Scales. Section 1: General overview.* San Antonio, TX: Harcourt Assessment.

Raven, J. C. (1936). *Mental tests used in genetic studies: The performance of related individuals on tests mainly educative and mainly reproductive* (Unpublished MSc thesis, University of London, England).

Ravindra, K., & Naik, D. N. (1999). *Applied multivariate statistics with SAS software* (2nd ed.). Cary, NC: SAS Institute.

Raykov, T. (1998). Cronbach's alpha and reliability of composite with interrelated nonhomogenous items. *Applied Psychological Measurement*, *22,* 375–385.

Raykov, T. (2001a). Bias of coefficient alpha for congeneric measures with correlated errors. *Applied Psychological Measurement*, *25,* 69–76.

Raykov, T. (2001b). Estimation of congeneric scale reliability via covariance structure analysis with nonlinear constraints. *British Journal of Mathematical and Statistical Psychology, 54,* 315–323.

Raykov, T. (2002). Examining group differences in reliability of multiple-component measuring instruments. *British Journal of Mathematical and Statistical Psychology, 55,* 145–158.

Raykov, T. (2004). Estimation of maximal reliability: A note on a covariance structure modeling approach. *British Journal of Mathematical and Statistical Psychology*, *57,* 21–27.

Raykov, T. (2007a). Evaluation of criterion validity for scales with congeneric measures. *Measurement and Evaluation in Counseling and Development*, *40,* 110–118.

Raykov, T. (2007b). Evaluation of weighted scale reliability and criterion validity: A latent variable modeling approach. *Measurement and Evaluation in Counseling and Development, 40,* 42–52.

Raykov, T. (2009). Evaluation of scale reliability for unidimensional measures using latent variable modeling. *Measurement and Evaluation in Counseling and Development*, *42,* 223–232.

Raykov, T. (2011). Evaluation of convergent and discriminant validity with multitrait–multimethod correlations. *British Journal of Mathematical and Statistical Psychology*, *64,* 38–52.

Raykov, T., Dimitrov, D. M., & Asparouhov, T. (2010). Evaluation of scale reliability with binary measures using latent variable modeling. *Structural Equation Modeling*, *17,* 265–279.

Raykov, T., & Grayson, D. A. (2003). A test for change of composite reliability in scale development. *Multivariate Behavioral Research, 38,* 143–159.

Raykov, T., & Hancock, G. H. (2005). Examining change in maximal reliability in multiple-component measuring instruments. *British Journal of Mathematical & Statistical Psychology*, *58,* 65–82.

Raykov, T., & Marcoulides, G. A. (2006a). *A first course in structural equation modeling* (2nd ed.). Mahwah, NJ: Erlbaum.

Raykov, T., & Marcoulides, G. A. (2006b). On multilevel model reliability estimation from the perspective of structural equation modeling. *Structural Equation Modeling, 13,* 130–141.

Raykov, T., & Shrout, P. E. (2002). Reliability of scales with general structure: Point and interval estimation using a structural equation modeling approach. *Structural Equation Modeling, 9,* 195–212.

Reichardt, C. S., & Coleman, S. C. (1995). The criteria for convergent and discriminant validity in a multitrait–multimethod matrix. *Multivariate Behavioral Research, 30,* 513–538.

Reips, U. D., & Funke, F. (2008). Interval-level measurement with visual analog scales in internet-based research: VAS generator. *Behavior Research Methods, 40,* 699–704.

Reise, S. P., Waller, N. G., & Comrey, A. L. (2000). Factor analysis and scale revision. *Psychological Assessment, 12*, 287–297.

Rensvold, R. B., & Cheung, G. W. (2001). Testing for metric invariance using structural equations models: Solving the standardization problem. In C. A. Schriesheim & L. L. Neider (Eds.), *Research in management* (pp. 25–50). Greenwich, CT: Information Age Publishers.

Reynolds, W. M. (2002). *Manual for the Reynolds Adolescent Depression Scale—Second Edition* (RADS–2). Lutz, FL: Psychological Assessment Resources.

Rice, K. G., & Aldea, M. A. (2006). State dependence and trait stability of perfectionism: A short-term longitudinal study. *Journal of Counseling Psychology, 53,* 205–212.

Ridley, D., & Novak, J. (1983). Sex-related differences in high school science and mathematics enrollments: Do they give males a critical headstart toward science- and math-related careers? *Alberta Journal of Educational Research, 29,* 308–318.

Roessler, R., Rumrill, P., & Hennessey, M. (2001). *Employment concerns of people with multiple sclerosis: Building a national employment agenda*. New York, NY: National Multiple Sclerosis Society.

Rogers, C. R. (1959). A theory of therapy, personality and interpersonal relationships as developed in the client-centered framework. In S. Koch (Ed.), *Psychology: A study of a science. Formulations of the person and the social context* (Vol. 3, pp. 181–256). New York, NY: McGraw-Hill.

Rogers, C. R. (1961). *On becoming a person: A therapist's view of psychotherapy.* London, England: Constable.

Rost, J. (1988). Measuring attitudes with a threshold model drawing on a traditional scaling concept. *Applied Psychological Measurement, 12*, 397–409.

Rummel, R. J. (1970). *Applied factor analysis*. Evanston, IL: Northwestern University Press.

Safir, M. A. (1937). A comparative study of scales constructed by three psychological methods. *Psychometrika, 2,* 179–199.

Salvia, J., & Ysseldyke, J. E. (2004). *Assessment in special and inclusive education* (9th ed.). Boston, MA: Houghton Mifflin.

Samejima, F. (1969). Estimation of latent ability using a response pattern of graded scores. *Psychometrika Monograph Supplement*, No. 17.

Saris, W. E., & Aalberts, C. (2003). Different explanations for correlated disturbance terms in MTMM studies. *Structural Equation Modeling, 10,* 193–213.

Saris, W. E., Satorra, A., & Coenders, G. (2004). A new approach to evaluating the quality of measurement instruments: The split-ballot MTMM design. *Sociological Methodology, 34,* 311–347.

Sass, D. (2010). Factor loading estimation error and stability using exploratory factor analysis. *Educational and Psychological Measurement, 70,* 557–577.

Satorra, A. (2000). Scaled and adjusted restricted tests in multi-sample analysis of moment structures. In R. D. H. Heijmans, D. S. G. Pollock, & A. Satorra (Eds.), *Innovations in multivariate statistical analysis. A Festschrift for Heiz Neudecker* (pp. 233–247). London, England: Kluwer Academic.

Satorra, A., & Bentler, P. M. (1994). Corrections to test statistics and standard errors in covariance structure analysis. In A.von Eye & C. C. Clogg (Eds.), *Latent variables analysis: Applications for developmental research* (pp. 399–419). Thousand Oaks, CA: Sage.

Satorra, A., & Bentler, P. M. (1999). *A scaled difference chi-square test statistic for moment structure analysis* (UCLA Statistic Series, No. 260). Retrieved from UCLA Statistics Electronic Publications website: http://preprints.stat.ucla.edu

Satorra, A., & Bentler, P. M. (2001). A scaled difference chi-square test statistic for moment structure analysis. *Psychometrika, 66,* 507–514.

Scheier, M. F., & Carver, C. S. (1985). Optimism, coping, and health: Assessment and implications of generalized outcome expectancies. *Health Psychology, 4,* 219–247.

Schmid, J., & Leiman, J. M. (1957). The development of hierarchical factor solutions. *Psychometrika, 22,* 53–61.

Schmidt, F. L., & Hunter, J. E. (1977). Development of a general solution to the problem of validity generalization. *Journal of Applied Psychology, 62,* 529–540.

Schmidt, F. L., Hunter, J. E., & Caplan, J. R. (1981). Validity generalization results for two groups in the petroleum industry. *Journal of Applied Psychology, 66,* 261–273.

Schonemann, P. H., & Tucker, L. R. (1967). A maximum likelihood solution for the method of successive intervals allowing for unequal stimulus dispersions. *Psychometrika, 32,* 403–427.

Schumacker, R. E., & Lomax, R. G. (1996). *A beginner's guide to structural equation modeling*. Mahwah, NJ: Erlbaum.

Schwarz, G. (1978). Estimating the dimension of a model. *Annals of Statistics, 6,* 461–464.

Schwarzer, R. (2001). Social–cognitive factors in changing health-related behavior. *Current Directions in Psychological Science, 10,* 47–51.

Schwarzer, R., & Luszczynska, A. (2008). *Perceived self-efficacy*. Available at National Cancer Institute website: http://cancercontrol.cancer.gov/brp/constructs/self-efficacy/self-efficacy.pdf

Scullen, S. E. (1999). Using confirmatory factor analysis of correlated uniquenesses to estimate method variance in multitrait–multimethod matrices. *Organizational Research Methods, 2,* 275–292.

Scullen, S. E., Mount, M. K., & Goff, M. (2000). Understanding the latent structure of job performance ratings. *Journal of Applied Psychology, 85,* 956–970.

Searing, L. M. (2008). *Family functioning scale validation: A Rasch analysis* (Doctoral dissertation, University of Illinois at Chicago). Source: DAI-B 70/01; Publication No. 3345542. Available at http://gradworks.umi.com/33/45/3345542.html

Shavelson, R. J., & Webb, N. M. (1991). *Generalizability theory: A primer*. Newbury Park, CA: Sage.

Sheperis, C. J. (2001). *The development of an instrument to measure racial identity in juvenile offenders* (Unpublished doctoral dissertation). University of Florida, Gainesville.

Sheperis, C. J., Davis, C., & Doggett, R. A. (2007). How tests are constructed. In B. T. Erford (Ed.), *Assessment for counselors* (pp. 319–355). Boston, MA: Lahaska Press.

Shrout, P. E., & Fleiss, J. L. (1979). Intraclass correlations: Uses in assessing rater reliability. *Psychological Bulletin, 86,* 420–428.

Simpson, E. H. (1951). The interpretation of interaction in contingency tables. *Journal of the Royal Statistical Society (Series B), 13,* 238–241.

Smith, E. V., Jr. (2002). Detecting and evaluating multidimensionality using fit statistics and principal component analysis of residuals. *Journal of Applied Measurement, 3,* 205–231.

Smith, E. V., Jr. (2005). Effect of item redundancy on Rasch item and person estimates. *Journal of Applied Measurement, 6,* 147–163.

Smith, E. V., Jr., & Johnson, B. D. (2000). Attention Deficit Hyperactivity Disorder: Scaling and standard settings using Rasch measurement. *Journal of Applied Measurement, 1,* 3–24.

Smith, E. V., Jr., & Smith, R. M. (Eds.). (2007). *Rasch measurement: Advanced and specialized applications*. Maple Grove, MN: JAM Press.

Smith, E. V., Jr., & Stone, G. E. (Eds.). (2009). *Criterion-reference testing: Practice analysis to score reporting using Rasch measurement models*. Maple Grove, MN: JAM Press.

Smith, E. V., Jr., Wakely, M. B., de Kruif, R. E. L., & Swartz, C. W. (2003). Optimizing rating scales for self-efficacy (and other) research. *Educational and Psychological Measurement, 63,* 369–391.

Smith, R. M. (1991). The distributional properties of Rasch item fit statistics. *Educational and Psychological Measurement, 51,* 541–565.

Smith, R. M. (1994). Detecting item bias in the Rasch rating scale model. *Educational and Psychological Measurement, 54,* 886–896.

Smith, R. M. (1996a). A comparison of methods for determining dimensionality in Rasch measurement. *Structural Equation Modeling, 3,* 25–40.

Smith, R. M. (1996b). Polytomous mean-square fit statistics. *Rasch Measurement Transactions, 10,* 516–517.

Smith, R. M. (2000). Fit analysis in latent trait measurement models. *Journal of Applied Measurement, 1,* 199–218.

Smith, R. M. (2004). Fit analysis in latent trait measurement models. In E. V. Smith, Jr., & R. M. Smith (Eds.), *Introduction to Rasch measurement* (pp. 73–92). Maple Grove, MN: JAM Press.

Smith, R. M., & Miao, C. Y. (1994). Assessing unidimensionality for Rasch measurement. In M. Wilson (Ed.), *Objective measurement II: Theory into practice* (pp. 316–327). Greenwich, CT: Ablex.

Smith, R. M., Schumacker, R. E., & Bush, M. J. (1998). Using item mean squares to evaluate fit to the Rasch model. *Journal of Outcome Measurement, 2,* 66–78.

Smith, T. B., Rosenstein, I., & Granaas, M. M. (2001). Intake screening with the Self-Rating Depression Scale in a university counseling center. *Journal of College Counseling, 4*, 133–141.

Snider, J. G., & Osgood, C. E. (1969). *Semantic differential technique: A sourcebook.* Chicago, IL: Aldine.

Snow, R. E., & Lohman, D. F. (1989). Implications of cognitive psychology for educational measurement. In R. Linn (Ed.), *Educational measurement* (3rd ed., pp. 263–331). New York, NY: Macmillan.

Snyder, C. R. (1997). *Marital Satisfaction Inventory—Revised manual.* Los Angeles, CA: Western Psychological Services.

Spearman, C. (1927). *The abilities of man: Their nature and measurement.* New York, NY: Macmillan.

Spielberger, C. D., Gorsuch, R. L., Lushene, R., Vagg, P. R., & Jacobs, G. A. (1983). *Manual for State–Trait Anxiety Inventory.* Palo Alto, CA: Consulting Psychologists Press.

Stacy, A. W., Widaman, K. F., Hayes, R., & DiMateo, M. R. (1985). Validity of self-reports of alcohol and other drug use: A multitrait–multimethod assessment. *Journal of Personality and Social Psychology, 49,* 219–232.

Steger, M. F. (2007). Structural validity of the Life Regard Index. *Measurement and Evaluation in Counseling and Development, 40,* 97–108.

Steger, M. F., Frazier, P., Oishi, S., & Kaler, M. (2006). The Meaning in Life Questionnaire: Assessing the presence of and search for meaning in life. *Journal of Counseling Psychology, 53,* 80–93.

Steiger, J. H. (1990a). Some additional thoughts on components, factors, and factor indeterminacy. *Multivariate Behavioral Research, 25*, 41–45.

Steiger, J. H. (1990b). Structural model evaluation and modification: An interval estimation approach. *Multivariate Behavioral Research, 25,* 173–180.

Steinmetz, H., Schmidt, P., Tina-Booh, A., Wieczorek, S., & Schwartz, S. H. (2009). Testing measurement invariance using multigroup CFA: Differences between educational groups in human values measurement. *Quality and Quantity, 43,* 599–616.

Stevens, J. P. (2002). *Applied multivariate statistics for the social sciences* (4th ed.). Mahwah, NJ: Erlbaum.

Stowe, R. W. (1985). Convergent and discriminant validity of Crites's Career Maturity Inventory Attitude Scale, Counseling Form B-1. *Educational and Psychological Measurement, 45,* 763–770.

Su, Y. H., Sheu, C. F., & Wang, W. C. (2007). Computing confidence intervals of item fit in the family of Rasch models using the bootstrap method. *Journal of Applied Measurement, 8,* 190–203.

Subkoviak, M. J. (1976). Estimating reliability from a single administration of a mastery test. *Journal of Educational Measurement, 13,* 265–276.

Symonds, P. M. (1931). *Diagnosing personality and conduct.* New York, NY: Appleton Century.

Tabachnick, B. G., & Fidell, L. S. (2007). *Using multivariate statistics* (5th ed.). Boston, MA: Pearson Education.

Tanaka, J. S. (1987). "How big is big enough?": Sample size and goodness of fit in structural equation models with latent variables. *Child Development, 58,* 134–146.

Taris, T. W., Bok, I. A., & Meijer, Z. Y. (1998). Assessing stability and change of psychometric properties of multi-item concepts across different situations: A general approach. *Journal of Psychology, 132,* 301–316.

Tatsuoka, K. K., Corter, J. E., & Tatsuoka, C. (2004). Patterns of diagnosed mathematical content and process skills in TIMSS–R across a sample of 20 countries. American *Educational Research Journal, 41,* 901–926.

Tatsuoka, K. K., & Tatsuoka, M. M. (1983). Spotting erroneous rules of operation by the individual consistency index. *Journal of Educational Measurement, 20,* 221–230.

Taylor, J. B., Ptacek, M., Carithers, M., Griffin, C., & Coyne, L. (1972). Rating scales as measures of clinical judgment III: Judgments of the self on personality inventory scales and direct ratings. *Educational and Psychological Measurement, 32,* 543–557.

Templin, J. L., & Henson, R. A. (2006). Measurement of psychological disorders using cognitive diagnosis models. *Psychological Methods*, *11,* 287–305.

Thompson, B. (1990). SECONDOR: A program that computes a second-order principal components analysis and various interpretation aids. *Educational and Psychological Measurement*, *50,* 575–580.

Thompson, B. (2004). *Exploratory and confirmatory factor analysis: Understanding concepts and applications*. Washington, DC: American Psychological Association.

Thompson, B., & Daniel, L. G. (1996). Factor analytic evidence for the construct validity of scores: An historical overview and some guidelines. *Educational and Psychological Measurement, 56*, 197–208.

Thompson, D. R., Webster, R. A., & Meddis, R. (1990). In-hospital counseling for first-time myocardial infarction patients and spouses: Effects on satisfaction. *Journal of Advanced Nursing, 15,* 1064–1069.

Thorndike, E. L. (1918). The nature, purposes, and general methods of measurements of educational products. In *National Society for the Study of Educational Products: Seventeenth Yearbook* (pp. 16–24). Bloomington, IL: Public School Publishing Company.

Thorndike, R. L. (2005). *Measurement and evaluation in psychology and education* (6th ed.). Upper Saddle River, NJ: Prentice Hall.

Thurstone, L. L. (1927a). A law of comparative judgment. *Psychological Review, 34,* 278–286.

Thurstone, L. L. (1927b). The method of paired comparisons for social values. *Journal of Abnormal and Social Psychology, 21,* 384–400.

Thurstone, L. L. (1928). Attitudes can be measured. *American Journal of Sociology, 33,* 529–554.

Thurstone, L. L. (1947). *Multiple factor analysis*. Chicago, IL: University of Chicago Press.

Tomás, J. M., & Oliver, A. (1999). Rosenberg's Self-Esteem Scale: Two factors or method effects. *Structural Equation Modeling, 6,* 84–98.

Torgerson, W. S. (1958). *The theory and methods of scaling*. New York, NY: Wiley.

Tovar, E., & Simon, M. A. (2010). Factorial structure and invariance analysis of the Sense of Belonging Scale. *Measurement and Evaluation in Counseling and Development, 43,* 199–217.

Tovar, E., & Simon, M. A., & Lee, H. B. (2009). Development and validation of the College Mattering Inventory with diverse urban college students. *Measurement and Evaluation in Counseling and Development, 42,* 154–178.

Trochim, W. M. (2006). *The research methods knowledge base* (2nd ed.). Retrieved December 12, 2008, from http://www.socialresearchmethods.net/kb

Tucker, L. R., & Lewis, C. (1973). A reliability coefficient for maximum likelihood factor analysis. *Psychometrika, 38,* 1–10.

Turner, S. L., Alliman-Brissett, A., Lapan, R. T., Udipi, S., & Ergun, D. (2003). The Career-Related Parent Support Scale. *Measurement and Evaluation in Counseling and Development, 36,* 83–94.

Uebersax, J. S. (2006). *Likert scales: Dispelling the confusion*. Retrieved December 12, 2008, from http://ourworld.compuserve.com/homepages/jsuebersax/likert2.htm

Vandenberg, R. J., & Lance, C. E. (2000). A review and synthesis of the measurement invariance literature: Suggestions, practices, and recommendations for organizational research. *Organizational Research Methods, 3,* 4–70.

Velicer, W. F. (1976). Determining the number of components from the matrix of partial correlations. *Psychometrika, 31,* 321–327.

Velicer, W. F., & Jackson, D. N. (1990). Component analysis versus common factor analysis: Some issues in selecting an appropriate procedure. *Multivariate Behavioral Research, 25,* 1–28.

Vigliocco, G. (2000). Language processing: The anatomy of meaning and syntax. *Current Biology, 10,* R78–R80.

von Davier, M. (2005). *A general diagnostic model applied to language testing data* (ETS Research Report No. RR-05-16). Princeton, NJ: Educational Testing Service.

Waller, N. G. (2001). *MicroFACT 2.0: A microcomputer factor analysis program for ordered polytomous data and mainframe size problems* [Computer software and manual]. St. Paul, MN: Assessment Systems Corporation.

Wang, T. (1998). Weights that maximize reliability under a congeneric model. *Applied Psychological Measurement, 22,* 179–187.

Ward, W. C. (1982). A comparison of free-response and multiple-choice forms of verbal aptitude tests. *Applied Psychological Measurement, 6,* 1–11.

Wechsler, D. (1999). *Manual for the Wechsler Abbreviated Scale of Intelligence (WASI)*. San Antonio, TX: Psychological Corporation.

Welch, C., & Hoover, H. D. (1993). Procedures for extending item bias techniques to polytomously scored items. *Applied Measurement in Education, 6,* 1–19.

Werts, C. E., Grabdy, J., & Schabacker, W. H. (1980). A confirmatory approach to calibration congeneric measures. *Multivariate Behavioral Research, 15,* 109–122.

Westby, C. E. (1994). The effects of culture on genre, structure, and style of oral and written texts. In G. P. Wallach & K. G. Butler (Eds.), *Language learning disabilities in school-age children and adolescents* (pp. 180–218). New York, NY: Merrill/Macmillan.

Wewers, M. E., & Lowe, N. K. (1990). A critical review of visual analog scales in the measurement of clinical phenomena. *Research in Nursing & Health, 13,* 227–236.

Whiston, S. C. (2005). *Principles and applications of assessment in counseling* (2nd ed.). Belmont, CA: Thomson Brooks/Cole.

Whitman, D. S., Van Rooy, D. L., Viswesvaran, C., & Kraus, E. (2009). Testing the second-order factor structure and measurement equivalence of the Wong and Law Emotional Intelligence Scale across gender and ethnicity. *Educational and Psychological Measurement, 69,* 1059–1074.

Whitney, D. R. (1978). An alternative test for use with Likert-type scales. *Educational and Psychological Measurement, 38,* 15–18.

Widaman, K. F. (1985). Hierarchically nested covariance structure models for multitrait–multimethod data. *Applied Psychological Measurement, 9,* 1–26.

Widaman, K. F. (1993). Common factor analysis versus principal component analysis: Differential bias in representing model parameters? *Multivariate Behavioral Research, 28,* 263–311.

Widaman, K. F., & Reise, S. P. (1997). Exploring the measurement invariance of psychological instruments: Applications in the substance use domain. In K. J. Bryant, M. Windle, & S. G. West (Eds.), *The science of prevention: Methodological advances from alcohol and substance abuse research* (pp. 281–324). Washington, DC: American Psychological Association.

Williams, L. J., & Anderson, S. E. (1994). An alternative approach to method effects by using latent-variable models: Applications in organizational behavior research. *Journal of Applied Psychology, 79,* 323–331.

Wilson, D., Wood, R., & Gibbons, R. D. (1991). *TESTFACT: Test scoring, item statistics, and item factor analysis* [Computer software]. Mooresville, IN: Scientific Software.

Wilson, M. (2005). *Constructing measures: An item response modeling approach*. Mahwah, NJ: Erlbaum.

Windle, M., & Dumenci, L. (1999). The factorial structure and construct validity of the Psychopathy Check List—Revised (PCL–R) among alcoholic inpatients. *Structural Equation Modeling, 6,* 372–393.

Wirth, R. J., & Edwards, M. C. (2007). Item factor analysis: Current approaches and future directions. *Psychological Methods, 12,* 58–79.

Wolfe, E. W. (2008). RBF.sas (Rasch Bootstrap Fit): A SAS macro for estimating critical values for Rasch model fit statistics. *Applied Psychological Measurement, 32,* 535–586.

Wolfe, E. W., & Nogle, S. (2002). Development of measurability and importance scales for the NATA Athletic Training Educational Competencies. *Journal of Applied Measurement, 3,* 431–454.

Wolfe, E. W., Ray, L. M., & Harris, D. C. (2004). A Rasch analysis of three measures of teacher perception generated from the school and staffing survey. *Educational and Psychological Measurement, 64,* 842–860.

Wolfe, E. W., & Smith, E. V., Jr. (2007a). Instrument development tools and activities for measure validation using Rasch models: Part I Instrument development tools. *Journal of Applied Measurement, 8,* 97–123.

Wolfe, E. W., & Smith, E. V., Jr. (2007b). Instrument development tools and activities for measure validation using Rasch models: Part II Validation activities. *Journal of Applied Measurement, 8,* 204–234.

Wood, A. M., Linley, P. A., Maltby, J., Baliousis, M., & Joseph, S. (2008). The authentic personality: A theoretical and empirical conceptualization and the development of the Authenticity Scale. *Journal of Counseling Psychology, 55,* 385–399.

Wood, J. M., Tataryn, D. J., & Gorsuch, R. L. (1996). Effects of under- and overextraction on principal axis factor analysis with varimax rotation. *Psychological Methods, 1,* 354–365.

Wothke, W. A. (1993). Nonpositive definite matrices in structural modeling. In K. A. Bollen & J. S. Long (Eds.), *Testing structural equation models* (pp. 256–293). Newbury Park, CA: Sage.

Wright, B. D. (1994). Rasch sensitivity and Thurstone insensitivity to graded responses. *Rasch Measurement Transactions, 8,* 382–383.

Wright, B. D., & Linacre, J. M. (1989). Observations are always ordinal; measurement, however, must be interval. *Archives of Physical Medicine and Rehabilitation, 70,* 857–860.

Wright, B. D., & Linacre, J. M. (1992). Combining and splitting categories. *Rasch Measurement Transactions, 6,* 233–235.

Wright, B. D., & Linacre, J. M. (1994). Reasonable mean-square fit values. *Rasch Measurement Transactions, 8,* 370.

Wright, B. D., & Masters, G. N. (1982). *Rating scale analysis*. Chicago, IL: MESA Press.

Wright, B. D., & Panchapakesan, N. (1969). A procedure for sample-free item analysis. *Educational and Psychological Measurement, 29,* 23–48.

Wright, B. D., & Stone, M. H. (1979). *Best test design*. Chicago, IL: MESA Press.

Wu, A. D., & Zumbo, B. D. (2007). Decoding the meaning of factorial invariance and updating the practice of multi-group confirmatory factor analysis: A demonstration with TIMSS data. *Practical Assessment, Research & Evaluation, 12,* 1–26.

Wu, M. L., Adams, R. J., & Wilson, M. R. (1998). *ACER ConQuest: Generalized item response modeling software* (Version 1.0) [Computer program]. Melbourne, Australia: Australian Council for Educational Research.

Wu, P.-C., & Chang, L. (2008). Psychometric properties of the Chinese version of the Beck Depression Inventory—II using the Rasch model. *Measurement and Evaluation in Counseling and Development, 41,* 13–31.

Yaffee, R. A. (1998). *Enhancement of reliability analysis: Application of intraclass correlations with SPSS/Windows v.8*. Retrieved from New York University website: http://www.nyu.edu/its/statistics/Docs/intracls.html

Yamaguchi, J. (1997). Positive versus negative wording. *Rasch Measurement Transactions, 11,* 567.

Yin, P., & Fan, X. T. (2003). Assessing the factor structure invariance of self-concept measurement across ethnic and gender groups: Findings from a national sample. *Educational and Psychological Measurement, 63,* 296–318.

Yoon, M., & Millsap, R. E. (2007). Detecting violations of factorial invariance using data-based specification searches: A Monte Carlo study. *Structural Equation Modeling, 14,* 435–463.

Young, J. F. & Mroczek, D. K. (2003). Predicting intraindividual self-concept trajectories during adolescence. *Journal of Adolescence, 26,* 586–600.

Yu, C.-Y. & Muthén, B. (2002, April). *Evaluation of model fit indices for latent variable models with categorical and continuous outcomes*. Paper presented at the meeting of the American Educational Research Association, New Orleans, LA.

Yuan, K. H. (2005). Fit statistics versus test statistics. *Multivariate Behavioral Research, 40,* 115–148.

Yung, Y.-F., & Bentler, P. M. (1996). Bootstrapping techniques in analysis of mean and covariance structures. In G. A. Marcoulides & R. E. Schumacker (Eds.), *Advanced structural equation modeling: Issues and techniques* (pp. 195–226). Mahwah, NJ: Erlbaum.

Zhu, W. (2002). A confirmatory study of Rasch-based optimal categorization of a rating scale. *Journal of Applied Measurement, 3,* 1–15.

Zieky, M. (2006). Fairness review in assessment. In S. M. Downing & T. M. Haladyna (Eds.), *Handbook of test development* (pp. 359–376). Mahwah, NJ: Erlbaum.

Zimmerman, B. (1989). Models of self-regulated learning and academic achievement. In B. J. Zimmerman & D. H. Schunk (Eds.), *Self-regulated learning and academic achievement: Theory, research, and practice* (pp. 1–25). New York, NY: Springer.

Zimmerman, B., & Kitsantas, A. (2005). The hidden dimension of personal competence: Self-regulated learning and practice. In A. J. Elliot & C. S. Dweck (Eds.), *Handbook of competence and motivation* (pp. 509–526). New York, NY: Guilford.

Zung, W. (1965). A Self-Rating Depression Scale. *Archives of General Psychiatry, 12*, 63–70.
Zwick, R., Donoghue, J. R., & Grima, A. (1993). Assessment of differential item functioning for performance tasks. *Journal of Educational Measurement, 30,* 233–251.

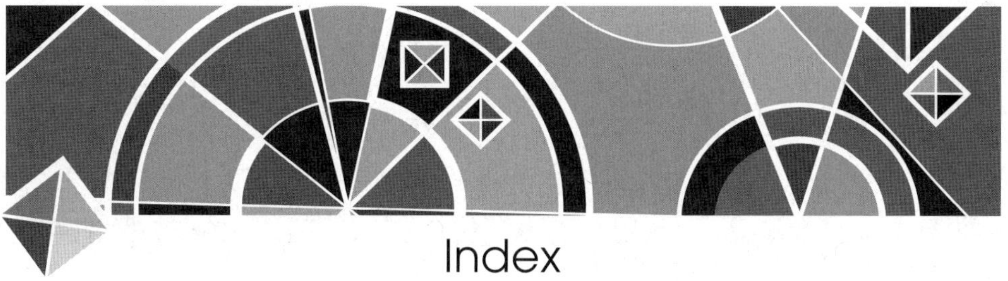

Index

Figures and tables are indicated by f and t following page numbers.

D

E

F

G

H

I

J

K

L

M

N

O

P

Q

R

S

T

U

V

W

Y

Z